THE KOREAN NEO-CONFUCIANISM OF YI T'OEGYE AND YI YULGOK

SUNY SERIES IN KOREAN STUDIES

SUNG BAE PARK, EDITOR

THE KOREAN NEO-CONFUCIANISM OF YI T'OEGYE AND YI YULGOK

A Reappraisal of the "Four-Seven Thesis" and Its Practical Implications for Self-Cultivation

Edward Y. J. Chung

STATE UNIVERSITY OF NEW YORK PRESS

Published by
State University of New York Press, Albany

Printed in the United States of America

For information, address State University of New York Press,
State University Plaza, Albany, NY 12246

Production by Dana Foote
Marketing by Nancy Farrell

Library of Congress Cataloging-in-Publication Data

Chung, Edward Y. J.
The Korean neo-Confucianism of Yi T'oegye and Yi Yulgok : a reappraisal of the "Four-Seven Thesis" and its practical implications for self-cultivation / Edward Y. J. Chung.
p. cm. — (SUNY series in Korean studies)
Includes bibliographical references and index.
ISBN 0-7914-2275-5 — ISBN 0-7914-2276-3 (pbk.)
1. Four beginnings and seven feelings thesis. 2. Neo-Confucianism—Korea. 3. Yi, Hwang, 1501–1570. 4. Yi, I, 1536–1584. 5. Philosophy, Korean. I. Title. II. Series.
BH253.F68C48 1995
181'.112—dc20 94-25830
CIP

10 9 8 7 6 5 4 3 2 1

For Agnes Eun-hee Chung

Contents

Foreword

This book represents the completion of an ambitious project. After all, Yi T'oegye and Yi Yulgok are the two greatest traditional Korean thinkers, both of whom lived in the sixteenth century, a time of great creativity. Each has been the focus of much scholarly attention. Edward Chung, however, has dared to study each of these two thinkers in comparision with the other. The issue choosen for discussion was central to the whole of traditional Korean philosophy: the relationship between human nature and the emotions, the so-called Four-Seven debate, which once divided philosophical opinion for centuries in Korea.

Basing his work on original sources, and consulting a massive amount of secondary works in Chinese, Korean, and Japanese as well as English, the author of this book places T'oegye's and Yulgok's ideas in specific contexts, drawing out the practical implications of their positions for what concerns ethics and spiritual cultivation. For us in the twentieth century, the book may not explain why the intellectual circles of sixteenth century Korea and even much later were so taken by such introspective questions. But the book gives us a taste of the atmosphere of those times, while spelling out for us, in textual analysis, the hidden meanings of the Four-Seven debates, with their metaphysical implications, their psychological concerns, as well as their considerations for ethics and spirituality. It also places the philosophical debates and discussions in Korea against the perspectives of the development of the matrix of these ideas in China, going back to Confucius, Mencius, and Chu Hsi (1130–1200).

It is my pleasure to see this book in print, and I know that it will serve its readers well.

Julia Ching
University Professor
Department of Religious Studies and
Department of East Asian Studies
University of Toronto
Fellow, Royal Society of Canada

Preface

There is a definite need to study more closely and seriously the philosophy of Yi Hwang (T'oegye, 1501–1570) and Yi I (Yulgok, 1536–1584), the two leading thinkers of Korean Neo-Confucianism. T'oegye and Yulgok established the characteristic patterns of the Korean Neo-Confucian tradition from the late sixteenth century up to the opening of the present century, exerting a profound influence on the metaphysical and ethical systems of the Yi Chosŏn dynasty (1393–1910). Both of them were followers of the so-called Ch'eng-Chu school (*Chŏngjuhak*)[1] or Chu Hsi school" (*Chujahak*),[2] a Neo-Confucian legacy associated with the Sung Chinese thinkers such as Ch'eng I (1033–1107) and Chu Hsi (1130–1200). Also known as the school of human nature and principle (*sŏngnihak/hsing-li hsüeh*),[3] this tradition served as the orthodox school of Neo-Confucianism for five centuries in Chosŏn Korea.

T'oegye has often been called the Master Chu Hsi of Korea. His philosophical, ethical, and spiritual synthesis of Sung Neo-Confucianism not only assured the dominance of Sŏngnihak in Chosŏn Korea, but also facilitated its spread to, and development in, Tokugawa Japan. Yulgok came thirty-five years after T'oegye, and he has been respected not only as a great scholar of Korea, but also as a distinguished statesman who had a good deal of knowledge about social and political matters. Most modern Koreans still admire both men as their two greatest scholars of the past, from whom the proud and inspiring source of learning, self-cultivation, and cultural identity is still drawn.[4] T'oegye and Yulgok are presented as the Korean models of education and morality, conveying the general public view that one's proper understanding of them is an important part of educational curriculum in the country.[5]

As we know, the Neo-Confucian traditions of China and Japan have already been studied to a great extent in the West, but this is not yet the case for the Korean tradition. There appears to be a growing interest in Korean philosophy and religion in both East Asia and North America. Recently, William T. de Bary, for instance, has pointed out: "There has been increasing recognition of the importance of Korea in East Asian civilization . . . in the premodern period (twelfth to nineteenth centuries) as an active contributor to the new Neo-Confucian culture."[6] For the English-speaking world, however, we have a translation of, and commentary on, T'oegye's *Sŏnghak sipto*

(Ten Diagrams of the Learning of the Sages),[7] a study of Yulgok's Neo-Confucianism,[8] and several exploratory works by distinguished scholars of Confucian thought.[9] As far as I know, there is, as yet, no full-length and comparative study of T'oegye and Yulgok.

This book examines the Korean Neo-Confucianism of T'oegye and Yulgok with special focus on the so-called Four-Seven thesis (*sach'illon*) and its implications for self-cultivation. As a common intellectual, moral, and spiritual discourse, the topic itself is significant for not only Confucian/Neo-Confucian studies, but also Korean philosophy, religion and intellectual history. In general, it constitutes the metaphysical and ethical essentials of each Korean thinker's thought; in particular, it is a sophisticated and fascinating Neo-Confucian controversy for understanding the status of human nature and the role of the mind and feelings. This volume deals with such a topic by addressing the major philosophical and moral questions and issues, as well as their practical implications for self-cultivation, the central and vital theme of Neo-Confucianism.

Special mention must be made of the Four-Seven debate (*sach'il nonpyŏn*), one of the historically most important and philosophically most challenging debates in the whole history of East Asian Neo-Confucianism. It was initiated by T'oegye in 1559, and Yulgok took it over thirteen years later. The term *four-seven* refers to the focus of the debate in terms of "Four Beginnings" (of virtue) and "Seven Emotions," two of the most important concepts in the entire Confucian tradition of metaphysics and ethics.[10] Indeed, the Four-Seven debate determined a common set of philosophical, moral and psychological issues for many more generations to come in Chosŏn Korea. Lasting for three more centuries, it engendered a profound intellectual and political controversy among many Korean Neo-Confucians. It was probably the most significant event in the history of Korean thought, one that divided the whole Korean intellectual world into the two mainstreams of the Chu Hsi school in Chosŏn Korea. Unfortunately, however, it has long been characterized as basically a textual and theoretical debate on Neo-Confucianism. We have yet to understand the moral and spiritual dimensions of T'oegye's and Yulgok's Four-Seven philosophies.

There are many important questions about the subject matter, but all of them cannot be stated here. Some of the major ones include the following. First, was the debate itself merely textual and theoretical or was it rather the apparent result of philosophical and moral reasoning from T'oegye's and Yulgok's own experiences and insights? Second, how does it relate to each thinker's Neo-Confucianism? Third, what is historically important about the Four-Seven debate, and why did it continue for three centuries after T'oegye and Yulgok? Fourth, what motivated T'oegye and Yulgok to inquire into the fundamental problems of the relationship between human nature and feelings? Fifth, what practical implications do these problems have for the Confucian way of life? Sixth, in what sense, and to what extent, do T'oegye and Yulgok differ from each other? Finally, how does the Four-Seven thesis relate to our own understandings of the role of feelings in the practice of moral cultivation?

The consideration of these and related issues accords with my reasons for choosing the Four-Seven thesis and its practical implications as the focus of the present volume. As far as I know, modern studies of T'oegye and Yulgok, which are available in Korean, Japanese, and even English, do not treat the Four-Seven controversy carefully enough, and there is, as yet, no comprehensive and systematic work on this fascinating topic. My approach differs from that used in contemporary Korean and other works, which tend to see it as little more than a textual legacy that maintained and promoted the orthodox Ch'eng-Chu school of Sung Neo-Confucianism in Chosŏn Korea. This has been the most conventional treatment of the Four-Seven thesis, one that need not be rehearsed here; as a result, the common understanding of it has been a theoretical or sketchy one especially among contemporary Korean scholars,[11] who did not inquire deeply into its subtle meanings and its practical implications. Cautioning against such a narrow or shallow view, I discuss T'oegye and Yulgok as thinkers, moralists, and educators whose insights and experiences provide us with an interesting and practical philosophy of life. I also argue that the Four-Seven debates significantly affected the ways in which they offer two unique guides to the Neo-Confucian way of learning and self-cultivation.

On the whole, I consider my task to be that of a textual analysis. As an interpreter of words, phrases, sentences, and their meanings, which are clear in some cases or often subtle in other cases, I present a philosophically comprehensive and systematic inquiry into the subject matter. The literary genres, philosophical concepts, and moral meanings and implications contained in the primary sources, such as *T'oegye chŏnsŏ* (Complete Works of T'oegye) and *Yulgok chŏnsŏ* (Complete Works of Yulgok),[12] led me to such an approach. Given the ambiguity and difficulty of Ch'eng-Chu teachings, both T'oegye and Yulgok cited many original texts to enable their challengers and readers to go beyond their philosophical speculations on Neo-Confucian metaphysics and its moral and psychological philosophy of human nature and feelings. Because the Neo-Confucian vocabulary presented in this book is essential to T'oegye's and Yulgok's philosophy, this approach allows the readers to generate certain reflections in their own ways of reading and philosophizing. For this reason, I present a great deal of translation[13] and analyze the theoretical meanings and practical implications of the relevant words and texts. This then becomes the first objective of my approach. The ways in which T'oegye and Yulgok presented the Four-Seven thesis often reveal their own experiences, concerns, and hermeneutical categories. It is, therefore, necessary to look at previously *untranslated* materials, including not only their "Four-Seven letters," but also their philosophical discourses, political treatises, biographical accounts, and other philosophical letters. This will facilitate us in following a textual analysis essential to any careful understanding of Neo-Confucianism in general and the Korean Four-Seven thesis in particular.

The fundamental argument that I present in this book is this: for T'oegye and Yulgok, the significance of the Four-Seven debate is its compelling implications for the practice of moral/spiritual cultivation and its related matters. And this is still relevant to the role and problem of feelings in moral life and actions. I should emphasize, however, that the Korean Four-Seven thesis is a highly sophisticated system of metaphysics and ethics at the same time. T'oegye's and Yulgok's words and sentences often reveal multilevel meanings, involving philosophical concepts as well as moral and psychological issues. Accordingly, our main concern is systematic and interpretive, rather than exegetic and apologetic. I have used "hermeneutical" analyses that are, in my view, reflective, suggestive, and sometimes interesting because they help the readers to acquire their own ideas about the underlying meanings and implications of the subject matter. The extent to which I present them make up the six main chapters of this book, representing the spirit of the whole Four-Seven legacy.

Given the fact that T'oegye and Yulgok each had a debate with another scholar on the Four-Seven problem and developed their own views and insights, my method is philosophically a dialectic one to provide a way of analysis, comparison, criticism, and interpretation. The uniqueness of Korean Neo-Confucianism is its strong commitment to Ch'eng-Chu orthodoxy; this is especially true of both T'oegye and Yulgok, the two leading thinkers of the Ch'eng-Chu tradition, who formulated new meanings of the old vocabulary. Therefore, it would be appropriate for me to do a comparative study of T'oegye and Yulgok. The last three chapters of the book, especially the concluding chapter, indicate similarities and differences in their views and insights. This comparative analysis can also clarify the fundamental patterns of continuity, change, and synthesis between Chu Hsi, T'oegye, and Yulgok. The question is, To what extent, and in what sense, did T'oegye and Yulgok tend to depart from the general norms of Chu Hsi's philosophy, each in his own way? This is another objective of my study.

To accomplish such a task, I have used early Chinese works, including the Four Books and the standard Neo-Confucian texts of the Ch'eng-Chu tradition. The latter include especially *Chu Tzu yü-lei* (Classified Conversations of Master Chu) and *Chu Tzu wen-chi* (Collected Literary Works by Master Chu) by Chu Hsi,[14] *Erh-Ch'eng ch'üan-shu* (Complete Works of the Two Ch'engs) by Ch'eng Hao (1032–1085) and Ch'eng I, and *Chang Tzu ch'üan-shu* (Complete Works of Master Chang) by Chang Tsai (1020–1077).[15] When a primary reference is cited, I assist the reader by considering both the efficiency and the reliability of the East Asian reference libraries. As a guiding principle, my first choice is to cite the *Ssu-pu pei-yao* (abbreviated as SPPY throughout). If the quoted passage is already available in English and if it is translated properly, I adopt it and indicate its source (e.g., Wing-tsit Chan, D. C. Lau, etc.)[16] in the Notes. Otherwise, I use my own translation. Furthermore, when it is appropriate, I cite a few prominent secondary sources written by contemporary Chinese, Japanese, and Korean scholars.[17]

The historical context of Korean Neo-Confucianism is important, especially for each Korean thinker's philosophy in general and his Four-Seven thesis in particular. Given the available historical information, it would be possible to present an interpretation consistent with it. Hence, this book begins with a survey of the historical background of Korean Confucianism prior to and including T'oegye's and Yulgok's lifetimes, that is, up to the late sixteenth century. Most readers will find that understanding the unfolding of Korean Confucianism, both historically and philosophically, assists them in becoming aware of the intellectual setting within which the Four-Seven debates took place in Chosŏn Korea. In addition, the Epilogue presents a brief study of the later philosophical development of T'oegye's school and Yulgok's school, with special reference to the Four-Seven controversy. This was necessary because several works available in English lack sufficient information about a few relevant historical facts.[18]

In the introductory chapter of philosophical background, I address some textually subtle passages and theoretically ambiguous points of the Chinese Confucian tradition. This is done by examining the early Confucian texts and Ch'eng-Chu Neo-Confucian commentaries. Furthermore, the key philosophical questions and moral and other related issues raised in the Korean Four-Seven controversy are listed and briefly discussed; these questions and issues, of course, constitute the centrality and vitality of T'oegye's and Yulgok's philosophies. This can facilitate the reader in following other chapters.

The four main chapters are tightly structured and connected by means of a clearly headed combination of comprehensive method, textual documentation, philosophical analysis, and systematic interpretation. To address the specific aspects of the Four-Seven thesis and its related topics, I discuss the link between Neo-Confucian metaphysics and ethics, between philosophical doctrines and moral practices, and between theoretical goals and practical methods. The second chapter deals with T'oegye, and the next chapter with Yulgok. These two chapters discuss the meaning and role of human nature, mind, and feelings and their problems for self-cultivation, as well as their relationships with Neo-Confucian metaphysics of *i/li* (principle) and *ki/ch'i* (material force). The fourth and fifth chapters present the implications of the Four-Seven thesis in the Neo-Confucian context of self-cultivation and related matters, such as learning, sagehood, T'oegye's religious thought, and Yulgok's ethico-political thought. These two chapters analyze the ways in which each man's interpretations moved beyond the textual and theoretical norms of the subject matter.

Whenever appropriate or relevant, I give my own interpretation. But most of my own opinions and insights are presented in the last three chapters, especially the concluding chapter. The readers can seriously consider some of the philosophical assumptions and moral arguments behind Korean Neo-Confucianism. I should also point out that I have limited myself to few brief, noted indications of certain parallels especially between Yulgok's theory of emotion and well-known Western philosophers' theories of emotion. A good deal of comparative analysis can be made between two Korean thinkers and those of the Western European tradition regarding human nature and emotions. However, such a task cannot be adequately covered in this book due to its limited scope and focus. Accordingly, a comprehensive presentation of the Korean Four-Seven thesis is more relevant here within the context of Neo-Confucianism.

The concluding chapter interprets the results of the preceding chapters, especially in terms of certain similarities and differences between T'oegye and Yulgok. This is done by comparing and contrasting at closer range their philosophies, while making necessary references to Chu Hsi and other Chinese and Japanese Neo-Confucians. A critical analysis of certain methodological and theoretical problems evident in both thinkers is presented. From a comparative perspective, this chapter also points out the uniqueness of each thinker's Four-Seven philosophy and its relevant contribution to the Neo-Confucian tradition as a whole. It argues that T'oegye and Yulgok made two valuable contributions to the transformation of Korean Neo-Confucianism: the former's inner-directed, contemplative approach with its ethico-spiritual tendency and the latter's outer-directed, active approach with its ethico-political overtone. Finally, the question that we need to address is, Are the implications of the Korean Four-Seven thesis still relevant for us in the modern world?

Supplementary information is presented in the Appendices, including T'oegye's and Yulgok's explanatory diagrams on human nature and feelings and two brief annotated, chronological lists of T'oegye's writings and Yulgok's writings cited in this book. The Glossary gives the major philosophical terms, personal names, and book titles presented in the text and notes. Finally, the Bibliography offers both generalists and specialists an updated and thorough catalogue of the primary sources and modern secondary works in the Korean, Chinese, and Japanese languages and a few English works including translations and articles. For convenience, the Chinese characters are given for the East Asian authors' names, as well as for the titles of their early or modern works.

I hope that this book makes a scholarly contribution in several ways. My translation, analysis, and interpretation make clear that, for both T'oegye and Yulgok, the breadth and depth of the Four-Seven thesis are the unifying Confucian thread for understanding the fundamental questions and issues that extend from Neo-Confucian metaphysics through its moral philosophy and psychology to the practice of self-cultivation and its related matters. I believe this book offers the first comprehensive and systematic study in English of the two leading Korean Neo-Confucians as an integrated philosophy for the Confucian way of life. Providing its readers with a conceptual vocabulary essential to any careful understanding of Neo-Confucianism, it can clarify and extend our present knowledge about Korean Neo-Confucianism. To generalists in humanities and social sciences, it presents a few critical points about the fundamental controversy on the relationship between mind, human nature, and emotions in the practice of philosophical reasoning and moral self-cultivation that are still relevant to our own philosophies of life and culture. Regardless of academic discipline, one can appreciate that the basic concepts and their practical implications discussed in this book are significant for both Neo-Confucianism and Korean thought. To specialists in East Asian philosophy, religion, or intellectual history, the book offers certain insights about not only Neo-Confucianism in general, but also the Korean tradition in particular. One can understand the Korean contribution to the development of East Asian thought. Those specialists in Korean studies will find this volume useful in studying the Korean Neo-Confucianism of T'oegye and Yulgok, with a broader and deeper comprehension of its Four-Seven thesis.

More studies are yet to be done. I hope that this volume will shed some refreshing light on the essential philosophical, moral, and cultural features of the topic that may go beyond the scope and focus of my own investigation. I also hope that it will stimulate others to undertake more specialized studies of Korean Neo-Confucianism or its related areas.

Acknowledgments

It is my pleasure to acknowledge here the debt of gratitude that I incurred in completing this book. Many people deserve credit and thanks. My warm thanks go to my teacher and friend Julia Ching, professor of East Asian thought and comparative religion at University of Toronto. I have been privileged to receive her inspiring knowledge of Neo-Confucianism. In the course of my study on East Asian religion and philosophy in general and Korean Neo-Confucianism in particular, I have received her encouraging help and counsel for almost one decade. Through her serious commitment to, and sympathetic appreciation of, modern scholarship, she has helped me receive a broader knowledge of Confucian studies and its related fields. It was, in fact, Professor Ching who suggested that Korean Neo-Confucianism is an important and interesting subject in East Asian philosophy, religion, and intellectual history and who advised me that a comparative study of Yi T'oegye and Yi Yulgok can make a valuable contribution to current scholarship in Neo-Confucian studies. This then resulted in my doctoral dissertation on the topic of T'oegye's and Yulgok's Four-Seven thesis (University of Toronto, 1990). The present volume grew out of my further study of it, together with editorial changes and the refreshing insights of revised argumentation.

Others also deserve thanks. In particular, my genuine gratitude goes to Professor Tu Wei-ming of Harvard University, an influential scholar in Chinese philosophy and history, whose works in Chinese Neo-Confucianism and T'oegye's philosophy have been a rich source of scholarly inspiration for my research on Korean Neo-Confucianism. After reading my doctoral dissertation, the earlier version of the present volume, he gave me positive comments and thoughtful suggestions, and I am certainly indebted to him. I thank also Professor Williard Oxtoby, a specialist in comparative religion, and Professor Richard Guisso, a Sinologist, from whom I received a good deal of academic advice and encouragement in the direction of my graduate studies in East Asian thought and comparative religion at University of Toronto. Furthermore, I am indebted to the East Asian Studies Library of that institution, which provided me useful information on the Chinese Neo-Confucian literature. During my research visits to Seoul, Korea, I received a few scholarly comments from Professor Yi Tong-jun, a specialist in Korean Confucian thought, at Sŏnggyun'gwan University. My research benefited from kind help offered by the Korean Studies Library staff of this university. I also thank Professor Chŏng In-jae of Sŏgang University, a specialist in Chinese Confucianism, who visited University of Toronto during the academic year of 1989–1990. He gave me useful comments on Korean Neo-Confucianism. Lastly, I must express a profound debt to my wife Agnes. Her endless patience and support have sustained this book from its beginning stage.

The substantial portion of the fourth chapter ("Practical Implications for T'oegye") was previously published as two articles: "Yi T'oegye on the Neo-Confucian Learning of Principle and Mind: A Religious Way of Self-Cultivation," *Asian Profile* 20, no. 5 (Oct. 1992): 353–365, and "Yi T'oegye on the Learning of Reverential Seriousness (*Kyŏnghak*): A Korean Neo-Confucian Spirituality," *Korea Journal* 32, no. 1 (Spring 1992): 61–71. Most of the former (copyright 1992 by Asian Research Center of Hong Kong and Vancouver) is reprinted with permission in the first and second sections of this chapter ("Principle and Self-Cultivation" and "The Learning of the Mind-and-Heart"); portions of the latter (copyright 1992 by the National Korean Commission for UNESCO) are reprinted with permission in the third section of this chapter ("Sagehood and the Learning of Reverential Seriousness"). I would like to thank both publishers for their permission to incorporate most portions of these papers that previously appeared in their journals. I should also point out that I have revised a few sentences and paragraphs for the purpose of the present book.

A Note on Style and Translation

The romanized Korean names, titles, and philosophical terms are given according to the standard McCune-Reischauer system. The Chinese forms are given according to the Wade-Giles system, and the Japanese according to Hepburn system. East Asian names are written according to the Sino-Korean and Japanese custom, except for contemporary persons (like myself) outside East Asia, who follow the Western custom. In other words, Korean thinkers, such as T'oegye and Yulgok, and other historical persons are initially referred to by the conventional order of the family name (*sŏng/hsing*) and the private (given) name (*myŏng/ming*), followed by the honorific name (*ho/hao*) in brackets. Afterwards, the Koreans are, according to the accepted style, referred to their honorific names (e.g., T'oegye). However, I made a few exceptions: the private name is used if it is better known.

For romanizing the Korean given names, I follow the accepted style of including hyphens between characters (syllables); for example, Pae Chong-ho, not Pae Chongho. As for the honorific names, the standard style of omitting hyphens between characters is used; for example, Yulgok, not Yul-gok. In this way, the readers can distinguish the Korean private names from the honorific names. For the primary and secondary Korean sources cited, only the Korean titles are given, as it is the standard style. The titles of the early Chinese Confucian and Neo-Confucian sources that T'oegye and Yulgok often quoted are given in both Korean and Chinese. With some exceptions, the romanized philosophical terms are provided in both languages. When both forms are given, the Korean always precedes the Chinese with a slash between (e.g., *i/li*).

Consistency in the translation of Confucian philosophical terms is usually a difficult goal because they are both subtle and flexible in meaning, involving diverse renderings and diffused implications according to their different contexts. Therefore, my approach to this difficult task is to maintain the standard English renderings of most philosophical terms as much as possible. For example, the Neo-Confucian term *i/li* is translated as "principle." Etymologically speaking, however, it refers to the "veins in jade" or "polishing jade." In both ordinary and philosophical languages, it signifies reason, truth, pattern, and so on. "Principle" is accepted as the best English equivalent for the Neo-Confucian understanding of it. In the Chu Hsi tradition, for example, it is conceived as the "formless principle" or "ground of being" that underlies all concrete things and phenomena. In relation to Chu Hsi's moral and psychological philosophy, it is identified also as *sŏng/hsing*, one of the most important single terms in Neo-Confucian metaphysics and ethics. The *sŏng/hsing* is translated as "human nature," which is thought to be full of truth, goodness, and moral principles.

In addition, I use variations when appropriate; some key words are translated according to their different contexts, without attempting to fix their meanings in English. For example, the Sino-Korean term *sim/hsin* is rendered sometimes as "mind," "heart," or even better "mind-and-heart," using them interchangeably. This is an important philosophical term in all forms of Neo-Confucianism (as well as Buddhism and Taoism); it is closely related to not only their metaphysics, but also their moral and psychological philosophies. Western philosophies often distinguish "mind" from "heart" and, thus, "reason" from "emotion." But to both traditional and modern East Asians, that kind of distinction is neither definite nor clear from a Confucian perspective. In fact, the etymology of *sim* indicates that the character *sim* itself corresponds to the physical shape of the organ of the human heart; this, of course, points to Confucian belief in the intellectual, ethical, and spiritual interaction and continuum of the mind-and-heart as a whole. T'oegye's and Yulgok's idea of *simhak/hsin-hsüeh* is translated as the "learning of the mind-and-heart."

Another important term, *chŏng/ch'ing*, is translated as the singular "feeling" in some cases, or the plural "feelings" in other cases, depending on its textual or situational context. In the case of *ch'ilchŏng/ch'i-ch'ing*, I always render it as the "Seven Emotions" (often abbreviated as the Seven), although I am aware of the difference in nuance between the meaning of "feeling" and that of "emotion." Furthermore, I use the standard rendering of *sadan/ssu-tuan* as the "Four Beginnings" (often abbreviated as the Four), although I realize that we can render it as the "four roots" (of virtue) as well. These problems are discussed in the introductory chapter of philosophical introduction to the Four-Seven legacy in China. As for T'oegye's concept of *kyŏng/ching*, I combine two standard English translations, "reverence" and "seriousness," into "reverential seriousness," since it often means both. Therefore, *kyŏnghak/ching-hsüeh* is translated as the "learning of reverential seriousness." Yulgok's idea of *sil/shih* is translated as "practical" or "real" (as an adjective) in some cases or "practicality" (as a noun) in other cases. And that of *sirhak/shih-hsüeh* is translated as "practical learning," indicating the fact that Yulgok was much concerned with the practical and pragmatic aspects of Neo-Confucian learning and self-cultivation. Throughout the book, most philosophical concepts are explained within either the text or notes. Last, on account of the difficulty of translating some of them accurately and comprehensively, I use the following romanized forms: *i* ("principle"), *ki* ("material force" or "ether"), *kyŏng*, *simhak*, *sirhak*, and so on.

Abbreviations

TC Yi T'oegye. *T'oegye chŏnsŏ* (Complete Works of Yi T'oegye), enlarged edition, 5 vols. Seoul: Sŏnggyun'gwan University Press, 1986.

YC Yi Yulgok. *Yulgok chŏnsŏ* (Complete Works of Yi Yulgok). 2 vols. Seoul: Sŏnggyun'gwan University Press, 1985.

CTYL Chu Hsi. *Chu Tzu yü-lei* (Classified Conversations of Master Chu Hsi). Comp. Li Ching-te, 1880.

CTWC Chu Hsi. *Chu Tzu wen-chi* (Collection of Literary Works by Master Chu Hsi). In *Chu Tzu ta-ch'üan* (Great Compendium of Works by Master Chu Hsi). SPPY ed.

Historical Background: Korean Neo-Confucianism

Confucianism was the most common intellectual, moral and cultural heritage of East Asia. Korea had a long and rich tradition of Confucianism since the early period. Particularly in the Chosŏn dynasty, it affected Korean philosophy, religion, social and political systems, and ways of life. For many centuries in Korea, it has been a code of family and social ethics and an intellectual discourse, as well as a political ideology. It also maintained some religious dimension in terms of its spiritual teaching and practice and its ritualistic tradition. And yet, it differs from other religious or philosophical traditions because it tends to integrate most aspects of human life and culture, including learning, moral and spiritual self-cultivation, family regulation, social harmony, political order, and cultural identity.

In the Three Kingdoms period (57 B.C.E.–668 C.E.),[1] Confucianism, Taoism, and Buddhism were all officially accepted by the ruling class and later spread to the commoners. In fact, each of three kingdoms supported Confucianism not only as an important part of Chinese learning, but also as an institutional means of maintaining its aristocratic power and its sociopolitical order. In addition, Confucian ritualism was embodied in official court ceremonies, including the veneration of deceased kings and other leaders. The people of Silla, for example, learned Confucian ethics and put it into practice in their daily life. The impact of Confucianism on Silla society indicates that even some Buddhist monks tried to incorporated certain Confucian moral teachings.[2] The people of Silla had a custom of a three-year mourning for the death of parents, one that originates from the Confucian rite system.[3] Another good example of Confucian influence is Silla's Hwarangdo (way of the flower youth), a quasi-religious and military academy for aristocratic sons, which promoted the Confucian way of learning and self-cultivation.[4] This academy was particularly important in welding together Silla Korean society. The Confucian virtue of loyalty, its cohesive force, facilitated Silla not only to maintain the authority of the throne, but also to unify two neighboring kingdoms.

In the Unified Silla period (668–935), Confucianism began to rival Buddhism. In the eighth and ninth centuries, many Korean students were sent to T'ang China and studied Confucianism at its national academy. Still, Confucianism was studied mainly in Buddhist temples and monasteries, the academic and religious centers of Unified Silla. Meanwhile, Confucian scholars promoted Confucianism as an alternative system of learning, self-cultivation, and political ideology for building a bureaucratic state in which they and their followers could prosper under state patronage. The establishment of the state examination system clearly reflects Unified Silla's decision to promote Confucian learning, rather than noble lineage, as the basis of selecting government officials.

The Rise of Neo-Confucianism in the Koryŏ Period

On the whole, there is not enough evidence to argue that Confucianism was important to everyone in the Three Kingdoms and Unified Silla periods. It played a subordinate role to the traditional ideas and institutions maintained by noble families and hereditary aristocrats, as well as by the Buddhist tradition. Not until the rise of Neo-Confucianism in the late thirteenth century did the Confucian tradition begin to exert a profound impact on Korean thought, religion, socio-political systems, and ways of life.

Confucian Academies and State Examinations

In the Koryŏ dynasty (918–1392), there was a serious blow to high officials of aristocratic origin. King Kwangjong (949–975), following the model of T'ang China, appointed many Confucian scholars who had passed the state examination (*kwagŏ*) to official government positions.[5] The civil service examination system consisted of three major sections: the composition examination (*chesul kwa*), the classics examination (*myŏnggyŏng kwa*), and the miscellaneous examination (*chap kwa*).[6] All members of aristocratic families and the freeborn peasants were allowed to sit for the examinations, but the low-born slaves and the children of Buddhist monks were ineligible. During the Unified Silla period, the criteria for selecting government officials tended to privilege the members of hereditary aristocratic families. However, the Koryŏ people of local elite groups had their opportunities to advance into the central bureaucracy. It was possible for more young men to become government officials in the Koryŏ period.

While relying on the views of Confucian scholars, Sŏngjong (r. 981–997), the sixth king of Koryŏ, instituted a reform of the local government structure and laid the new foundation of Koryŏ's aristocratic order. He liked Confucianism and was well versed in Confucian classics. In the second year of his reign (982), a portrait of Confucius, the tableware used in Confucian ceremonies, and the texts regarding the achievements of the "Seventy-two Worthies" (Confucius' disciples) were brought to Koryŏ Korea from Sung China. In fact, these stimulated the observance of Confucian ceremonies for the veneration of the Confucian sages throughout the country.

Meanwhile, Buddhism and Confucianism maintained a mutually supportive relationship. However, Confucian scholars, who had more interest in promoting their own scholarship as well as in capturing the political power of the central government, urged that Confucianism be fully established as the state ethico-political ideology. For example, in his *Simu sippal cho* (Twenty-Eight Proposals for Government Administration) submitted to the king, Ch'oe Sŭng-no (927–989) describes Buddhism as the religious foundation for personal salvation and Confucianism as the moral and socio-political basis of ordering the state and governing the people.[7] Following Ch'oe's and others' recommendations, King Sŏngjong, built the first national Confucian shrine, called Sajik tang, in 991 and then another one, Taemyo (Great Shrine), for venerating the Confucian sages of China.[8] More important, he organized a national Confucian academy (Kukchagam) in the following year, which quickly led to establishing Koryŏ's educational system on the basis of Confucian learning.[9]

In a state committed to the principle of rule by civil officials in accordance with Confucian political ideals, Confucianism began to prosper from the early eleventh century. According to Confucianism, a centralized state should be governed by a benevolent ruler and his loyal ministers, whose political legitimacy is sanctioned by a morally rational view of the harmony of human beings, society, government, and the universe. As such an ethico-political thinking gradually received more nationwide support among the leading elite classes of the Koryŏ dynasty, Confucianism, which previously had little political power in comparison with Buddhism, began to develop into an institutionalized state ideology from the middle of the eleventh century. Local Confucian academies centers were not yet fully organized during Sŏngjong's reign. To spread Confucian education in local areas, King Sŏngjong first brought young students from the countryside to the capital.[10] When this program failed, however, he sent Confucian scholars to the countryside to establish regional schools known as Hyanggyo and to teach students in local areas.[11] Such an educational system, despite its high cost, expanded to produce a new elite class of scholar-officials. But as the state gained social mobility and political stability, it relied more on its examination system, which cost much less to recruit new qualified officials, thereby no longer being able to adequately support its educational institutions in local areas. Consequently, private Confucian schools began to appear and quickly became popular among most aristocratic sons, who depended on the quality of these private academies founded by some of the famous former scholar-officials.

In Munjong's reign (1046–1083), for example, the great Confucian scholar, Ch'oe Ch'ung (984–1068), who held a top government position as chancellor, established a specialized Confucian academy, called the Nine-Course Academy, where lectures were given in nine specialized areas of study.[12] This academy offered aristocratic sons who planned to take state examinations the following three basic programs: the Five Classics and Four Books; the Three Histories; and the study of literature.[13] Also known as Master Ch'oe's Assembly, it, in fact, marked the beginning of private Confucian academies in Korea. For this reason, Ch'oe's followers called their master the Confucius of Korea. His academy and eleven other private academies were known as the Twelve Assemblies (*sibi to*).[14] In fact, most instructors in these Confucian schools were eminent scholar-officials of the day, and many of them supervised the state examinations. This circumstance and the emphasis placed on aristocratic lineage background led many aristocratic sons to consider it a great honor to attend one of these private academies. However, one serious problem was that such a trend helped the private academies, instructors, and students monopolize the state examination system in the capital. The examiner was called an examination master, and his student who passed the examination was called his disciple; that is, the master-disciple relationship formed a very close personal relationship.[15] This tradition later became a major factor for causing and maintaining academic and political factionalism. In addition to the financial burden, this is why the freeborn peasant youth found it virtually impossible to attend these academies and take part in the civil service examinations.

As the state academies declined in popularity, the private schools flourished. This led King Yejong (r. 1103–1122) in 1107 to establish seven programs in the specialized fields of Confucian classics at the National Confucian Academy.[16] He appointed distinguished instructors in each area. After establishing a scholarship foundation called *yanghyŏn'go* (Fund for Nurturing Worthies), he built more Confucian institutes in the palace and recruited young scholars for promoting the study of Chinese Confucian classics and histories. During the early twelfth century, then, this brought about a number of famous Confucian scholars. Among them was Kim Pu-sik who is well-known for his *Samguk sagi* (History of the Three Kingdoms), an important book on the early history of Korea in the annalistic form. Another eminent Confucian scholar was Yun On-i, who studied Confucianism in Sung China for seven years and who wrote two important works, *Yŏkhak* (Philosophy of Changes) and *Yŏkhae* (*Book of Changes* Explained), which had been lost.[17] While continuing to support state institutes on the basis of Confucian learning, King Injong (r. 1122–1146), Yejong's successor, completed Koryŏ's education system by establishing the so-called Six Colleges of the Capital at the National Confucian Academy, as well as by building more local academies in the countryside.[18] The first three colleges were designed especially for the study of the following Confucian texts: Five Classics, Four Books, *Hsiao-ching* (Classic of Filial Piety), *Tso chuan* (Tso's Commentary on the Spring and Autumn Annals), *Chou li* (Rites of Chou), and *I li* (Rules of Rites).

During the most of the Koryŏ period, however, Korea was isolated from Sung China because of the Liao and Chin states that occupied northern China. However, following Koryŏ's surrender to the Mongols after thirty years of struggle, the Korea-China relationship began to improve.[19] This historical event then reopened channels of intellectual contact between Sung China and Koryŏ Korea. Thus many of the Koryŏ scholars traveled to Sung China and studied the new form of Confucianism, known as the Ch'eng-Chu school. This then introduced Sung Neo-Confucianism to Korea in the late thirteenth, or early fourteenth, century.

The Introduction of Neo-Confucianism to Korea

There has been some dispute over when and how Neo-Confucianism was brought to Koryŏ. Some say that the scholar-official An Hyang (1243–1306) introduced it during the reign of Ch'ungyŏl (1274–1308). This claim is based on the biography of An Hyang,[20] and modern historians tend to favor it.[21] However, others argue that Paek I-jong (fl. 1275–1325) was the first Korean scholar to propagate Sung Neo-Confucianism in Korea, and this occurred a few years later in King Ch'ungsuk's reign (1313–1339). This view corresponds to the biography of Paek I-jong,[22] and some early Korean historians accepted it, without giving further historical evidences.[23]

An Hyang was a member of the new elite class of Confucian scholar-officials. He believed that the most effective way to confront the entrenched aristocrats and corrupt Buddhists was to follow the Chinese model of adopting Sung Neo-Confucianism as the new state religion and ideology. In 1290, he accompanied King Ch'ungyŏl on a royal trip to Beijing, where he met Chinese Neo-Confucian scholars. After becoming deeply impressed by Chu Hsi's writings in particular, he brought home in the following year a copy of

Chu Tzu ch'üan-shu (Complete Works of Master Chu).[24] As a high-ranking government official, he then revitalized the National Confucian Academy to disseminate Neo-Confucian learning.[25] He also found it necessary to expand the state schools so that they could overcome the popularity of private academies. For this task, he established a scholarship fund to support state academies and purchase Sung Neo-Confucian texts from China. In recognition of these accomplishments, he was later appointed as the head of the Confucian Shrine. These facts support the view that An Hyang was the first Korean who introduced Neo-Confucianism to Koryŏ Korea.

According to another view, An Hyang's junior Paek I-jong brought Neo-Confucianism to Korea in 1314. Paek is considered as "the first Korean to study the Ch'eng-Chu learning" in China where Neo-Confucianism was flourishing under the state support of the Yüan dynasty.[26] He stayed with King Ch'ungsŏn (r. 1298 and 1308–1313) in the Yüan capital for about a decade, and there he devoted himself to the study of Sung Neo-Confucianism.[27] When he returned to Koryŏ, he taught it to Yi Che-hyŏn (1287–1367), Pak Ch'ung-hwa (1287–1349), and other Korean scholars. Several historical points are relevant here. Although An Hyang might not have had sufficient time to study Sung Neo-Confucianism or teach it to other Koreans, he actually laid the foundation for the transmission of Sung Neo-Confucianism in Korea. On the other hand, we have to give a good deal of credit to Paek I-jong for mastering Neo-Confucianism in China, as well as for helping to propagate it in Korea.

From the late Koryŏ period, the Ch'eng-Chu school in Korea began to receive strong support from the new class of Confucian scholar-officials who did not find fulfilment either in Buddhism or in the old tradition of philology-centred Confucianism. Its development can be divided into three stages: first, the early fourteenth century when it was first introduced to Korea; second, its increasing acceptance a half century later; and third, its expansion with a harsh criticism against Buddhism during the last years of the Koryŏ dynasty. During the first stage, a great number of Sung Neo-Confucian writings were imported from China. An Hyang, for instance, sent Kim Mun-jong to bring back portraits of Confucius and his seventy-two disciples, Neo-Confucian texts, and officials vessels for performing Confucian rituals.[28] With an increasing recognition of Neo-Confucianism, the government renamed Kukhak (National College) as Sŏnggyun'gwan (Royal College) in the early fourteenth century. It sent two instructors of the Sŏnggyun'gwan to China, and they brought home more Confucian classics and Neo-Confucian writings, numbering over 10,000 volumes. The Sŏnggyun'gwan instructed these texts to its students, a few of whom became famous Neo-

Confucian scholars, such as Kwŏn Po (1262–1346), Yi Chin (1244–1321), U T'ak (1263–1342), and Yi Che-hyŏn (1287–1367) in the late Koryŏ period. In the Chosŏn dynasty, this Confucian academy produced many more eminent Neo-Confucians, especially T'oegye and Yulgok, and continued to serve as the most important center for education, scholarship, and political influence in Korea up to 1910.[29]

Kwŏn Po was a student of An Hyang, who published Chu Hsi's *Ssu-shu chi-chu* (Collected Commentaries on the Four Books) with his own comments. According to his biography, "Korean commentaries on Neo-Confucianism began with Kwŏn Po."[30] U T'ak was well-known for mastering Chu Hsi's commentary on the *Book of Changes*. It is said that after teaching it to his students, the Ch'eng-Chu school began to prosper in the late Koryŏ period.[31] Yi Che-hyŏn was Kwŏn Po's friend and a student of Paek I-jong. He went to the Yüan capital with King Ch'ungsŏn. At the Hall of Ten Thousand Volumes, a library built by the Korean king,[32] he met several leading Chinese Neo-Confucian scholars, including Yao Sui (1238–1313), a disciple of the eminent Yüan Neo-Confucian Hsü Heng (1209–1281). There, Yi Che-hyŏn developed friendly relationships with them and was fully exposed to current Neo-Confucian thought. These circumstances then led to the development of Neo-Confucianism in fourteenth century Korea.

Chŏng Mong-ju and Other Neo-Confucian Scholars

The second stage of development began when Neo-Confucian scholar-officials especially Yi Saek (Mogŭn, 1328–1396), Chŏng Mong-ju (Poŭn, 1337–1392), Yi Sung-in (Toŭn, d. 1392), Kim Ku-yong (1339–1384), and Pak Sang-chung (1332–1375) began to institute the state education system at the Sŏnggyun'gwan and attack the Buddhist institutions. These men strongly supported the status of the Sŏnggyun'gwan as the national center for Confucian education. In 1363, for example, Yi Saek proclaimed that everyone, who wished to take any state examination, must first study Neo-Confucianism at the Sŏnggyun'gwan. Several years later, at the request of him and others, the Sŏnggyun'gwan revised its programs to establish specialized course offerings in the Five Classics and Four Books.[33] They taught Sung Neo-Confucianism to such brilliant students as Chŏng To-jŏn (Sambong, 1342–1398), Kwŏn Kŭn (Yangch'on, 1352–1409), and Kil Chae (Yaŭn, 1353–1418), all of whom became influential Neo-Confucian scholars in the transitional Koryŏ-Chosŏn period. Thereafter, the Sŏnggyun'gwan continued to flourish, many more students came to study there, and the Koryŏ government finally closed the private academies in 1391.

Chŏng Mong-ju, like Yi Saek, was an influential scholar-official and served as an instructor at the Sŏnggyun'gwan. He was well versed in the Five Classics, Four Books, and Chu Hsi's commentaries on the Four Books.[34] Yi Saek once praised Chŏng's knowledge of Sung Neo-Confucianism highly, saying that Chŏng's understanding of Ch'eng-Chu teachings was accurate, rich, and original. He even called Chŏng the "founder of the school of principle (*ihak/li-hsüeh*) in Korea." The term *ihak* is one of the common terms used for referring to Sung Neo-Confucianism; it is usually reserved for the Ch'eng-Chu school as something opposed to the Lu-Wang "school of the mind" (*simhak/hsin-hsüeh*), a main outgrowth of Neo-Confucianism associated with the Ming philosopher Wang Yang-ming (1472–1529) and his predecessor Lu Hsiang-shan (1139–1192) in Sung China.[35] Chŏng seriously learned Sung Confucianism and put it into his practice of the moral life. For this reason, his contemporaries praised him as the first Korean who elevated Confucianism in Korea to the level of philosophical thinking and moral self-cultivation.[36] Of course, this claim is valid partly because Confucianism, ever since its introduction to early Korea, was studied from the standpoint of either literary composition or political ideology.

To propagate Neo-Confucian ethics, Chŏng Mong-ju encouraged others to use the Confucian custom of a three-year mourning for the death of parents.[37] At the same time, he criticized the traditional Buddhist 100-day mourning and observed the Confucian custom for the death of his father.[38] This was especially noteworthy because other Neo-Confucians scholars saw it as crucial to changing a social and ethico-religious practice on the basis of Neo-Confucianism. Furthermore, Chŏng was the first Korean Neo-Confucian who also advocated study and practice of Chu Hsi's *Chia li* (Family Rituals).[39] Following Chu Hsi's recommendation, he strongly urged every family to build a Confucian shrine called *sadang* (place of worship) for performing ancestor veneration and other Confucian rituals.[40]

The Criticism of Buddhism in the Late Koryŏ Dynasty

Toward the end of the Koryŏ dynasty, the state patronage of Neo-Confucianism gained its stronger momentum. Most leading Neo-Confucians began to attack Buddhism, criticizing its spiritual and institutional decay. From Confucian perspectives, Koryŏ Buddhism was charged with causing corruption in government institutions. Criticizing the Buddhist monastic life, Chŏn Mong-ju, for example, said: "The Confucian way is simply about our daily affairs. It is the way of Yao and Shun. The Buddhist teaching is not natural not only because it ignores parents and family and neglects the distinction between men and women, but also because it urges people to sit in caves away from society."[41] Yi Saek also argued that, although the Buddha was a great "sage," Korean Buddhist monks had corrupted Koryŏ society, and that the government should be reformed according to Neo-Confucian ideals.[42]

Another serious critique of Buddhism was on economic grounds. For centuries, Koryŏ scholar-officials were dissatisfied with the political factionalism of Buddhist institutions, as well as with their control over estates, slaves, and financial monopolies. Yi In-jok (?–1395), for example, demanded that the Buddhist temples and their lands and slaves must be subject to the secular state control, and that one should be prohibited from becoming a monk unless one has an official approval from the state.[43] Kim Cha-su (fl. 1374) criticized Buddhist rituals for being "superstitious" and, therfore, argued that they should be supervised by the state.[44] Furthermore, Pak Cho (1367–1454) attacked Buddhism in several ways: Buddhism is a religion that distorts human nature and creates evil; Buddhist monks should be subject to military service; and Buddhist texts be destroyed.[45]

As the Koryŏ dynasty was falling apart, most Neo-Confucian scholars of this time supported Sung Neo-Confucianism as a new philosophy of life with emphasis on the self, family, society, and government; as an educational system focused on rational learning and moral cultivation; and as a practical religion whose spiritual teachings support a concrete set of ethical and political guidelines for governing the people. In short, it offered them the hope of creating a new moral and socio-political order out of the old society dominated by the Buddhist tradition.

Neo-Confucianism in the Early Chosŏn Dynasty

Instead of his duty to fight the Ming Chinese forces in 1388, General Yi Sŏnggye, who had already witnessed the collapse of the Yüan empire and the rise of the Ming dynasty, withdrew his army from the Yalu River and marched toward the Koryŏ capital to seize political power. This led to the beginning of the Yi Chosŏn dynasty (1392–1910). Liberal Neo-Confucian scholar-officials, such Chŏng To-jŏn and Kwŏn Kŭn, supported Yi's claims of the legitimacy of the new dynasty. However, others like Chŏng Mong-ju opposed Yi's revolt by maintaining that it was an immoral act and the new regime could never, according to Confucian moral principles, achieve political legitimacy. As a result, Chŏng was murdered by one of Yi's sons, and Koryŏ quickly fell. Chŏng is still admired by modern Koreans not only because he suffered martyrdom to defend his loyalty to Koryŏ, but also as a Korean paradigm of the Confucian virtues of loyalty and righteousness.

Chŏng Mong-ju's followers, such as Yi Saek (Mogŭn), Kil Chae (Ch'iŭn), and Yi Sung-in (Toŭn), chose to have the term *ŭn* (literally, "retirement") as the second character of their pen names. To them, this was important not only for sharing the same second character of Chŏng's pen name (P'oŭn), but also for paying respect to their spiritual leader. These Neo-Confucians, in fact, retired from the political world of the day; therefore, they and their followers became known as the Mountain-Grove School (*sallim hakp'a*), referring to their retirement to the countryside.[46] For example, Kil Chae withdrew to his home province of Kŏyngsang, the southeastern Yŏngnam area of the Korean peninsula, and established an academy there to train his students in Neo-Confucianism. Many eminent Neo-Confucian scholars, especially Yi T'oegye and his followers, came from this region during the later period. In fact, they developed the famous Yŏngnam school that became closely associated with the school of the primacy of principle (*churip'a*), one of the two leading schools of Korean Neo-Confucianism.

Chŏng To-jŏn: The Establishment of Neo-Confucianism as the State Religion and Political Ideology

In a period of dynastic and ideological transition, Sung Neo-Confucianism facilitated Yi Sŏnggae to ascend to the throne and to begin the Chosŏn dynasty as King T'aejo (r. 1392–1398). As a military man rather than a scholar, he was initially not interested in Neo-Confucianism partly because he tended to remain faithful to Buddhism. Although he condemned the political corruption of Koryo Buddhism especially in terms of its corrupt monks, its land holdings, and its control over slaves, he did not quite reject the basic religious doctrines of Buddhism.[47] Nevertheless, by taking advantage of Yi's rise to power, many Neo-Confucian scholar-officials began to establish Sung Neo-Confucianism as the new state religion and ideology. These men were concerned with the social, political, and economic problems of this time; therefore, the Ch'eng-Chu school offered them not only the hope of creating a new socio-political order out of the corrupt old society but also an ethical and religious system of thought that provided a refreshing set of goals and methods to legitimize the authority of the new dynasty.

Among Yi's close supporters was Chŏng To-jŏn (Sambong, 1342–1398) who assisted his ascent to power.[48] Sambong was a graduate from the Sŏnggyun'gwan and a disciple of the eminent late Koryŏ scholar Yi Saek. As an influential Neo-Confucian and a close friend of Yi, he laid the foundation of the major institutional structures of the new government, thereby playing a crucial role in establishing the Ch'eng-Chu tradition of Neo-Confucianism as the ethical and religious basis for it. His first approach to reform was a revision of the legal code according to Neo-Confucian ethical and political ideals. As the principal architect of the new dynasty, he wrote major political works, such as the *Chosŏn kyŏngguk chŏn* (Chosŏn's Codes for Governing the Country),[49] *Kyŏngje mun'gam* (Historical Mirror for Managing the World and Saving the People),[50] and *Kyŏngje mun'gam pyŏlchip* (A Supplement to *Kyŏngje munŭgam*).[51] All of these provided a general framework of the polity and social order of the new dynasty, becoming the basis of his *Kyŏngguk taejŏn* (Great Codes for Governing the Country), the new dynasty's political canon. In addition, he wrote the first draft of a history of Kory that constitutes the core of Koryŏ's official history known as the *Koryŏsa.*

At the same time, Sambong launched a serious attack against Buddhism. He was, in my view, the first Korean Neo-Confucian to formulate a systematic philosophical criticism of Buddhist doctrines, as revealed in his two essays: *Simgii p'yŏn* (On Mind, Material Force, and Principle) and *Pulssi chappyŏn* (Arguments Against the Buddha). The three-part work *Simgii p'yŏn* is a critical comparative analysis of Taoism, Buddhism, and Neo-Confucianism in which Sambong quotes Confucius, Mencius, and Chu Hsi to criticize both Buddhism and Taoism.[52] Sambong's main argument is that Neo-Confucianism is metaphysically and ethically superior to the other two traditions, which are, according to him, "false teachings." The Buddhist method of self-cultivation is concerned too much with what he calls the "subjective calmness" of mind (*sim/hsin*), ignoring the objective reality of things, society, and culture, whereas the Taoist teachings of Lao Tzu and Chuang Tzu are charged for emphasizing only the attainment of physical longevity by means of nourishing "material force" (*ki/ch'i*).[53] Sambong's conclusion is that the Neo-Confucian learning of human nature (*sŏng/hsing*) and principle (*i/li*) is more valuable in the context of not only integrating both Buddhist and Taoist teachings, but also emphasizing the objective reality of learning, self-cultivation, and socio-political orders.

The *Pulssi chappyŏn* is a more systematic critique of Buddhism, one that presents Sung Neo-Confucianism as the orthodox tradition of learning and self-cultivation, defending Ch'eng-Chu metaphysics and ethics.[54] Following two Sung Neo-Confucians, Ch'eng I and Chu Hsi,[55] he addressed the following points: first, the Buddhist ideas of *samsara* and *karma* and their implications for "rewards and punishments" are "wrong and immoral";[56] second, the Buddhist theory of knowledge neglects objective principles because it regards the phenomenal world as only an "illusion";[57] and finally, its ethico-spiritual teachings on the method of self-cultivation are focused too much on the "emptiness" of the mind, ignoring the family and society.[58]

Kwŏn Kŭn and Neo-Confucian Scholarship

In addition to Sambong, Kŏwn Kŭn (Yangch'on, 1352–1409) was an important Neo-Confucian, a former dean of the Sŏnggyun'gwan who helped the new government in establishing Neo-Confucianism as the basis of its state religion and ideology. He did so by preparing a number of influential scholarly works. Most of his writings are collected in *Yangch'on munjip* (Collected Literary Works of Yangch'on),[59] which contains a good deal of historical information as well. Among them are *Yegi ch'ŏngyŏk nok* (Commentary on the *Book of Rites*) and *Sangjŏl karye* (Annotated Edition of *Family Rites*); these are, in fact, the first Korean Neo-Confucian commentaries on Confucian rituals and ceremonies. These texts facilitated the promotion of the state rituals of the Chosŏn dynasty during it first century. Yangch'on wrote another important text, *Ogyŏng ch'ŏngyŏng nok* (Commentary on the Five Classics), which is now lost. Finally, his name was also known for his annotation of Sambong's anti-Buddhist literature.

Yangch'on was a close friend of Sambong. Like Sambong, he used Ch'eng-Chu Neo-Confucian doctrines to criticize Buddhism. He argued that Buddhism is "partial," whereas Neo-Confucianism is "correct"[60] and that the Confucian virtue of filial piety is the greatest virtue to be cultivated and put into practice.[61] In his view, Neo-Confucianism is superior to Buddhism because it "perfects both substance and function"; that is to say, its way of self-cultivation integrates both inner life and outer life.[62] Thus, he emphasized the unity of knowledge and action in learning and self-cultivation.

Yangch'on's most famous work is the *Iphak tosŏl* (Diagrammatic Treatise for the Commencement of Learning), the first systematic formulation of Neo-Confucian metaphysics and ethics in Korea.[63] He completed it in 1397, and then it was published fifty-five times in both Korea and Japan, due to its highly scholarly significance. It consists of twenty-six diagrams relating to the Five Classics, Four Books, and Sung Neo-Confucian writings. The first diagram is the *Ch'ŏnin simsŏng habil to* (Diagram of the Unity and Oneness of Heaven, Human Beings, Mind, and Nature); it is especially significant because it summarizes the basic teachings of Neo-Confucian metaphysics, ethics, and psychological theory.[64] Yangch'on based it partly on the *T'ai-chi t'u* (Diagram of the Great Ultimate) by the Sung Neo-Confucian Chou Tun-i (1017–1073), as well as on Chu Hsi's commentaries on the *Great Learning* and *Doctrine of the Mean*.[65] Presenting Ch'eng-Chu teachings, it mentions, for the first time in Korea, the ideas of benevolence, righteousness, propriety, and wisdom that pertain to the "Four Beginnings"; more to the point, it lists the emotions of pleasure, anger, sorrow, fear, love, hatred, and desire and briefly describes them in terms of principle (*i/li*) and material force (*ki/ch'i*). In Korea, Yangch'on was, then, the first Neo-Confucian who spoke of the Four-Seven topic. Although he did not directly spoke of the terms "Four Beginnings" and "Seven Emotions" in his *Ch'ŏnin simsŏng habil chi to*, he assigned benevolence, righteousness, propriety, and wisdom to human nature (*sŏng/hsing*), and the list of Seven Emotions to the mind-and-heart (*sim/hsin*). As we will see later, this aspect of his diagram had some influence on the initial stage of the Four-Seven debate.

Upon the impact of Chŏng's and Kwŏn's writings in particular, the Chosŏn dynasty declared Sung Neo-Confucianism as the basis of its orthodox school. The announcement was made memorable in King Sejong's royal edict of 1421. According to it, even the king, his sons, and all scholar-officials, should go to the Confucian shrine and humble themselves before the sages and worthies.

The question is, To what extent was Neo-Confucianism compatible with the social and political conditions of the Koryo-Chosŏn transitional period? Undoubtedly, the first step for scholar-officials was to establish it as the state religion and ideology by giving an ethico-spiritual and political justification for the new dynasty's legitimacy. For the new elite class, it meant a renewed commitment to China and its Confucian tradition. For example, Sambong and Yangch'on supported the new dynasty to promote the Ch'eng-Chu school. They argued that because the old dominance of Buddhism was morally and spiritually corrupt, cultural progress must involve a reform to bring about moral, social, and political orders according to Confucian principles. Their rejection of what the Ch'eng-Chu tradition saw as a "pessimistic" Buddhist worldview was not a difficult matter in an environment whose culture had already been considerably Confucianized from early times.

Why did this generate such irreversible enthusiasm and conviction in the Korean context? As we have seen in Sambong's and Yangch'on's writings, Neo-Confucianism was considered as the new intellectual, ethical and spiritual guide for scholar-officials to sustain a centralized, bureaucratic Confucian state. Following the Four Books and Neo-Confucian commentaries, they found an inseparability of Confucian scholarship and politics. Confucian ethics emphasizes the essential link between learning, self-cultivation, family regulation, social harmony, political order, and cultural prosperity. To Korean scholar-officials, it represented a cultural universalism based on the harmony of the natural, social, and political orders, which reflects the "secular as sacred" symbol (to use Herbert Fingarette's terminology).[66] Of course, the entire Confucian tradition tends to reveal certain complexity about the notion of "sacredness." In addition to the family as the basic locus of sacredness and continuity, the Korean Neo-Confucians took the socio-political order as another source of them. They saw no separation between the church and the state, as well as no room for any utopian spiritual sanctuary outside the world of here and now. The Ch'eng-Chu tradition was considered a convincing force that could universalize an ethico-political ideology and an educational and social system. In other words, the state itself assumed a good deal of ethico-religious significance.

To Sambong and his fellow scholar-officials, Neo-Confucian metaphysics, moral teachings, and political ideologies were an effective alternative to the corrupt Buddhist tradition of the Koryŏ dynasty, one that had a concrete and practical way to govern the country including educational, social, and spiritual matters. This was addressed in the light of what Neo-Confucianism, especially its statecraft tradition, calls *kyŏngse/ching-shih* ("to manage the world"), *chemin/chi-min* ("to save the people"), and *kyŏngguk/ching-kuo* (or *ch'iguk/chi-kuo*; "to rule the country"). In fact, Sambong used all of these ideas not only to address the essentials of Confucian political thought, but also to title his writings, such as the *Chosŏn kyŏngguk chŏn*, *Kyŏngje mun'gam*, and *Kyŏngje mun'gam pyŏlchip*. For example, the Sino-Korean term *kyŏngje* (or *kyŏng-che* with a hyphen) in the last two titles is the combined form of the *kyŏngse* and the *chemin*. For Sambong and his followers, then, even economic issues were to be addressed in the Confucian context of administrating a political economy. These Neo-Confucian political ideas and concerns were the focus of their statecraft school; in the later period, they also played a major role in the works of other eminent Korean Neo-Confucians, especially Cho Kwang-jo (Chŏngam, 1482–1519) and Yi Yulgok.

Neo-Confucian Education and State Examination System

With the establishment and spread of Neo-Confucianism, the state examination system, which was put into effect in Koryŏ as a way of recruiting government officials, took on a more central role in the Chosŏn dynasty. The Neo-Confucian literati had great socio-political might in the entire society. They devised a system of administrative law infused with ethico-political ideals of Confucianism. They constituted *yangban*, the privileged two orders of civil and military officials. The term *yangban* distinguishes them from other social classes.[67] Given the fact that marriage between *yangban* and lower classes was prohibited, the *yangban* state became exclusively hereditary in this Confucian society. As a result, social classes of literati and commoners were strictly separated according to birth and lineage. For example, occupational distinctions maintained a hierarchical order with the *yangban* class occupying the highest place. Rights and duties were prescribed for each group by law. Although the elite class enjoyed political, social, and cultural privileges, its men became government officials through civil-service examination or by the merit of their ancestors to the state. They commanded the administration of government, economy, and culture. We may designate this Confucian society as an elite, *yangban*-dominant society.

One of the most fascinating facts about the entire Confucian tradition in East Asia is Korea as the most thoroughly Confucianized state during the five centuries of the Chosŏn dynasty. From the early fifteenth century, Chosŏn society accepted Neo-Confucianism; by the eighteenth century, almost all levels of the whole society became transformed into what JaHyun Kim Haboush calls a *Confucian normative society*.[68] As the conscious attempt of the *yangban* elite to Confucianize the whole society became stronger, many elite families and Neo-Confucian bureaucrats began to compete in their power struggle. Indeed, one can argue that Neo-Confucianism played a powerful intellectual and ethico-political role that engendered an elite *yangban* society, on the one hand, and a conservative bureaucratic tradition, on the other. This has been the most popular area in current scholarship in traditional Korean history, society, and politics, one that need not be rehearsed here.[69]

To protect common interests of the whole *yangban* class, the early Chosŏn dynasty found it wise to put primary emphasis on state examinations. From the early fifteenth century, then, Confucian education thus became a primary gateway to personal and family success. However, note that, although any commoner of free-born status theoretically was allowed to write examinations, the *yangban* quickly monopolized the state examination system, partly because financial and educational opportunities to attend Confucian academies and, thus, to prepare for the examinations were available almost exclusively to the sons of the *yangban* class.

These examinations were conducted at two levels: lower examinations (*sokwa*) and higher examinations (*taekwa*).[70] The former included the classics licentiate examination (*saengwŏn si*) on the Five Classics and the Four Books and the literary licentiate examination (*chinsa si*) on skill in composing such

Chinese literary works as poetry, documentary prose, and problem essays. The texts used in the examinations also included Neo-Confucian commentaries, histories, and other books. The most important ones among the Neo-Confucian texts were the *Hsing-li ta-ch'üan* (Great Compendium on Human Nature and Principle), Chu Hsi's *Hsiao-hsüeh* (Elementary Learning) and *Chin-ssu lu* (Reflections on Things at Hand), and the *Ssu-shu chang-chü chi-chu* (Collected Commentaries on the Words and Phrases of the Four Books). The first three were especially important to the extent that, in the early fifteenth century, many copies of these texts were regularly brought from Ming China. Hence, the government continued to develop its public academies, which was, in fact, significant for Neo-Confucian scholar-officials to establish a thoroughly Confucian society on the basis of the state examination and education systems. However, as they began to accumulate more political power throughout the whole country, this soon led to the severe purges of Neo-Confucian literati.

The Purges of Neo-Confucian Literati

During King Sŏngjong's reign (1469–1494), many rural Neo-Confucian intellectuals were appointed to high-ranking government positions. The Sino-Korean term *sarim* (forest of literati) commonly designated groups of these Neo-Confucian literati who maintained their academic bases in the countryside. In the southeastern Kyŏngsang province, a few Neo-Confucians carried on the teachings of Kil Chae, a follower of the late Koryŏ scholar-official Chŏng Mong-ju, who had retired to his home province. Like their spiritual masters, Chŏng and Kil, these men had remained faithful to the declining Koryŏ court, refusing to accept any government positions under the Yi Sŏnggae faction. Their leading figures were Kim Chong-jik (1431–1492), Kim Il-son (d. 1498), and the former's disciples, Kim Koeng-p'il (1453–1504) and Chŏng Yŏ-ch'ang (1449–1504). Their scholarship was generally based on an idealistic philosophy of learning and self-cultivation, one that significantly differed from the statecraft tradition of scholar-bureaucrats in the capital. They made their appearance and exerted their political influence on the central government when King Sŏngjong appointed these *sarim* Neo-Confucians in an effort to prevent the further expansion of the dominant power of the court aristocrats. Consequently, severe political conflict developed between the two forces: the Neo-Confucian literati and the aristocrats in the central bureaucracy. This, then, led to a series of political events known as *sahwa* (literati purges) that continued from the mid-fifteenth century to the early sixteenth century.

Under the power of the tyrannical king Yŏnsan'gun, the first two purges of 1498 (*muo sahwa*) and 1504 (*kapcha sahwa*) resulted in the banishment or death of many members of the aristocratic elite, as well as numerous *sarim* Neo-Confucian scholars.[71] King Chungjong (1506–1544), who highly respected the Neo-Confucian literati, brought forward the young Neo-Confucian Cho Kwang-jo (Chŏngam, 1482–1519) to a succession of influential government positions. Cho's primary political objective was a rational reform of the state in accordance with the Neo-Confucian ideal. For example, he proposed the village code (*hyangyak*),[72] a model of local self-government; encouraged the translation of basic Confucian writings to promote and spread its moral and social teachings among the populace at large; and put into practice a much more simplified examination system for recruiting men of virtue.[73] As his political power grew quickly, a greater number of Neo-Confucian scholars who supported Cho were appointed to high-ranking official positions, and his reform group became known as the school of political thought.[74] However, the aristocratic families managed to get rid of him and his reform faction, and this political event was the third literati purge of 1519 (*kimyo sahwa*). T'oegye and Yulgok later praised Chŏngam highly as a true Neo-Confucian political thinker. Another literati purge occurred in 1545 after a series of factional events surrounding the successive enthronement, which once again broke the political power of the Neo-Confucian scholar-officials.

The circumstances of these four persecutions of Korean Neo-Confucians differed in each case, but their major cause was the factional struggle for political power between the aristocratic class and the Neo-Confucian elite. The latter suffered a setback as victims in this political strife. However, the result was not entirely unfruitful because most of them retired to their home regions and continued to build private academies (*sŏwŏn*) for promoting Confucian scholarship.[75] With their solid bases in the countryside, the power of the Neo-Confucian literati became stronger. In fact, these Neo-Confucians controlled the village codes, thereby solidifying the economic, social, and political power in their own regions.

The Paegundong Academy is the most famous *sowŏn* established in the Yŏngnam region in 1543. It adopted the rules that Chu Hsi laid down for his Pai-lu-tung Academy in Sung China. Obviously, the Korean Neo-Confucian scholars built the *sowŏn* as something that came to occupy a significant position in Chosŏn society exactly like that maintained by the Buddhist temples in the Koryŏ period. It must be emphasized, therefore, that, during the difficult period of the literati purges, they found in these private academies the hope for laying the intellectual basis for their revival, as well as for their return to political power. Historically speaking, this trend also led many of the Korean Neo-Confucians to maintain serious dedication, more than ever, not only to the education of the younger generations but, more significant, to the philosophical development of Sung Neo-Confucianism.

Unfortunately, however, another historical fact is that most private Confucian academies gradually became stronger breeders of political and intellectual factionalism. Nevertheless, they served as the important local centers for Neo-Confucian education and scholarship through which many retired scholars were able to make a significant progress in the study of Ch'eng-Chu teachings from the middle of the sixteenth century. Indeed, during this period, the most glorious period in the entire history of Korean Neo-Confucianism, many eminent thinkers emerged, including T'oegye and Yulgok. This, then, brings us to the philosophical scene of Korean *sŏngnihak* (school of human nature and principle) prior to, and including, T'oegye's and Yulgok's lifetime.

Sŏngnihak Before T'oegye and Yulgok in Sixteenth-Century Korea

Sŏ Hwadam's Philosophy of Ki

Sŏ Kyŏng-dŏk (Hwadam, 1489–1546), T'oegye, and Yulgok are known as the "Three Masters" (*samja*) of Korean Neo-Confucianism, who determined the unique patterns of its *sŏngnihak*. After turning his back on the political world of the Chosŏn dynasty, Hwadam dedicated himself to the study of Sung Neo-Confucianism and became the first Korean Neo-Confucian to have formulated a philosophy of material force (*kihak*). His well-known works include the *Wŏn iki* (Principle and Material Force as the Origin of Things), *Iki sŏl* (Principle and Material Force Explained), and *T'aehŏ sŏl* (Great Vacuity Explained).[76] In these short philosophical treatises, he presented his own metaphysics, especially in terms of the working of *ki* in the process of all cosmic transformation.

Following especially Chang Tsai (1020–1077), a Sung Neo-Confucian who based his whole philosophy on the dynamic role of *ki*, Hwadam identified the "Great Vacuity" (*t'aehŏ/t'ai-hsü*) with *ki*, the creative and transformative source of the universe: "The Great Void is empty and yet not empty. The void is identical with material force. The void is inexhaustible and all-embracing; material force is likewise inexhaustible and all-embracing. If it is called the void, how can it be called material force? When the void is in repose, it is the substance of material force. Coagulation and disintegration are its function."[77] In the *Wŏn iki*, Hwadam also asserted that *ki* is the "fundamental substance" of the universe, and everything in it is "pure and void."[78] He considered *ki* as the formless and unlimited force that creates and transforms all phenomena. By contrast, principle is only an element inside of *ki*. In the *Iki sŏl*, he argued that "there is no *i* outside of *ki*."[79] For Hwadam, then, *i* by itself has no ontological status and no creative or transformative power. Life and death are the fusing and intermingling activities of *ki*, and the operation of everything is founded on the dynamic activity of *ki*, not *i*. *Ki* is the actual energy and creative entity, whereas *i* plays only the supportive role of *ki*'s activity; *i* is taken as nothing but the ground for the activity of *ki*. In general, Hwadam's emphasis on *ki* tends to underestimate Chu Hsi's philosophy of *i*. It took an objective and empirical view of Neo-Confucian epistemology that what governs the material world and what becomes manifest in it are *ki*, not *i*.

Hwadam's philosophy of *ki* was carried on by his disciples such as Yi Ku (d. 1573), Pak Sun (n.d.), Hŏ Yŏb (n.d.), and Min Sun (n.d.) in the sixteenth and seventeenth centuries. In his Four-Seven debate with Ki Tae Sŭng (Kobong, 1529–1592), T'oegye later criticized Hwadam for misinterpreting Chu Hsi's metaphysics of *i* and *ki*; in T'oegye's view, he saw the essence of *ki* as *i*.[80] However, in his Four-Seven debate with Song Ugye (1535–1598), Yulgok praised Hwadam's originality. Yulgok pointed out that, although Hwadam's interpretation of *i* and *ki* is incomplete, he clearly saw the inseparability of *i* and *ki* and that his thinking is quite independent compared to T'oegye's.[81]

Yi On-jok's Philosophy of Principle

In contrast to Hwadam, Yi On-jok (Hoejae, 1491–1553) formulated an early Korean philosophy of principle (*ihak/li-hsüeh*) during the first half of the sixteenth century, before T'oegye. His major works include the following: *Taehak changgu poyu* (Supplement of the *Ta-hsüeh chang-chü*), a commentary on textual ambiguities and problems of the Ch'eng-Chu commentary on the words and phrases of the *Great Learning*; *Chungyong kugyŏng yŏn'ŭi* (Extended Meaning of the Nine Rules of the *Doctrine of the Mean*), an elaborated explanation of governing the state and society, outlined in Chapter 20 of the *Doctrine of the Mean*; and *Kuin nok* (Records in Search of Humanity), a commentary on collected quotations on the Confucian concept of benevolence (*in/jen*).

Hoejae is better known as the first Korean Neo-Confucian who emphasized principle with respect to cosmology and morality. Although he generally followed Chu Hsi's theory of *i* and *ki*, his philosophy focuses on the status of *i* as the basis of all activities of *ki*, emphasizing the metaphysical and ethical concept of *i*.[82] His entire metaphysics can be summarized in terms of his theory that "since *i* is substance and *ki* is function, the former is prior and the latter is posterior." Principle is the same as the Great Ultimate, the essence of cosmic transformation and moral self-cultivation. In fact, T'oegye liked his philosophy of *i* and praised Hoejae as one of the "Four Confucian Worthies of Korea."

Other important thinkers were Yi Hang (Ilchae, 1499–1575), Cho Sik (Nammyŏng, 1501–1572), Chŏng Chi-un (Ch'uman, 1509–1561), and No Su-sin (Sojae, 1515–1570), who followed the Ch'eng-Chu school. They were T'oegye's contemporaries but interpreted Ch'eng-Chu teachings in different ways, developing their own ideas and views.

Yi Iljae on the Relationship of I *and* Ki

Yi Iljae emphasized the inseparability of *i* and *ki*. Following Chu Hsi, he argued that, if viewed from the standpoint of unity, *i* and *ki* are one; if viewed from the standpoint of duality, they are two. For him, then, although *i* and *ki* are ontologically and conceptually two, they are always one in concrete phenomena.[83] In this regard, he was probably influenced by Lo Ch'in-shun, a Ming Chinese Neo-Confucian of the Ch'eng-Chu school, who emphasized the inseparability of *i* and *ki*, as well as the dynamic and empirical role of *ki* in all phenomena. Apparently, Lo's *K'un-chih chi* (Knowledge Painfully Acquired) was an influential text among Korean Neo-Confucians.[84]

It is precisely for this reason that T'oegye later criticized Yi Ilchae's theory of the "oneness of *i* and *ki*" for being no different from Lo's philosophy of *ki*. According to T'oegye, such a theory is incorrect because it tends to affirm *i* as *ki*. As we will see in his Four-Seven thesis, this already indicates T'oegye's full commitment to formulating a theory, which comes from Chu Hsi himself, that *i* and *ki* are ontologically and conceptually distinct and never mixable in phenomena. This is the whole basis of T'oegye's metaphysics and ethics. In his Four-Seven debate, Yulgok compared Lo with two Korean thinkers, Hwadam and T'oegye, arguing that Lo really understood the Neo-Confucian metaphysics of *i* and *ki* in terms of their inseparability in phenomena. Of course, Yulgok studied the *K'un-chih chi* and praised Lo as a great thinker of the Ch'eng-Chu school in China.

Chŏng Ch'uman on the Four and the Seven

Chŏng Ch'uman is well-known for his *Ch'ŏnmyŏng to* (Diagram of Heaven and Destiny).[85] In this diagram, he summarized basic Ch'eng-Chu teachings on metaphysics and ethics. In fact, Chŏng's *Ch'ŏnmyŏng to* was modeled after Kwŏn's *Ch'ŏnin simsŏng habil chi to* (Diagram of the Oneness of Heaven and Human Beings, Mind, and Nature), the first diagram of Kwŏn Kŭn's *Iphak tosŏl* (Diagrammatic Treatise for the Commencement of Learning),[86] which is the earliest Korean diagrammatical treatise on Ch'eng-Chu Neo-Confucianism. As mentioned before, the *Iphak tosŏl* was the earliest Korean text that lists the "Seven Emotions" and describes them in terms of mind, human nature, and feelings, as well as in terms of principle (*i/li*) and material force (*ki/ch'i*).

Without giving a clear explanation, Chŏng stated: "The Four Beginnings are manifest from *i*, whereas the Seven Emotions are manifest from *ki*."[87] Note that this statement, in fact, initiated T'oegye's Four-Seven debate with Ki Kobong who asked T'oegye to clarify such a statement. This was, then, the beginning stage of the Four-Seven controversy in Korea.

No Sojae on the Moral Mind and the Human Mind

Sojae was an independent scholar who became interested in the Neo-Confucian theory of the "moral mind" (*tosim/tao-hsin*) and "human mind" (*insim/jen-hsin*).[88] In fact, his most famous work is the *Insim tosim pyŏn* (Discourse on the Human Mind and the Moral Mind), which contains a diagram.[89] Although he spent nearly twenty years in exile, he was well acquainted with the intellectual trends of Ming China, especially Lo Ch'in-shun's reinterpretation of Ch'eng-Chu teachings. After studying Lo's *K'un-chih chi*, he praised it: "Its content is upright and subtle. It formulated underdeveloped ideas and, thus, made a great contribution to the Ch'eng-Chu learning."[90] His dependence on it points to his critical study of Sung Neo-Confucianism. In the *K'un-chih chi*, Lo asserted: "The mind is one, but one speaks of it as two because of the distinction of activity and tranquility and the difference between substance and function."[91]

Following Lo's theory of the oneness of the moral mind as "substance" (*ch'e/t'i*) and the human mind as "function" (*yong/yung*), Sojae criticized Chu Hsi for implying that there are two minds as the two separate sources of goodness, one from the moral mind and the other from the human mind. He states: "The moral mind is Heaven's principle; it is called the human mind when it is manifest by *ki*. The human mind necessarily involves feelings that both attained and did not attain their due degree and measure; therefore, it is said to be precarious."[92] His *Insim tosim pyŏn* drew a critical reaction from

T'oegye who criticized both Lo and Sojae for viewing the moral mind and the human mind merely as one.

Yi Hwang (T'oegye, 1501–1570)

Yi Hwang is commonly known by his honorific name, T'oegye, and often referred to as the Master Chu Hsi of Korea. Tu Wei-ming calls T'oegye "a major source of inspiration for creative scholarship on Confucian philosophy and its modern scholarship."[93] The contemporary Japanese scholar Abe Yoshio considers T'oegye as "the greatest scholar of the Ch'eng-Chu school in Korea."[94] In Chosŏn Korea, Yulgok had praised his senior: "Only after T'oegye explained the learning of the Way (*tohak/tao-hsüeh*, or Neo-Confucianism), our scholars in Korea finally understand the essence of Neo-Confucianism."[95] Moreover, "T'oegye's scholarship is unchallenged by any other Korean scholars."[96] T'oegye was the first Korean thinker who studied Neo-Confucianism thoroughly while writing many significant works.

T'oegye's thought exerted a good deal of influence on the development of the *Shushigaku* (Chu Hsi school) in Tokugawa Japan as well. Fujiwara Seika (1561–1619), the founder of the Japanese Chu Hsi school, and his disciple Hayashi Razan (1583–1657) respected him as the Korean transmitter of the Ch'eng-Chu tradition.[97] These Japanese Neo-Confucians and their followers studied Neo-Confucianism through reading his original works, as well as the Korean editions of the Sung, Yüan, and Ming writings of the Chinese Ch'eng-Chu school compiled by him. This facilitated Seika and Razan to establish the orthodox Ch'eng-Chu school in Tokugawa Japan. Razan, for example, mastered T'oegye's *Ch'ŏnmyŏng tosŏl* (Diagrammatic Treatise on Heaven's Imperative) and his annotation of Chu Hsi's dialogue with Li Yen-p'ing (*Yen-p'ing ta-wen*). He respected the former so much that he published it in 1651, introducing Chu Hsi's philosophy and T'oegye's commentary on it. After Seika and Razan, Yamazaki Ansai (1618–1682) respected the teaching and character of the Korean scholar, regarding T'oegye as the most distinguished scholar of the Korean Chu Hsi school. Ansai was inspired especially by his philosophy of self-cultivation through reading the latter's own writings.[98] Ansai studied the *Chasŏng nok* (Record of Self-Reflection),[99] a collection of about 100 letters written by T'oegye, *Chujasŏ chŏryo* (Essentials of Master Chu's Letters),[100] Chu Hsi's philosophical letters collected by T'oegye, and *T'oegye sŏnsaeng munjip* (Collected Works of Master T'oegye). Among Japanese scholars, who studied T'oegye's works extensively, were especially Ansai's disciples who respected him as the champion of the

Ch'eng-Chu orthodoxy in Korea. Sato Naokata (1650–1719), for example, claimed that T'oegye's remarkable scholarly achievement stand unchallenged by any of the Yüan and Ming Chinese Neo-Confucians. In Meiji Japan as well, a few Neo-Confucians claimed that the development of the Japanese Chu Hsi school was greatly influenced by T'oegye who inherited the Ch'eng-Chu legacy in Korea.

It is appropriate to mention a few facts about T'oegye's life.[101] We can divide his life into three major periods: first, the study period until age thirty-three; second, the official period until age forty-nine; and finally, the period of retirement, teaching, and writing for twenty years until his death at age seventy. T'oegye was by nature a modest, sincere, and friendly person. At age twelve, T'oegye learned the *Analects* from his uncle Yi U (Songjae, 1469–1517), a stern teacher who helped his nephew master this text from the first to the last chapter, without missing a single character. His uncle had a reputation for poetry, so T'oegye also learned it from him and developed a serious lifelong dedication to it. He composed over 2,000 poems of various types.[102] He was attracted particularly to the poetry of T'ao Yan-ming (365–427), a famous Chinese poet, who wrote many poems especially about rural retirement and closeness to nature. In fact, this aspect of life exerted certain influence on T'oegye's mature philosophy directed toward the inner-directed and contemplative way of life.

At age nineteen, T'oegye obtained a copy of the *Hsing-li ta-ch'üan* (Great Compendium of Human Nature and Principle), a seventy-fascicle encyclopedic compendium of the discussions of the Sung and Yüan Neo-Confucian thinkers, topically arranged to cover the most fundamental doctrines and concepts in the Ch'eng-Chu school.[103] This text first inspired T'oegye to dedicate his life to the study and practice of Neo-Confucianism.[104] He was a quiet and introspective man by nature, who always liked reading and study. Even in the early years of his life, he practiced quiet-sitting meditation and reflection over what he learned from books, especially when his mind recovered its serenity at night.

While studying in Seoul, the young scholar T'oegye obtained a copy of the *Hsin ching/Simgyŏng* (Classic for the Mind-and-Heart) written by Chen Te-hsiu (1178–1235), a leading follower of the Ch'eng-Chu school in late Sung China.[105] The main emphasis of this text is on the way of moral self-cultivation. It had a good deal of impact on T'oegye's mature philosophy of self-cultivation. According to T'oegye's biography, ever since his encounter with it in his early days, it had been a continuous source of inspiration for his study and practice of *simhak* (learning of the mind-and-heart).[106] Chen's *Hsin ching* circulated in Korea in an expanded version, entitled *Hsin ching fu-chu/Simgyŏng puju* (Classic for the Mind-and-Heart Supplemented and Annotated), compiled by the Ming scholar Ch'eng Min-cheng (1445–1499). The *Hsin ching fu-chu* was published in China in 1492, but it is unclear when it was introduced to Korea. In his later years, T'oegye used it as a standard text for lectures at the court and to his students. Holding it in great veneration, he ranked it along with the Four Books, *Chu Tzu ta-ch'üan* (Great Compendium of Chu Hsi's Works), *Hsing-li ta-ch'üan* (Great Compendium of Human Nature and Principle), as well as Chu Hsi's *Chin-ssu lu* (Reflections on Things at Hand).[107] In his *Simgyŏng huron* (Epilogue to the *Hsin ching*), he affirmed his faith in Chen's *Hsin ching* as his "divine spirit" and "parents."[108] Partly due to T'oegye's influence, it was printed in Korea seventy years later and became one of the most important Neo-Confucian texts in there, leading to twenty-five more printings from the sixteenth to nineteenth century.

During the second period of his life, from 1534 to 1549, T'oegye served in a total of twenty-nine official positions in which he utilized his scholarly and literary talents. Although he carried out his official posts sincerely, he always wanted retire because he had no political ambition. In 1543 he got hold of the *Chu Tzu ta-ch'üan* (Great Compendium of Master Chu Hsi) that was printed in Korea for the first time. He had not previously known such a work. He began to study it, and his resolve to resign from public life grew from this date. This compendium became another important Neo-Confucian text that shaped T'oegye's mature thought. He became familiar with Chu Hsi's ideas to the extent that he often quoted them in his own writings.

Obviously, T'oegye's longing for an opportunity to devote himself to the study of Chu Hsi at home corresponds to his strong dissatisfaction with the political problems of his time. In 1549 he finally left his official post, without permission, and went to T'ogye (renamed T'oegye later), a small place near a stream not far from his birth place. Here began the third period of his life, in which he studied, taught, and wrote. But as he became more famous, he was forced to accept few government positions throughout the twenty-one years of his retirement period.[109] T'oegye wrote fifty-three documents to resign from, or refuse, many high-ranking government positions.[110] In these documents, he gave a number of reasons including a chronic illness, old age, lack of knowledge, and so on. In reality, however, he could not explicitly express his reasons in public. First, his retirement was due to the series of three serious purges of the Neo-Confucian literati that occurred during his lifetime. The painful aftermath of such purges made him finally extricate himself in 1549 from pubic life. Second, he had no ambition for political power and always wished to return to his home, so that he could fulfil his lifelong desire to devote himself to the Neo-Confucian way of learning and self-cultivation. Furthermore, he had a serious interest in teaching and writing.

T'oegye wrote many significant works during his sixties. Among them are the following: *Paeksa Sigyo Chŏnsŭmnok ch'ojŏn insŏ kihu* (Postscript to Conveyed Copy of Ch'en Hsien-chang's *Instructions Through Poetry* and Wang Yang-ming's *Instruction for Practical Living*); *Chŏnsumnok nonbyŏn* (Critique of Wang Yang-ming's *Instruction for Practical Living*); *Heoam sŏnsaeng haengjang* (Biographical Account of Master Chu Hsi); *Yukcho so* (Six-Article Memorial), T'oegye's greatest political treatise; *Sŏnghak sipto* (Ten Diagrams on the Learning of Sagehood), a massive summation and synthesis of the whole framework and linkage of the Ch'eng-Chu metaphysics and ethics; *Sasŏ haeŭi* (A Commentary on the Four Books), the first Korean commentary in contemporary Korean, readable for nonscholars; *Samgyŏng haeŭi* (Commentary on the Three Classics); and *Sim mu ch'eyong pyŏn* (Critique on the Saying "the Mind Does Not Have Substance and Function"), an essay on the Neo-Confucian philosophy of the mind.[111]

For seven years from early 1559 to late 1566, T'oegye carried on his Four-Seven correspondence with the young bright scholar Ki Kobong (1529–1592).[112] In this debate, he formulated a highly sophisticated philosophy of mind, human nature, and feelings in relation to the Neo-Confucian metaphysics of *i* and *ki*. Soon the debate generated a great deal of scholarly and philosophical controversy, setting the philosophical agenda for generations to come. A few years later, it divided the whole Korean intellectual world into two different transmissions of the Ch'eng-Chu school. T'oegye's Four-Seven thesis is the best source for understanding not only the philosophical and intellectual dimensions of his Neo-Confucianism, but also the ethical and spiritual patterns of his life and character.

Until T'oegye's time, there was no accepted custom of any form of free debate between a master and a disciple or between a senior scholar and a junior scholar. It was unthinkable for a disciple to engage himself either formally or informally in a free debate with his master; similarly, a junior scholar would not dare challenge or criticize, by any means, a senior scholar with reputation and fame. However, T'oegye's Four-Seven debate with Ki Kobong broke this tradition for the first time in Korean intellectual history. Before the debate began, T'oegye was sixty years old and the most highly respected scholar of the day; he had not only served as the head of the Sŏnggyun'gwan seven years earlier, but also resigned from, or refused, a number of high-ranking government positions. Kobong was, by contrast, thirty-two years old and a young scholar who just began his official career after passing civil-service examinations. As a virtuous man and serious scholar, however, T'oegye welcomed Kobong's challenge and accepted his criticism. Actually, he could have followed the old tradition simply by ignoring Kobong's challenge or considering his views inferior or wrong. He often praised Kobong's thoughtful comments and did not hesitate even to revise his own views whenever he discovered their shortcomings. When Kobong expressed a point of view contrary to his, T'oegye never considered it incorrect at once, but kindly explained to him why and how he had reached a different interpretation. This clearly indicates T'oegye's modest moral character and serious scholarly attitude toward seeking the truth. The T'oegye-Kobong debate stimulated the rather quiet scholarly environment of the time in Chosŏn Korea, thereby giving rise to a unique philosophical development in the whole history of Korean Neo-Confucian thought.

The underlying structure and content of T'oegye's Four-Seven philosophy focus on the primary role of principle with respect to both metaphysics and ethics. As we will see shortly, his entire Neo-Confucianism addresses such a concept of principle and its implications for self-cultivation. It reveals certain patterns of the philosophical continuity of the Ch'eng-Chu school. Many passages in his Four-Seven letters and other writings indicate T'oegye's highest respect for Chu Hsi and his faithful followers, especially the late Sung thinker Chen Te-hsiu, who had a good deal of impact on the development of T'oegye's mature philosophy. T'oegye was, indeed, a Korean paradigm of Ch'eng-Chu orthodoxy, who sought to ground his Four-Seven philosophy on the metaphysical, ethical, and spiritual grounds of the Ch'eng-Chu tradition. He was, in fact, the first major Korean critique of the Lu-Wang school of the mind. As revealed in his Four-Seven thesis in particular, his Neo-Confucianism emphasizes a way to cultivate sagehood, the ultimate truth of human nature, calling for a Neo-Confucian way of life that integrates intellectual insight, moral effort, contemplative discipline, and spiritual cultivation.

After T'oegye, this transmission of Korean Neo-Confucianism was carried on by his disciples including Yu Sŏng-nyong (1542–1607), Kim Sŏng-il (1538–1598), and Chŏng Ku (1543–1620). As part of the Yŏngnam school (*Yŏngnam kakp'a*), it became closely identified as the "school of the primacy of principle" (Churip'a). This, then, is a brief outline of T'oegye's biography.

Yi I (Yulgok, 1536–1584)

T'oegye and Yulgok are often mentioned together as the two greatest minds of Chosŏn Korea. Modern Koreans respect Yulgok not only as a great

Neo-Confucian scholar, but also as a distinguished politician and reformer. As a thinker, statesman, and educator, his short life of forty-nine years was filled with many remarkable accomplishments. No other Korean Neo-Confucian before and after Yulgok can match his far-reaching vision of history, practical learning, and politics. As an original and liberal political thinker, he advocated Confucian principles to reform the contemporary political, economic, social, and military institutions of the Chosŏn dynasty.

When Yulgok was a young boy, many people praised him as a genius. For example, at age five, Yulgok began to commit himself seriously to mastering literary Chinese and basic Confucian classics, under the guidance of his mother, Lady Sim-sa-im-dang, who was so highly respected not only for her intellectual and ethical devotion to the education of her son, but also for her knowledge of Confucianism and her talent in painting and poetry. Unlike most other sons of elite families, Yulgok, at age twelve, passed the preliminary literary licentiate examination (*chinsa ch'osi*) on skills in composing Chinese literary works such as poetry, rhymed prose, documentary prose, and problem essays. In his teens, Yulgok was attracted to both Buddhism and Taoism as well. When he found the Confucian texts not quite sufficient for his needs, he began to study Lao Tzu, Chuang Tzu, and Zen Buddhist scriptures. His mother's early death in May 1551, when Yulgok was only fifteen years old, left him with a deep sorrow. He built a small hut near his mother's grave and mourned her for three years. In this period, he devoted himself to extensive reading in Neo-Confucianism, Zen Buddhism, and philosophical Taoism. As his memory of his late mother grew more painfully, he underwent a profound conversion of his mind. In March 1554, Yulgok, then eighteen years old, went to a Zen Buddhist monastery in the Diamond Mountains. Reading a Buddhist scripture, he became deeply moved by its doctrines on the problem of life and death unanswered by Confucianism; consequently, he decided to pursue a Buddhist monastic life of study and meditation. According to a biographical account of Yulgok by his leading disciple Kim Chang-saeng, Yulgok's renunciation was only an "experiment" to test Zen Buddhism. Kim, of course, meant to defend his master against charges that he was interested in studying Buddhism or influenced by it.

In my view, however, the fundamental reason for Yulgok's interest in Buddhism was quite serious, in both intellectual and spiritual contexts. Yulgok himself later confessed to the king in one of his memorials: "Your minister was originally a student of Confucianism. Unfortunately, however, when I lost my mother, I studied Buddhist scriptures seriously to erase my sorrow. I then retreated to a mountain in an attempt to devote myself to Zen."[113] It is true that his initial interest in Buddhism helped relieve the sorrow of his beloved mother's death. Another apparent reason he could not tell others was that his stepmother did not get along with him. [114] According to an account of Yulgok by Song Si-yŏl (Uam, 1607–1689),[115] "At the age of ten, Yulgok already mastered the Confucian classics, but he began to doubt the Way of the Sages and Worthies. As result, he studied both Taoist and Buddhist texts as well. After entering the Diamond Mountains, he united Neo-Confucianism and Zen."[116] Of course, Yulgok's early interest in Buddhism and Taoism was to fulfill his diverse pursuit for learning and self-cultivation. After he decided to leave home, he told his friends: "Material force (*ki/ch'i*) can be transformed by nourishing it. Everyone is born with it. When it is well nourished, the mind can control it; when it is not nourished properly, the mind becomes its servant. When the mind controls *ki*, the body can serve as the master; therefore, one can become a sage or wise person. . . . It was Mencius who, among ancient people, nourished *ki* well. . . . Where can wise and benevolent people go to except mountains and water in order to nourish their *ki*? I'll go to a Buddhist monastery."[117] This passage indicates not only Yulgok's serious interest in searching for the truth revealed in the Buddhist scriptures,[118] but also his strong determination to lead a Buddhist monastic life of study and meditation for spiritual self-cultivation.[119] During his stay in the Diamond Mountains, Yulgok often practiced Zen meditation and debated with a few Buddhist monks on the conflicting issues on Buddhism and Neo-Confucianism. He won a good deal of admiration from the Buddhist monks who called him a reincarnation of the Buddha.

After a year-long stay in a Buddhist monastery, Yulgok came back to the secular world in the spring of 1556. On the way to Seoul, he went to his native place where he spent one year, leading another short period of intensive meditation and reading. There he experienced another change of his mind, a second turning; he was uncertain in choosing between Neo-Confucianism and Buddhism as his lifelong pursuit. He finally decided upon Neo-Confucianism and wrote his famous *Chagyŏng mun* (Letter of Resolution),[120] a self-disciplinary letter consisting of eleven articles. In this letter, he confessed that the Buddhist way of meditation and mind cultivation is less valuable than the Confucian way of learning, self-cultivation, family regulation, political order, and social prosperity. Another interesting passage illustrates the point further: "When I was young, I was wrong to think that the Zen method of *koan* is the fastest and most excellent approach for entering the Way. Although I studied it for several years, I returned to Confucianism, realizing that the Buddha's teaching is not right learning."[121] It should be emphasized that both Zen Buddhism and philosophical Taoism gave Yulgok an opportunity to reexamine the truth of Neo-Confucianism; in fact, this proved to be a great help for him in achieving a mature philosophy in his later years.

In the spring of 1558 Yulgok, then twenty-two years old, went to Ye-an to pay a courtesy visit to T'oegye, the most famous scholar of the time. He stayed with the old master for a couple of days, composing poems and exchanging questions on Neo-Confucian learning and self-cultivation. He was impressed by T'oegye's character and scholarship. Recognizing Yulgok as a great future scholar, T'oegye praised the young man's intelligence and his knowledge of Neo-Confucianism. He said in a letter to his friend: "Yulgok is a very bright man who is now devoting himself to our learning. It is said that young students should be treated with respect and fear. Now I can see that the former sages told the truth."[122] In a long letter to Yulgok, however, he expressed his sincere concern about Yulgok's early devotion to Zen Buddhism, although he praised Yulgok as an outstanding young scholar. T'oegye told Yulgok that he made a wise decision to follow the Ch'eng-Chu learning by overcoming his early mistake of studying and practicing Zen.[123] Subsequently, Yulgok felt more confidence in his decision to pursue the Neo-Confucian way of learning and self-cultivation.

In the winter of the same year, Yulgok took a civil-service examination in Seoul and finished first. The philosophical essay he wrote in this examination is the famous *Ch'ŏndo ch'aek* (Treatise on the Way of Heaven) on Ch'eng-Chu Neo-Confucian metaphysics and ethics, one that astonished many people, who praised Yulgok as a true Confucian genius in producing such an excellent thesis on a difficult subject in a short time. It is said to be highly sophisticated to the extent that the senior examiners themselves needed several days to understand it. The *Chŏndo ch'aek* is 2,500 words long and demonstrates Yulgok's early, mature knowledge of Neo-Confucian history, metaphysics, and ethics. It gained a high reputation in Korea and was introduced also to Ming China where it received admiration from Ming scholars.

Yulgok initially was not interested in pursuing a public official career rather than a scholarly life. However, under the pressure of his father and two older brothers, Yulgok was often forced to take more civil-service examinations (altogether nine including his early literacy-composition exam), finishing among top candidates. His official career began in 1559 when he was twenty-three years old. After that, his scholarly and official life was a busy one. But a chronic illness, especially since his late thirties, made him to retire a few times. Nonetheless, he served many top-ranking government positions including minister of home affairs (1581), minister of justice (1582), minister of civil affairs (1582), and minister of defense (1583). The king reappointed

Yulgok as minister of civil affairs in the winter of 1583, but he became very ill in the spring of 1584 and died at age forty-eight.

As a distinguished Neo-Confucian politician in Korea, he wrote extensively, producing many important political writings of high quality. Among those presented to the king include the following: *Tongho mundap* (Tongho Questions and Answers), a famous political memorial consisting of critical eleven articles of political reform; *Manŏn pongsa* (Ten Thousand Character Memorial), another political memorial about the practical way of Confucian learning, self-cultivation, and government administration; *Simu yukcho kye* (Six Article Memorial of Current Affairs), a systematic work containing six specific and urgent reform proposals; *Hakkyo mobŏm* (Model for an Academy), an educational treatise on the goals and methods of the education of youth; *Kyŏngyŏn ilgi* (A Diary of Lectures Before the Throne), a critical record of crucial historical and political events of Korea; and *Kyŏngmong yokyŏl* (Essential Instructions of Kyŏngmong), a systematic guide of learning.[124]

These works demonstrate the practical and pragmatic aspects of Yulgok's thought, including government administration, economy, social reform, and popular education. Yulgok addressed an urgent need to abolish political corruptions maintained by the traditional rules and customs of government and to establish new institutions, programs, and strategies to bring about the economic, social, and political harmony and progress of the country.[125] For example, given the emphasis on service by the capable, he urged for liberation of talented slaves and advocated a reform measure so that sons of secondary wives of the *yangban* class could be appointed to both civil and military government offices.[126] With a clear vision of history, Yulgok even predicted the potential for a Japanese invasion and proposed the preparation of 10,000 soldiers for such an emergency. However, most conservative politicians found Yulgok's reform ideas too radical for existing socio-political systems in sixteenth century Korea. His advocacy of strengthening national defense met opposition by Prime Minister Yu Sŏngnyong (one of T'oegye's disciples) and his powerful Easterners (*tongin*) faction; Yu argued that to train such a large army in peacetime for no specific reason would result in an economic and social disaster.[127] If Yulgok's reform measures were accepted by the government, they might have facilitated a possible process of reform and modernization in sixteen century Korea. As the unfolding history of the late Chosŏn dynasty indicates, the combination of internal economic, social, and political stresses and external pressures exerted by the Japanese and Western imperial powers created a national crisis that eventually led to various criticisms of the Ch'eng-Chu tradition by the reformers of the Practical Learning (Sirhak) school, especially in the nineteenth century.

Yulgok was a follower of Confucius and Mencius in his attitude of learning and self-cultivation, as well as in his serious concerns for social and political matters. He always emphasized that any benevolent ruler should adopt the sagely way of learning and self-cultivation before he could govern the people. Learning, self-cultivation, and government administration, in the true Confucian spirit, could never be separated from one another. In comparison to T'oegye who had no serious interest in politics, Yulgok was an active statesman who utilized Confucian principles and ideals to formulate his political thought in terms of reform. Historically speaking, T'oegye had to overcome three Neo-Confucian literati purges, which made him stay away from politics as much as possible; in addition, he was more interested in reading and writing, as well as in a contemplative way of self-cultivation. By contrast, Yulgok lived in a period when the government was relatively stable, and this tended to allow him to participate more actively in politics. This corresponds to the fact that Yulgok highly respected the late Neo-Confucian politician Cho Kwang-jo as a true Confucian political thinker.

The *Sŏnghak chipyo* (Essentials of the Learning of Sagehood) is Yulgok's most famous philosophical work that contains the fundamentals of Confucian metaphysics, ethics, self-cultivation, and statecraft. His other major philosophical works include the following: *Insim tosim tosŏl* (Diagrammatic Treatise on the Human Mind and the Moral Mind), a short but sophisticated discussion of the Neo-Confucian philosophy of mind, human nature, and feelings; *Yŏksu ch'aek* (Treatise on the *Book of Changes*), an interesting essay on explanation of Chu Hsi's metaphysics especially in terms of *i* and *ki*; *Sŏngch'aek* (Treatise on Sincerity); *Saja ŏnsŏng ch'aek* (Treatise on Questions About the Statements on Sincerity in the Four Books); and *Sasaeng kwisin ch'aek* (Treatise on Life and Death, Ghosts and Spirits).[128] Furthermore, among numerous philosophical letters are his famous Four-Seven letters.[129]

In 1572 Yulgok, then thirty-six years old, began the Four-Seven debate with Sŏng Hon (Ugye, 1535–1598) by exchanging up to ten letters on the subject that T'oegye and Kobong had discussed a decade ago. In this debate, Yulgok gave a detailed and systematic interpretation of Ch'eng-Chu philosophy of mind, human nature, and feelings. As we shall see in his Four-Seven thesis, Yulgok criticized T'oegye's Four-Seven thesis, especially his emphasis on principle; in challenging his senior's philosophy, he emphasized the status and role of *ki* with respect to both learning and self-cultivation. The basic content of his Neo-Confucianism has its metaphysical and ethical grounds in Ch'eng-Chu teachings. His Neo-Confucianism focuses on an empirical philosophy of *ki* that appears to be influenced by the early Ming Neo-Confucian Lo Ch'in-shun in particular. His philosophy of practical learning with strong emphasis on the unity of knowledge and action indicates some unmistakable imprints of Wang Yang-ming's thought as well. Furthermore, Buddhism and Taoism, which he had studied in his early years, also had a strong impact on the development of his mature philosophy.

In the late sixteenth and early seventeenth centuries, Yulgok's Neo-Confucianism was maintained by his disciples Kim Chang-saeng (1548–1631), Chŏng Yŏp (1563–1625), Yi Kui (n.d.), and others, who referred to their tradition as the Kiho school (Kiho hakp'a).[130] Although Yulgok, in a strict sense, was not a philosopher who emphasized *ki* only, followers of the Yŏngnam school that was associated with T'oegye's "school of the primacy of principle" (Churip'a) criticized Yulgok's followers as "the school of the primacy of *ki*" (Chugip'a). According to T'oegye's followers, Yulgok emphasized the priority of *ki* in metaphysics and ethics. On account of the Four-Seven controversy, then, two different schools of thought, the Churip'a and Chugip'a factions, emerged within the Korean Ch'eng-Chu school, each of which underwent further development for three more centuries in the hands of successive thinkers. I shall treat this topic further in the Epilogue. The next topic of our investigation deals with the question of why the Four-Seven controversy developed in Chosŏn Korea.

Why the Four-Seven Controversy Developed in Korea: Some Historical Reflections

The Four-Seven controversy was a powerful philosophical and moral issue not only for T'oegye and Yulgok, but also among their disciples and followers from the late sixteenth century on. Philosophical views and interpretations depended on different thinkers, groups, and academies, so they served a crucial historical function as well. In the intellectual sphere, for example, the controversy contributed enormously to the development of Sung Neo-Confucianism in Chosŏn Korea from the late sixteenth century, producing divergent and sophisticated views of Chu Hsi's philosophy. It definitely established a distinctive intellectual agenda for many Neo-Confucians and, thus, initiated a unique feature of Korean Neo-Confucianism, one that demonstrated an exclusive loyalty to the Ch'eng-Chu school and inhibited any significant spread of Wang Yang-ming's thought in the Chosŏn dynasty's intellectual domains.

The crucial question we have to address here is, Why did the Four-Seven controversy begin in sixteenth century Korea and develop further among later generations? There is no simple answer to this challenging question because it involves a few historical circumstances related to the intellectual and political settings of sixteenth century Korea. We have look at some of these specific circumstances. Although the fundamental metaphysical and ethical issues of T'oegye's and Yulgok's Four-Seven debates are significant for the entire Neo-Confucian tradition in East Asia, they had never been raised with the same urgency and intensity in China, either before or after T'oegye and Yulgok. With the issue of Ch'an (Zen) Buddhism in the background, the famous "Goose-Lake" debate between two Chinese Neo-Confucian thinkers, Chu Hsi and Lu Hsiang-shan (1139–1193), did not alter the general direction of Chinese Neo-Confucianism in the twelfth century.[131] On the contrary, the Four-Seven debate between T'oegye and Kobong and that between Yulgok and Ugye determined the characteristic patterns of Korean Neo-Confucianism for later generations.

It is interesting to speculate what would have happened if the Four-Seven debate had occurred in Sung or Yüan China before the rise of the Wang Yang-ming school in the Ming period. In Ming China, most Neo-Confucians were instead occupied with philosophical issues concerning human nature and the mind as rival topics in the competing Ch'eng-Chu and Lu-Wang schools of thought. By contrast, there was no such competition in Chosŏn Korea where the Ch'eng-Chu Sŏngnihak (school of human nature and principle) dominated the whole scholarly and political enterprise since the beginning of the Chosŏn dynasty in the late fourteenth century. This was part of the reason why, in sixteenth-century Korea, T'oegye, Yulgok, and their challengers addressed those ambiguous questions and issues that relate not only to Chu Hsi's metaphysics and ethics, but also to the entire Confucian literature, including the early classics, in regard to its moral and psychological philosophy of mind, human nature, and feelings and its implications for the practice of self-cultivation.

From an intellectual perspective, then, the Korean Neo-Confucians wished to interpret the basic problematic inherent in Chu Hsi's philosophy through a broader and deeper inquiry into the Four-Seven controversy of mind, human nature, and feelings and its relationship to Chu Hsi's metaphysics of *i* and *ki*. In comparison to China, their absolute dependence on the Ch'eng-Chu tradition as the orthodox school of Neo-Confucianism contributed to the rise and development of the Four-Seven controversy. As the state permitted no schools of thought other than Sŏngnihak, the academic and scholarly circles of the Chosŏn dynasty were restricted to it. In a historical context, then, this limited but focused scholarship led to specific studies and challenging debates on it, which resulted in many sophisticated interpretations of it.

This historical setting can be explained from a political perspective as well. Most Korean Neo-Confucians were proud of being faithful to Ch'eng-Chu orthodoxy and used it as a weapon against any new schools of thought including the Wang Yang-ming school. As I have pointed out elsewhere, "In Korea, a full commitment to the heritage of the Chu Hsi school was the basis of political ideology and legitimacy," and Korean Neo-Confucian scholar-officials maintained this scholarly commitment to the heritage of Chu Hsi orthodoxy.[132] In the sixteenth century, T'oegye and others eventually came to see themselves as the faithful guardians of the Ch'eng-Chu tradition, calling it "right learning" (*chŏnghak*).[133] This tendency was, in fact, established by Chŏng To-jŏn, Kwŏn Kŭn, and their followers at the beginning of the Chosŏn dynasty; in other words, there had already been an exclusive political tendency toward the view that only one orthodox teaching should be allowed to exist.

By the time of T'oegye, the champion of Ch'eng-Chu orthodoxy in Korea, other teachings were regarded as "heretical" and, therefore, had no solid grounds on which to stand. For example, the Korean Neo-Confucians felt extremely uncomfortable about the fact that contemporary Ming thought in the form of the Wang Yang-ming school of the mind had displaced the Ch'eng-Chu school in the homeland of orthodox Neo-Confucianism. Although the Wang Yang-ming school was introduced to Korea sometime in the middle of the sixteenth century, T'oegye immediately condemned as "heretical learning" and became the first major critic of Wang Yang-ming. His strong faith in the Ch'eng-Chu school is expressed in his famous biographical work of the Ch'eng-Chu school, the *Songgye Wŏn Myŏng ihak t'ongnok* (Records of the School of Principle in the Sung, Yüan, and Ming Dynasties),[134] as well as in his essay, the *Chŏnsŭmnok nonpyŏn* (Critique of Wang Yang-ming's *Instructions for Practical Living*).[135] Especially in the latter, he seriously criticized Wang Yang-ming's reformulation of Neo-Confucianism as "false," "anti-Chu Hsi," and "Zen Buddhist." His own scholarly discipline resulted in the view that any deviation from Ch'eng-Chu orthodoxy was "heretical." For T'oegye and others, then, right learning meant a full commitment to the Ch'eng-Chu school, setting absolute standards for scholarly pursuits. As a result, the Wang yang-ming school could not develop into an independent school of thought that could compete with the Ch'eng-Chu school.

In Ming China and Tokugawa Japan, the Wang Yang-ming school developed by compromising with the Chu Hsi school, bringing about flexibility and diversity in Neo-Confucian thought. Chinese and Japanese Neo-Confucians took the Lu-Wang thesis that "the mind is principle" and were not led into any kind of the Four-Seven controversy on the specific issues of human nature and feelings in Chu Hsi's philosophy. By contrast, T'oegye, Yulgok, and their challengers took the Ch'eng-Chu school seriously, to the extent that they discovered its distinctive philosophical agenda. This was part of the reason for the initial rise of the Four-Seven debate in Korea that made a great contribution to the philosophical advancement of Sŏngnihak. Under the impact of T'oegye and Yulgok, then, the Wang Yang-ming school was not convincing to most Korean scholars in such a focused intellectual environment. As a result, the exclusive devotion of T'oegye's and Yulgok's followers to the Ch'eng-Chu tradition maintained the Four-Seven controversy until the end of the nineteenth century. They continued to formulate different views according to Chu Hsi's original thinking and their masters' interpretations. However, the Korean tradition of Sŏngnihak often served as a system of thought for the literati bureaucrats, including many of T'oegye's and Yulgok's followers, who engaged themselves constantly in political power struggles and factional disputes, some of which were, in fact, related to the Four-Seven controversy itself.

Neo-Confucian scholarship in Tokugawa Japan was more devoted to practical matters rather than doctrinal disputes; therefore, various schools of Neo-Confucian thought prospered, and criticism of the orthodox Shushigaku (Chu Hsi school) was kept comparatively free. This was possible through the development of the Wang Yang-ming school (Yōmeigaku), Yamazaki Ansai's Southern school (Nangaku), Ito Jinsai's Ancient Learning school (Kogaku), Ogyū Sorai's school of political Neo-Confucianism (Soraigaku), and the Mito school (Mitogaku), which produced flexibility and vitality in Japanese Neo-Confucian thought.[136] Unlike the Chinese or Japanese, who developed different schools of Neo-Confucianism, the Korean thinkers who came after T'oegye and Yulgok devoted their energy to the study of Sŏngnihak only and were always interested in philosophical debates on it. In addition to the Four-Seven debates, the "Horak Debate" also took place in the eighteenth century.[137] It was a hair-splitting philosophical debate between three leading followers of Yulgok's Chugip'a, Kwŏn Sang-ha (Sangam, 1641–1721), Han Nam-dang (Wŏnjin, 1682–1750), and Yi Kan (Oeam, 1677–1729), on the distinction of human nature and the nature of things.

The Four-Seven debates were significant both historically and philosophically. Undeniably, the T'oegye-Kobong and Yulgok-Ugye debates generated a convincing model of scholarly debate, giving rise to the unique Korean style of systematic inquiry and moral reasoning for later generations. In short, Korean Neo-Confucianism is characterized by a strong commitment to Ch'eng-Chu orthodoxy; the entire legacy of the Korean Four-Seven debates demonstrates this historical and philosophical fact. Given such a commitment to continuity, both T'oegye and Yulgok found it necessary to clarify the Ch'eng-Chu tradition of metaphysics and ethics.

As a philosophical introduction to the Four-Seven debate in Korea, let us now examine the textual legacy of Chinese Confucianism.

I

Philosophical Introduction: The Fruitful Four-Seven Legacy

The Four-Seven debates in Korea raised a number of challenging questions and significant issues. In a sophisticated and comprehensive way, T'oegye, Yulgok, and their challengers examined the existing Confucian literature including Ch'eng-Chu Neo-Confucian texts and commentaries. They concentrated their debates on understanding and interpreting not only textual ambiguities and philosophical questions about the Confucian ideas of the "Four Beginnings" of virtue and the "Seven Emotions," but also their specific moral-psychological meanings and implications for the practice of self-cultivation, which had not been articulated clearly in the Chinese Confucian tradition.

The *Locus Classicus* for the Ideas of the Four Beginnings and the Seven Emotions

The Confucian term *Four Beginnings* (*sadan/ssu-tuan*) originally comes from a famous passage in the *Book of Mencius:*

> A person without the "mind-and-heart" (*sim/hsin*) of commiseration is not human; a person without the mind-and-heart of shame and dislike is not human; a person without the mind-and-heart of courtesy and modesty is not human; and a person without the mind-and-heart of right and wrong is not human. The mind-and-heart of commiseration is the beginning of benevolence; the mind-and-heart of shame and dislike is the beginning of righteousness; the mind-and-heart of courtesy and modesty is the beginning of propriety; and the mind-and-heart of [moral discernment of] right and wrong is the beginning of wisdom. All human beings have these Four Beginnings (*sadan/ssu-tuan*) just

> as they have their four limbs. If one who has the Four Beginnings is unable [to develop them], one destroys oneself.[1]

In this vigorous passage, Mencius referred specifically to the human "mind-and-heart" (*sim/hsin*)[2] of commiseration, that of shame and dislike, that of courtesy and modesty, and that of moral discernment of right and wrong as the Four Beginnings of such key Confucian virtues as benevolence, righteousness, propriety, and wisdom. Hence, his assertion that all human beings have the Four Beginnings is based on the fundamental belief that they have what he calls "the mind-and-heart that cannot bear to see the suffering of others."[3] Every person's spontaneous and immediate response to an urgent case like a child "falling into a well" is Mencius' best illustration of his moral argument: "When one were, all of a sudden, to see a child on the verge of falling into a well, one will certainly experience the mind-and-heart of commiseration [to save the child]. This is not to gain friendship with the child's parents, not to seek the praise of one's neighbors and friends, nor because one dislikes the cry of the child. From this, we can understand that a person without the mind-and-heart of commiseration is not human."[4]

This passage suggests Mencius' ontological view that the Four Beginnings of virtue are originally and naturally rooted in the human mind-and-heart. Mencius considered the "mind-and-heart of commiseration" as identical to the "beginning of benevolence." He continues to say: "If one develops fully all of these Four Beginnings that one [naturally] possesses, the result would be like a fire starting up or a spring coming forth. When these are fully developed, one can protect the whole world within the four seas; however, if one fails to develop them, one will not be able even to serve one's parents."[5] The Four Beginnings are, then, our natural innate seeds of moral self-cultivation. In the light of the *Great Learning*, one must nourish them to cultivate oneself and to transform others and the world. Mencius' doctrine of the Four Beginnings corresponds to what Charles Fu calls the *fourfold beginning*[6] of virtue, which basically means that the Four Beginnings are the spontaneous manifestations of our moral nature. This conviction upon the Four Beginnings as our innate virtuous qualities is, of course, the basis of his doctrine of the original goodness of "human nature" (*sŏng/hsing*); evil is not inborn, but comes from one's neglect to express the natural goodness of human nature inherent in the mind-and-heart as the Four Beginnings.[7] Evil is due to one's "failure" to control bad external influences.[8] In Mencius' own words, the way of self-cultivation necessarily involves one's commitment "to realize the mind-and-heart to the utmost" or "to preserve the mind-and-heart and to nourish human nature."[9] Wing-tsit Chan correctly points out:

"Mencius did not deviate from the general direction determined by Confucius. What we have in Mencius is, therefore, orthodox Confucianism, developed along with idealistic lines."[10]

The *locus classicus* for the Confucian term *Seven Emotions* (*ch'ilchŏng/ch'i-ch'ing*)[11] is the *Book of Rites* according to which pleasure, anger, sorrow, fear, love, hatred, and desire are basic human feelings "not acquired through learning from the outside."[12] As this list is too long, the *Doctrine of the Mean* draws special attention to the first three and adds joy representing the Seven Emotions: "What Heaven imparts to human beings is called human nature. To follow human nature is the Way. . . . Before [the emotions of] pleasure, anger, sorrow, and joy are aroused, it is called equilibrium. When these are aroused and all of them attain their due degree and measure, it is called harmony. Equilibrium is the great foundation of the world; harmony is the universal path. When equilibrium and harmony are realized to the utmost degree, Heaven and Earth will achieve proper order and all things flourish."[13] According to these two quotations, the Seven Emotions refer to physical and mental states that are understood as basic human feelings and emotions in a natural, common sense. The Seven Emotions are not learned from the outside; however, they are still the aroused states of the mind and body in response to the external things. As the *Doctrine of the Mean* indicates, therefore, the way of mind cultivation demands a measure of control over them because their problem is excessiveness and disharmony.[14] On the one hand, the purpose of self-cultivation is to retain the state of "equilibrium" before the Seven Emotions are aroused; on the other hand, it is to attain the state of "harmony" after they are aroused. This topic and its correlation with the Four Beginnings became one of the major issues in the Korean Four-Seven debates

Note that we have no evidence to show that Mencius was aware of the idea of the "Seven Emotions" mentioned especially the *Doctrine of the Mean*. He never paid any special attention to the Seven Emotions. Neither did he relate his belief in the ontological and moral status of the Four Beginnings to the physical and mental characteristics of the Seven Emotions. According to Chu Hsi, Tzu-ssu (Confucius' grandson) wrote the *Doctrine of the Mean* and transmitted it to his disciple Mencius. Chu Hsi and other Sung Neo-Confucians generally believed that the Mencian interpretation of the original goodness of human nature had came from Tzu-ssu, the alleged author of the *Doctrine of the Mean*; in other words, it was basically a further development of Tzu-ssu's original theory of "Heaven-imparted human nature." But modern scholarship on this subject suggests that the *Doctrine of the Mean* was written from a significantly different perspective that came later than the *Book of Men-*

cius.[15] Both texts deal with the Confucian way of self-cultivation according to their own contexts. But the fundamental difference is that the former deals more with the early Confucian metaphysical psychology of emotional integration and self-cultivation in terms of the Seven Emotions, whereas the latter addresses its moral theory of human nature and its ethical concerns in terms of the Four Beginnings.

On the whole, however, Mencius did not clarify what he meant by mind-and-heart (*sim/hsin*), human nature (*sŏng/hsing*), and feelings (*chŏng/ch'ing*); more to the point, he did not explain how they relate to one another. For example, the following passage illustrates this ambiguity:

> As far as human "feelings" (*chŏng/ch'ing*) are concerned, people are capable of becoming good. This is what I mean by [saying that human nature is] good. If one becomes evil (*pulsŏn/pu-shan*; literally no goodness), it is one's fault. All human beings have the mind-and-heart (*sim/hsin*) of commiseration, the mind-and-heart of shame and dislike, the mind-and-heart of respect and reverence,[16] and the mind-and-heart of moral discernment of right and wrong. The mind-and-heart of commiseration pertains to benevolence. . . . Benevolence, righteousness, propriety, and wisdom are not welded into us from the outside; rather, they are within us originally [in our nature].[17]

Although the term *chŏng/ch'ing* in the preceding passage can be rendered as "feelings," it is not clear what Mencius means by it. The left character of this term is identical to the term *sim/hsin* itself; in the Mencian context, then, the *chŏng/ch'ing* can be translated as the "mind-and-heart" as well.[18] In general, Mencius tended to emphasize the status of human nature in terms of the mind-and-heart. For example, he says: "What the superior person (*kunja/chün-tzu*) calls human nature (*sŏng/hsing*) refers to benevolence, righteousness, propriety, and wisdom rooted in the mind-and-heart (*sim/hsin*)."[19] Another passage illustrates this point further: "Our mouths desire tastes, our eyes desire colors, our ears desire sounds, our noses desire smells, and our limbs desire ease and comfort. These desires are certainly due to our nature. But there is also fate (*ming*). This is why the superior person does not call these desires human nature (*sŏng/hsing*)."[20] For Mencius, the Four Beginnings are to be considered as the four roots of moral goodness inherent in human nature. But he did not spell out whether by *feelings* he meant only the Four Beginnings as the mind-and-heart. What about those physical desires that he mentioned in the preceding passage; did he consider them as feelings as well? This was a sign of ambiguous legacy at the heart of Mencius' teaching, one that the Four-Seven debates in Korea addressed while generating a wellspring of creative thought. T'oegye, Yulgok, and their challengers cited and discussed some of the quoted passages.

What Mencius intended is, of course, to distinguish general physical desires and physiological sensations from the Four Beginnings of moral virtue. To him, the Four Beginnings do not come from the outside, but are inherent in the mind-and-heart (*sim/hsin*). At the same time, according to the *Book of Rites* and *Doctrine of the Mean*, other feelings, like the Seven Emotions, also do not come from the outside, but arise from within under external influence. Taken together, Mencius definitely meant that benevolence, righteousness, propriety, and wisdom are moral virtues pertaining to human nature (*sŏng/hsing*); the Four Beginnings, such as commiseration, are our moral roots and expressions pertaining to the mind-and-heart (*sim/hsin*). This is his ontological and moral conviction that these "beginnings" of virtue are fundamental qualities of human nature. In other words, all human beings are born good because they naturally possess the Four Beginnings.

But the crucial question is, How do human nature and the Four Beginnings relate to what Mencius calls *feelings* (*chŏng/ch'ing*) in general? His vigorous view that the "mind-and-heart of commiseration" is the "beginning of benevolence" does not answer the question at all. For Mencius, however, we have little doubt that there can be no discussion of human feelings outside of the context of the Four Beginnings of virtue. He seems to have suggested that the Four Beginnings are our innate, good feelings (*chŏng/ch'ing*). Another problem is revealed in the following key passage: "The ability that human beings possess without learning is their innate ability (*yangnŭng/liang-neng*); the knowledge that human beings possess without deliberation is their innate knowledge (*yangji/liang-chih*). Young children all know to love (*ae/ai*) their parents. As they grow, they all know to respect their elder siblings as well. Loving one's parents is benevolence, and respecting one's elders righteousness. These [innate ability and knowledge] are universal in the world, that is all."[21]

In my own reading, Korean Neo-Confucians including T'oegye and Yulgok never cited such a key passage that indicates another main aspect of ambiguity. What does Mencius mean by *love* in the context of the Four Beginnings and the Seven Emotions? It is possible that he was unaware of the fact that love is one of the Seven Emotions mentioned in the *Book of Rites*. In any case, he meant that love ("loving parents" in his own terminology), one of the Seven Emotions, is a natural human feeling, part of what he calls the "innate ability" and "innate knowledge" of human nature to do good.

As Wing-tsit Chan correctly comments on Mencius, "since human nature is good, love is therefore an inborn moral quality."[22] But the whole problem is precisely this: Mencius identified the innate feeling of "love" with the moral virtue of "benevolence," which he referred to not only as an ontological and moral quality of human nature itself, but also as the mind-and-heart of commiseration, one of the Four Beginnings. The question is, Can love be benevolence? Surely there is likely a meaningful link between them. Sung Chinese Neo-Confucians, especially Ch'eng I and Chu Hsi, commented on this kind of issue, which later became an important part of the Korean Four-Seven debates. On the whole, however, they did not directly pay much attention to the Four-Seven controversy in detail.

The Ch'eng-Chu Interpretation in China

Commenting on Mencius, Ch'eng I briefly argued that Mencius' saying that "the mind-and-heart (*sim/hsin*) of commiseration is benevolence" does not imply that love (one of the Seven Emotions) is also benevolence.[23] A passage from his commentary illustrates this point further: "The 'mind-and-heart of commiseration' is certainly an expression of 'love.' However, love is a feeling (*chŏng/ch'ing*), whereas benevolence is human nature (*sŏng/hsing*). How can love be taken simply as benevolence? Mencius said that 'the mind-and-heart of commiseration is benevolence,' for it is 'the beginning of benevolence.'"[24] Ch'eng I generally meant that "the mind-and-heart of commiseration" pertains to a seed of benevolence inherent in what Mencius calls the "original goodness of human nature." By contrast, love is to be understood as a common mental feeling that is not, in the Mencian sense, a virtuous root of morality. When asked whether "joy and anger come from human nature," Ch'eng I answered "yes, of course" and said: "As there is human nature, there must be feelings as well. Without the former, how can there be the latter?"[25] The Four Beginnings and the emotions like joy and anger are all feelings aroused not from the outside; they "arise within under external influence." Ch'eng I did not discuss the Seven Emotions specifically; neither did he clarify any connection between the Four Beginnings and the emotions like joy and love he mentioned. Using an interesting analogy of water and waves, he said: "It is the nature of water to be clear, level, and tranquil like a mirror. But when water strikes sand and stone, or when the ground underneath it is not level, water immediately begins to move. When wind moves over it, water immediately gives rise to waves and currents. . . . *In human nature there are only the Four Beginnings without any form of evil.* Nevertheless, without water, how can there be waves? Similarly, without human nature, how can there be feelings?"[26]

Though obscure in itself, this passage implies that the Four Beginnings are truly the defining characteristics of human nature. To put this in another way, the Four are the innate, autonomous, and moral manifestations of human nature, just as the clear, level, and tranquil state of water is the fundamental nature of water. To Ch'eng I, the Four Beginnings and the emotions of joy, love, and anger are aroused feelings coming from human nature; however, joy, love, and anger should be understood as our psychological and physiological states, just as the waves of water represent a temporary state conditioned by external influence. This distinction was important for him to address the way of self-cultivation in the light of Mencius and the *Doctrine of the Mean* together. He argued that the practice of self-cultivation involves what Mencius calls "preserving [the mind-and-heart] and nourishing [human nature],"[27] which means to retain what the *Doctrine of the Mean* calls "the state of equilibrium before [the emotions of] pleasure, anger, sorrow, and joy are aroused."[28] Of course, Mencius meant that self-cultivation requires one to realize and nurture the Four. On the other hand, Ch'eng I asserted that one also has to maintain what the *Doctrine of the Mean* calls "the state of harmony after pleasure, anger, sorrow, and joy are aroused," which can be done by letting aroused feelings to "attain due degree and measure."[29] This line of reasoning became another important issue in the Four-Seven controversy in Korea.

But the whole subject matter became much more complicated when Chu Hsi systematized a coherent synthesis of the entire Confucian tradition of metaphysics and ethics. According to him, Ch'eng I was correct in saying that "love is a feeling, whereas benevolence is human nature."[30] Chu Hsi said: "Although the spheres of human nature (*sŏng/hsing*) and feelings (*chŏng/ch'ing*) are different, their mutual penetration is like the bloodstream in which each part has its own relationship [with other parts]."[31] Commenting on the Mencian doctrine of the Four Beginnings, Chu Hsi distinguished human nature from feelings: "Commiseration, shame and dislike, courtesy and modesty, and [moral discernment of] right and wrong are feelings (*chŏng/ch'ing*). Benevolence, righteousness, propriety, and wisdom are human nature (*sŏng/hsing*)."[32] These passages, of course, correspond to Ch'eng I's interpretation of Mencius. In other words, what Mencius calls the *Four Beginnings* are inherent moral "feelings" aroused from moral virtues, such as benevolence, righteousness, propriety, and wisdom, which constitute the essence of human nature. As Chu Hsi emphasized, the Four Beginnings are "illuminating virtues (*myŏngdŭk/ming-te*)" or "great virtues (*taedŭk/ta-te*)."[33] "The Four

Beginnings are the principles of the Way (*to/tao*) . . . and moral feelings (*ŭri chŏng/i-li ch'ing*)."[34]

Throughout his writings, however, Chu Hsi hardly discussed the Four Beginnings in relation to the Seven Emotions. He made a vague statement in terms of their origins: "The Four Beginnings are manifestations of *li* (*sadan si ijibal/ssu-tuan shih li-chih-fa*); the Seven Emotions are manifestations of *ch'i* (*ch'ilchŏng si kijibal/ch'i-ch'ing shih ch'i-chih-fa*)."[35] The term *pal/fa* in this passage is rather ambiguous and means "issue forth," "arise," or "manifest." So, the same statement can be translated in another way: "The Four Beginnings are issued from *li*; the Seven Emotions are issued from *ch'i*." This isolated and unexplained statement in the *Chu Tzu yü-lei* (Classified Conversations of Master Chu) does indicate a great deal of ontological separability and conceptual distinction between the Four and the Seven. Without explaining it, Chu Hsi might have meant that the Four Beginnings are the roots of virtue pertaining to *li*, whereas the Seven Emotions are not necessarily so and, therefore, pertain to *ch'i*. Undoubtedly, he did not explain anything about the Four-Seven relationship and its implications for learning and self-cultivation. Consequently, this issue became the main focus of the Four-Seven debates in Korea, one that T'oegye, Yulgok, and others debated extensively quoting Chu Hsi's ambiguous Four-Seven statement repeatedly.

Nevertheless, we can approach it by addressing Chu Hsi's metaphysics of principle and material force, which has been researched and interpreted by modern scholars.[36] Obviously, there is a remarkable convergence of opinion on the general theme of Chu Hsi's metaphysics. As distinguished from concrete things and phenomena that must exist "within form," *li* is the metaphysical principle that remains "without form," "unitary," omnipresent, and so on. It is understood as the ground of being present in each phenomenon in its fullness. On the other hand, material force (*ch'i*) is the actual physical agent that brings everything into concrete existence; it always remains "within form" and determines the individuality and transformation of everything. In a moral sense, *li* is always good, pure, and unchanging, whereas *ch'i* is what may cause impurity and evil.

Given this consistent pattern of Chu Hsi's philosophy of *li* and *ch'i*, it was reasonable for him to assert that the Four are manifest from *li*, and the Seven from *ch'i*. Commenting on Chu Hsi's theory, Tang Chün-i, a contemporary Chinese scholar, makes an interesting but unclear point: the Four and the Seven can be distinguished in terms of "human nature characterized by feelings" and "stimulated feelings," respectively. Of course, Tang argues that the former means "moral feelings," and the latter "the selfishness of human desires."[37] This can be explained in the following manner: because the Four, as emphasized by Mencius, are innate, moral expressions of the original goodness of human nature, it follows that they must be aroused by *li*; by contrast, the Seven must be aroused by *ch'i* because they, as mentioned in the *Doctrine of the Mean*, are physical feelings and mental emotions that are capable of becoming good or evil depending on their harmony or excessiveness, respectively. According to Chu Hsi, the mind-and-heart itself is where *li* and *ch'i* are united. To him, then, feelings can be the manifestation of either *li* or *ch'i*. Because both the Four and the Seven are all human feelings, Chu Hsi might have assumed that those moral feelings aroused by *li* should be represented by the Four, whereas those physical and mental emotions aroused by *ch'i*, which may not be fundamentally virtuous, should be represented by the Seven. This issue became another main topic in the Koran Four-Seven debates.

On the whole, Chu Hsi paid more attention to the Mencian understanding of the Four Beginnings. But this becomes much more complex in the context of his philosophy of mind-and-heart, human nature, and feelings. Chu Hsi provided a sophisticated explanation by taking as a basic precept Chang Tsai's assertion that "the mind-and-heart commands human nature and feelings."[38] To convince the Mencian creed that human nature is originally good, just as water naturally flows downward, Chu Hsi also utilized Ch'eng I's theories that "human nature is principle (*i/li*)"[39] and that "that which is inherent in things is called principle, and that which is endowed in human beings is called human nature."[40] For Chu Hsi, human nature is principle and full of moral and spiritual goodness inherent in the mind-and-heart,[41] and all the principles inherent in the mind-and-heart are, therefore, called human nature. The mind-and-heart serves as "the master of the self."[42]

Following Mencius and his senior Sung Neo-Confucians, Chu Hsi meant that all human beings have the mind-and-heart consisting of moral feelings such as commiseration, shame and dislike, courtesy and modesty, and discernment of right and wrong. He argued that this view corresponds the Mencian doctrine of human nature:

> Benevolence, righteousness, propriety, and wisdom are human nature. They are called principles. Their beginnings refer to the mind-and-heart of commiseration, shame and dislike, courtesy and modesty, and right and wrong. Commiseration, shame and dislike, courtesy and modesty, and right and wrong are feelings (*chŏng/ch'ing*). Benevolence, righteousness, propriety, and wisdom are human nature (*sŏng/hsing*). Hence, "the mind-and-heart commands human nature and feelings."[43] The beginnings

> are aroused feelings that come from the original essence of human nature. . . . When Mencius spoke of "the mind-and-heart of commiseration," for example, he discussed the mind-and-heart (*sim/hsin*), not the human nature (*sŏng/hsing*). The mind-and-heart is one thing, and human nature is another thing. . . . Mencius' theory of the Four Beginnings is best explained by three points: commiseration is a feeling; the mind-and-heart of commiseration is the mind-and-heart; and benevolence is human nature.[44]

Implicit in this passage is an ontological and conceptual perspective that the "mind-and-heart," "human nature," and "feelings" are three different things that can be discussed separately. From a standpoint of concrete reality, however, "the mind-and-heart includes human nature and feelings."[45] "The Four Beginnings are all manifest from the mind-and-heart"[46] and "the mind-and-heart includes the four virtues [of benevolence, righteousness, propriety, and wisdom] and penetrates the Four Beginnings."[47] The mind-and-heart is to be conceived as something that "includes" and "commands" both human nature and feelings. Futhermore, because the Four and the Seven are both feelings, it follows for Chu Hsi that "the Seven Emotions cannot be separated from the Four Beginnings"[48] and that "the Four Beginnings can be understood from the standpoint of the Seven Emotions."[49] Interestingly, in their Four-Seven debates, T'oegye, Yulgok, and their debaters were not familiar with these two statements by Chu Hsi, which suggest that the Four Beginnings do not belong to an independent kind of feelings and, therefore, should be understood in the context of addressing the Seven Emotions.

According to Chu Hsi, the mind-and-heart has its two states: the "unmanifest" (*mibal/wei-fa*) and the "manifest" (*ibal/i-fa*). Human nature is its unmanifest "substance" (*ch'e/t'i*), and feelings are its manifest "function" (*yong/yung*).[50] The former is the mind-and-heart in itself before manifestation, whereas the latter is its function after manifestation. Commenting on the Mencian idea of the Four, Chu Hsi said: "The mind-and-heart commands human nature and feelings. . . . Human nature is the principle (*i/li*) of the mind-and-heart, and the feelings are the function of the mind-and-heart. . . . The mind-and-heart is the master of human nature and feelings."[51] As "the master of the self," it commands human nature and feelings, uniting and apprehending them. In other words, it participates in the whole process of integrating all faculties of human experience, including moral principles and feelings, rational reasoning, emotional feelings, and physical desires. Chu Hsi's philosophy is quite different from the Mencian doctrine of human nature that seems to be focused on the ontological status of human nature as the mind-and-heart in itself.[52] This was, in fact, one of the major issues debated by the Korean scholars in the Four-Seven controversy.

Chu Hsi's interpretation of the mind is also discussed in terms of the so-called moral mind (*tosim/tao-hsin*; literally the "mind of the Way") and human mind (*insim/jen-hsin*).[53] Commenting on the *Doctrine of the Mean*, he argued that the former is aroused from "the correctness of Heaven and destiny" and the latter from "selfishness identified with physical form"; more to the point, the former is "subtle," "impartial," and "good," whereas the latter is "partial" and "prone to error," involving both good and evil.[54] In Chu Hsi's view, then, the moral mind pertains to moral principles such as benevolence, righteousness, propriety, and wisdom, whereas the human mind pertains to our physical feelings and sensations, including the mouth's desire for taste, the eye's desire for color, and so on.[55] Furthermore, the moral mind is the mind-in-itself full of *li* only, whereas the human mind is the manifest mind mixed with selfish desires caused by *ki*.[56] But Chu Hsi did not discuss them with respect to the Four and the Seven; this was, in fact, another obscure area that the Korean Neo-Confucians especially Yulgok debated.

According to the Ch'eng-Chu tradition, human nature can be discussed in terms of its two names, *original* (human) *nature* (*ponyŏn chi sŏng/penjan chih hsing*) and *physical* (human) *nature* (*kijil chi sŏng/ch'i-chih chih hsing*). Ch'eng I and Chu Hsi explained the former with respect to *li* and the latter as its physical endowment conditioned by *ki*. Chang Tsai discussed the latter in terms of the transformation of *ki* as a way of self-cultivation. Interpreting the early classics and his senior Neo-Confucians including Chang Tsai, Chu Hsi argued that the original human nature and the physical human nature are not two separate natures with their own ontological grounds. Rather they are just two different names or concepts referring to the two realms of one nature. Chu Hsi said: "As there is Heaven-endowed nature (*ch'ŏnmyŏng chi sŏng/t'ien-ming chih hsing*), there is also physical nature."[57] The following passage illustrates his view further:

> Original human nature is purely good. This is the nature described by Mencius as good. Master Chou Tun-i described it as "pure and perfectly good,"[58] and master Ch'eng I called it "the fundamental character of our nature."[59]. . . . However, it would be wrong to say that physical human nature contains impurity. This is why [Chang Tsai said] "In physical human nature, there is that which the superior person declines to call original nature,"[60] and "If one learns to return to the original

> human nature endowed by Heaven and Earth, one will preserve it."[61] Accordingly, any discussion of human nature must include physical human nature, so that the discussion can be complete.[62]

The physical human nature is neither different nor separate from the original human nature; more to the point, "the latter runs through the former."[63] For this reason, Chu Hsi said: "The nature of all human beings is good; however, some people are good from their birth, while some people are evil from theirs. This is due to the difference in the physical endowment of *ki*. . . . The objective of learning is to transform one's physical endowment."[64] Despite Chu Hsi's extensive discussion of such a topic on the two dimensions of human nature, he did not address it terms of feelings; neither did he discuss it especially in relation to the Four Beginnings and the Seven Emotions.

Indeed, the Four-Seven debates in Korea addressed these and other problems with respect to Chu Hsi's Four-Seven statement, his metaphysics of *li* and *ch'i*, and his moral and psychological philosophy of mind-and-heart, human nature, and feelings. Consequently, various questions and issues centering around such ambiguous or underdeveloped areas of Chu Hsi's philosophy became the focus of the Four-Seven controversy in Korea.

Questions and Issues Raised in the Korean Four-Seven Debates

T'oegye, Yulgok, and their challengers addressed a number of challenging philosophical questions and moral issues in a hairsplitting, sophisticated way, citing the entire Confucian literature including Ch'eng-Chu commentaries. The goal was, of course, to understand a meaningful philosophical, ethical, and psychological link between the Four and the Seven, which had not been articulated clearly by the Chinese thinkers. Add to the general linguistic ambiguities the fact that the Four-Seven debates took place during the sixteenth century, when the philosophical development of Korean Neo-Confucianism was reaching its peak under the leadership of T'oegye, Yulgok, and others.

A key issue that simulated T'oegye, Yulgok, and their challengers was why Mencius singled out the Four Beginnings as evidence to explain the fundamental Confucian creed that "human nature" (*sŏng/hsing*) is originally good. Although Mencius described the Four as "feelings" (*chŏng/ch'ing*) in general, the ambiguity definitely lies in the fact that he referred to them specifically in terms of the "mind-and-heart" (*sim/hsin*). For example, he emphasized the spontaneous and natural rise of the "mind-and-heart of commiseration" when "one sees a child falling into a well." The Koreans were highly curious about how Mencius' doctrine of the original goodness of human nature—characterized by the virtues of benevolence, righteousness, propriety, and wisdom—should be understood in terms of what he calls the Four Beginnings, such as commiseration, shame and dislike, courtesy and modesty, and right and wrong, to which the mind-and-heart is referred.

The fundamental question was, If both the Four Beginnings and the Seven Emotions are basic human feelings, why make *any distinction* between them, using two different terms? Commenting on T'oegye's Four-Seven debate with Kobong, Michael Kalton correctly points out that whether the Four and the Seven are "only different names for the same reality looked at from differing perspectives, or rather truly point to some differentiation in the condition whence they arise" was a central issue.[65] More specifically, this issue had to deal with whether the Four-Seven relationship is purely arbitrary or has important philosophical meanings and moral implications. In other words, do the Four Beginnings (mentioned by Mencius) and the Seven Emotions (mentioned in the *Doctrine of the Mean* and *Book of Rites*) point to the two separate realms of human feelings? What about any meaningful connection between them? As Tu Wei-ming point outs, "Surely there is a meaningful connection between the two realms. The whole intellectual enterprise of the 'Four-Seven' debate, after all, was to define clearly what the connection is."[66]

For T'oegye and Yulgok, a fascinating question was whether the meaning and implication of the Four Beginnings are superior to those of the Seven Emotions from a conceptual and moral standpoint. It was the issue of addressing any ontological possibility that the Four Beginnings belong to a special group of moral feelings that exist independent of the Seven Emotions. In relation to this issue, another question was whether both the Four and the Seven are identically aroused by external stimuli and conditions and, therefore, have to be controlled by the mind-and-heart in the same way. For the Korean thinkers, these questions and issues were significant for addressing not only the Four-Seven relationship from a philosophical standpoint, but also its implications for *self-cultivation* in an ethico-spiritual context.

T'oegye, Yulgok, and their challengers addressed the question of whether the Four Beginnings, like the Seven Emotions, are feelings understood in general sense or they are to be conceived as what Julia Ching calls "moral intuitions" independent of the Seven Emotions.[67] Should the Four Beginnings rather be considered fundamental roots of the human potential for moral self-cultivation in the Mencian sense? Unlike the Chinese, the Korean thinkers debated on the question of whether the Four are "natural, spontaneous, and autonomous manifestations of the mind-heart" associated with moral "knowing and willing."[68] Evidently, the Koreans found this issue important in determining if the Four have such characteristics as "self-regulation" and "self-manifestation." Of course, such an issue was necessary to provide an ontological and moral justification for the Mencian doctrine of the original goodness of human nature. As for the Seven Emotions, they debated on the questions of whether the Seven Emotions are merely mental feelings and physiological states without any ontological or moral status in relation to the Four Beginnings. They addressed the following issues: first, why does the *Book of Rites* describe the Seven as feelings "not acquired through learning from the outside"; second, in what sense does the *Doctrine of the Mean* describe them in terms of "equilibrium" and "harmony," and why does it emphasize emotional control by attaining their "proper measure and degree"; third, why do the Seven Emotions bring about evil; fourth, do they represent the totality of feelings, whereas the Four Beginnings constitute the good side of the Seven; fifth, is there any continuum between harmonized emotions (e.g., love) and the Four Beginnings (e.g., commiseration); and finally, what do all these issues mean for the practice of self-cultivation?

Another topic, which had been left unexplained by Chu Hsi and his followers, was the issue of how to interpret the Four and the Seven in terms of principle (*i*) and material force (*ki*). This became a complicated issue for Korean thinkers who wanted to interpret Chu Hsi's statement that "the Four Beginnings are manifestations of *i* and the Seven Emotions are manifestations of *ki*."[69] In a sense, the issue was initially a textual one; however, it quickly became a significant issue, for it related directly to one's proper understanding of learning and self-cultivation. The compelling question was whether Chu Hsi's theory could be interpreted *dualistically* in the dichotomous system of *i* and *ki* (as T'oegye had done), or *nondualistically* in terms of the inseparability and oneness of *i* and *ki* (as Kobong and, in turn, Yulgok had done). In this regard, the unsettling issue was whether it is wiser to acknowledge that the Four Beginnings should be considered as a subset of good feelings within the Seven Emotions, instead of differentiating them according to the system of *i* and *ki*.

Note that the whole issue comes from Chu Hsi himself. The real problematic in Chu Hsi's metaphysics is that, despite his emphasis on the inseparability and interdependence of *i* and *ki* in concrete phenomena, he definitely affirmed that *i* and *ki* are ontologically and conceptually distinguishable. More to the point, this led him to suggest that, although the Four and the Seven are both feelings, they are, like *i* and *ki*, different from an ontological and conceptual frame of reference and, therefore, can be represented by *i* and *ki,* respectively. The question is, What did he really intend to mean? There is no clear answer to this question, but it can addressed in terms of his philosophy of the mind, human nature, and feelings. Of course, this was a central issue in the Korean Four-Seven debates.

According to Chu Hsi, the mind combines *i* and *ki* and commands human nature and feelings. Both the Four and the Seven are feelings, the aroused states of the mind. It follows that feelings can be manifestations of either *i* or *ki*. But Chu Hsi also argued that the Four are fundamentally moral feelings, and Seven can be selfish feelings or desires. Does this, then, imply that the Four cannot be energized by *ki* in the same manner that the Seven are? Should the Four be represented by *i* only? These questions were significant for the Korean Neo-Confucians. Other questions included the following. How can the Four Beginnings be discussed independent of material force? Futhermore, how can principle, which is explicitly interpreted by Chu Hsi as a passive and formless entity in itself, have its own *self-manifesting* power to emanate the Four Beginnings? Hence, Chu Hsi's whole metaphysics of *i* and *ki* and his moral and psychological philosophy were critically reexamined through the unique Korean style of systematic reasoning and creative interpretation.

In such a process, another crucial issue focused on the Confucian way of understanding the Four-Seven connection in terms of "good" and "evil," which had not been articulated by Chinese Neo-Confucians. Both T'oegye and Yulgok asked, Why does a human being whose nature is fundamentally good become evil in some cases? This question was debated seriously in the spirit of two classical perspectives, notably, the Mencian doctrine that the Four Beginnings are innate, moral characteristics of "the original goodness of human nature," and the thesis in the *Doctrine of the Mean* that the Emotions can be either good or evil depending on whether or not they are properly harmonized according to "due measure and degree." Furthermore, this issue, of course, relates to the fundamental Ch'eng-Chu doctrine that, although human nature is always full of goodness and moral principles backed up by *i*, one can become evil if one's physical endowment is disturbed by turbid *ki*, which can cause selfish desires, or if one's mind-and-heart does not control one's emotions and feelings.

Yet another major issue dealt with the Four-Seven problem in terms of what Sung Neo-Confucians call *original* (human) *nature* (*ponyŏn chi sŏng/pen-jan chih hsing*) and *physical* (human) *nature* (*kijil chi sŏng/ch'i-chih chih hsing*). According to Chu Hsi's philosophy, human nature is fundamentally one. On the one hand, when human nature is spoken of as undisturbed by *ki* or unmixed with physical endowment, it is called *original human nature* ("human nature in itself"), which consists of good (*i*) only; on the other hand, when viewed from a concrete standpoint of physical endowment, it is called *physical human nature,* which includes both good and evil, consisting of *i* and *ki* together. For the Korean scholars, however, the critical subject was whether or not the Four-Seven relationship could be interpreted in the same manner. That is to say, do the Four belong to the original human nature and the Seven to the physical human nature? And can the former be viewed as something included inside the latter, just as the physical human nature includes the original human nature?

The last characteristic feature of the Four-Seven controversy, especially that between Yulgok and Ugye, focused on Chu Hsi's philosophy of the mind. The question was, If the mind is ontologically one, how can it be discussed in term of what Chu Hsi calls the *moral mind* (*tosim/tao-hsin*) and the *human mind* (*insim/jen-hsin*)? Does this not suggest that the Four Beginnings and the Seven Emotions can be interpreted according to these two aspects of the mind? In other words, this issue focused on any conceptual possibility of whether the Four Beginnings and the Seven Emotions belong to the "purely good" moral mind and the "precarious" human mind, respectively. How can there be two origins of feelings? In what sense, then, does such a hypothetical categorization of the mind have practical implications for self-cultivation? Accordingly, Chu Hsi's philosophy and his approach to mind cultivation faced a good deal of criticism and reinterpretation. As Yulgok realized, How can there be two different kinds of the mind as two separate sources of goodness?

In short, the main intellectual reason for the rise of the Four-Seven debate in Korea pertains to most of these questions and issues, which saw very little discussion in China. To T'oegye, Yulgok, and their debaters, the vital thrust of the whole debate was to clarify conscientiously the constructive meanings and implications of the Four-Seven link. They discussed them systematically and creatively according to the Four Books and the Neo-Confucian tradition of metaphysics and ethics. This was, indeed, necessary to provide a concrete way of understanding the *moral-spiritual* teachings of the former Confucian sages and worthies, especially in regard to the critical issue of the role of human feelings in self-cultivation. Both T'oegye and Yulgok realized the crucial implications of the Four-Seven enterprise for self-cultivation, and offered a more adequate set of explanatory categories and practical guidelines in two unique directions. This, then, brings us to T'oegye's Four-Seven thesis.

II

T'oegye's Four-Seven Thesis

The Four-Seven debate between T'oegye and Kobong began in the form of correspondence in the spring of 1559 and lasted for about eight years until the winter of 1566, producing six long letters of high quality.[1] As Yi Sang-ŭn said, "it was genuinely a scholarly and philosophical debate in the history of Korean Confucianism, resulting in a great development of Sung Neo-Confucianism in Korea."[2] Unquestionably, the T'oegye-Kobong debate is the most important intellectual event in the entire history of Korean Confucian thought. As Tu Wei-ming pointed out correctly, "it symbolizes a major landmark of philosophical sophistication in the tradition of East Asian Confucianism."[3] It is a highly challenging and penetrating debate on two of the most important problems in the Ch'eng-Chu tradition of Neo-Confucianism; namely, its metaphysics of principle and material force, and its moral and psychological philosophy of mind, human nature, and feelings. Indeed, the T'oegye-Kobong exchange generated the Korean model of sophisticated scholarly communication for subsequent generations of the Ch'eng-Chu school in Chosŏn Korea.

The initial correspondence appeared to T'oegye nothing more than a textual matter of clarifying the *Chŏnmyŏng to* (Diagram of the Heaven's Imperative)[4] composed by Chŏng Chi-ŭn (Ch'uman, 1509–1575). But it became the starting point of the Four-Seven debate. Chŏng's diagram summarizes the basic teachings on Neo-Confucian metaphysics and ethics. As indicated before, it was influenced by the *Ch'ŏnin simsŏng habil chi to* (Diagram of the Oneness of Heaven and Human Beings, Mind, and Nature), the first diagram of Kwŏn Kŭn's *Iphak tosŏl,* which is the earliest Korean diagrammatical treatise on Ch'eng-Chu Neo-Confucianism.[5] The important aspect of Chŏng's *Ch'ŏnmyŏng to* is the following statement: "The Four Beginnings are manifest from *i* (*sadan palŏi/ssu-tuan fa yü li*); the Seven Emotions are manifest from *ki* (*ch'ilchŏng palŏki/ch'i-ch'ing fa yü ch'i*)."[6] Indeed, Chŏng was the first Korean Neo-Confucian to mention the distinction between the Four and the Seven. And yet, his Four-Seven statement appears to have originated from Chu Hsi's unexplained saying that "the Four Beginnings are manifestations of *i*; the Seven Emotions are manifestations of *ki*."[7]

T'oegye revised Chŏng's saying into a slightly different version that is the same as Chu Hsi's saying: "the Four Beginnings are manifestations of *i* (*sadan ijibal/ssu-tuan li-chih-fa*) and the Seven Emotions are manifestations of *ki* (*ch'ilchŏng kijibal/ch'i-ch'ing ch'i-chih-fa*)."[8] With some doubt about the feasibility of separating the Four and the Seven into such a dichotomous system of *i* and *ki*, T'oegye wrote a short but unconvincing note to Kobong and asked him for his feedback on the revised version of Chŏng's original Four-Seven statement. In addition, T'oegye politely requested Kobong to consider the following revised version of Chŏng's another statement: "The issuance of the Four Beginnings [involves] purely *i* and, therefore, does not have evil (literally, "that which is not good"); the issuance of the Seven Emotions includes *ki* also and, accordingly, has [both] good and evil."[9]

Kobong's Challenge to T'oegye: The Continuum of the Four and the Seven

In his response to T'oegye's question, Kobong wrote a thorough and convincing three-page critique[10] of the dualistic tendency implicit in T'oegye's thinking. In this first letter to T'oegye, he maintained that the Four Beginnings (the mind-and-heart of commiseration, the mind-and-heart of shame and dislike, the mind-and-heart of courtesy and modesty, and the mind-and-heart of discernment of right and wrong) and the Seven Emotions (pleasure, anger, sorrow, fear, love, hatred, and desire) are all basic human feelings (*chŏng/ch'ing*). In other words, the *Book of Rites*, *Mencius*, and *Doctrine of the Mean* all refer to a theory of feelings. Kobong argues:

> Tzu-ssu's saying [in the *Doctrine of the Mean*] referred to the totality [of all feelings], and Mencius singled out [the Four Beginnings]. In general, human nature is the unaroused mind-and-heart, and feelings are the aroused mind-and-heart. Fundamentally speaking, human nature is always good, whereas feelings involve both good and evil. What Tzu-ssu and Mencius each intended to mean is not the same; there is only a simple distinction between the Four and the Seven. But it is not that outside of the Seven Emotions, there are the Four Beginnings. If we say [as Chŏng has said] that "the Four Beginnings are manifest from *i* and, therefore, purely good; the Seven Emotions are manifest from *ki* and, accordingly, can have either good or evil," then we

> mean that *i* and *ki* are certainly two things in opposition to each other. Furthermore, this implies that the Seven Emotions do not come from human nature, and the Four Beginnings do not ride on *ki*. This is, of course, wrong in wording, and later scholars will have doubts about it. Your revised theory that "the manifestation of the Four Beginnings involves purely *i* and, therefore, does not have any evil; the manifestation of the Seven Emotions involves *ki* also and, accordingly, have both good and evil" is, in my view, still unsatisfactory, although it is a little better than the previous theory [Chŏng's original statement].[11]

Kobong's fundamental thesis is that the Seven represent the "totality" of all feelings because Mencius deliberately selected the Four a set of good feelings to refer to them as the "good side" of the Seven. In other words, the Four do not exist outside the Seven; they were mentioned by Mencius especially to explain his belief that human nature (*sŏng/hsing*) is originally good and all human beings are good because they naturally possess the Four Beginnings of virtue or the "fourfold" mind-and-heart (*sim/hsin*). Kobong, of course, meant that, because the Four do not have their own ontological ground outside the Seven, it follows from a standpoint of Neo-Confucian epistemology that the former cannot be spoken of separately from the latter and, therefore, must be discussed in the context of understanding the latter. Although he did not argue exactly in this way, his understanding of the Four-Seven relationship seems to correspond to Chu Hsi's two brief statements that "the Seven Emotions cannot be separated from the Four Beginnings," and that "the Four Beginnings can be understood from the standpoint of the Seven Emotions."[12] Interestingly, however, Kobong was not aware of these statements by Chu Hsi.

Given the consistent patterns of Kobong's Four-Seven thesis, it was reasonable for Kobong to argue that, instead of differentiating the Four and the Seven according to a metaphysical dichotomy of the *i-ki* opposition, the Four should be taken as good feelings that constitute a good part of the Seven. In another passage, he criticizes his fellow Neo-Confucians for misinterpreting the Four-Seven issue: "Recently, scholars discuss the distinction of the Four Beginnings and the Seven Emotions, without seeing carefully the question of why Mencius intended to single out the good side [of the Seven]."[13] For Kobong, the Four Beginnings must "come from the totality of the Seven Emotions and are those feelings that attain due degree and measure"; that is to say, the Four are good "harmonized feelings" of the Seven.[14] Moreover, the basis of good and evil is, "What is manifest and harmonized is called good; what is manifest but not harmonized is called evil."[15] When human nature is manifest, the Seven Emotions arise, but there may be good, harmonized feelings in some cases and bad, disharmonized feelings in other cases. Hence, we have the problem of good and evil, depending on whether or not feelings are harmonized. For Kobong, the good, harmonized feelings refer to the Four Beginnings. In the light of the *Doctrine of the Mean*, he also means that before the Seven emotions are aroused, the mind-and-heart is in the state of equilibrium that refers to human nature in itself or the "original substance of human nature" (*sŏng chi ponch'e/hsing chih pen-t'i*).[16] In other words, human nature (*sŏng/hsing*) is originally good; however, when it is manifest and disturbed by external things, an access of feelings can lead one to evil, presumably in one's selfish desires, intentions, and actions. Emotional control and integration are the universal path to self-cultivation, as it is indicated in the *Doctrine of the Mean*.[17]

A convincing feature of Kobong's argument is that Mencius paid special attention to the Four and considered them as those good and harmonized feelings that come out of the Seven, the totality of all feelings. For Kobong, one cannot talk about two different kinds of feelings in terms of the Four and the Seven,[18] especially in terms of the contrast of *i* and *ki* or that of good and evil.[19] The Four constitute a "subset" of the Seven, and the latter, if expressed properly "through attaining due degree and measure," can also become good.[20] So far as feelings are concerned, both the Four and the Seven involve *i* and *ki* together. T'oegye's assertion that the Four and the Seven can be spoken of in terms of the dichotomy of "manifestation of *i*" and "manifestation of *ki*" is, in Kobong's view, not right because it separates the one side (Four) from the totality (Seven). If the Seven are said to be "manifestations of *ki* only," it must mean that, in the issuing process of the Seven, only *ki* is manifest without any participation by *i*.

By selecting and explaining a few key quotations from *Mencius*, the *Doctrine of the Mean*, and Ch'eng-Chu teachings, Kobong carefully argues that *good* refers to "the original nature of heaven and earth," and *evil* refers to the excessiveness or deficiency of "physical endowment." For him, "the essence of *i* is nothing but what is naturally manifest when *ki* acts without any excess or deficiency."[21] Quoting Chu Hsi's saying that "the mind unites *i* and *ki*," he argues that "if *ki* obeys *i*, *i* is naturally manifest." T'oegye's statement that "the issuance of the Four is good because it involves *i* only" is, in his view, incorrect. Kobong maintains, on the contrary, that the issuance of the Four involve both *i* and *ki* and that the Four are said to be good because, when they are aroused, *i* is undisturbed by *ki*. The issuance of the Seven can bring about either good or evil; evil arises when *i* is disturbed by the activity of *ki* that can often be either excessive or deficient.[22] This argument is somewhat based on Chu Hsi's theory of the inseparability of *i* and *ki* in regard to concrete phenomena including the mind and feelings. Because "*i* is the master of *ki*, and *ki* is the material stuff of *i*,"[23] it follows that *i* and *ki* can be conceptually distinct. And yet, Kobong maintains: "From the standpoint of things and phenomena, *i* and *ki* are intermingled with each other and, therefore, inseparable from each other."[24]

For this fundamental reason, Kobong argues that T'oegye's Four-Seven theory is not convincing because it analyzes the Four and the Seven in terms of the *i-ki* dualism and the good-evil opposition and affirms *i* and *ki* as being independent from each other in both metaphysical and ethical contexts. In Kobong's view, T'oegye's theory is wrong, for it not only affirms the Four and the Seven as two different kinds of feelings, but also implies that there are two different kinds of goodness, one belonging to the Four and the other to the Seven. Kobong makes a concluding remark especially on learning: "Those who pursue learning should know that *i* cannot exist outside of *ki*. When *ki* is naturally manifest without excess and deficiency, it is actually [literally, 'none other than'] the original substance of *i*. If one understands this fact well, while giving one's full effort [to learning and self-cultivation], there will be no mistakes."[25] Explicit in Kobong's argument means that "*i* cannot exist outside of *ki*" with regard to all concrete phenomena including feelings. As revealed in the preceding passages, this is not just a philosophical argument, but also a *moral* argument expressed from a concrete standpoint of self-cultivation. It emphasizes that what is called *good* necessarily involves one's effort at maintaining harmonized feelings in the practice of self-cultivation. To put it in another way, Kobong means to justify his belief that the key to the Confucian "learning of the Way" (*tohak/tao-hsüeh*) is emotional control and moral integration. The whole foundation of his argument is morally oriented emphasizing one's control of *ki* for self-cultivation. Indeed, this is a vital part of the entire Confucian tradition.

On the whole, Kobong's vocabulary suggests what we may call a *nondualistic* interpretation of the Four-Seven relationship. His Four-Seven thesis acknowledges the fundamental inseparability of *i* and *ki*. The Four and the Seven are not two separate kinds of feelings, rather they belong to one realm of all human feelings in the sense of maintaining their "subset-totality" relationship. It is in this context that we should qualify our use of the term *nondualistic*. From a nondualistic epistemological and ethical perspective, Kobong definitely affirms the "harmony-disharmony" link between the Four and the Seven; that is to say, their fundamental difference is due only to the problem of whether feelings are harmonized by "attaining their due degree and measure." This is, of course, a moral argument from a Confucian standpoint of self-cultivation. Embedded in this argument includes three points: first, good and evil can never be two separate realities each with its own ground according to T'oegye's dualistic system of *i* and *ki*; second, there is, therefore, neither the good-evil contrast nor the Four-Seven contrast; and finally, there must be a close link between the Four and the Seven and between good and evil. Although avoiding any extreme form of dualism, Kobong means the relationship of continuum between the Four and the Seven in terms of what we may call a metaphysical *i-ki* complementarity and an ethical good-evil link. For this reason, he criticizes T'oegye for maintaining a strict Four-Seven contrast in terms of *i* and *ki*. Hence, T'oegye is, in his view, wrong for considering good feelings as the Four ("manifestations of *i*") and evil feelings as the Seven ("manifestations of *ki*").

The originality and depth of Kobong's argumentation are grounded on selected elements of fundamental ideas found in early Confucian texts and Ch'eng-Chu teachings. Out of his intellectual confidence and scholarly commitment, he formulated constructive meanings and implications of the Four-Seven controversy. Nevertheless, Kobong's entire interpretation points to a philosophy that emphasizes the role of *ki* in learning and self-cultivation; in fact, this line of philosophical and moral reasoning later had some impact on Yulgok's Four-Seven thesis.

How did T'oegye respond to Kobong's challenge? T'oegye criticized such a tendency of Kobong's Four-Seven thesis, arguing that Kobong failed to realize the fundamental "distinction" between the Four and the Seven and, in turn, that between *i* and *ki*.

T'oegye's Response to Kobong's First Challenge: The Distinction of the Four and the Seven

In his first eight-page response to Kobong's preliminary challenge,[26] T'oegye gives an elaborated presentation of his Four-Seven thesis. He begins by asserting that although the Four and the Seven, as Kobong has pointed out, involve both *i* and *ki* in the process of their emanation, they are significantly different in several ways:

> The former Confucian scholars had understood the distinction between human nature (*sŏng/hsing*) and feelings (*chŏng/ch'ing*). But they briefly mentioned that the Four Beginnings and the Seven Emotions are both feelings. I have not seen any theory that explains them clearly in terms of *i* and *ki*. Last year, I saw

> Chŏng Chi-un's *Ch'ŏnmyŏng to* (Diagram of Heaven's Imperative). According to it, "The Four Beginnings are manifest from *i* and the Seven Emotions are manifest from *ki*." Since I feared that Chŏng's distinction [of the Four and the Seven] is too strict, I have modified it by adding such phrases as "purely good," "involves *ki* also," and so on....Generally speaking, the Four Beginnings are feelings, and the Seven Emotions are also feelings. They are all feelings.[27]

In this passage, T'oegye generally agrees with Kobong's view that the Four and the Seven are all basic human feelings. If the Four and the Seven, as both T'oegye and Kobong agreed, are the aroused feelings or states of the mind, why would there be two different terms, the Four and the Seven? Is the distinction purely arbitrary and textual? Should the Four Beginnings (mentioned by Mencius) and the Seven Emotions (mentioned in the *Doctrine of the Mean* and *Book of Rites*) point to the two separate realms of human feelings? For T'oegye, these were three critical questions. As Tu Wei-ming points out, "The dilemma for T'oegye was to formulate a correct interpretation of the Mencian idea of human nature in the light of Chu Hsi's concept of mind. If there was a conceived conflict between the two orientations, his task was to see that it be satisfactorily resolved."[28]

After accepting Kobong's citation of Chu Hsi's theory of the inseparability of *i* and *ki*, T'oegye states: "Generally speaking, *i* and *ki* need, and depend on, each other: one being 'substance' *(ch'e/t'i)* and the other 'function' *(yong/yung)*. Certainly, there is no *i* without *ki*, and no *ki* without *i*. However, what is spoken of is not the same; there is a distinction between them."[29] T'oegye means the fundamental Ch'eng-Chu doctrine that, from the standpoint of a concrete thing, *i* and *ki* are inseparable in the process of cosmic transformation. Under Kobong's challenge, T'oegye moves a step away from his previous Four-Seven theory that tends to affirm the Four-Seven contrast in terms of not only *i* and *ki* but also good and evil. He agrees with Kobong that, because the Four and the Seven are all feelings, it follows that they are the aroused states of the mind and that the process of their emanation involves both *i* and *ki*. Nevertheless, he still maintains that the Four and the Seven can be, and should be, understood separately in terms of *i* and *ki*. To articulate this point further, he addresses the concept of human nature in the tradition of the *Doctrine of the Mean*, Mencius, and Ch'eng-Chu teachings:

> The term "human nature" *(sŏng/hsing)* is what Tzu-ssu in the *Doctrine of the Mean* meant by "the nature endowed by Heaven," and what Mencius called "the original goodness of human nature." What do these two phrases about "human nature" mean? Do they refer to the original being of *i*, as well as the physical endowment of *ki*? What they refer to is *i* without any existence of *ki*. They all meant pure goodness without any evil. If one says that human nature [in itself] includes *ki* as well because *i* and *ki* are inseparable from each other, then one is not talking about the original essence of human nature (*sŏng chi pon'yŏn/hsing chih pen-jan*). Tzu-ssu and Mencius spoke of it in this manner and understood the whole essence of the Way. . . . They meant that if one speaks of human nature combined with *ki*, the original goodness of *i* (*i chi ponsŏn/li chih pen-shan*) will not be understood correctly. It is only from the period of Ch'eng I, Chang Tsai, and Chu Hsi that there emerged inevitable debates on "physical human nature" (*kijil chisŏng/ch'i-chih chih hsing*). . . . Being reckless, I have considered that the distinction between the Four Beginnings and the Seven Emotions is similar to that between original human nature and physical human nature. Why can we not analyze feelings in terms of *i* and *ki*, if human nature is already spoken of in terms of *i* and *ki*?[30]

T'oegye means that both Tzu-ssu and Mencius refered specifically to what he calls the "original essence of human nature" or human nature in itself, unmixed with the physical endowment by *ki*. For him, what they meant is the "pure" and "original" goodness of *i* that refers to *i* in itself, before being disturbed or conditioned by external stimuli. In fact, the Chinese Neo-Confucians like Chu Hsi did not pay any attention to the Four-Seven relationship in terms of original human nature and physical human nature. T'oegye was the first Korean Neo-Confucian to address this topic. Citing the Sung Neo-Confucians like Chu Hsi, he attempted to explain the distinction of the Four and the Seven. Of course, he wanted to convince Kobong the following point: because human nature can be understood in terms of its two names, it logically follows that feelings can be discussed in terms of their two names, the Four and the Seven.[31] When understood in terms of *i* and *ki*, the Four-Seven relationship is, he asserts, similar to the original nature–physical nature relationship. For him, then, the Four pertain to the original human nature, and the Seven to the physical human nature. As he writes, "Where do the feelings of commiseration, shame and dislike, courtesy and modesty, and discernment of right and wrong come from? These are nothing but manifestations of human nature characterized by the virtues of humanity, righteousness, propriety, and wisdom. Where do the feelings of pleasure, anger, sorrow, fear, love, hatred, and desire come from? These are aroused as physical form comes into contact with external things."[32]

Arguing in the Mencian sense,[33] T'oegye means that the Four come from human nature in itself and that they should be understood as the inborn moral qualities or fundamental seeds of goodness. For this reason, the Four belong to the original human nature. On the contrary, the Seven Emotions, according to T'oegye, come from the physical human nature; that is to say, pleasure, anger, sorrow, fear, love, hatred, and desire are basic feelings that arise from external influence. They should be understood as conditional and short-lived expressions of our psychological and physiological states. Certainly, the Mencian doctrine of human nature is supported by his argument that the Seven, unlike the Four, are not moral feelings, the genuine roots of morality. As the Mencian idea of "making the desires few"[34] implies, it means, from a perspective of self-cultivation, that a moral nourishment of the Four and a measure of emotional control over the Seven are quite relevant here.

In his *Sim t'ong sŏngchŏng tosŏl* (Diagrammatic Treatise on the Saying "the Mind Commands Human Nature and Feelings"),[35] the sixth of his famous *Sŏnghak sipto* (Ten Diagrams of the Learning of Sagehood),[36] T'oegye argues that the original human nature refers to what Tzu-ssu called the *nature endowed by Heaven*, what Ch'eng I meant by "human nature is *i*," what Chang Tsai and Chu Hsi referred to as the *nature of Heaven and Earth*, and what Chu Hsi meant by saying "what flows from the origin has nothing but good."[37] In T'oegye's view, they all meant *i* alone, referring to the "original essence of human nature"; otherwise, one cannot understand the Confucian doctrine of human nature.[38] On the other hand, when one speaks of concrete "human nature mixed with *ki*" in the factual, concrete sense, one is referring to what Chang Tsai and Chu Hsi called *physical nature*.[39] T'oegye's basic philosophical position generally comes from Chu Hsi's own philosophy: the original human nature is basically the unmanifest and perfectly good state before the feelings are aroused, whereas the physical human nature is the manifest state involving both good and evil after the feelings are aroused. For him, then, the Four should be represented by the original human nature, and the Seven by the physical human nature.

By pointing out the importance of analyzing the divergence as well as the convergence of the Four and the Seven, T'oegye asserts that the Four and the Seven are different in several fundamental ways. From an ontological perspective, their "origins" are different.[40] In an epistemological context as well, the Four and the Seven are not the same in terms of "what is spoken of" and "what is referred to."[41] To T'oegye, Mencius explained the Four by referring principally to *i* because human nature is characterized by moral virtues, such as benevolence, righteousness, propriety, and wisdom, which exist purely and naturally in the mind-and-heart. While accepting Kobong's convincing view that the emanation of Seven includes both *i* and *ki*, T'oegye argues, however, that in this case "what is spoken of refers principally to *ki*."[42] Of course, this is based on the Ch'eng-Chu doctrine that physical form is always in movement and thus stimulated easily by the external things that represent *ki* and can lead to evil. Chu Hsi said that "the Seven Emotions cannot be separated from the Four Beginnings" and that "the Four Beginnings can be understood in the context of the Seven Emotions."[43] As mentioned before, these secluded and unexplained statements, which both Kobong and T'oegye were never aware of,[44] seem to contradict Chu Hsi's Four-Seven statement that "the Four are manifestations of *li*; the Seven are manifestations of *ch'i*."[45] Although Chu Hsi did not describe the precise relationship of the Four and the Seven, he seems to have meant that the Four and the Seven cannot be spoken of as two separate realms of human feelings. Hence, T'oegye's interpretation, though he never noticed, does not seem to accord with the intended meaning of Chu Hsi's original thinking.

The question is *why*. In T'oegye's view, the Four are all good because they are expressed by *i*; therefore, Mencius said that "a person without the mind-and-heart of the Four Beginnings is not human."[46] The Seven are either good or evil because they are expressed by *ki*, so it is said that, if they all "attain their due measure and degree after they are aroused, it is called harmony."[47] T'oegye believes that although Kobong understood the relationship between *i* and *ki*, he went too far in stressing only their inseparability, without acknowledging their distinction:

> We know that the Four Beginnings and the Seven Emotions are not outside of *i* and *ki*. But in each case, there is what is principally referred to as origin and what is principally important. Why can we not say that something belongs to *i*, while something belongs to *ki*? You have carefully observed and strongly argued that *i* and *ki* move each other and are inseparable from each other. You also think that there is no *ki* without *i* and no *i* without *ki*, saying that the Four Beginnings and the Seven Emotions do not have different meanings. Even though this is almost cor-

> rect, it still has some inadequacy when I compare it with the opinions of the former sages and worthies.[48]

The vocabulary presented in this quotation suggests T'oegye's view that Kobong was mistaken in asserting that the Four and the Seven do not have different origins and meanings. In other words, they are different in both ontological and conceptual contexts. T'oegye was, of course, concerned with the orthodox tradition of the classical texts, including Ch'eng-Chu teachings. He informs Kobong further: "In discussing 'equilibrium' and 'harmony,' Tzu-ssu mentioned pleasure, anger, sorrow, and joy[49] but did not quite include the Four Beginnings in his explanation.... Ch'eng I talked about [the Seven Emotions such as] pleasure, anger, sorrow, fear, love, hatred, and desire,[50] but he too did not pay any significant attention to the Four Beginnings. This indicates that *i* and *ki* need each other and are 'merged one into the other [in concrete phenomena].'[51] And yet, this does not necessarily mean that *i* and *ki* are not distinct."[52]

T'oegye was well aware of the Ch'eng-Chu doctrine that *i* and *ki* are inseparable from each other in concrete things and phenomena; however, he chose to emphasize that one must not neglect another fundamental point that each of *i* and *ki* is "an entity in itself."[53] After seeing Chu Hsi's Four-Seven statement in the *Chu Tzu yü-lei* (Classified Conversations of Master Chu), he became even more confident and made a naive but strong statement to praise Chu Hsi and to support his own argument: "I have recently read the *Chu Tzu yü-lei*. . . . According to it, 'the Four Beginnings are manifestations of *i* and the Seven Emotions are manifestations of *ki*.'[54] Did the ancient people not say, 'Do not trust yourself, but trust your teacher.' Chu Hsi is my teacher who is respected by the whole world. After reflecting myself on this saying, I now believe that Chŏng Chi-un's statement and my explanation are not absurd."[55] In T'oegye's view, the Four are "purely good" and, therefore, should be expressed "principally by *i*," whereas the Seven are capable of becoming good or evil and, therefore, should be expressed "principally by *ki*." Accordingly, there is nothing wrong with Chu Hsi's saying that "the Four Beginnings are manifestations of *i* and the Seven Emotions are manifestations of *ki*."

On the whole, T'oegye's vocabulary suggests what we may call a *dualistic* interpretation of the Four-Seven issue. There are several fundamental reasons for this: first, his Four-Seven thesis definitely affirms that *i* and *ki* are distinct from, and unmixable with, each other; second, in the same manner it interprets the Four and the Seven as two different realms of human feelings; third, when understood in the context of *i* and *ki*, the Four-Seven contrast is identical to the original nature–physical nature contrast; and finally, one should comprehend it in terms of origin, meaning, and quality. In these contexts, then, T'oegye meant to do full justice to what appears to be a dualistic standpoint. Hence, we can qualify our use of the term *dualistic* in analyzing the basic philosophical position of his Four-Seven thesis; in fact, it originates partly from Chu Hsi's own reasoning. Unlike Kobong's nondualistic position, the underlying theme of T'oegye's thesis focuses on his strong commitment to maintaining the unmixability and distinction between *i* and *ki*.

The question is, What motivated T'oegye to maintain it in such a way? More specifically, why did he prefer to set the Four over the Seven in terms of an *i-ki* dualism? This is a *moral* issue with profound implications for the practice of self-cultivation: the whole dilemma for T'oegye was to formulate a convincing interpretation of the Four-Seven contrast that must be addressed in *both* philosophical and moral contexts. Throughout the whole debate, he criticizes Kobong for maintaining what he considers as an unconvincing view that the Four and the Seven cannot be analyzed separably in terms of *i* and *ki* simply because *i* and *ki* are inseparable in concrete phenomena including feelings. Of course, his argument is morally grounded. In other words, T'oegye maintains the distinction between the Four and the Seven in terms of what we may call an ontological and conceptual *i-ki* dichotomy and an ethical good-evil contrast. To Kobong's way of thinking, it is, however, not possible to divide feelings into two groups: the Four as good ("manifestations of *i*"), and the Seven as good or evil ("manifestations of *ki*"). Of course, T'oegye's basic mission was to emphasize the former in the light of the Mencian doctrine of the goodness of human nature, insofar as the Four should be considered as the genuine roots of moral self-cultivation. He means that the Four have their own status of self-manifestation and self-regulation outside the Seven, whereas the Seven should be understood as basic physical and mental feelings and desires. It is, therefore, crucial to distinguish the Four from the Seven in both theoretical and practical contexts.

T'oegye's Four-Seven thesis is a good example to illustrate his strong commitment to Ch'eng-Chu orthodoxy. Given this commitment to transmitting it in Korea, it was natural for him to quote and interpret the existing vocabulary of Chu Hsi's philosophy. He was also clearly aware of certain impact of Lo Ch'in-shun (Cheng-an, 1465–1547)[56] on some of his contemporary Neo-Confucians in Korea (including Kobong, as T'oegye has claimed); in his Four-Seven letter to Kobong, T'oegye condemned Lo's criticism of Chu Hsi as well as his theory of the oneness of *i* and *ki*.[57]

In the *K'un-chih chi* (Knowledge Painfully Acquired), Lo had criticized Chu Hsi's dualistic philosophy of *li* and *ch'i*, including his statement that "*li* and *ch'i* are definitely two things."[58] Seeing *li* and *ch'i* as one and inseparable, he said that "I doubt he [Chu Hsi] finally achieved unity," and that "*li* is not a separate entity."[59] Because he accepted only the Ch'eng-Chu doctrine that "*li* is one; its manifestations are diverse (*li-i fen-shu*),"[60] it follows for him that "the oneness of principle" must always be understood from the standpoint of "the diversity of its manifestations" before it can be thoroughly perceived. As Lo pointed out, Mencius' saying that "human nature is good"[61] refers to the oneness of *li*; his disciple's statement that "the nature of some is good, and the nature of others is not good"[62] refers to the diversity of its particularizations.[63] Furthermore, he criticized the Sung Neo-Confucians, including Ch'eng I, Chang Tsai, and Chu Hsi, for not understanding the oneness of the original nature and the physical nature. As he said, "To a single nature, they applied two different names."[64]

The defensive way in which T'oegye formulated his Four-Seven thesis concludes with his claim that Kobong's interpretation of *i* and *ki* is influenced by, and no different from, Lo's argument found in the *K'un-chih chi.*[65] Following Lo, Kobong went too far in emphasizing the inseparability of *i* and *ki*, thereby making what T'oegye calls a "serious mistake" in acknowledging the oneness of *i* and *ki* and that of original nature and physical nature. T'oegye politely instructs Kobong that if one does not distinguish clearly *i* from *ki*, it may lead one to an "unfortunate consequence" of misidentifying the moral qualities aroused by Heaven's principle (*ch'ŏlli/t'ien-li*) with the selfish "human desires" (*inyok/jen-yü*) aroused by external stimuli. For this reason, T'oegye urges Kobong to grasp a clear conceptual and ethical distinction between the Four and the Seven in terms of *i* and *ki.*[66]

How did Kobong, then, respond to T'oegye's critique of his first challenge? T'oegye's systematic and serious argument stimulated Kobong to further clarify the basic features of his Four-Seven thesis, especially in the context of emphasizing the inseparability of *i* and *ki* and the oneness of human nature.

Kobong's Second Challenge: The Inseparability of *I* and *Ki* and the Oneness of Human Nature

In the summer of 1560, more than a year after he had sent his preliminary letter to T'oegye, Kobong wrote to a systematic forty-two page and twelve-point critique that analyzes T'oegye's first letter point by point.[67] Before reformulating his Four-Seven position, he first makes an interesting insight that any references to "orthodox" interpretations of the classical texts (including those by Chu Hsi) need to be supplemented by personal views and reflections. He seems to have meant that the whole purpose of his debate with T'oegye was to clarify the apparent legacy of fretful ambiguity at the heart of Ch'eng-Chu orthodoxy. In other words, the Four-Seven debate had to serve a wellspring of creative thought among those (like T'oegye) who avowed that orthodoxy and those (like Kobong) who wanted to move beyond it.

Generally speaking, however, Kobong agrees with T'oegye that the Four mentioned by Mencius refer to "good feelings" aroused by *i*, and that those feelings like joy and anger, which are mentioned in the *Doctrine of the Mean*, refer to the Seven that are capable of becoming either good or evil. He also agrees with T'oegye that the issuance of all feelings involve both *i* and *ki*.[68] But Kobong challenges T'oegye by arguing that his senior's Four-Seven theory is not correct because it implies that there are two different kinds of feelings and, in turn, of goodness, one issued from *i* and the other from *ki*. T'oegye's dualistic interpretation is, Kobong asserts, unreasonable because in all concrete things and phenomena, *i* and *ki* are never separated from or act in opposition to each other. Furthermore, he reiterates his basic position that the Four and the Seven belong to "one realm of feelings," for the former constitutes the "good side" of the latter, the totality of feelings.[69] Accordingly, he rejects T'oegye's view that the Seven are potentially evil; the Seven, like the Four, are good if they become harmonized.

To Kobong, there are simply two terms such as the *Four* and the *Seven*.[70] Although he agrees with T'oegye that the Four and the Seven are different in terms of "origin" and "what is spoken of," he criticizes T'oegye for misinterpreting the Four-Seven relationship. In his view, T'oegye misunderstood the Four and the Seven as two separate and independent kinds of feelings in opposition to each other.[71] His challenging question to T'oegye is, If the Four and the Seven all come from human nature, how can they have two different origins? T'oegye is, Kobong asserts, wrong in arguing, from an ontological and moral standpoint, that the Four come from original human nature, whereas the Seven from physical human nature. In other words, divergent ways of addressing the same reality can simply be a matter of "emphasis"; therefore, the Four and the Seven should refer to the same reality of feelings understood from two complementary angles.

Kobong's critique of T'oegye is founded on analyzing what the latter meant by "origin." The word *origin* is not appropriate in discussing the Four-Seven relationship. Following basic Ch'eng-Chu doctrines of mind, nature, and feelings, he reiterates and explains six points of his basic argument to convince T'oegye.[72] First, he supports Ch'eng I's and Chu Hsi's views that when human nature is manifest, it becomes feelings, and that all feelings arise from human nature, under external stimuli. In other words, the beginnings of virtues and the emotions like joy and anger all come from human nature. Second, the Four and the Seven involve both *i* and *ki*, for *i* and *ki* are inseparable in the context of concrete phenomena. Because the mind unites both *i* and *ki*, the Four and the Seven should be understood in the same way that feelings are aroused when the mind is stimulated by external things. Third, in the case of the Seven, "*ki* is manifest," and "*i* makes the manifestation of *ki* possible." Fourth, it is, Kobong asserts, unreasonable to address the Four-Seven issue, as T'oegye has done, in terms of the ethical good-evil contrast; rather, it should be understood in the light of the *Doctrine of the Mean*. The Four-Seven continuum must be discussed in terms of whether aroused feelings are harmonized according to "due degree and measure." This, Kobong argues, is due to the fact that "the goodness of the Four" and "the goodness of the Seven" belong to the "same realm of goodness" that must include all harmonized feelings. Fifth, the Four are said to be good because, when they are aroused, "*i* is undisturbed by *ki*" as the former "rides on" the latter. Sixth, T'oegye's statement that "the Four are purely good" is unreasonable; this is because even the Four, as aroused feelings, are capable of becoming evil if they do not attain their due degree and measure.

The first three points of Kobong's argument are based on Ch'eng-Chu teachings. But the last three points are uniquely his own perspectives that he developed through his debate with T'oegye. After discussing these six fundamental points in a systematic manner, Kobong then opposes T'oegye's dualistic thesis based on the distinction of the different "origins" of the Four and the Seven. In the spirit of the *Doctrine of the Mean*, the fourth point of Kobong's argument in particular can be convincing, insofar as one cannot talk about the two different "origins" of the Four and the Seven on the basis of both the *i-ki* dichotomy and the contrast of original human nature and physical human nature. This certainly corresponds to Kobong's previous view that the real basis of good and evil is only a matter of whether or not aroused feelings are harmonized. Since the Seven actually refer to the total realm of all aroused feelings, including those in harmony and those in disharmony, the Four must, Kobong argues, refer to those harmonized, good feelings of the Seven.[73] For this reason, he criticizes T'oegye's Four-Seven thesis for implying the following three points: first, the Four have their own ontological status outside the Seven; second, the Four and the Seven are, therefore, two distinct kinds of feelings; and finally, the goodness of human nature has two different sources, one originating from the Four and the other from the Seven. The basic difference of the Four and the Seven, as understood by

Kobong, pertains merely to whether one speaks of feelings as referring to the "subset" of good, harmonized feelings or the "totality" of all feelings (both harmonized and disharmonized).

The whole dilemma for Kobong was to interpret Mencius and Ch'eng-Chu doctrines in the spirit of the *Doctrine of the Mean*. He wished to convince T'oegye that the Four Beginnings can be understood as moral roots of the Seven Emotions. If any of the Seven is harmonized, it is certainly a good, moral feeling. This striking feature of Kobong's thought can be explained in the following manner: the emotion of "love" (one of the Seven Emotions), if properly harmonized, is identical to "the mind-and-heart of commiseration," "the beginning of benevolence," which is one of the Four Beginnings. At the same time, the "the mind-and-heart of commiseration" is equivalent to the moral root of love. Although Kobong did not argue exactly in this way, it is obvious that he did decide to go beyond Ch'eng I's and Chu Hsi's views that commiseration is an innate seed of the virtue of benevolence inherent in what Mencius calls the "original goodness of human nature" and that love is a common mental feeling that cannot be a virtuous root of morality in the Mencian sense. Undoubtedly, the fundamental implication of Kobong's Four-Seven thesis is a significant moral issue for Kobong, who emphasizes emotional integration in the practice of self-cultivation.

The next main topic of Kobong's critique focuses on T'oegye's dualistic theory that the Four Beginnings come from original human nature and the Seven Emotions come from physical human nature. According to Kobong, there are no two separate kinds of human nature. "That which is called good" refers to the original human nature; "that which is called evil" refers to the excessive or deficient dimension of the physical human nature. Quoting Ch'eng-Chu doctrines of human nature, he agrees with T'oegye that the original human nature pertains to what Chang Tsai and Chu Hsi call the *nature of Heaven and Earth*. When one speaks of this nature, one is talking about to *i* alone.[74] It is the nature that exists before physical form; in human beings, it is called *original human nature*. As Chu Hsi pointed out, "when one speaks of physical nature endowed by *ki*, one is referring to *i* and *ki* combined."[75] Nevertheless, Kobong states: "When we speak of physical human nature, it is not a separate nature because substance [original nature] already exists in the physical human nature."[76] In other words, the original human nature is human nature in itself prior to existing in physical form; with respect to existing in physical form, it is called *physical human nature*. However, Kobong, like Chu Hsi, argues that the original human nature must be understood in the concrete context of the physical human nature. For him, then, only two conceptual "terms" are used in discussing the subject matter;

surely, he presented what we may call a theory of *one nature and two names*.[77] What Ch'eng-Chu Neo-Confucianism means by *human nature* in a concrete sense is actually the "physical human nature"; the so-called original human nature is only an abstract ideal.

Kobong makes a compelling conclusion that, to a single nature, T'oegye misapplied two terms and spoke of them as the two separate origins of the Four and the Seven, as if they were independent from and in opposition to each other. *Original human nature* and *physical human nature* are, according to Kobong, used for simple convenience to explain "one reality" of human nature by referring to *i* only, or *i* and *ki* combined; they are not two different human natures but rather one and united. Kobong, therefore, rejects T'oegye's theory. Both the Four and the Seven must belong to one human nature. This is why Kobong found it impossible to accept T'oegye's dualistic view of *i* and *ki* and of original human nature and physical human nature, which, however, originates significantly from Chu Hsi's original thinking. To formulate a theory of the oneness of human nature, he maintains a philosophical and moral view in favor of the continuum the Four and the Seven.

In short, Kobong means that T'oegye's Four-Seven thesis is unreasonable because it dualistically emphasizes the two different "origins" of the Four and the Seven. To him, good and evil are never two opposing realities of feelings pertaining to the Four, on the one hand, and the Seven, on the other hand. In other words, he emphasizes the Four-Seven continuum in the context of addressing an *i-ki* complementarity and an ethical good-evil link. The fundamental difference of the Four and the Seven is due only to the problem of whether feelings are harmonized. This is, of course, another moral argument from the Confucian standpoint of self-cultivation, especially in the light of the *Doctrine of the Mean*. One may call it a nondualistic approach to philosophical thinking and moral reasoning.

Note that Kobong's philosophy of human nature is strikingly similar to that of Lo Ch'in-shun: both thinkers argued that two "names" are applied to describe one human nature. This is partly why, T'oegye, in his first letter to Kobong, criticized the latter for presenting an interpretation of *i* and *ki* and of original human nature and physical human nature on the basis of Lo Ch'in-shun's *K'un-chih chi*. Here, an interesting matter of debate is that, in his second challenge to T'oegye, Kobong denies his senior's claim that he was influenced by Lo's *K'un-chih chi*. He claims that he had never seen such a text. This claim appears to be true,[78] which suggests that Kobong's interpretation of *i* and *ki* and of human nature did not come directly from Lo's philosophy but was his own original thinking. For T'oegye, however, this was never the real issue of the debate, and what was more important was to debate further on their divergent views. The seriousness and thoroughness with which Kobong analyzed and criticized his senior's first response forced T'oegye further to modify some of his views once more.

T'oegye's Revised Four-Seven Theory of "Alternate Manifestation"

As a scholarly appreciation of Kobong's systematic and critical argument, T'oegye revised his first letter and sent its revised version to his challenger in the fall of 1560, three months after he had received Kobong's second critique. Also, he enclosed a comprehensive response consisting of forty-six pages of careful summations of, and reflections on, Kobong's points.[79] In the revised version of the first letter, T'oegye made four short and two long corrections. For example, he deleted a long statement claiming that Kobong's position is no different from Lo's critique of Chu Hsi's philosophy; of course, he means that he was mistaken in assuming that Kobong had actually advocated a theory of the oneness of *i* and *ki* according to Lo's philosophy.[80] Futhermore, he gave a more positive view of the Seven Emotions, suggesting that they are "originally good" rather than "both good and evil."[81] Although agreeing with Kobong, he carefully pointed out that "they can easily become evil," if they are not in harmony and depart from proper measure and expression.[82] Despite his willingness to accommodate some of Kobong's convincing views and insights, he maintained his basic position that the Four and the Seven are different in terms of origin, meaning, and quality. In other words, the core of his Four-Seven thesis still remains intact.

In his second letter, T'oegye considered Kobong's interpretation thoroughly and carefully, adopting basically the same style of communication. After rearranging Kobong's twelve-point critique into five sections, T'oegye outlined the following points: first, he apologizes for misreading and thus misinterpreting a statement in Kobong's first letter; second, he wishes to revise his four statements that, through Kobong's thoughtful insights, he found inadequately expressed; third, there are thirteen agreed items that he does not wish to clarify further; fourth, eight points of dispute, which he initially considered as being resolvable, are less agreeable and, therefore, require a reinterpretation; and finally, nine incompatible issues on which he totally disagrees with Kobong need more debate.[83]

After giving such an outline with a few general comments, T'oegye discusses the eight points of dispute and the nine incompatible issues in an organized and systematic manner. He begins by clarifying his basic Four-Seven position in terms of *i* and *ki*:

> You have argued: "The nature of Heaven and Earth refers only to *i*; the physical nature refers to both *i* and *ki* combined.[84] This means that the manifestation [of the Four] from *i* is certainly correct, but the manifestation [of the Seven] from *ki* does not refer to *ki* only." To me, the nature of Heaven and Earth, as you have said, certainly refers to *i* only. But can there be *i* without *ki*? In the universe, there is no *i* without *ki*. It is not that there is only *i*. However, if the nature of Heaven and Earth can be spoken in terms of *i* only, then why can we not speak of the physical nature by referring to *ki* [only], even though *i* and *ki* are combined in it?[85]

Interestingly, T'oegye softened his dualistic position by recognizing more of a continuum between the original nature [the nature of Heaven and Earth] and the physical nature and by accepting Kobong's emphasis on the inseparability of *i* and *ki* in all concrete phenomena. He decided not to insist too much on one of his initial points that *i* and *ki* are ontologically two and unmixable. But he still argues: "The nature of Heaven and Earth [the original human nature] can be spoken in terms of *i* only because *i* is what dominates; the physical human nature can be spoken in terms of *ki* because *ki* is what dominates."[86] In other words, the physical human nature pertains mainly to *ki*, conditioning and controlling the process of physical endowment, whereas the original nature pertains mainly to *i*, constituting the whole goodness of human nature. T'oegye means that although *i* and *ki* are inseparable from a phenomenalistic standpoint of concrete things, the original human nature and the physical human nature can be discussed separately in terms of *i* and *ki* respectively. For him, this is a simple matter of *emphasis*.

By addressing this matter, however, Toegye wishes to maintain his basic thesis that *i* and *ki* are distinct from a conceptual perspective of separation. As he argues further, "Regarding Heaven, Earth, human beings, and things, it is not that *i* exists outside of *ki*. And yet, *i* and *ki* can be spoken of separately. Although we say, in regard to human nature and feelings, that *i* is in *ki* and human nature is in its physical endowment, why can we not talk about *i* and *ki* separately?"[87] In this passage, T'oegye reaffirms the Ch'eng-Chu doctrine of the inseparability of *i* and *ki* in all concrete phenomena. But he still maintains the basis of his dualistic position that, because the original human nature is full of goodness and, therefore, refers to *i*, it logically follows that the physical human nature can be expressed by referring mainly to *ki*, although both *i* and *ki* are present in it. Hence, one can discuss feelings in terms of the Four and the Seven by referring principally to *i* or *ki*, respectively.

T'oegye then claims that he does not see why Kobong accepted the first part (the Four as "manifestations of *i*") of his Four-Seven statement but rejected the second part of it (the Seven as "manifestations of *ki*"). In his view, although the issuance of the Seven involve both *i* and *ki*, it can refer mainly to *ki*. To Kobong, however, this was not a convincing argument at all. From a logical standpoint, T'oegye makes a strong point that if Kobong agreed with him that "*i* manifesting" (*ibal/li-fa*), in the case of the Four, refers mainly to *i*, then he should also accept logically that "*ki* manifesting" (*kibal/ch'i-fa*), in the case of the Seven, refers mainly to *ki*. Otherwise, as T'oegye asserts, Chu Hsi would not have said that "the Four Beginnings are manifestations of *i*" and that "the Seven Emotions are manifestations of *ki*."[88] Here, T'oegye, of course, means to defend Chu Hsi and justify what appeared to be a naive attempt in Kobong's view. Obviously, he had to accept his junior scholar's view that both the Four and the Seven involve *i* and *ki* that are never separable in all phenomena including feelings.

Given the conceptual distinction of *i* and *ki*, however, it is, T'oegye argues, possible to say that the Four are "not without *ki*," but "said to be manifestations of *i*"; similarly, the Seven are "not without *i*," but "said to be manifestations of *i*."[89] To put it in a clearer perspective, although the issuing process of the Four involves some participation of *ki*," the Four themselves can still be considered as manifestations of *i*; although the issuing process of the Seven involves some participation of *i*," the Seven themselves can still be considered as manifestations of *ki*. As Kobong himself realized, such an interpretation, though obscure and confusing from a philosophical standpoint of argumentation, clearly bears T'oegye's basic presupposition that the origin of the Four Beginnings should be *i* and the origin of the Seven Emotions should be *ki*. The interesting matter is that T'oegye adopted Kobong's theory that "*i* is manifest" in the case of the Four because "*i* is undisturbed by *ki*" and that "*i* rides on the Seven." In response to Kobong's challenging views on the inseparability of *i* and *ki*, T'oegye utilizes it to articulate his revised Four-Seven theory in terms of what he calls an *alternate manifestation of i and ki* (*iki hobal/li-chi hu-fa*): "I and *ki* are manifest alternatively. When they are about to be manifest, they need each other. Since they are manifest with each other, we can understand that there is a distinctive emphasis in each case. They can be spoken of separately as distinctive entities because the manifestation of each entity has what is principal in itself."[90] T'oegye means that the relationship between *i* and *ki* is one of *hobal,* which can also mean "reciprocal issuing" or "mutual manifestation." Critically speaking, however, this theory is the slightly revised version of Kobong's own argument. It is T'oegye's attempt to accommodate Kobong's points that the Four and the Seven belong to one reality of feelings seen in two interrelated perspectives with a matter of "emphasis" and that T'oegye's idea of "origin" is inappropriate in discussing the Four-Seven relationship. In his view, *i* and *ki* do not manifest themselves at the same time: in the issuing process of the Four and the Seven, "there is a distinctive emphasis in each case." This specific reference to "distinction" and "emphasis" still indicates T'oegye's dualistic position on the Four-Seven relationship in terms of *i* and *ki*.

T'oegye, then, raises the following question: "Why is it not possible to distinguish the origin of the Four Beginnings from that of the Seven Emotions?"[91] He seems to mean, in an epistemological context of "emphasis," "distinction," and "separation," that the origin of the Four is *i*, whereas the origin of the Seven is *ki*. In response to Kobong's view that the Four do not belong to an independent kind of feelings outside the Seven, he agrees with Kobong that the issuance of the Four certainly involves the participation by *ki*.[92] But what Kobong does not recognize is, T'oegye argues, the fact that what Mencius singled out as the Four cannot refer to any manifestation of *ki* at all. As T'oegye states, "If you say that it refers to *ki* also, it should not be called the Four Beginnings."[93] He gives an ambiguous statement to criticize Kobong for opposing his analysis of the Four and the Seven: "Your argument states: 'In its state of equilibrium, the mind is stimulated by external things and does not lack *i*. Both the Seven and the Four respond to external stimuli.' I think this statement is certainly correct, but it refers to the realm of undifferentiation [before the mind is aroused]. Using this you oppose my explanation that I have formulated from a standpoint of distinction and separation. . . . I did not make such a theory of distinction and separation. In Heaven and Earth, there was originally such a principle. . . . If you focus only on one principle, neglecting the other, are you not one-sided?"[94] Surely, T'oegye agrees with Kobong that both the Four and the Seven are aroused feelings after the mind is stimulated by external things. He is well aware of Kobong's nondualistic position based on the inseparability of *i* and *ki*; as a result, he accepts Kobong's view that the issuance of the Seven involves both *i* and *ki*. And yet, the Four and the Seven can be compared and contrasted in an epistemological context of "distinction" and "separation." As T'oegye argues, "in the case of the Seven, *ki* is that which is principally referred to"; similarly, "in the case of the Four, *i* is that which is principally referred to."[95] He writes further: "I do not say that the Seven Emotions have nothing to do with *i*. . . . In this regard, the Four Beginnings, which move when stimulated by external things, are no different from the Seven Emotions."[96]

T'oegye's final *hobal* thesis is: "In the case of the Four Beginnings, *i* is manifest and *ki* follows it; in the case of the Seven Emotions, *ki* is manifest and *i* rides on it."[97] Clearly, this revised theory is somewhat softened in comparison with his original theory that "the Four Beginnings are manifestations of *i*; the Seven Emotions are manifestations of *ki*." In other words, the former is less strict than the latter in the sense of separating *i* and *ki*. But it still involves his dualistic position that the Four are manifest from *i* and the Seven from *ki*; more specifically, he explicitly emphasizes the primary role of *i* in the issuance of the Four and the primary role of *ki* in the issuance of the Seven. The following passage illustrates it further in terms of the popular rider-horse analogy used by Chu Hsi:

> In old days, people compared a rider's coming and going by riding on a horse with *i*'s moving as riding on *ki*. This is a good comparison. In general, a rider without a horse cannot come and go; a horse without a rider will lose its right track. Therefore the rider and the horse need each other and are inseparable from each other. Someone said in this regard: "If viewed simply from the standpoint of going, both rider and horse are all included." This is exactly like the case when we speak of the Four and the Seven without differentiation. When we say that "a rider going [somewhere]," we know that a horse is also said to be going [somewhere], without having to mention the horse at the same time. This is similar to the case of the Four Beginnings. On the other hand, when we say that "a horse going [somewhere]," we know that a rider is also said to be going [somewhere], without having to mention the rider at the same time. This is similar to the case of the Seven Emotions.[98]

In T'oegye's view, Kobong's standpoint of inseparability means that "a rider and a horse are going together at the same time," not that "a rider is going [somewhere]" and "a horse is going [somewhere]." If viewed from T'oegye's standpoint of separation and distinction, we can say that "a rider is going," although we really mean that not only the rider but also the horse are going together. Similarly, we can say that "a horse is going," although we really mean that both the horse and the rider are going together. Implicit in this analogical reasoning is T'oegye's view that "a horse is going" refers to "*i* manifesting," whereas "a rider is going" refers to "*ki* manifesting." In other words, in the case of the Four, *i* (rider) is manifest (going) and *ki* (horse) follows;[99] in the case of the Seven, *ki* (horse) is manifest (going) and *i* (rider) rides on it. T'oegye means that in the former case, *i* is "what dominates" and "what is principally referred to," even though *ki* plays its role of following *i*; in the latter case, *ki* is "what dominates" and "what is principally referred to," even though *i* plays its role of riding on *ki*.

The interesting fact here is that Kobong's convincing challenge forced T'oegye to revise his original theory and defend his new theory. But the revised version of T'oegye's theory is formulated to accommodate Kobong's insistence on the fundamental inseparability of *i* and *ki* in the emanation of feelings. Nonetheless, its underlying theme still does not accord with Kobong's belief that what is manifest in all phenomena including feelings is *ki*, not *i*. But T'oegye criticizes Kobong:

> If I speak of the Four Beginnings and the Seven Emotions from the standpoint of distinction and separation, you oppose me by using a theory from the standpoint of nondifferentiation. This is the same as saying that when a rider and a horse are going [somewhere], they are one and, thus, cannot be separated. If I speak of the Seven Emotions in terms of the manifestation of *ki*, you still oppose me by asserting [your theory of] the manifestation of *i*. This is the same as saying that a rider is going [somewhere] when a horse is going [somewhere]. If I speak of the Four Beginnings in terms of the manifestation of *i*, you oppose me by insisting on [your theory of] the manifestation of *ki*. This is the same as saying that a horse is going [somewhere] when a rider is going [somewhere].[100]

To justify his belief that the Four are never the same as the Seven, T'oegye synthesizes it with the Mencian doctrine of the Four. He argues that the Four constitute the pure existence of goodness in human nature represented by *i*:

> Can you see that Mencius' explanation of the Four Beginnings refers to the manifestation of *ki*? Do you view the Four as manifestations of *ki*? To what extent do you really comprehend [what Mencius calls] "the beginning of humanity" and "the beginning of righteousness," as well as four terms such as humanity, righteousness, propriety, and wisdom? If these are understood as involving even a little bit of participation by *ki*, then they do not belong to the original essence of Heaven's

> Principle. . . . According to your view, humanity, righteousness, propriety, and wisdom pertain purely to *i* because they are the names in the unmanifested state; the Four Beginnings cannot move without *i* and, thus, pertain to *ki* because they are the names in the manifested state. In my opinion, however, although the Four Beginnings ride on *ki*, what Mencius meant does not refer to the context of *i*'s riding [on *ki*]; it refers only to the manifestation of pure *i*.[101]

According to this quotation, the Four are the names of what is already aroused; therefore, the process of their issuance involves *ki*'s participation. But T'oegye still argues what Kobong refused to recognize is the fundamental fact that the Four, the innate roots of morality, do not really refer to any manifestation of *ki* itself. In his second letter to T'oegye, Kobong states: "If we trace the fundamental origin, it is not that there are two different meanings."[102] By contrast, T'oegye asserts that, if we trace the fundamental origin, then there is a difference between *i* and *ki*, and "there are different meanings between the Four and the Seven."[103] For him, then, there must necessarily be a clear "difference" between the manifestation of *i* and the manifestation of *ki*.[104] Even though Kobong is correct in seeing that the Four cannot exist separately outside of the Seven, "it would be incorrect to consider that the Four and the Seven are no different."[105]

Obviously, Kobong's view that the Four lack their own ontological status, belonging to a separate kind of feelings, does not convince T'oegye that the Four and the Seven are the same kind of feelings.[106] In T'oegye's opinion, what Mencius meant by the Four refers to *i* only, Ch'eng I spoke of physical human nature including both *i* and *ki*, and this is why Chu Hsi emphasized that *i* and *ki* are distinct.[107] If the origin of the Four is *i*, then it logically follows that the origin of the Seven would be *ki*.[108] T'oegye argues that "*i* is manifest and *ki* follows" can simply be considered as referring "principally to *i*," although "this statement does not mean that *i* exists outside of *ki*"; similarly, "*ki* is manifest and *i* rides on it" can be taken as referring "principally to *ki*," although "this statement does not mean that *ki* exists outside of *i*."[109] On the whole, these passages correspond to T'oegye's basic argument that, from his epistemological standpoint of "distinction" and "separation," one can discuss the Four and the Seven according to *i* and *ki*.

An inevitable question arises here, Why did T'oegye keep emphasizing such an argument? As emphasized before, this, of course, becomes a crucial moral issue relevant to the practice of self-cultivation. In his view, the Seven Emotions--pleasure, anger, sorrow, fear, love, hatred, and desire--are not necessarily moral virtues and feelings like the Four Beginnings; therefore, they come from *ki,* which can always disturb *i* to transform them into "precarious" psychological feelings and "selfish" physical desires. Even though the Seven are said to be "originally good," they can easily turn to evil. This is the main reason T'oegye intended to distinguish the Four from the Seven, presenting a solid moral argument to support his Four-Seven thesis from a concrete standpoint of self-cultivation. He concludes by quoting Ch'eng Hao's doctrine[110] on the calming of the nature: "The mind (*sim/hsin*) can easily become aroused. What is difficult to comprehend is that its emotion of anger [one of the Seven Emotions] is especially excessive and difficult to control. When one is angry but immediately forgets one's anger and examines the right and wrong of the matter at hand according to principle (*i/li*), then one will understand it is not true that one hates only external temptations."[111]

In this passage, T'oegye wants to convince Kobong that the emotion of anger can never be a manifestation of *i.* Otherwise, Ch'eng Hao and, in turn, Chu Hsi would not have urged to forget anger by means of grasping moral principles and virtues (such as benevolence, righteousness, propriety, and wisdom) represented by *i.* T'oegye asks Kobong, "In general, which one is easily manifest and hard to suppress: *i* or *ki*?"[112] T'oegye's answer is *ki,* not only because it is always in motion, but also because its activity varies according to different physical conditions. As he writes, "this indicates a way of suppressing *ki* by means of *i,*" and the method of "suppressing *ki*" is to control the Seven that can easily turn to evil.[113] For him, then, anger should be understood as a manifestation of *ki.* To overcome the dehumanizing tendencies (like anger) stimulated by *ki,* one should hold fast to the Four issued from *i.* In fact, T'oegye's entire philosophy of self-cultivation is based on such a theme; it developed especially as a fruitful result of his debate with Kobong. The impact of his Four-Seven thesis on it is quite profound. I shall discuss this further in the fourth chapter of the present volume.

Undeniably, T'oegye maintains a moral argument for the Mencian and Ch'eng-Chu doctrine that the original goodness of human nature must be preserved. All human beings are perfectly capable of doing it by realizing this inborn, moral quality of human nature as principle. On the one hand, the way of self-cultivation is to nourish the Four Beginnings; on the other, it means to control the Seven Emotions because their fundamental problem is their excessiveness. In this context of moral self-cultivation, T'oegye emphasizes one's clear understanding of the Four and the Seven from a standpoint of conceptual "distinction" and logical "separation."

How did Kobong respond to the philosophically revised and morally strengthened version of T'oegye's Four-Seven thesis? The depth and breadth of T'oegye's argument, which is presented with a series of relevant quotations, sequential arguments, and personal insights, stimulated Kobong to articulate his Four-Seven thesis further in the light of another popular Neo-Confucian discourse, namely, the "moon-moonlight" metaphor.

The Last Exchange on the Moon-Moonlight Analogy: Unity or Duality?

Several months after receiving T'oegye's second letter, Kobong responded in the first month of 1561 with a long, itemized review of it. Enclosed were his comments on the revised version of T'oegye's first letter as well. In his third and last Four-Seven letter to T'oegye, Kobong admitted that among the thirty items of dispute, eighteen items are already compatible, but fundamental disagreement still remained in twelve areas. As he claimed, the eighteen agreed items are the major issues of the debate, and twelve problem items are only minor ones that can be settled through further clarification.[114] He first presented a solid point that the principle of the Way transmitted by the former Confucian sages and worthies should be discussed and understood from the standpoint of "unity," not from the standpoint of "duality." He then warned T'oegye politely that nobody is to win the whole debate because it began with a scholarly motivation to clarify the Confucian "Way of the sages and worthies." T'oegye was asked to continue presenting honest and correct opinions in order to solve those problem items.

Kobong begins by criticizing T'oegye's idea of "origin." Specifically, he argues that he could not accept T'oegye's opinion that, regarding "what is principally referred to,"[115] there is a clear "difference" between the saying that "*i* dominates" in the case of the Four and the saying that "*ki* dominates" in the case of the Seven.[116] As he states, "Mencius did not speak of the Four Beginnings by referring to *i* only. In mentioning the Seven Emotions, Tzu-ssu must have referred to *i* and *ki* together."[117] In other words, both Tzu-ssu and Mencius did not mean the "origins" of the Four and the Seven. Kobong charges T'oegye with misunderstanding Mencius' and Tzu-ssu's teachings; more to the point, he criticizes him for formulating an inconsistent logical view that "Mencius referred to the Four Beginnings as the manifestation of *i*; therefore, it follows that Tzu-ssu described the Seven Emotions by referring to *ki*."[118] Here, the fundamental difference of opinion between T'oegye and Kobong is clear: for the latter, in the process of issuing both the Four and the Seven, what is manifest is *ki*, and what rides on it is *i*.

To Kobong, T'oegye's Four-Seven theory, which is formulated from a standpoint of the "distinction" and "separation," does not apply especially to the Seven, the "totality" of all feelings, because their issuance should be explained in terms of both *i* and *ki* combined. Kobong makes an interesting epistemological statement: "Chu Hsi's saying that 'the Four Beginnings are manifestations of *i*, and the Seven Emotions are manifestations of *ki*'[119] was viewed from a standpoint of causal relation, not from a standpoint of dichotomy."[120] Had Chu Hsi really meant it from the standpoint of *i-ki* dichotomy, then he is, Kobong argues, completely wrong.[121] The way in which Kobong interprets Chu Hsi reveals that Chu Hsi must have meant from the standpoint of *relation* that the Four and the Seven are all feelings connected with each other and that there are merely two related "names" for "one realm of feelings" described in terms of *i* and *ki* together. This argument reemphasize his basic belief that, in the light of Neo-Confucian metaphysics and ethics, the Four-Seven issue should be understood in the context of "unity," not "duality." In this regard, we can use an argument made by Cho Sŏng-ki (Chosuljae, 1638–1687) who attempted to find a compromise between T'oegye and Yulgok. In his famous *T'oeYul yangsŏnsaeng sadan ch'ilchŏng ikisŏl hupyŏn* (Second Treatise on Two Masters T'oegye and Yulgok and Their Theories of the Four and the Seven, *I* and *Ki*),[122] Cho criticized T'oegye's Four-Seven thesis for focusing too much on the dualistic distinction and separation of *i* and *ki*. Like Kobong, he argued that, although *i* and *ki* are ontologically unmixable and conceptually distinct, it is equally true that they are inseparable in concrete phenomena including feelings.

Kobong requests T'oegye to accept his initial argument that, instead of differentiating the Four and the Seven according to what he considers as a dualistic system of *i* and *ki*, the Four should be understood as a "subset" of the Seven. For Kobong, "they cannot be distinguished from each other according to what is manifest [*i* or *ki*]."[123] He points out that T'oegye can understand his argument better if he were to draw a diagram of the Four and the Seven on a piece of paper and put the Four and the Seven separately in opposition to each other. In fact T'oegye later found this argument helpful for compiling his *Sim t'ong sŏngchŏng tosŏl* (Diagrammatic Treatise on the Saying "the Mind Commands Human Nature and Feelings), the sixth of his famous *Sŏnghak sipto*. The impact of Kobong's argument is very evident in this diagrammatic treatise.[124]

To Kobong, T'oegye is not correct in analyzing the origins of the Four and the Seven from the standpoint of "separation" and "distinction." In other words, T'oegye's approach does not accord to the true essence of classical texts. Addressing the issue of interpreting orthodox Ch'eng-Chu teachings, Kobong challenges T'oegye by requesting him to answer two specific questions: "Where do the aroused and harmonized feelings of pleasure, anger, sorrow, and joy that attained their due degree and measure issue from, *i* or *ki?*" and "Is the goodness of these feelings the same as that of the Four Beginnings?"[125] Obviously, his answer to the first question is *ki* and that to the second question is yes. Embedded in Kobong's argument is that the Four do not exist outside of the Seven but constitute a good side of the latter. The goodness of the Four is, therefore, no different from the goodness of harmonized emotions; more specifically, there must be a certain continuum between the harmonized emotion of "love" (one of the Seven) and the "mind-and-heart of commiseration" (one of the Four—beginning of benevolence).

In the emanation process of the Four and the Seven, what really acts and becomes manifest is *ki*, not *i*.[126] This is the foundation of Kobong's Four-Seven thesis, and it is for this reason why he could not accept the first half of T'oegye's *hobal* theory that "in the case of the Four, *i* is manifest and *ki* follows." In general, Kobong's argument corresponds to Chu Hsi's view that *ki* is the active physical agent that exists "within form," activating and transforming all concrete phenomena, whereas *i* is the passive metaphysical principle or "the ground of being" that has neither form nor manifesting power on its own. If, as T'oegye has suggested, *i* is able to manifest itself in the case of the Four, then it means incorrectly that *i* must have form and action. To put it in another way, Kobong means *i* has no self-manifesting power, and what T'oegye meant by saying "*i* is manifest" is that "*ki* is manifest as it follows *i*, without disturbing it."

To convince T'oegye further, Kobong criticizes another dualistic aspect of T'oegye's Four-Seven thesis expressed in terms of original human nature and physical human nature. Using Chu Hsi's analogy of the moon in the sky and its reflections on the water,[127] he argues: "The nature endowed by Heaven refers to Heaven and Earth; the physical nature refers to the physical endowment of human beings and things. If we view them from a standpoint of the moon, the Heaven-endowed nature is the moon in the sky, while the physical nature is the moon on the water. Although there is a difference between [two phrases] 'in the sky' and 'on the water,' the moon [as such] is only one. Thus, we cannot say that the one in the sky is the [real] moon, but the other one on the water is not [the real moon]."[128] For Kobong, "the moon in the sky" is one, and "the moon on the water" can be many as its many reflections are seen on "thousands of rivers." The reality of the moon is one; we simply have two "names" used in describing one reality of the moon from a standpoint of "different locations." Although "the moon in the sky is the original moon, and the moon on the water is its reflection," the former is identical to the latter. In other words, it is not that there are two different or separate moons.[129] This moon-moonlight analogy, though obscure in itself, supports the basic Ch'eng-Chu doctrine that "principle is one, but its particularizations are diverse" (*iil punsu/li-i fen-shu*).[130] There is only one reality of principle, but its manifestations are many. The previously-mentioned passage indicates that original human nature and physical human nature are simply two "names" used in describing one human nature from two perspectives. From this epistemological standpoint of "unity," then, there cannot be two different human natures. The original human nature represents "the moon in the sky," and the physical human nature represents "the moon on the water."

In a systematic manner, Kobong continues further: "What Mencius referred to as the original goodness of human nature represents the moon in the sky, but he viewed it from a standpoint of the moon reflected on the water."[131] In other words, Mencius spoke of human nature in itself from a concrete viewpoint of aroused feelings (the Four). Ch'eng I and Chu Hsi described human nature in a context of understanding human nature combined with physical form; they referred to the physical human nature that represents the moon reflected on the water.[132] All of them, Kobong asserts, addressed human nature in the context of aroused feelings.

The Four and the Seven are aroused feelings pertaining to the physical human nature (represented by *i* and *ki* combined) that includes its original goodness (represented by *i* only), just as the moon on the water reflects the original moon in the sky. Kobong argues that the Four-Seven relationship can be expressed in terms of the moonlight on the water that represents the physical human nature: "The Four represent especially the bright side [the moonlight on the water], while the Seven represent both bright and dark sides [the moonlight on the water]."[133] In other words, the Four are good feelings (bright moonlight), and the Seven Emotions include both good feelings (bright moonlight) and bad feelings (dark moonlight). This corresponds to Kobong's initial theory that the Seven, the totality of feelings, include the Four as its "subset" of good feelings and that both the Four and the Seven pertain to the physical human nature. The reality of human nature is one, just as the reality of the moon is one; therefore, the reality of feelings is one, and the Four and the Seven neither have two different sources (*i* and *ki*) nor belong to two separate human natures (the original and the physical). According to Kobong, T'oegye's theory of "alternate manifestation" incorrectly points to the different origins of the Four and the Seven, the Four representing the bright side that came from "another source of light" independent of the moonlight. To emphasize the Four-Seven relationship in the context of inseparability and continuum, Kobong concludes by reiterating his fundamental points: the Four and the Seven pertain to one realm of feelings; they do not have two independent sources; and there is only one concrete reality of goodness including the goodness of the Four and the goodness of the harmonized Seven.

How did T'oegye respond to these points of Kobong's Four-Seven thesis? In 1592 he responded with a short letter. In this last reply to Kobong, T'oegye did not wish to revise his *hobal* Four-Seven thesis claiming that he had already clarified it in his previous letter to Kobong. For him, so much had been gained through the debate that it was no longer necessary to push the debate further for complete agreement. One problem area, on which he finally agreed with Kobong, is that "the goodness of the Four is the same as that of the Seven." After being impressed by Kobong's theory of the oneness of human nature, he also accepted Kobong's view that the physical human nature is never another nature independent of the original human nature. But he rejected Kobong's view that both the Four and the Seven are issued from *ki*. To maintain his belief in the moral significance of the Four, he argued that the original human nature is the true nature of human beings: "The moon in the sky is the real one, whereas the moon on the water is only its reflection. Therefore, if one speaks of the former, one gets the truth; if one tries to grasp the latter, one gets nothing. The moon reflected on the water is also the moon. Even when the water flows quietly and clearly, the movement of the moon depends on its movement. But the existence of the moon and the shape of the moonlight depend on the degree to which the water's surface moves."[134] Embedded in this statement is that T'oegye accepts Kobong's view that "the moon in the sky" is "the real moon," representing the original human nature, and "the moon on the water" represents the physical human nature. That is to say, the original human nature is our true good nature in the Mencian context, whereas the physical human nature means its physical endowment after it comes into contact with physical form. This, in fact, corresponds to Chu Hsi's philosophy. From T'oegye's standpoint of "distinction" and "separation," his convincing argument is that "the moon reflected on the water" is not as authentic and stable as the real moon in the sky. The movement and shape of the water (and, thus, the reflected moon on it) are always conditioned by the external movement and physical flow of the water and wind. In other words, the original human nature (like the real moon in the sky) is unchangeable and its goodness remains intact, whereas the physical human nature (like the reflected moon) always changes according to, and is conditioned by, external stimuli (like the movement and flow of the water and wind). Of course, this argument applies to T'oegye's contrast of the Four Beginnings and the Seven Emotions.

T'oegye's line of reasoning is similar to Ch'eng I's, although he did not quote Ch'eng I directly. Using an analogy of water and waves, Ch'eng I argued that the emotions of joy and love are unstable like the waves and currents of the water that change according to the physical and movement of wind.[135] To Ch'eng I, as well as to T'oegye, the emotions of love and anger should be understood as the temporary states of our psychological and physiological expressions conditioned by external stimuli, just as the waves and currents of water represent temporary states conditioned by physical conditions. As Ch'eng I said, "In human nature [in itself], there are only the Four Beginnings without any form of evil."[136] Like Ch'eng I and Chu Hsi (who supported the former's argument), T'oegye meant that the Four are truly the moral qualities of human nature. The Four are the autonomous manifestations of what Mencius calls its "original goodness," just as "the clear, level, and tranquil state of water is the fundamental nature of water."[137]

T'oegye argues that Kobong's conclusion that "the manifestation of *i* is none other than the manifestation of *ki* when *ki* follows *i*" tends to acknowledge *ki* as *i*.[138] As he said in his second letter to Kobong, Kobong's Four-Seven thesis based on such a theory can be a "dangerous" deviation from the whole metaphysical and ethical basis of Ch'eng-Chu Neo-Confucianism, according to which "human nature is *i*." The question is, Why did T'oegye consistently reject that part of Kobong's interpretation and is there any significant reason behind T'oegye's intention for doing so? This is an important question that should be readdressed here. T'oegye wanted to convince Kobong that there must be a certain contrast between the Four Beginnings and the Seven Emotions. The Four-Seven contrast has important implications for the way of moral self-cultivation in the light of Mencius and Ch'eng-Chu teachings. The centrality and vitality of T'oegye's Four-Seven thesis have a substantial portion of moral argument. The key to self-cultivation is to realize that the true reality of human nature is the original goodness of it that remains intact in the Four Beginnings, just as that of the moon itself is the "real moon in the sky." In other words, the ultimate reality of human nature should never be confused with the physical formation of human nature both theoretically and practically.

T'oegye seems to mean that the fundamental aim of self-cultivation depends on one's realization of one's inner, moral nature in itself. It must involve what Mencius calls *preserving* (the mind-and-heart) *and nourishing* (human nature), which requires one to realize and extend the Four Beginnings. Indeed, it is precisely this fundamental framework of Ch'eng-Chu Neo-Confucianism in which T'oegye attempted to convince Kobong from the beginning of the debate. Although T'oegye himself did not argue exactly in this way, his Four-Seven thesis does have significant implications for the practice of *moral and spiritual self-cultivation.* Chapter IV will treat this topic more specifically by discussing his other major philosophical writings as well, especially those written after his debate with Kobong.

In 1566, eight years after the beginning of the debate, Kobong wrote a general summary statement of T'oegye's Four-Seven thesis according to his senior's basic position.[139] T'oegye accepted it with pleasure; he finally was overjoyed to receive such a conciliatory letter from his junior friend. He found that Kobong's summary is somewhat a representation of his own ideas, though it did not fully accommodate his entire Four-Seven thesis. However, the interesting point of this finale is that Kobong somehow gave up pushing his challenge further, especially about T'oegye's theory that *i* has its own self-manifesting capability in the case of issuing the Four (it is precisely this issue on which Yulgok subsequently focused his systematic critique of T'oegye's interpretation). Although this is a disappointing scholarly matter in the context of our own investigation, Kobong was probably satisfied with his impressive performance in the debate with T'oegye and knew that his senior scholar would not revise his basic position any further.[140] Obviously, Kobong respected T'oegye as the leading scholar of the Ch'eng-Chu tradition in Korea, who had politely welcomed his challenge for nearly eight years. Also, T'oegye praised some of Kobong's ideas and insights. Taken together, then, this probably led Kobong to accept the fundamental features of his senior's interpretation.

III

Yulgok's Four-Seven Thesis

Yulgok's Four-Seven thesis is found in his correspondence with his close friend Sŏng Hon (Ugye, 1536–1598), a scholar who had studied Ch'eng-Chu thought through reading T'oegye's works in particular. T'oegye's writings were quite influential during his time, and Ugye respected T'oegye highly. Ugye wrote to Yulgok asking for clarification especially regarding T'oegye's Four-Seven theory of "alternate manifestation of *i* and *ki*" (*iki hobal/li-ch'i hu-fa*). Yulgok and Ugye, then, began a wide ranging debate that covers not only the whole ground the T'oegye-Kobong debate had traversed, but also new philosophical concepts and moral issues. Their principal exchanges took place in 1572, six years after the end of the T'oegye-Kobong debate and a year after the death of T'oegye. Yulgok, then thirty-six years old, already had established his reputation as one of the leading scholar-officials and had written a few important philosophical works of outstanding quality while serving several high-ranking government positions.

The Yulgok-Ugye debate includes nine queries and responses, some of which are especially lengthy.[1] Note that, even though Yulgok was writing to Ugye, his real debate was with T'oegye; Ugye simply provided him with T'oegye's perspectives. In general, Yulgok's letters are longer and better organized than Ugye's; the former's arguments tend to be original, clearer, and more systematic, whereas the latter's views are usually unclear and copied after T'oegye, lacking originality and systematic thinking.

Human Mind and Moral Mind: The Unity and Duality of the Mind

In his first letter to Yulgok, Ugye initiates the debate by supporting the basic ideas of T'oegye's Four-Seven thesis. After studying T'oegye's *Sim t'ong sŏngchŏng tosŏl* (Diagrammatic Treatise on the Saying "the Mind Commands Human Nature and Feelings"), the sixth of his well-known *Sŏnghak sipto*,[2] Ugye defends T'oegye's Four-Seven theory of "alternate manifestation of *i* and *ki*" (*iki hobal/li-ch'i hu-fa*).[3] Like T'oegye, Ugye argues: "The Four Beginnings are purely good without any evil."[4] Although supporting T'oegye's *hobal* theory, he sees nothing wrong with analyzing the Four and the Seven dualistically, assigning the former to *i* and the latter to *ki* as their respective origins.[5] He argues further: "The Four Beginnings refer to one side of the Seven Emotions and are those feelings that are issued from *i*. The Seven Emotions refer to those feelings that do not attain their due degree and measure, and this is due to the deficiency and excess of *ki*'s activity that leads one to evil."[6] This passage reveals Ugye's commitment to the *Doctrine of the Mean* that the Seven might lead to evil if they are harmonized according to their "due degree and measure." Both the Four and the Seven are feelings, so it follows for him that, in trying to draw a diagram of human nature and feelings, one should put both the Four and the Seven inside a circle of feelings.[7] Ugye's argument means T'oegye's original thesis that one should not be confused between the manifestation of *i* and the manifestation of *ki*.[8] Ugye also makes Kobong's point that the Four can be conceived as a "good side" of the Seven.

To defend T'oegye's Four-Seven theory that feelings can be spoken of in terms of *i* or *ki*, Ugye appends his own view that it is logically correct to discuss the Four and the Seven in terms of the "moral mind" (*tosim/tao-hsin*) and the "human mind" (*insim/jen-hsin*), respectively. The *locus classicus* for the ideas of the "moral mind" and the "human mind" is the so-called Sixteen-Character Transmission of the Mind-and-Heart, an obscure passage from the *Book of History*, which reads: "The human mind is precarious; the moral mind is subtle. Remain refined and single-minded. Hold fast to the Mean."[9] This instruction of sage-king Shun to his successor Yü contrasts the precariousness of the human mind with the subtlety of the moral mind; it emphasizes the necessity of mind cultivation with a "refined and single-minded" concentration to hold on to the truth of equilibrium before feelings are aroused. It was, of course, taken by Chu Hsi, as well as by his followers like the late Sung scholar Chen Te-hsiu,[10] as a short formula of the Neo-Confucian philosophy of mind cultivation.

We can recall here that, according to Chu Hsi's philosophy, the moral mind is aroused from "the correctness of heaven and destiny," whereas the human mind is aroused from "selfishness identified with physical form."[11] The former is described as "subtle," "impartial," and "good," whereas the latter as "partial" and "prone to error," involving both "good and evil." Furthermore, the human mind refers to our physical feelings and sensations such as the mouth's desire for taste and the eye's desire for color, whereas the moral mind refers to moral principles and virtues such as benevolence, righteousness, propriety, and wisdom.[12] According to Chu Hsi's formula, then, the moral mind is the unaroused state of the mind in itself that is pure and always good; the human mind is the aroused state of the mind mixed with desires that includes both good and evil.[13] But Chu Hsi never discussed the moral mind and the human mind with respect to the Four and the Seven, and this is a significant area of the Four-Seven debate between Ugye and Yulgok. Neither did T'oegye discuss the Four-Seven contrast specifically in terms of the moral mind and the human mind. This was a real problem of Ugye's interpretation to the extent that Yulgok criticized not only Ugye's way of thinking, but even T'oegye for causing such an unreasonable influence on Ugye.

Quoting Chu Hsi's theory, Ugye writes to Yulgok:

> "The mind (*sim/hsin*) is one in its pure intelligence and consciousness."[14] Why do we, then, have the two terms, "human mind" and "moral mind"? In some cases, "it is born of the partial physical form"; in other cases, "it originates from the correctness of Heaven and destiny."[15] *I* and *ki* differ in their manifestations (*pal/fa*); therefore, there are two terms such as the "moral mind" and the "human mind" that differ in their functioning. One is "precarious," whereas the other is "subtle." *Is this [relationship], then, the same as [the relationship between] the Four Beginnings and the Seven Emotions? It would be correct to call the moral mind the Four Beginnings, but it would not be correct to call the human mind the Seven Emotions.* Moreover, the Four Beginnings and the Seven Emotions refer to what is manifest from human nature (*sŏng/hsing*), whereas the moral mind and the human mind refer to what is manifest from the mind (*sim/hsin*). The names and meanings are not the same. I would welcome your instruction on the right way [of understanding this issue].[16]

In this passage, Ugye means that the mind is ontologically one but called differently depending on whether it rises from selfishness identified with physical form or is based on virtuous behavior. For him, then, it is incorrect to say that the moral mind is one thing and the human mind is another.[17] However, the mind may be two on account of the difference between *i* and *ki* because *i* and *ki* are the sources of the moral mind and the human mind, respectively. By contrasting the goodness of the "subtle" moral mind and the "instability" of the human mind involving both good and evil, he suggests, though he did not argue explicitly, that there can be some correlation between the moral mind and the human mind.

In his response to Ugye's first letter, Yulgok presents a systematic discussion of the Four-Seven relationship. Being sharply aware of the textual ambiguities at the heart of classical texts and Ch'eng-Chu writings, he first points out that the words and explanations of the former sages and worthies are clear in some cases and subtle in other cases. He emphasizes that one should not follow them blindly without one's careful reflection, and one should interpret them correctly with one's own experiences and views.[18] This is the first objective of his thinking; it demonstrates his fundamental view that any subtle and unclear old teachings must be clarified to appreciate them fully.

For Yulgok, T'oegye's *hobal* theory is improper for understanding the Four-Seven relationship, for it implies incorrectly that *i* and *ki* are "two separate entities," one being prior and the other being posterior, each appearing independently."[19] Yulgok, then, criticizes Ugye's Four-Seven view in terms of the moral mind and the human mind. He refuses to assume any ontological division of the mind. Rejecting Ugye's strict "distinction" of the moral mind and the human mind, he emphasizes their mutual "relationship" of interdependence and harmony. From such a standpoint, Yulgok addresses the oneness of the mind: "The mind is one. To call it 'moral' or 'human' is to distinguish nature and destiny from physical form."[20] How can there be two terms for the mind? Yulgok states: "There are two names according to the source of primary manifestation."[21] This, he argues, is why Chu Hsi said: "What is precarious [human mind] is the sprout of human desires, and what is subtle [moral mind] is the deep mystery of Heaven's principle. The mind is one; however, its name varies only according to whether or not it is rectified."[22] The human mind and the moral mind are intertwined being "each other's beginning or end."[23] In other words, the human mind can overcome itself to become the moral mind, and the latter can end up with the former: "The mind of human beings comes straight from 'the correctness of nature and destiny.'[24] Although it began as the moral mind, it ends up as the human mind if it does not follow the correctness of nature and destiny and becomes mixed with selfish intentions. When it is aroused by physical form and does not deviate from the principle of form, it will not act against Heaven's principle. If it does deviate from the principle of correctness and knows what is wrong and what is to be overcome, without following selfish desires, then it will end up as the moral mind, even though it began as the human mind."[25] Implicit in this passage is Yulgok's emphasis on the mutual relationship of continuum and interdependence between the moral mind and the human mind. From a moral standpoint of self-cultivation, he means that, although one has a good intention and begins initially with the moral mind, one will end up with the human mind if one falls into "selfish intentions." In this regard, Yi Pyŏng-do makes an interesting but unclear point that Yulgok saw the moral mind and the human mind as sharing "the possibility and relationship of overcoming each other."[26] To put in a correct way, the human mind can be overcome by the moral mind, as the latter serves its role as the former's master. Furthermore, even if one begins with the human mind mixed with selfishness, one can still transform it into the moral mind if one decides to follow moral principles and overcome selfish desires.

In regard to *i* and *ki*, the mind is one because, as Chu Hsi argued, it unites *i* and *ki*. From a nondualistic standpoint of the metaphysical *i-ki* inseparability and the ethical good-evil link, Yulgok, like Kobong, argues that the basic difference between good and evil is only a matter of whether "*ki* disturbs *i*" or "*ki* does not disturb *i*."[27] Criticizing Ugye's Four-Seven theory for separating the mind and human nature into two, Yulgok, like Chu Hsi, writes: "Human nature is *i*, the centre of the mind. The mind is the vessel that contains human nature."[28] In other words, the original goodness of human nature, in the Mencian sense, is inherent in the mind that includes and commands both human nature and feelings. For Yulgok, Ugye was wrong in considering human nature and the mind as two independent entities and in maintaining the distinction between "manifesting from human nature" and "manifesting from the mind." Both the human mind and the moral mind are manifest from human nature, so it follows for Yulgok that "what is disturbed by *ki*" pertains to the human mind, and "what is undisturbed by *ki*" pertains to the moral mind.[29] If one follows moral principles, then one can always transform the human mind into the moral mind. By contrast, if one cannot do so, then one's feelings become more selfish, the human mind becomes more "precarious," and the moral mind becomes more "subtle." For Yulgok, then, it is not possible for our mind to have two ontological or ethical foundations.

Ugye was not easily persuaded. In his second letter to Yulgok, he claims that, after reading Chu Hsi's theory of the moral mind and the human mind, he rather wants to follow T'oegye. Defending T'oegye's dualistic theory of human nature, Ugye argues that, because human nature can be spoken of by referring to *i* or *ki*, it logically follows that feelings can also be spoken of in terms of *i* or *ki*.[30] He states: "If the moral mind and the human mind can be spoken of in terms of *i* and *ki*, then the Four Beginnings and the Seven Emotions can also be spoken of in terms of *i* and *ki*."[31]

In his third letter to Ugye, Yulgok maintains that when stimulated, one wishes to "abide in benevolence," "follow righteousness," "be filial to parents," "be faithful to friends," and so on.[32] Following Chu Hsi, Yulgok argues that these kinds of feelings, which exist in one's moral and virtuous behavior, have *i* as principal backing and, therefore, are called the *moral mind.* "What stimulates and moves is certainly physical form; however, what is manifest comes straight from moral principles . . . that are not disturbed by the physical form."[33] Hence, the moral mind can be understood principally in terms of *i*, as it is based on the Four Beginnings that have *i* as their principal backing. As Yulgok argues, one's innate virtuous behavior comes from the moral mind, although it is still subject to physical endowment by *ki*. By contrast, our common instincts, such as "desiring to eat when hungry" and "desiring to put on clothes when cold," all refer to the basic characteristics of the human mind, with *ki* as their principal backing.[34] According to Yulgok, these kinds of desires also originate from the same Heaven-endowed nature of human beings, although they are aroused for the individual needs and responses. These physical desires and physiological feelings, like the Seven, are not moral feelings pertaining to "the original essence of principle." However, both the moral mind and the human mind are manifest from "one human nature"; therefore, they cannot be separated into "two kinds, one as issuing from *i* and the other issuing from *ki*." Also, all feelings, desires, and responses, including the Four and the Seven, come from "one human nature."

Yulgok continues to argue: "If the consciousness of the mind is aroused from physical dispositions and sensations, then we call it the 'human mind.' The human mind is originally good, but it easily turns to evil, for which reason it is said to be 'precarious.' If the consciousness of the mind is aroused from human nature characterized by benevolence, righteousness, propriety, and wisdom, we call it the 'moral mind.' The moral mind is purely good; therefore, one should give full effort to extend it."[35] In this passage, Yulgok wants to convince Ugye that, although there are two "names" of one mind, there is, in reality, only one consciousness of the mind. He compares the moral mind and the human mind, giving some of the traditional metaphoric examples:

> The manifestation of the moral mind is as difficult to understand as the kindling of a flame and the initial rising of a spring. For this reason, the moral mind is said to be "subtle." The manifestation of the human mind is as difficult to control as the jumping up and down of a freed eagle untying its strings and of an unbridled horse going out of its tracks. For this reason, the human mind is said to be "precarious." Although the human mind and moral mind are two names, their source is only one. The mind

> is manifest in favor of moral principles in some cases and in favor of eating and sexual desire in other cases; therefore, the two names vary only according to their respective manifestations.[36]

In other words, the mind is ontologically one in its unmanifest state, and its two names, *moral mind* and *human mind*, are used in describing the manifest mind according to whether it is manifest from moral principles or physical desires and sensations. In the manifested state, the mind can appear in two ways. Embedded in the afore-mentioned passages is a moral issue. The so-called precarious human mind is originally good, for it comes from human nature; however, it can easily turn to evil if it does not follow moral principles that constitute the original goodness of human nature. The key to self-cultivation is, then, to give full effort to control the human mind, so that it can be transformed into, and remain, the moral mind.

As concrete phenomena, the moral mind and the human mind both pertain to aroused feelings. Following Chu Hsi, Yulgok asserts that the mind unites *i* and *ki* in a perfect harmony. Although the moral mind is inseparable from *ki*, it is founded on *i* as the source of moral principles, and the human mind consists of both *i* and *ki*. In his famous *Insim tosim tosŏl* (Diagrammatic Treatise on the Human Mind and the Moral Mind),[37] Yulgok states: "The mind is not two. . . . It is only that there are two beginnings when manifestation occurs. What issues the moral mind is *ki*; however, there is no moral mind without nature and destiny. The human mind is founded on *i*; however, there is no human mind without the physical form."[38] Both are originally founded on what Mencius calls the *goodness of human nature*. Yulgok's interpretation can be articulated further by examining his *Simsŏngchŏng sŏl* (Treatise on the Mind, Human Nature, and Feelings), a short philosophical section included in the famous *Sŏnghak chipyo* (Outline of the Learning of the Sages) that is Yulgok's most important work, compiled in 1575, three years after the Yulgok-Ugye Four-Seven debate.[39] He discusses the same argument on the basis of Chu Hsi's philosophy:

> Someone [probably Ugye in his debate with Yulgok] asked: "If the moral mind and human mind are two kinds of the mind, can the Four Beginnings and the Seven Emotions be considered as two kinds of feelings?" I replied: The mind is one. How can there be two minds? There are two names according to what is principally manifest, and that is all. Hence, Chu Hsi said: "What is precarious [human mind] is the sprout of human desires, while what is subtle [moral mind] is the deep mystery of Heaven's

> principle. The mind is one, but its name varies only according to whether or not it is rectified. It is not that one takes the moral mind to be one mind and the human mind to be another."[40] From this point of view, we can know that the mind is not two.[41]

From Yulgok's standpoint of "mutual relationship," then, the mind is always "one" in both ontological and epistemological contexts. This is an ethical issue as well. Good and evil are never two separate principles or entities directly opposed to each other; therefore, the moral mind and the human mind should not be related to good and evil in an exclusively antithetical way.

In his third letter to Ugye, Yulgok argues that Ugye's argument implies that "Even when nothing is manifest, there is already the sprout of the human mind and the moral mind. . . . When *i* is manifest, it becomes the moral mind; when *ki* is manifest, it becomes the human mind."[42] This is, Yulgok argues, incorrect because it means that our mind has "two foundations."[43] Following Chu Hsi's perception of the mind, Yulgok then criticizes Ugye for defending T'oegye:

> Chu Hsi said that "the mind is only one in its pure intelligence and consciousness."[44] . . . The so-called [cosmic] source or production refers to what is already manifest and established. If manifestation is in favor of virtuous behavior, you can see its origin. Where does the mind of *virtuous behavior* come from? It comes from nature and destiny [inherent] in the mind; therefore, we have the moral mind. If manifestation is in favor of eating and sexual desire, for example, you can see its origin. Where do the thoughts of *eating* and *sexual desire* come from? They come from our temperament complete in physical form; therefore, we have the human mind.[45]

Ugye was not convinced. In his fourth letter to Ugye, Yulgok writes: "Is it the moral mind or the human mind that does not originate from *i*? The source is one, but there are two ways. Could it be possible that Chu Hsi did not know this? Of course, not. He set up the words to help other people understand."[46] He continues: "The sages regarded the moral mind as those feelings that are aroused straight from the original essence of nature. They also regarded the human mind as those feelings that are not aroused straight from the original essence of human nature due to the disturbance of *ki*."[47] As a moral guideline, therefore, they taught others to preserve and nourish their moral mind, as well as to control their human mind by examining its excessive and deficient expression in feelings. For Yulgok, what commands the human mind is "the activity of the moral mind," the master of the human mind.[48] He states further: "If one can fill and extend the moral mind by regulating the human mind so that physical shape and color each follow their rules, then one's action, tranquility, and speech will all accord with the original essence of nature and destiny. Since ancient times, this has been the sages and worthies' fundamental doctrine of the 'method of the mind' (*simbŏp/hsin-fa*)."[49]

From a concrete standpoint of moral self-cultivation, Yulgok explains the moral mind and the human mind by comparing the sages and inferior persons in terms of the physical endowment of their nature. In his view, the sages' physical endowment is clear and pure; therefore, the entire substance of their nature does not have any selfishness. Their physical desires and mental feelings follow moral principles. However, "only after their learning of self-cultivation was established, their original human nature was able to be manifest correctly and straightforwardly, without being disturbed by physical form."[50] In this case, the human mind follows the moral mind., On the contrary, the physical endowment of inferior people is, Yulgok asserts, highly "turbid" and "impure." The moral mind is lost, and the original essence of the nature of these people is disturbed by physical form; this is because their effort at self-cultivation is incomplete. As Yulgok writes, "Because the human mind dominates, the manifestation of the original essence of their nature is controlled by physical form. Hence, although their moral mind is manifest, they neither preserve nor realize it if they devote themselves only to the selfishness of physical form."[51] In this case, there is only the human mind in control. This is why the desires of inferior people can arise excessively and violently, as the human mind does not follow the moral mind.

To convince Ugye further, Yulgok articulates his position metaphorically by utilizing the traditional rider-horse analogy, the one that T'oegye quoted to explain his *hobal* theory of *i* and *ki*:

> If we compare it to a person riding a horse, [we can say that] the rider is human nature and the horse is its physical disposition. The reason that the horse's nature is obedient or disobedient is due to the clarity and turbidity of the physical endowment of *ki*. When a rider goes out riding a horse, the horse follows the rider's wishes in some cases, or the rider goes out by simply depending on the legs of the horse in other cases. In the case that

> the horse follows the rider, the rider is the master in control, just as the moral mind [is the master of the human mind]; in the case that the rider follows the horse, the horse is the master in control, just as the human mind [is the master of the moral mind].[52]

In this passage, Yulgok is emphasizing what he calls the *interdependent relationship* of the moral mind and the human mind from an empirical standpoint of concrete phenomena. The moral mind and the human mind are one, just as the rider and the horse are one. In Yulgok's analogical view, the horse that follows the rider's will can be viewed as the moral mind, and the horse that does not follow the rider's will as the human mind. As he argued in his first letter, the human mind and the moral mind are "each other's beginning or end." Although the horse's nature is gentle, there can be a situation when the rider rides his horse only by following its lead and depending on its legs. In a comparative context, Yulgok writes: "If the horse used to be disobedient to the rider and happens to take the right path, without being guided by the rider, then this case would be the same as the fact that the sages follow their desires without transgressing what is right."[53]

The sages and ordinary people must be born the same in the sense that they all have basic instincts and desires. As Yulgok states, "The sages cannot avoid eating when hungry, drinking when thirsty, putting on clothes when cold, and scratching when itchy."[54] However, their human mind of having such desires follows their moral mind and becomes identical to it, just as the horse's will follows the rider's will and becomes identical to it. As for the ordinary people, Yulgok argues that their physical nature is not as pure as the sages's physical nature; therefore, "when the mind is aroused, it can become evil if the moral mind is not maintained as the master of the human mind."[55] This situation is similar to the case that "if the rider follows the horse's lead without guiding or controlling it, the horse may go on its own, without following the right path."[56] In short, embedded in Yulgok's argument is its basis on what we might call a nondualistic standpoint of inseparability and interdependence. The practical implication of this argument is, of course, a *moral* one: from a moral standpoint of self-cultivation, Yulgok means that, even when one begins with the human mind mixed with basic human feelings, one can always transform it into the moral mind if one follows moral principles to overcome selfish desires.

Responding to Ugye's view of the Four-Seven relationship in terms of the moral mind and the human mind, Yulgok states: "The Four Beginnings refer to the moral mind, while the Seven Emotions refer to the moral mind and the human mind together as a whole."[57] The Four are to be understood as "the good side of the moral mind and the human mind together."[58] In other words, because the mind is one, it follows for Yulgok that the moral mind that pertains to the Four is included inside of the human mind and the Seven includes both the moral mind and the human mind as a whole. This interpretation is quite different from Ugye's explanation, which divides the Four and the Seven antithetically into the moral mind and the human mind separated from each other.[59] One's innate virtuous behavior comes from the moral mind that is the good part of the human mind. And both Four and the Seven are included in the human mind. According to Yulgok, then, T'oegye's interpretation is incorrect because the Seven include both the moral mind and the human mind. In the *Insim tosim tosŏl* as well, he argues that the Seven are "the whole name of the human mind and the moral mind, good and evil," criticizing T'oegye for considering the Four as the moral mind and the Seven as the human mind.[60]

Yulgok makes a strong point, in his seventh letter to Ugye, that T'oegye was wrong in considering the moral mind and the human mind antithetically as inner manifestation and outer manifestation respectively: "On the whole, T'oegye referred to internal manifestation as the moral mind and external feelings as the human mind. On the contrary, I believe that the human mind and the moral mind are both manifest from the inside, and both are stimulated by external feelings."[61] In the strict sense, however, Yulgok's criticism is not justifiable in the textual context. T'oegye, in his Four-Seven debate with Kobong and in his other writings, did not explicitly discuss the Four and the Seven in terms of two kinds of the mind. Instead, in articulating the Ch'eng-Chu way of self-cultivation, he generally followed Chu Hsi's philosophy that the human mind is aroused from "selfishness identified with the physical form," whereas the moral mind is founded on "moral principles." T'oegye emphasized a distinction between the moral mind and the human mind in terms of the metaphysical *i-ki* contrast and the ethical good-evil opposition.[62] For him, evil is due to "selfish desires" caused by the human mind mixed with *ki*.[63] The path to self-cultivation requires the command of one's moral mind over the instability of one's human mind, so that one can control the selfish desires issued from the human mind. In other words, it also involves one's nourishment of moral principles associated with the Four. As mentioned before, this is the basic philosophical and moral basis of T'oegye's Four-Seven thesis.

Yulgok's criticism of T'oegye is not valid. Given that Ugye defended T'oegye's way of thinking and Yulgok was familiar with his senior's Four-Seven philosophy, Yulgok must have read T'oegye's Four-Seven letters and perhaps his other major writings. In any case, Yulgok understands T'oegye as implying that the Four belong to the moral mind and the Seven belong to the human mind. Of course, Ugye himself would also be partly responsible, not only because he indicated that his Four-Seven thesis is based on T'oegye's, but also because he engendered Yulgok to interpret T'oegye in such a way. What Yulgok presents is, however, a more positive view that basic human desires are a natural part of human nature and, therefore, can be controlled to become good feelings like the Four. In his view, T'oegye overemphasized one's distinction of moral principles and human desires to the extent that T'oegye saw the human mind only as the cause of selfish desires and evil.

On the whole, Yulgok refused to make any dualistic metaphysical or ethical contrast between the moral mind and the human mind that do not have two separate "origins." His argument is based on "the oneness of the mind" in both metaphysical and ethical contexts.[64] As Young-chan Ro correctly points out, Yulgok affirms neither a separate existence nor a clear-cut division between the moral mind and the human mind.[65] In other words, the moral mind and the human mind are not two different minds; rather, they simply refer to two realms of one mind. The distinction between them should be conceived in such a way that they are two related phenomena of the mind. From Yulgok's epistemological standpoint of "mutual relation," there must be continuum between them. The reality of the mind is ontologically one, and there are only two conceptual terms according to two interrelated perspectives used in describing intellectual, moral, physical, and psychological dimensions of the mind as a whole. According to Neo-Confucian thought in general and Yulgok's interpretation in particular, the mind participates in manifold realms including those of moral principles and virtues, intellectual rationality, psychological emotions and feelings, and physical desires. Surely, virtuous and ethical phenomena (pertaining to the moral mind) and physical and emotional phenomena (pertaining to the human mind) are different; however, this difference, Yulgok argues, is never the absolute factor for separating them into two different minds or feelings. Hence, the whole philosophical and ethical issue here deals with the two different yet related tendencies of the mind. As Yulgok argues, this does not necessarily imply two separate sources of feelings; in other words, they are not two directly opposing entities and, therefore, cannot discussed in terms of the Four and the Seven, respectively. The relationship of the moral mind and the human mind should be understood with a correct understanding of the inseparability of not only *i* and *ki* but also feelings.

For this reason, Yulgok wanted to convince Ugye that "The Four refer to the moral mind in particular; the Seven refer to the moral mind and the human mind combined as a whole."[66] Accordingly, the Four and the Seven cannot be considered dualistically as belonging to two separate minds.[67] To put in another way, just as the reality of the mind is "one," the reality of feelings is also "one" and not divided into the Four and the Seven. This was, of course, not only the basis of Yulgok's Four-Seven thesis, but also a criticism of T'oegye's dualistic Four-Seven thesis. The next topic of our investigation addresses this issue more closely.

The Continuum of Feelings: The Four in the Seven

In his first letter to Ugye, Yulgok explains the basic Four-Seven relationship: "The Four Beginnings cannot include the Seven Emotions; however, the Seven Emotions include the Four Beginnings. . . . The Four Beginnings are not like the totality of the Seven Emotions, while the Seven Emotions are not like the purity of the Four Beginnings."[68] This statement is almost identical to Kobong's Four-Seven thesis. Yulgok added only that "the Four Beginnings cannot include the Seven." Like Kobong, he argues that the Four are good, moral feelings included in the Seven and that they should be understood in the context of in the Seven, the "totality" of feelings. He also adopted Kobong's argument that one cannot affirm the difference between the Four and the Seven on the basis of any metaphysical or ethical dualism. As he states, "To call feelings the 'Four' or 'Seven' is only due to the distinction between speaking only of *i* or speaking also of *ki*."[69] The Four-Seven relationship is not exactly like the moral mind–human mind relationship because the Four and the Seven are not "each other's beginning and end" as are the moral mind and the human mind.[70] Three points of Yulgok's argument are evident here: first, to talk about feelings, one should refer to both the Four Beginnings and the Seven Emotions; second, to address feelings in terms of good and evil, one should acknowledge the Seven as the "totality" of feelings; and finally, the Four should be understood as the "good side" of the Seven deliberately selected by Mencius.[71] Of course, these three points are similar to those of Kobong's Four-Seven thesis. Yulgok added one point that to explain the mind, one has to clarify the human mind and the moral mind.

Surely, the Four are mentioned by Mencius to convey the idea that human nature is originally and naturally good; that is to say, all human beings are naturally good because they possess the Four as innate roots of virtue. For this reason, Yulgok sees the Four as simply "the good side of the Seven." In other words, the Four and the Seven are conceptually distinguishable, although they do not fit into the scheme of the moral mind and the human mind. But Yulgok, like Kobong, does not argue that the Four have any ontological or moral status independent of the Seven. As aroused moral feelings, the Four do not exist outside the Seven, the totality of all feelings. By suggesting that any of the Seven can be related to the Four in one way or another, Yulgok means that the Four and the Seven are not two different realms or kinds of feelings that exist in opposition to each other. For instance, the Four can serve as the virtuous source of any good feelings. From a standpoint of self-cultivation, Yulgok means that the Four cannot have their own moral ground other than that of the Seven and that all of the Seven have the moral potential to become good feelings like the Four.

As Yulgok points out, if *i* is in control when *ki* does not disturb it, we have the Four; if *ki* already disturbs *i*, we refer to both good and evil of the Seven. In his first letter to Ugye, he criticizes T'oegye for interpreting the Four and the Seven as two separate kinds of human feelings: "It would be appropriate for scholars to view Chu Hsi's saying dynamically. Master T'oegye refers to the Four Beginnings as good [feelings] but says that the Seven Emotions are also good. If he is right, this means that there are good feelings outside of the Four Beginnings. Where do these feelings come from? Mencius described them [the Four] generally; therefore, he gave only four examples such as 'commiseration,' 'shame and dislike,' 'courtesy and modesty,' and 'discernment of right and wrong.'[72] However, other good feelings also belong to the Four Beginnings, and scholars should understand this fact as well."[73] Asking how human feelings can become good, without being grounded in moral principles (such as benevolence, propriety, righteousness, and wisdom), Yulgok maintains that the Four are already "good feelings." This is why Mencius referred to the Four as the *mind-and-heart of commiseration, the mind-and-heart of shame and dislike*, and so on, implying that they, like the Seven, are concrete feelings aroused from human nature. If "there are good feelings in addition to the Four," this implies incorrectly that the mind has two ontological foundations.[74] Given Yulgok's critique of T'oegye's theory and his interpretation of the Four as the "good" feelings of the Seven, an obvious question thus arises: How do we recognize the issuance of the Four? Yulgok argues that the Four can be recognized when the good side of the Seven is influenced by the external stimuli. For example, commiseration occurs after seeing a small child falling into a well; in other words, without experiencing any external object, one cannot have the aroused feeling of commiseration. Like Kobong, Yulgok, though he never noticed, accords with Chu Hsi's statements that "the Seven Emotions cannot be separated from the Four Beginnings" and that "the Four Beginnings can be understood in the context of the Seven Emotions."[75]

In his second letter to Ugye, Yulgok enclosed an interesting diagram of the Four and the Seven, called the *Simsŏngchŏng to* (Diagram of Mind, Human Nature, and Feelings), articulating his view of the Four-Seven relationship in terms of mind, human nature, and feelings.[76] He drew a large circle and indicated it as representing the mind as a whole. In addition, a small inner circle at the center of the large outer circle represents human nature. This circle represents what he calls the *unmanifested state of the mind* or the mind before feelings are aroused. In other words, as "the centre of the mind with no evil," human nature "constitutes *i*."[77] In the light of Mencius, the *Doctrine of the Mean*, and Ch'eng-Chu teachings, this diagram presents three basic points of Yulgok's argument: first, "human nature, in its unmanifest state, is originally good without being mixed with any evil"; second, "the mind [as a whole] refers to what is conditioned by physical endowment with various differentiations of purity"; and third, "when the mind is stimulated by external things, feelings issue from it, giving rise to either good or evil."[78]

Furthermore, the Four, as the good side of the Sevens, are placed on the top of the Seven because they, Yulgok argues, "serve as the beginnings of benevolence, righteousness, propriety, and wisdom."[79] Speaking from a perspective of emotional harmonization emphasized in the *Doctrine of the Mean*, he also asserts that the Four are "good feelings" that always attain their "due degree and measure" after they are aroused.[80] The Four are taken as a set of good feelings that already exist inside of the Seven. The Seven, like the Four, are considered as originating in "the goodness of moral principles." But Yulgok asserts that they can "end up serving diametrically opposite ends, thereby doing injury to the virtues."[80] In other words, "evil feelings" arise when one neglects the original goodness of human nature, and this is due to one's failure to harmonize the Seven according to their due degree and measure. It is incorrect to say that human nature, which refers to "the unmanifested state of the mind," has both good and evil.[82] If "it is called 'equilibrium' before the feelings of pleasure, anger, sorrow, and pleasure are aroused,"[83] one cannot say that human nature includes both good and evil. The reason that the mind of an ordinary person is confused and disorderly is "due to its confinement to physical and material desires."[84]

Sharply aware of Ch'eng-Chu teachings, Yulgok points out: "What is called principle [in reality] refers to the principle that circulates by riding on material force. But it does not refer to the original essence of principle (*i chi ponyŏn/li chih pen-jan*)."[85] That is to say, "*i* in itself is purely good; however, when it moves by riding on *ki* [in the process of cosmic transformation], it divides into myriad variations which can lead to both good and evil. Hence, the physical endowment of human nature has both good and evil."[86] Yulgok continues to argue:

> You [Ugye] said: "There can be the sprout of evil in human nature before feelings are aroused." After thinking it over, I have discovered a serious flaw in this statement; your misunderstanding of the great fundamental [of the former sages' and worthies' teachings] lies right in it. What is unmanifest pertains to the original essence of human nature, the mystery of the Great Ultimate, the Mean, and the important foundation [of Confucian teaching]. If, as you said, there is the sprout of evil in it, then this implies . . . that the Mencian doctrine of human nature as good is absurd, and not everyone can become a [sage like] Yao and Shun. The former wise people of the past, including Tzu-ssu in the *Doctrine of the Mean*, generally said [for all people] that "before feelings such as pleasure, anger, sorrow and joy are aroused, it is called the Mean"; they did not mean this specifically for superior persons only. Accordingly, your statement is absolutely wrong.[87]

For Yulgok, then, it is misleading to suggest that human nature in itself, before feelings are aroused, has any beginning of evil or even the slightest sign of it. Of course, he means to do full justice to the Mencian doctrine that human nature is originally good in the context of its innate roots of virtue.

It is clear that Yulgok supports Kobong's Four-Seven thesis. In the context of the *Doctrine of the Mean*, both thinkers see the difference between the Four and the Seven as the problem of whether or not aroused feelings are. Of course, this is a concrete ethical issue for the practice of self-cultivation. But the relevant question is, Where does *evil* come from? Like Kobong, Yulgok argues that evil does not have its own ontological ground other that the Seven, the totality of the feelings. Another key question is, If human nature is originally and naturally good, why and how does evil become apparent in human feelings? For Yulgok, as well as for Kobong, the problem of good and evil must come from the physical endowment of human nature; when the Seven are not properly directed, they may not end up with good and can lead to evil. As indicated in his diagram of mind, human nature, and mind Yulgok asserts that the Four are harmonized moral feelings that constitute the good part of the Seven.[88] Before the Seven are aroused, the unmanifest state of human nature is good; however, when it is stimulated by external things, either good or evil can arise, depending on whether the Seven become harmonized. Therefore, any of the Seven, if harmonized properly according to moral principles, is a good feeling like the Four. In short, then, this is the fundamental basis of Yulgok's understanding of good and evil, one that corresponds to Kobong's original thinking. That which becomes harmonized is good, and that which does not become harmonized is evil. Like Kobong, Yulgok means that there are no two different "origins" of the Four and the Seven and that the Four-Seven relationship cannot be discussed from an ontological or ethical perspective of the good-evil opposition. Good and evil are never *two opposing realities* of feelings pertaining to the Four, on the one hand, and the Seven, on the other hand.

In his third letter to Ugye, Yulgok underscores that the Four Beginnings are only "other names of good feelings."[89] To him, it is never possible for the "good side" and the "totality" to be divided into the two kinds of feelings that are separate from, or in opposition to, each other. Thus, "Chu Hsi's saying that 'the Four Beginnings are manifestations of *i*; the Seven Emotion are manifestations of *ki*'[90] is meant only in a general sense"; he would not expect others to separate the Four and the Seven in terms of *i* and *ki* too much.[91] Yulgok continues: "Contemporary scholars are unable to grasp the meaning [of Chu Hsi's theory] and simply defend it by distinguishing their explanations and by dragging in quotations. How could they arrive at the truth of its real meaning?"[92] Implicit in his claim is a criticism of T'oegye's Four-Seven thesis; that is to say, T'oegye misunderstood and misinterpreted Chu Hsi, and his problem is his dualistic view of the Four and the Seven in terms of *i* and *ki*.[93]

Yulgok repeatedly tried to convince Ugye that the Four do not exist outside of the Seven, and the former are only the good side of the latter. "According to Tzu-ssu [in the *Doctrine of the Mean*], it is called 'equilibrium' before the Seven Emotions are aroused, and it is called 'harmony' after they are aroused."[94] But he discussed human nature and feelings in terms of the Seven Emotions.[95] In the *Sŏnghak chipyo*, Yulgok also argues: "Outside of the Seven Emotions, Mencius selected the good feelings and saw them as the Four Beginnings."[96] In the *Non simsŏngchŏng* (A Ttreatise on the Mind, Human Nature, and Feelings) as well, Yulgok criticizes T'oegye's theory while praising Kobong for correctly interpreting the Four and the Seven as belonging to one kind of feelings.[97]

In his third letter to Ugye, Yulgok articulates specific examples to emphasize the Four-Seven relationship of continuum in a convincing way:

> Now as regard to human nature (*sŏng/hsing*), we are joyous when we should be joyous; we are sorrowful on account of bereavement; we are pleased in seeing those we love; and we desire to investigate principles when we see them and we desire to be equal to the worthies when we meet them. These are the four feelings (*chŏng/ch'ing*) of joy, sorrow, love, and desire that refer to the beginnings of benevolence. We are angry when we

> should be angry, and we dislike something when we should dislike it. These are the two feelings of anger and dislike that refer to the beginnings of righteousness. We fear our superiors and nobles when we see them. This is the feeling of fear that refers to the beginning of propriety. To know that we should be joyous, angry, sorrowful, or fearful when we should have a feeling of joy, anger, sorrow, or fear, and to know that we should not be joyous, angry, sorrowful, or fearful when we should not have a feeling of joy, anger, sorrow, sorrow, or fear belongs to the feeling of right and wrong . . . this is the beginning of wisdom.[98]

The underlying theme of this argument reveals three crucial points: first, the Four are the moral norms of the Seven; the Seven, if expressed properly, are identical to the Four; and therefore, there is definite continuum between the Four and the Seven. For example, to be pleased in seeing others that one loves is the feeling (*chŏng/ch'ing*) of love and to be sorrowful on account of bereavement is the feeling of sorrow. Note that love and sorrow are, in fact, two of the Seven Emotions; more to the point, these feelings, according to Yulgok, refer to "the beginning of benevolence." The noticeable feature of his argument here is that these feelings are identical to what Mencius calls *the mind-and-heart of commiseration*, one of the Four Beginnings. To be angry when one ought to be angry is the feeling of anger, one of the Seven Emotions; this is, Yulgok asserts, identical to "the beginning of righteousness" or what Mencius calls *the mind-and-heart of shame and dislike*. Furthermore, to know properly when one should, or should not, be joyous (angry, sorrowful, or fearful) is the feeling of right and wrong or the beginning of wisdom that is identical to what Mencius calls *the mind-and-heart of right and wrong*, one of the Four Beginnings.

Obviously, Yulgok's interpretation is significantly different from T'oegye's, according to which the Seven are never inborn moral qualities like the Four. For T'oegye, the Seven are conditional, short-lived, and "precarious" expressions of our physical and psychological feelings and desires.[99] The whole dilemma for Yulgok was to interpret the Four-Seven relationship meaningfully and creatively in the entire legacy of Mencius, the *Doctrine of the Mean*, and Ch'eng-Chu doctrines, presenting his philosophical views and his experiential and hermeneutical insights. He wanted to convince Ugye that the Four should be considered as moral roots of the Seven and that, if any of the Seven is harmonized, it is certainly a good feeling that corresponds to one of the Four. This is remarkably similar to Kobong's original views. We can recall that, without giving a clear-cut explanation, Kobong moved beyond Ch'eng I and Chu Hsi[100] and generally argued that the emotion of "love" (one of the Seven), if properly harmonized, can be considered as "the mind-and-heart of commiseration" or "the beginning of benevolence" (one of the Four). As I have discussed, Kobong did not articulate such a topic either explicitly or clearly in his debate with T'oegye. This is exactly the area of the Four-Seven debate to which Yulgok makes his own contribution.

On the whole, Yulgok emphasizes the relationship of continuum between the Four and the Seven in the context of addressing not only the inseparability and complementarity of *i* and *ki* in all feelings, but also the ethical link of good and evil. In this regard, Kobong has a significant impact on Yulgok's thinking. But Yulgok's Four-Seven thesis is presented more specifically; it is, indeed, a critique of T'oegye's interpretation. In his view, T'oegye overemphasized the Four-Seven contrast dualistically in terms of distinction and separation. The fundamental implication of Yulgok's argument is a significant *moral issue* from a Confucian standpoint of self-cultivation. To emphasize a concrete way of emotional integration, he utilizes a *nondualistic* approach and definitely affirms the "harmony-disharmony" link between the Four and the Seven in the sense that their fundamental difference relates to the issue of whether feelings are expressed and harmonized properly. The goodness of the beginnings of virtue is no different from the goodness of the harmonized emotions. The feelings fundamentally pertain to one kind, just as the entire reality of human nature is one.

For Yulgok, if the basic distinction between the Four and the Seven were to be discussed, then it can done in terms of the distinction between original human nature and physical human nature.

The Oneness of Human Nature

The topic of the Four-Seven relationship in terms of original human nature and physical human nature was one of the major issues in the T'oegye-Kobong debate. Obviously Ugye and Yulgok debated this issue, and the latter presented more original insights into those sophisticated ideas that were interpreted by both of his predecessors.

In response to Ugye's challenge, Yulgok began his first letter by saying: "Original human nature is spoken of without including physical endowment, whereas physical human nature includes the original human nature. Similarly, the Four Beginnings cannot include the Seven Emotions; rather, the latter includes the former."[101] In the Ch'eng-Chu context, Yulgok means that the original human nature is the pure, unmanifested nature referring to *i* only, and the physical human nature is always spoken of in terms of *i* and *ki* together; therefore, the latter must include the former. Like Kobong, he argues that both the Four and the Seven belong to the physical human nature. Accordingly, the Four are aroused "when *i* is in control and *ki* does not disturb it"; the Seven are aroused and give rise to both good and evil "when *ki* has already disturbed *i*."[102]

Ugye is not easily convinced. He maintains that if one could discuss human nature by referring "principally to *i*" (original human nature) and "principally to *ki*" (physical human nature), then one should also be able to discuss the Four and the seven in the same manner.[103] In his third letter, Yulgok argues, however, that Ugye's argument is wrong. Following Ch'eng-Chu teachings carefully,[104] he points out: "The original human nature refers to *i* only, without mentioning *ki*; however, the physical human nature refers to both *i* in *ki* combined."[105] In other words, one cannot use Ugye's theory to separate human nature arbitrarily into the original human nature and the physical human nature, especially given the fact that Ugye took the original human nature and the physical human nature to be two different human natures in opposition to each other. Ugye chooses to defend T'oegye's argument that the Four and the Seven can be discussed separately according to what is principally manifest in each case, just as original human nature and physical human nature can be spoken of separately.[106]

In his fifth letter to Ugye, Yulgok encloses a poem on the inseparability of *i* and *ki* in concrete phenomena, presenting a theory of "one nature with two names."[107] In the concrete reality, "human nature" is the physical human nature that "already includes the original human nature"; this is, he asserts, because *i* already exists in *ki*.[108] The underlying message of this argument accords with the Ch'eng-Chu doctrine that original human nature refers to the pure ideal state of *i* only, and that it is called *physical human nature* in terms of *i and ki* when it is to be understood in a concrete context of addressing its physical endowment. For Yulgok, then, the so-called original human nature is only an abstract concept of human nature; from an empirical perspective, one has to talk about the physical human nature. Note that his explicit interpretation of the oneness of human nature appears to have been influenced by Lo Ch'in-shun's original thinking and Kobong's interpretation, according to which two names are used in discussing one human nature.

Yulgok maintains, in his fifth letter to Ugye, that "human nature is what unites *i* and *ki*; only after *i* is in *ki*, is there human nature that we can speak of."[109] Nevertheless, he affirms the Ch'eng-Chu doctrine that "if one speaks of *i* without including physical form, it is called original human nature."[110] Yulgok states further: "Tzu-ssu and Mencius spoke of original human nature, whereas Ch'eng I and Chang Tsai spoke of physical human nature. Although the original human nature and the physical human nature are, in reality, one human nature, what is spoken of principally in each case is not the same. . . . Human nature is always one.[111] Certainly, Yulgok means to do full justice to the general agreement that Mencius singled out the original goodness of human nature as the Four, whereas Ch'eng I and Chang Tsai spoke of the physical human nature that already includes the original human nature in it. The following quotation taken from his sixth letter to Ugye illustrates his view of the oneness of human nature on the basis of Ch'eng-Chu teachings: "Did Chu Hsi not say that 'physical human nature is only this one nature that fell into physical endowment'? There is only one human nature in the context of physical endowment. . . . From this point of view, physical human nature and original human nature are not two [different] natures. When viewed from a standpoint of referring to *i* only, without referring to the physical endowment of our nature, we call it the original human nature. However, when *i* and *ki* are spoken of together as a whole, we call it the physical human nature."[112]

Yulgok continues to articulate his argument by criticizing T'oegye's mode of thinking in the following words: "Since human nature is already one, how can there be two [kinds of] feelings? Only after there are two human natures, there can be two kinds of feelings. If T'oegye's dualistic interpretation is correct, the original human nature is at the east and the physical human nature is at the west. In other words, the moral mind is manifest from the east and the human mind from the west. How can this be right at all?"[113] In Yulgok's view, then, aroused feelings cannot have two sources such as *i* and *ki*. If there are two natures of the human being, this means incorrectly that there are two different kinds of feelings, the Four and the Seven. Hence, T'oegye's theory that the Four belong to the original human nature, whereas the Seven belong to the physical human nature is, Yulgok argues, unreasonable.

In his *Non simsŏngchŏng* (A Treatise on Mind, Human Nature, and Feelings), Yulgok asserts that the Four pertain to the original human nature, and the physical human nature simply refers to the original human nature contained in the physical endowment.[114] The original human nature and the physical human nature are not two separate natures of a human being; similarly, we do not have two different kinds of feelings. Analogically speaking, Yulgok declares, it is like the relationship between the "container" and "water": human nature is like the water, and its physical endowment is like the container.[115] Using this analogy, he distinguishes "three grades of human beings" based on the purity of physical endowment: "Those who have water in the clear and pure container are the sages; those who have sand and soil are ordinary people; and those who have only mud are the people of the lowest class."[116] The original human nature is "the unmanifested state" of human nature that is not mixed with evil; however, the "manifest state" of human nature is the physical endowment of human nature that gives rise to both good and evil."[117] On the whole, Yulgok means that physical human nature is not a separate nature because original human nature already exists inside of it and that, in the concrete sense of reality, the former refers to human nature. Like Lo Ch'in-shun and Kobong, he emphasizes that "two names" are used in describing *one single human nature from two angles*: the original human nature and the physical human nature are "one in union." For this reason, he rejects T'oegye's assertion that the Four, which are purely good, should be represented by the original human nature, and the Seven, which are either good or evil, should be expressed by the physical human nature. Yulgok's conclusion is that to a single nature, one cannot, as T'oegye has done, apply two terms separately, using them as the two distinct origins of the Four and the Seven.

In short, embedded in Yulgok's whole interpretation underscores the following points: first, the Seven include the Four; second, both the Four and the Seven are issued from the physical human nature; and third, the difference between them is whether or not these feelings become harmonized. This, then, brings us to Yulgok's critique of T'oegye's Four-Seven theory of "alternate manifestation."

A Critique of T'oegye's Theory of Alternate Manifestation: The Working of *Ki*

In his first letter to Yulgok, Ugye defends T'oegye's Four-Seven theory of "alternate manifestation of *i* and *ki*": "In the case of the Four Beginnings, *i* is manifest and *ki* follows it; in the case of the Seven Emotions, *ki* is manifest and *i* rides on it."[118] Ugye asserts that he himself sees nothing wrong with analyzing the origins of the Four and the Seven dualistically, assigning the former to *i* and the latter to *ki*.[119] "In my view, when we speak of the Four Beginnings and the Seven Emotions from a standpoint of contrast, we can say [as T'oegye has said] that the Four Beginnings issue from *i*; the Seven Emotions issue from *ki*."[120]

In his response to Ugye, Yulgok argues that T'oegye's *hobal* theory is not convincing because it implies wrongly that *i* and *ki* are two separated entities, each manifesting independently.[121] He criticizes Ugye for following such an incorrect view. "If *i* and *ki* manifest themselves independently," as T'oegye has claimed, then "*i* and *ki* would be two entities, each with its own root and ground."[122] As Yulgok argues, the former sages' and worthies' teachings on mind cultivation do not support T'oegye's dualistic theory of the alternate manifesting of *i* and *ki*.[123] With regard to all concrete phenomena, it is not true that *i* is manifest in some cases and *ki* is manifest in other cases. Rather, *i* and *ki* are always inseparable in concrete things, and there is neither priority nor posteriority between *i* and *ki*.[124]

Yulgok continues to argue that Chu Hsi must have meant something by his statement that "the Four Beginnings are manifestations of *i*; the Seven Emotions are manifestations of *ki*."[125] But Chu Hsi would not expect later scholars (like T'oegye) to overemphasize the Four-Seven contrast in the dichotomous system of *i* and *ki*.[126] It is important to grasp the real meaning of Chu Hsi's statement: "What Chu Hsi intended to mean is simply that in the case of the Four Beginnings, only *i* is spoken of, whereas in the case of the Seven Emotions, *ki* is spoken together [with *i*]. He did not mean that in the case of the Four Beginnings, *i* is manifest first, whereas in the case of the Seven Emotions, *ki* is manifest first."[127]

Embedded in this passage is that T'oegye misunderstood Chu Hsi's theory and, in turn, formulated his *hobal* theory that destroys the fundamental doctrine of the inseparability of *i* and *ki* in concrete phenomena including feelings. In his third letter to Ugye, Yulgok accepts only the last half of T'oegye's *hobal* theory that "in the case of the Seven Emotions, *ki* is manifest and *i* rides on it." He argues that this is true for the Four Beginnings also.[128] This argument, of course, is founded on Yulgok's cosmological view that, in the transformation of all concrete phenomena, "what is manifest (*palcha/fa-che*) is *ki*, and the reason for its manifestation (*soi palcha/so-i fa-che*) is *i*."[129] In other words, in the process of issuing feelings such as the Four and the Seven, *ki* is what becomes manifest. He argues strongly that this is the earlier Confucian scholars' opinion, and "even if a sage arises again, he cannot dare change this statement."[130] "Without *ki*, nothing can manifest; without *i*, there is nothing manifested."[131] In the Mencian context, this statement can be illustrated by the following example: when we see a child falling into a well, the actual rising of our feeling of commiseration is due to the activity of *ki*, and what makes us feel such a moral principle of commiseration is *i*. Yulgok prefers Kobong's argument over T'oegye's: "The Four-Seven debate between T'oegye and Kobong has as many as 10,000 words. Kobong's argument is clear. . . . Although T'oegye's argument is detailed, it is too repetitive and often unclear in principle; it has no real taste. But how can Kobong's learning be compared to T'oegye's at all? It is only that

Kobong had some talent and knowledge and understood the Four and the Seven."[132]

In this passage, Yulgok claims that T'oegye's interpretation of Chu Hsi's theory is not as convincing as Kobong's, though it is more detailed than the latter. He criticizes T'oegye's theory for implying that "the Four Beginnings are issued from the inside, whereas the Seven Emotions are issued from the outside."[133] Another quotation from Yulgok's third letter to Ugye conveys Yulgok's view of external stimuli in the issuance of all feelings: "How can there be any feelings aroused from the inside with no external stimulation? What is perceived has good or evil. . . . If what is issued from the inside independently without the external stimulation is taken to be the Four Beginnings, this means that filial piety is aroused without the presence of parents, loyalty is aroused without the presence of ruler, and reverence is aroused without the presence of elder brothers. Would these be our real feelings?"[134] Speaking in the Mencian sense, Yulgok then argues that commiseration is aroused after "one sees a child falling into a well."[135] What is sensed or perceived is the child who is an external stimulus. "How can there be commiseration aroused by itself without seeing a child falling into a wall? If there is, it would not be a real feeling."[136]

Comparing T'oegye with the Ming Chinese Neo-Confucian Lo Ch'in-shun, Yulgok criticizes the former for separating *i* and *ki* in terms of his *hobal* theory. The following passage taken from his third letter to Ugye illustrates his argument further: "A brilliant scholar like Lo Cheng-an (Ch'in-shun) with outstanding thought committed a small flaw in his view that *i* and *ki* are one.[137] T'oegye's learning is refined, detailed, prudent, and dense; there is no other man like T'oegye in recent years. Nonetheless, [the first half of] his theory that '*i* is manifest and *ki* follows' [in the issuance of the Four] also has some flaw in the sense that it tends to assert the priority and posteriority for *i* and *ki*. When I heard it before master T'oegye passed away, I knew it was wrong. However, because I was younger than him, and my learning was inferior to his, I did not dare challenge him."[138]

Yulgok also argues that the problem of Ugye's interpretation is that he blindly follows T'oegye's *hobal* theory that incorrectly affirms the self-manifesting capability of *i*. Ugye defends T'oegye again by citing the rider-horse parable used by T'oegye. In his fourth letter to Ugye, Yulgok points out that Chu Hsi set up the words to help other people understand.[139] "How can *i* and *ki*, which are inseparable and merged one with the other, manifest themselves alternately?"[140] Yulgok makes a strong point that if Chu Hsi really considered *i* and *ki* as capable of manifesting themselves alternately, he is not only making a big mistake, but also does not deserve so much respect as master Chu Hsi.[141] To Ugye, however, earlier Confucian thinkers referred to humanity and righteousness as the "manifestation of *i*" and physical desires for food and clothes as the "manifestation of *ki*."[142] Ugye challenges Yulgok's critique of T'oegye's *hobal* theory: "Although they [*i* and *ki*] are one, they are to be spoken of in terms of what is important. In other words, this refers to what T'oegye meant by 'alternate manifesting,' or your saying that 'the horse obeys the rider in some cases or the rider trusts the horse in other cases.'"[143] In Ugye's view, aroused feelings can be spoken of in terms of *i* and *ki* because some feelings are founded on *i*, and some on *ki*; therefore, one can speak of the Four and the Seven by referring to either *i* or *ki*.[144] To Yulgok, however, T'oegye's *hobal* theory is mistaken in language itself: "T'oegye's opinion that what issues from the inside and what is felt outside are distinct is very much different from my own view."[145] Consequently, T'oegye's belief that *i* can manifest itself is unacceptable. In the issuance process of both the Four and the Seven, *ki* is manifest and *i* is the reason for its manifestation. This is the key point that Yulgok maintained throughout his entire Four-Seven thesis. In his *Insim tosim tosŏl*, he says: "How can there be any distinction between the manifestation of *i* and the manifestation of *ki*?"[146] In the *Simsŏngchŏng sŏl*, he also argues: "The Four Beginnings refer exclusively to *i*, whereas the Seven Emotions refer to *i* and *ki* combined. But scholars [like T'oegye] took *i* and *ki* to manifest themselves alternately."[147]

Obviously, Yulgok's emphasis is on the role of *ki* in all phenomena including the issuance of the Four and the Seven. In contrast to T'oegye, he makes no attempt to relate the Four to the manifestation of *i* because, by doing so, the "passive" nature of *i* as "the reason for *ki*'s manifestation" will be confused with the "active" nature of *ki*. As the focus of the next section, we need to examine this crucial part of his Four-Seven thesis in terms of the inseparability and harmony of *i* and *ki*.

The Inseparability and Harmony of *I* and *Ki*

Yulgok's understanding of the Four-Seven relationship in terms of *i* and *ki* is articulated in most of his letters to Ugye. Generally speaking, Yulgok, like T'oegye, affirms the Ch'eng-Chu doctrines on the ontological and conceptual "distinction" of *i* and *ki*, as well as on their phenomenalistic "inseparability." Unlike T'oegye, however, he does not emphasize the *i-ki* distinction and contrast in addressing the Four-Seven relationship. He points out carefully that, although *i* and *ki* are inseparable in concrete phenomena, they cannot be referred to as one and the same thing.[148] For this reason, Chu Hsi said that *i* itself is *i* and *ki* itself is *ki*, and they are not mixable with each other.[149] In his second letter to Ugye, Yulgok begins with the Ch'eng-Chu doctrine of principle. The so-called oneness of principle refers to "the original essence of human nature" or "the mystery of the Great Ultimate."[150] This is, Yulgok argues, what the central Ch'eng-Chu doctrine of "principle is one; its particularizations are diverse" (*iil punsu/li-i fen-shu*) really means.[151] He argues further in an empirical context: "The original essence of *i* (*i chi ponyŏn/li chih pen-jan*) is purely good. But when it flows by riding on *ki*, it generates irregularities and nonuniformities.[152] *I* is everywhere existing in valuable things of extreme clarity and purity, as well as in invaluable things of extreme turbidity and impurity. In clear and pure things, *i* is also clear and pure; in turbid and impure places, *i* is also turbid and impure. Nevertheless, it would be incorrect to say that what is unclear and impure is not the original essence of *i*. It is incorrect to say that there is no *i* in dirty places."[153]

For Yulgok, "the original essence of *i*" refers to the oneness of *i*; however, "it moves by riding on *ki*." Both dimensions of *i* must be understood together; one should talk about not only "the original essence of *i*" (or *i* in itself), but also the *i* that moves by riding on *ki* to produce its diverse particularizations in concrete phenomena.[154] In other words, principle must be discussed both ontologically and phenomenalistically, without neglecting one or the other aspect. "The original *i*" (*ponyŏn chi i/pen-jan chih li*) is "one," "undifferentiated," and "purely good"; however, when it rides on *ki*, it generates myriad transformations due to the limiting role of *ki*. In the physical endowment of human nature are both good and evil; thus, we both good and evil in feelings.[155] Yulgok continues to argue:

> The original essence of *i* is one; however, when it flows and circulates, its particularizations are diverse. It is wrong to seek for the original *i* only while neglecting the *i* that flows and circulates. We have to consider and understand most seriously the four-character [Ch'eng-Chu] doctrine that "*i* is one, but its particularizations are diverse."[156] Knowing only "the oneness of *i*," but neglecting "the diversity of its particularizations," the Shakyamuni Buddha referred to the action and function [of *i*] as human nature. Knowing only "the diversity of *i*'s particularizations," but not comprehending its oneness, Hsün Tzu [fl. 298–238 B.C.E.] took human nature to be evil, and Yang Hsiung [53 B.C.E.–18 C.E.], in the later period, considered human nature to be a mixture of both good and evil.[157]

In this passage, Yulgok points out that Hsün Tzu and Yang Hsiung understood only particular principles without realizing the oneness of *i*. This is, he asserts, the reason why Hsün Tzu said that "human nature is evil" and Yang Hsiung said that "good and evil are mixed in human nature." Here, Yulgok also makes an interesting point that Mencius singled out only the original substance, without including the *i* that rides on *ki* (in things and phenomena) and, therefore, could not win Kao Tzu's full agreement.

From a standpoint of concrete phenomena, "unless there is *ki*, *i* has nothing to depend on; unless there is *i*, *ki* has nothing to lean to."[158] *I* and *ki* are "one yet two" because they are not one; they are "two yet one" because they are not two.[159] In his third Four-Seven letter, Yulgok argues that their relationship includes both unity and duality:

> Why is it said that *i* and *ki* are not one? *I* and *ki* are inseparable from each other; however, in their mysterious unity, *i* is *i* in itself, and *ki* is *ki* in itself. Since *i* and *ki* are not intermingled as such, they are not one. Why is it said that they are not two? Although *i* itself is *i* and *ki* itself is *ki*, they are still merged one into the other in perfect harmony, thereby having no space, no priority and posteriority, and no separation and union between them. Since *i* and *ki* are not seen as two as such, they are not two. For this reason, movement and tranquility have no beginning, and *yin* and *yang* have no starting point. Since *i* has no starting point, *ki* also has no starting point. In general, *i* is nothing but one. Fundamentally, in *i* there is no difference between the correct and the turbid, the pure and the impure. But the *ki* that is ridden by *i* ascends and descends, flies and flutters, and becomes blended and irregular everywhere. It never stops its breath, while producing the myriad things of Heaven and Earth that become correct or partial, penetrated or blocked, clear or turbid, pure or impure, and so on.[160]

Surely, this passage reveals Yulgok's point that *i* is one but takes on the myriad variations when it rides on *ki*. "What is irregular" in concrete phenomena must be due to the activity of *ki*. Because *i* and *ki* are interrelated without one being prior and the other posterior, it follows that they cannot be treated as two separate entities.[161] As Yulgok argues, *i* and *ki* cannot be mixed with each other: *i* remains *i*, and *ki* remains *ki*, even though they are combined in all things.[162] Of course, this affirms an ontological and conceptual distinction of *i* and *ki*. Yulgok continues to argue that the reason for the principle of people being equivalent to the principle of things is that *i* is "one" and "universal":

> Principle is one; however, its myriad particularizations are diverse when it rides on material force. In Heaven and Earth, *i* is the principle of Heaven and Earth; in the myriad things, it is the principle of the myriad things; and in human beings, it is the principle of human beings. Although Heaven, Earth, human beings, and things each have principle, the principle of Heaven and Earth is, in fact, the same as the principle of the myriad things, and the principle of the myriad things is, in fact, the same as our principle. This is the so-called One Great Ultimate in its whole self. Although it is called the "oneness of *i*," human nature is not the same as the nature of things, and the dog's nature is not the same as the cow's nature. This is what is meant by each having its own nature. If we ponder on the origin, *i* and *ki* are the father and mother of human beings and things. Heaven and Earth received what is perfectly upright and penetrating in *ki*; therefore, they have the fixed nature and, as result, there is no change in them. The myriad things received what is partial and blocked; however, they also have fixed nature and, as a result, no change in them.[163]

As J. Ching points out correctly, Yulgok is giving a philosophy for Chou Tun-i's explanation of the *Diagram of the Great Ultimate.*[164] But Yulgok means that what is not uniform in things and phenomena is due to the various grades of *ki*'s purity. As Ching argues, Yulgok's interpretation of Ch'eng-Chu metaphysics emphasizes the role of *ki* in all cosmic phenomena including self-cultivation.[165] For Yulgok, *i* is the ultimate reality for which *ki* generates regularities and irregularities. Human nature is not the same as the nature of things because *ki* is limited, particular, and causes *i*'s diverse particularizations. Among human beings, the sages "received the extremely penetrating, correct, clear, and pure *ki*, and their virtues are united with Heaven and Earth."[166] They have an unchanging nature that is never disturbed by physical form; therefore, they have ability to fulfill their status as the sages. As Yulgok writes, "Heaven and Earth are the models for the sages who are, in turn, the models for all other people."[167] This is, of course, a *moral* argument in the Confucian context of self-cultivation. The practice of moral cultivation is to follow the sages' instructions.

Yulgok also compares T'oegye with the Ming Chinese Neo-Confucian Lo Ch'in-shun, criticizing the former for separating *i* and *ki* in terms of his *hobal* theory.[168] Undoubtedly, he wanted to convince Ugye that both T'oegye and Ugye are wrong. According to Yulgok, although Lo Ch'in-shun saw correctly that *i* and *ki* are inseparable in concrete things, he went too far in seeing *i* and *ki* as fundamentally one and, therefore, *i* almost as *ki*. In other words, Lo ignored to discuss clearly the distinction of *i* and *ki* that happens to be part of the basis of Chu Hsi's philosophy. It is precisely in this sense of the inseparable and harmonious relationship of *i* and *ki* that Yulgok prefers his own interpretation.

In Ming China, Lo had opposed Chu Hsi's dualistic statements on the relationship of *i* and *ki*, such as "*i* and *ki* are definitely two things."[169] Without asserting their unmixability, Lo stated that "principle is not a separate entity which depends on material force in order to exist."[170] The following passage embodies his point further: "*Li* is only the *li* of *ch'i*. It must be observed in the phenomenon of revolving and turning of *ch'i*. . . . What acts and reacts is *ch'i*, while the fact that a particular action involves a particular reaction without there being the slightest possibility of error is principle. . . . I have therefore said that *li* must be identified as an aspect of *ch'i*."[171] Lo's view of the oneness of *i* and *ki* seems to have a significant impact on Yulgok's theory of the inseparability and harmony of *i* and *ki*, which serves as the philosophical core of his Four-Seven thesis. Unlike Kobong, Yulgok argues more systematically that what moves and becomes manifest is *ki*, while the reason for its movement and manifestation is *i*. The same kind of argument is evident also in his *Ch'ŏndo ch'aek* (Treatise of the Heavenly Way),[172] one of his early works: "That which is in movement and tranquility is *ki*; that which makes it move and become tranquil is *i*."[173]

Yulgok praises Lo as a distinguished Neo-Confucian scholar who had addressed the problem of Chu Hsi's dualistic philosophy of *i* and *ki*. But "Lo lost his reputation by misinterpreting the moral mind as substance and the human mind as function."[174] Nevertheless, T'oegye's mistake is, Yulgok asserts, greater than Lo's. Yulgok states: "According to Buddhism, it is said: 'Although bits of gold are very valuable, if put in one's eyes, they cause a disease.'[175] This explains the fact that although the sayings of sages and worthies are valuable, they can become harmful if we misunderstand them. . . . They would rather become harmful if we are confined to written words only, without understanding their intended meanings."[176] For Yulgok, certain textual ambiguities are at the heart of classical texts and Ch'eng-Chu writings; therefore, subtle old teachings should not be followed blindly, and one has to clarify them through one's own *reflections* and *experiences*.

In his fifth Four-Seven letter to Ugye, Yulgok enclosed a poem on the inseparability of *i* and *ki* to explain a Buddhist metaphor of "air" and "bottle":

The primal *ki*, where did it originate from?
The invisible is found in the visible.
The source, when found, is fundamentally one.

> If the variations are followed, the multitude of feelings are seen.
> Water takes the shape of a square or round according to its containers.
> Air makes itself small or big according to its bottles.[177]
> Let not the seeming duality confuse you.
> In silence, experience that human nature is feelings.[178]

Commenting on his poem, Yulgok argues that "*i* and *ki* are originally united" and "those who want to separate them into two do not understand the Way."[179] This is why he argues elsewhere that "*i* exists in *ki*,"[180] just as water exists in its container, and that "*i* must dwell in *ki*, and *ki* must carry *i*."[181] According to Yulgok, *i* and *ki* are "originally inseparable from each other," and "*i* is the master of *ki*," while "*ki* serves as the physical implement of *i*" in the entire process of cosmological transformation.[182] Following Chu Hsi's philosophy, he argues, in his sixth letter to Ugye, that *i* is "formless" (*muhyŏng/wu-hsing*) and "nonacting (*muwi/wu-wei*), whereas *ki* has form (*yuhyŏng/yu-hsing*) and is acting (*yuwi/yu-wei*).[183] In other words, *i* is the metaphysical and static principle, whereas *ki* is the physical and active material force. Therefore, *i* cannot manifest itself. This, of course, corresponds to Chu Hsi's original thinking in the sense that *ki* is the actual physical energy manifested in all phenomena, and *i* is the reason for *ki*'s manifestation.[184] This is why Yulgok criticizes T'oegye's theory of "alternate manifestation": "T'oegye could not quite understand the 'mysterious inseparability' of *i* and *ki*."[185]

Yulgok also formulates an original theory of his own: "*i* is penetrating and *ki* is limited" (*it'ong kiguk/li-t'ung ch'i-chu*)."[186] This theory systematizes the entire Ch'eng-Chu metaphysics of *i* and *ki*; also, it serves the basis of Yulgok's Four-Seven thesis. Yulgok explains it in his sixth letter to Ugye:

> Why is it said that "*i* is penetrating"? *I* has neither beginning nor end, neither priority nor posteriority; therefore, what is unmoved is not prior and what is moved is not posterior. For this reason, as *i* rides on the circulating movement of *ki*, it makes irregularities and nonuniformities. But its original mystery exists everywhere. Where *ki* is partial, *i* is also partial. What is partial is *ki*, not *i*; what is complete is *ki*, not *i*. *I* exists everywhere, even in dregs, ashes, excrement, soil, and dirt, each having its own nature. Yet, *i* suffers no injury in its original subtlety. This is what I meant by saying "*i* is penetrating." Why is it said, "*ki* is limited"? *Ki* already involves its physical form and traces; therefore, it has beginning and end, priority and posteriority. The foundation of *ki* is profoundly one, clear and pure. Why should

> there be the *ki* of dregs, ashes, excrement, soil, and dirt? Since *ki* moves without cease, ascending and descending, flying and fluttering, it becomes irregular and uneven and, thus, produces the myriad changes. . . . This is what I meant by saying "*ki* is limited."[187]

Yulgok means that metaphysically speaking, *i* is a transcendent and universal principle whose "mysterious" and "subtle" nature is one, unconditioned, and indeterminate, existing in all phenomena. From a standpoint of concrete phenomena, however, *i* is limited by the diverse activities and purities of *ki*. What is limited in things is the limitedness of *ki*. The following passage from his seventh Four-Seven letter illustrates this point further:

> In a dry tree, there is a [particular] *ki* of a dry tree; in dead ashes, there is a [particular] *ki* of dead ashes. How can there be things with only form, but no *ki*? Since the *ki* of the dry tree and dead ashes is not the same as the *ki* of the living tree and fire, it cannot flow and move because its living energy is disintegrated. In regard to the fact that *i* rides on *ki*, the *i* of the dry tree and dead ashes is limited by their *ki* and, thus, become a [particular] *i* of the dry tree and a [particualr] *i* of the dead ashes. If viewed from the standpoint of *i*-in-itself, although *i* is in the dry tree and dead ashes, it is still the same as the undifferentiated *i*. Although the *ki* of the dry tree and dead ashes is not the same as the *ki* of the living tree and fire, the *i* of the dry tree and dead ashes is, with respect to substance, the same as the *i* of the living tree and fire.[188]

What Yulgok is indicating here is that *i* is the reason for the manifestation of *ki* and that it plays the role of riding on the activity of *ki*, nourishing and transforming all cosmic phenomena. The cosmic production and transformation is possible only by *ki*. Without *i*, however, there can be no activity and manifestation of *ki*. Yulgok theory of "*i* is penetrating and *ki* is limited" (*it'ong kiguk*) corresponds to his understanding of the mutual relationship of inseparability and harmony between *i* and *ki* on which he based his moral and psychological philosophy of mind, nature, and feelings. For him, the pervasiveness of "penetrating" *i* implies transcendence, whereas the particularization of "limiting" *ki* implies cosmic transformation. Such a theory indicates some influence of both philosophical Taoism and Hua-yen Buddhism; this is never a surprising finding because Yulgok himself claimed that he had studied them seriously in his early years. His idea of the "original mystery of *i*"[189] is somewhat similar to the philosophy of *Tao*; more specifically, his saying that "*i* penetrates, existing everywhere even in the ashes, excrement and dirt" closely alludes to Chuang Tzu's theory of the omnipresence of *Tao*.[190] It might have been influenced by Buddhism as well. Yulgok's theory of *it'ong kiguk* is especially similar to the Hua-yen philosophy of the interaction of principle (*i/li*) and phenomenon (*sa/shih*).[191] One may argue that he formulated it according to the Hua-yen theory that principle is "penetrating" (*t'ong/tung*) and phenomena are "limited" (*kuk/chu*).[192] But we cannot say for sure that it came directly from Hua-yen Buddhism.[193] From an intellectual standpoint, Yulgok tended to tolerate certain Taoist and Buddhist ideas and insights to develop his own philosophy. In my own judgment, however, Yulgok's philosophy rather derives out of his Four-Seven thesis, which is based on his own views and insights. In the Ch'eng-Chu context, it still reveals some traces of the influence of Chu Hsi's metaphysics of *i* and *ki*, as well as the influence of Lo Ch'in-shun's nondualistic reformulation of it with emphasis on its doctrine of "the oneness of principle and the diversity of its particularizations."

In his eighth letter to Ugye, Yulgok argues that, after all, the sages and worthies intended certain meanings in their subtle teachings; therefore, as he points out, "not to seek these meanings, but to become trapped in their own words, is to do injury to their basic doctrine."[194] In his ninth and last letter, he utilizes Taoist terms to explain the *i-ki* relationship: "In the past, Lao Tzu said, 'Being is born from Non-being,'[195] and this saying is about the beginning of the Great One. If we suppose that *i* and *ki* had a beginning in time, they must be said to undergo the process of change so that there will be the moment when *ki* disappears. Since there was no beginning, there will be no end."[196]

For Yulgok, then, *i* and *ki* have no beginning and no end and cannot be spoken of as prior being or posterior being. But if one has to trace their origin logically and looks into the metaphysical "reason for being so" (*soiyŏn/so-i-jan*), then *i* is the normative principle that can unavoidably considered to be prior.[197] However, in the concrete phenomena, *i* and *ki* are never separable. To articulate his point further, he presents an analogy of the container and water: "The square and round containers are not the same, but water in these containers is one [and the same]. The large and small bottles are not the same, but air in these bottles is one [and the same]. The reason why *i* takes on the myriad variations is that *ki* is limited. In the original substance (*ponch'e/pen-t'i*), the circulating movement is complete. In its circulating movement, the original substance is preserved."[198] Embedded this passage is that the *i* of human beings is the same as the *i* of things, and this is due to the universal and pervasive nature of *i*. This relationship is equivalent to the analogical case of the water in containers and that of the air in bottles. Although the containers of various shapes are different (limited), the water in them is fundamentally the same water (universal). In Yulgok's view, this analogy conveys the fact that the oneness of *i* remains unchanged; it is similar to the case that the original essence of water (or that of air) remains one and unchanged in various containers. Moreover, the water in a vessel can take a particular shape, due to the shape of the vessel in which the water is placed. Similarly, human nature is not the same as the nature of things because the diversity of *i*'s particularizations is generated by the particular and limiting role of *ki*.

Yulgok comments on three thinkers such as Lo Ch'in-shun, Hwadam, and T'oegye, especially praising Lo's conception of the union of *i* and *ki* in things and phenomena:

> Recently, I have examined the sayings of the three masters such as Cheng-an [Lo Ch'in-shun], T'oegye, and Hwadam. Cheng-an is highest, T'oegye is next, and Hwadam is lowest. Cheng-an and Hwadam have a strong taste of independent and original thinking, whereas T'oegye has a strong taste of following, and depending on, others. Cheng-an saw the whole thing, but there is still something incomplete in his vision. He did not want to believe in Chu Hsi. . . . Consequently, there may be excessiveness in his words; that is, there are some flaws in his view that *i* and *ki* are one. In reality, however, he did not consider *i* and *ki* as one thing. It is only that, because what he viewed is incomplete, his words are, in some cases, mistaken or excessive. T'oegye, by contrast, believed strongly in Chu Hsi and tried very hard to search out Chu Hsi's instruction. The physical endowment of T'oegye's nature is refined, detailed and minute. What he studied is deep and accords with Chu Hsi's opinions.[199]

Yulgok means that, although T'oegye's scholarship is highly respectful, he did not quite understand *i* and *ki* penetratingly. What T'oegye understood is not clear, and his *hobal* theory "neglects the inseparability of *i* and *ki*."[200] On the whole, however, Yulgok still prefers his sincere way of learning over Hwadam's independent thinking:

> Although Hwadam was brighter than others, he lacked dignity and solemnity. In the process of his reading and his investigation of principles, he did not care about words and texts, while for-

> mulating many independent opinions. . . . He cleverly saw the mystery of the inseparability of *i* and *ki*. So, he was not the same as those [like T'oegye] who simply followed others. . . . But he also had some flaws in acknowledging *ki* as *i*. . . . As regards T'oegye, there is a strong taste of imitating and copying others; therefore, his words are restricted by prudence. Hwadam has a strong taste of independent thinking, but his words are imprudent. Being prudent leads to fewer errors. Hence, one should rather follow T'oegye's approach than Hwadam's independent thinking.[201]

To Yulgok, T'oegye did not understand the harmonious relationship between *i* and *ki* in all phenomena including feelings, and he lacked the originality of Hwadam's thinking. But he still respects T'oegye as a great scholar, praising his prudent approach to Neo-Confucian learning. The extreme type of Hwadam's philosophy of *ki* is accused of having a lot of errors, and his approach to learning is said to be much less sincere and serious than T'oegye's.

The question is, Why did Yulgok reject T'oegye's Four-Seven thesis? Undoubtedly, this is a significant moral issue in the Confucian context of self-cultivation. Philosophically speaking, what Yulgok intended to clarify is the mutual relationship of inseparability between *i* and *ki* from his epistemological standpoint of concrete phenomena. As he argues, for all aroused feelings, "what manifests is *ki*, and the reason for its manifestation is *i*." In this context, then, it was obvious for him to reject T'oegye's Four-Seven thesis, especially his view that *i* is manifest in the issuance process of the Four. Yulgok, like Kobong, means that the Four-Seven issue cannot be understood in terms of the metaphysical *dichotomy* of *i* and *ki* and the ethical *contrast* between good and evil. His argument definitely affirms the Four-Seven relationship of continuum in such a context. This is why Yulgok rejects T'oegye's Four-Seven theory: in his view, it means that the Four and the Seven are two different kinds of feelings, each with its own origin and meaning in both metaphysical and ethical contexts. Using a *nondualistic* approach to Neo-Confucian metaphysics and ethics, he emphasizes emotional integration and the transformation of one's *ki* as a practical way of self-cultivation. We shall examine this topic more closely in Chapter V. This concludes Yulgok's Four-Seven thesis and brings us to the practical implications of T'oegye's Four-Seven thesis.

IV

Practical Implications for T'oegye

Current scholarship on Korean Neo-Confucianism, especially research in T'oegye's thought, has made a significant contribution to our growing understanding of the subject. But most works, including those in English, are concerned primarily with the philosophical and historical patterns of T'oegye's Neo-Confucianism; modern interpreters of T'oegye have been impressed mainly by his philosophical writings, calling him the *Korean synthesizer* of the Ch'eng-Chu school.[1]

However, what is not yet clearly articulated is the moral and spiritual dimension of his thought, which is closely related to the basic philosophical motifs of T'oegye's Four-Seven thesis. The chapter addresses this neglected, but crucial, area in the context of his interpretation of principle (*i/li*) and what he emphasizes as the "learning of the mind-and-heart" (*simhak/hsin-hsüeh*) and "learning of reverential seriousness" (*kyŏnghak/ching-hsüeh*). Because T'oegye often presented his own experiences and insights in his later years, we shall look at a few previously untranslated materials as well, especially those from his philosophical works and biographical accounts compiled after his debate with Ki Kobong. In short, this chapter argues that the centrality and vitality of T'oegye's Four-Seven thesis intensify the Neo-Confucian path to self-transformation with an ethico-religious quest for sagehood. To analyze such a topic is significant for a broader and deeper comprehension of not only Ch'eng-Chu Neo-Confucianism in general, but, more important, T'oegye's Four-Seven thesis and its implications for self-cultivation.

Principle and Self-Cultivation

One of the common terms of Neo-Confucianism is *i/li*. This book has translated it as "principle," "reason," "the ground of being," "the principle of existence," and so on. It represents one of the most important Neo-Confucian concepts, especially in the Ch'eng-Chu "school of human nature and principle." In Chu Hsi's philosophy, its fundamental characteristic is that, as distinguished from concrete things and phenomena existing "within physical form" (*hyŏng i ha/hsing-erh-hsia*),[2] *li* is the metaphysical principle that must exist "without physical form" (*hyŏng i sang/hsing-erh-shang*).[3] His theory that "fundamentally there is only one Great Ultimate, yet each of the myriad things is endowed with it and each in itself possesses the Great Ultimate in its entirety"[4] implies the ontological omnipresence of principle. Although the particularization of principle takes myriad variations, principle in itself is always good, unchanging, and universal. Ontologically speaking, principle is unitary and transcendent; phenomenalistically speaking, however, its particularizations are many and different in concrete phenomena. This corresponds to the Ch'eng-Chu theory that "principle is one, but its particularizations are diverse (*iil punsu/li-i fen-shu*)."[5] In relation to the moral and psychological philosophy of the Ch'eng-Chu school, it is identified also as human nature (*sŏng/hsing*) and, thus, thought to be full of goodness and moral principles.

Chu Hsi's philosophy of principle and material force has been researched and interpreted by modern scholars.[6] Obviously, there is a remarkable convergence of opinion on the general theme of his metaphysics. For Chu Hsi, principle and material force (*ki/ch'i*) are conceptually "distinct," but they are "inseparable" in concrete things. Speaking from the standpoint of physical things, he said: "*Li* and *ch'i* must come together to form a concrete thing; therefore, they are inseparable from each other."[7] Logically speaking, however, they are distinct: "The two entities are each an entity in itself."[8] But they are never separated from each other in the phenomenal world. If viewed from the standpoint of unity, *li* and *ch'i* are one; if viewed from the standpoint of separability, they are two.[9] According to Chu Hsi's thinking, then, unity implies duality, and duality implies unity.

From an ontological standpoint of existence, principle "has neither form nor body,"[10] and material force has form to nourish and transform them.[11] And yet, if the concept of priority must be applied, principle is prior to material force.[12] What Chu Hsi really meant was the priority of *li* in a logical sense. For example, it is reasonable to assume using an analogy that the principle of a boat that floats on water must first be there already to be realized before there can be any concrete existence of a boat as such. *Li* is "the principle of existence";[13] accordingly, it is not capable of manifesting itself in the factual and empirical sense. The general hallmark of Chu Hsi's thinking is to take *li* as "the law of being" that underlies all concrete phenomena.[14] *Li* is the ultimate reality, rather than the actual, phenomenal activity; *ch'i* is the actual, material agent of creation and transformation. In other words, *li* brings into existence Heaven, Earth, and the myriad things; it is the principle behind the manifestation of *ki* in all cosmic phenomena.

How did T'oegye view Chu Hsi's philosophy of principle? As we have seen in his Four-Seven thesis, T'oegye generally followed it to support his arguments. But he preferred to emphasize the ontological and moral status of *i* in terms of the Four Beginnings and original human nature. Recent studies of his philosophy suggested that T'oegye clarified to the satisfaction of his contemporary challengers and followers some of the ambiguous messages in Chu Hsi's philosophy of principle and material force. For example, Tu Weiming argued that T'oegye formulated a "creative interpretation" of Chu Hsi's philosophy.[15] But we need to note that, although T'oegye seriously took Chu Hsi as his intellectual and spiritual guide, he tended to *misinterpret* the underlying content of Chu Hsi's metaphysics to a considerable extent. Strictly speaking, his interpretation of principle, as presented in his Four-Seven thesis, was a contradictory system of thought, although it brought about a new understanding of Chu Hsi's philosophy.

This is, as we have seen, vividly evident in his Four-Seven debate with Kobong on the moral and psychological philosophy of mind, human nature, and feelings, one that led T'oegye to reexamine the whole idea of principle in the context of its implications for self-cultivation. He had to accept the fundamental inseparability between *i* and *ki* in concrete phenomena including feelings (the Four Beginnings and the Seven Emotions). In his first and second letters to Kobong, he said that "*i* and *ki* need each other and are merged one into the other"[16] and that "how can there be *i* without *ki*? In the universe, there is no *i* without *ki*."[17] He made a clear-cut distinction of *i* and *ki* more explicitly than Chu Hsi did: "Regarding Heaven, Earth, human beings, and things, it is not that *i* exists outside of *ki*. And yet, *i* and *ki* can be spoken of separately . . . Why can we not talk about *i* and *ki* separately?"[18] "What is spoken of is not the same, and there should be a distinction between them."[19] T'oegye pointed out that, although *i* and *ki* are inseparable in things, this relationship, however, "does not necessarily mean that *i* and *ki* are not distinct."[20] Criticizing Kobong's strict emphasis on their inseparability in all phenomena, T'oegye argued that one must distinguish *i* from *ki* from a standpoint of "separation."

In his other philosophical writings, T'oegye explained *i* and *ki* in the same fashion. For example, in the *Pi iki wi ilmul pyŏnchŭng* (Treatise on the Saying That "*I* and *Ki* Are Not One"),[21] T'oegye, like Chu Hsi, states: "The distinction of the Way (*Tao*) and the concrete things is the same as that of *i* and *ki*."[22] He also argues elsewhere: "Principle neither integrates nor disintegrates," and it "has neither physical form nor body."[23] "Things are physical, whereas principle complete in them is metaphysical."[24] Because principle never ends and is not limited by material force, it is "the highest reality" that "commends things without being commended by them."[25] For T'oegye, *i* is "high," whereas *ki* is "low."[26] The entire undifferentiated state of principle before particularization is "*i*-in-itself and not confined to material force or limited by things."[27] *Ki* is purely physical and materialistic, whereas *i* is more fundamental and important than *ki*. For this reason, Tomoeda Ryūtarō correctly notes that *i* and *ki* are, in T'oegye's view, dialectical and opposed to each other.[28] Undoubtedly, T'oegye formulated an explicitly dualistic system of *i* and *ki*.

In general, T'oegye followed Chu Hsi to affirm the inseparability between *i* and *ki* in concrete things. However, he deliberately wanted to underscore much more the distinction of *i* and *ki*. In his debate with Kobong, he stated: "Know that *i* and *ki* are distinct. . . . To distinguish them as two distinct entities does not cause any harm to their relationship of inseparability; to unite them into one still makes them distinct."[29] His Four-Seven thesis focused on his commitment to maintaining the ontological unmixability and conceptual distinction of *i* and *ki*. He warned Kobong not to misunderstand *i* and *ki* as one, for such a mistake is a dangerous tendency of "misidentifying" *i* as *ki*.[30] To condemn Lo Ch'in-shun's theory of the oneness of *i* and *ki*,[31] he argued that Kobong, like Lo, is wrong in conceiving *i* and *ki* as one thing.[32] As we have seen, the final version of his Four-Seven thesis was revised in a way to accommodate Kobong's argument for the inseparability of *i* and *ki*; however, his theory of "the alternate manifestation of *i* and *ki*" and its "rider-horse" analogy certainly meant that T'oegye maintained his dualistic Four-Seven position in terms of reference to the "distinction" and "separation" of *i* and *ki*.

More important, T'oegye definitely affirmed *i* as an entity capable of manifesting itself in the process of cosmic transformation. This argument can be supported further by his other writings, in which principle is analyzed in terms of "substance" (reality) and "function" (manifestation) as well. For example, in his *Sim mu ch'eyong pyŏn* (Critique on the Saying "the Mind Does Not Have Substance and Function"), T'oegye argues that the actual manifesting power of *i* is "the active function of *i*," whereas "*i*-in-itself is the tranquil substance of *i*."[33] He also sees *i* as a self-manifesting principle, capable of both "movement" and "tranquility."[34] In contrast to Chu Hsi, he certainly understood the dynamic, autonomous nature of *i*. Yu Ch'i-myŏng (Chongjae, 1777–1861), one of the leading scholars of T'oegye's school in the nineteenth century, commented that T'oegye's entire philosophy is based on his belief that "*i* is the active entity." On the whole, then, T'oegye's interpretation of principle is a substantial departure from Chu Hsi's original philosophy. In Chu Hsi's philosophy, it is true that *i* is not capable of moving or manifesting by itself. According to Yulgok, T'oegye misunderstood and misinterpreted Chu Hsi's concept of principle, giving a more confusing interpretation in the name of defending his textual authority. As we have observed, Yulgok criticized his theory of *i* dynamism for not realizing that *i*, as the metaphysical principle for existence, can never be an acting agent that can manifest itself.

However, the crucial question that we must address here is, Why did T'oegye formulate such a contradictory theory of *i*? Also, what does he mean by arguing that *i* can manifest itself in the Four Beginnings? This is really the key issue that we need to comprehend in the context of his Four-Seven thesis in particular. As far as my own reading is concerned, T'oegye was aware of the fact that the dynamism of cosmic transformation is reserved, in Chu Hsi's philosophy, only to *ki*. Strictly speaking, however, he was not always consistent in explaining the relationship of *i* and *ki* with respect to Chu Hsi's metaphysics. He had to face the challenging problem of interpreting the crucial issue of whether or not principle, which is fundamentally a metaphysical and static concept, can manifest itself in the practice of self-cultivation. For this profound reason, T'oegye wanted to do full justice to his belief that *i* must necessarily have priority over *ki* in terms of both ontological and ethical contexts.

As de Bary correctly observes, T'oegye's synthesis of Ch'eng-Chu Neo-Confucian thought emphasizes "the moral and spiritual aspects of principle."[35] Obviously, this remark is relevant to our further discussion of T'oegye's philosophy of self-cultivation. One can also argue that T'oegye emphasized the "spontaneous issuance" of *i* as "something active," not "something passive" in moral practice.[36] As the ultimate "commander of things" (to use T'oegye's own terminology), *i* should be understood as "the moral master." Perhaps, T'oegye argued from his experiences, and self-cultivation proves to be the central feature of his philosophy of principle. We may identify it as a "new kind" of Ch'eng-Chu school that stresses mind cultivation.[37] Surely, he considered *i* as "a practical moral substance."[38] In other words, T'oegye's theory of the self-governing manifestation of *i* must be addressed in terms of his own understanding of self-cultivation.

More specifically, we have to understand it in the context of T'oegye's Four-Seven thesis. T'oegye tried to convince Kobong that *i* represents moral virtues (like the Four), whereas *ki* represents physical-psychological emotions and desires (like the Seven).[39] This is why he warned Kobong to grasp a clear distinction of *i* from *ki* in both the philosophical and moral contexts. He emphasized the Four-Seven distinction in terms of an ontological and conceptual *i-ki* dichotomy and an ethical good-evil contrast. His Four-Seven thesis is significant not only from a philosophical standpoint, but also in an ethical context. His holistic mission was to emphasize the transcendent, virtuous, and spiritual reality of *i* over the physical, emotional, and material reality of *ch'i*, insofar as the pure existence of *i* remains the original goodness of human nature, the indispensable potential for self-cultivation. T'oegye's philosophy of principle provides a philosophical and moral justification for the Mencian doctrine that human nature is naturally good as the Four Beginnings inherent in the mind-and-heart. For him, human nature, as principle, has to be an *active*, not passive, thing capable of manifesting itself in self-cultivation. Unlike Chu Hsi who emphasized the rationalistic "investigation of principles," he has a stronger tendency for the *self-realization* of principle. And his conviction was to take principle as the ultimate foundation of the Neo-Confucian learning for sagehood. This is why T'oegye's Four-Seven thesis and his other philosophical writings point to a philosophy of cultivating and nourishing *i*, not *ki*. Obviously, he fully committed himself to the practice of moral and spiritual self-cultivation in the tradition of Mencius and Ch'eng-Chu teachings. This is the focus of the next two sections.

Feelings and the Learning of Mind-and-Heart (*Simhak*)

A common term for Neo-Confucianism is *simhak/hsin-hsüeh* which has variously been translated as the "school of the mind," "philosophy of the mind," or even "learning of the mind-and-heart." This term was often reserved for the Lu-Wang school, an outgrowth of Neo-Confucianism identified with the Ming philosopher Wang Yang-ming (1472–1529) and his predecessor Lu Hsiang-shan (1139–1192), Chu Hsi's contemporary and rival in the Sung period. The two have been considered to be the Lu-Wang "school of the mind" as opposed to the so-called Ch'eng-Chu "school of principle" (*ihak/li-hsüeh*) or "learning of human nature and principle" (*sŏngnihak/hsing-li hsüeh*). Although this distinction is generally convenient for us to distinguish the two schools of thought, it is misleading in a strict sense. This is because the *simhak* occupies a central and vital part particularly in T'oegye's Neo-Confucianism closely relating to his Four-Seven thesis. Hence, the designation of this term can also be applied to the Ch'eng-Chu tradition especially T'oegye's philosophy and practice of mind cultivation.

Sung Chinese Neo-Confucians originally used the term *simhak* as an alternative to Chan Buddhism.[40] Its original doctrine was more explicitly expressed by the late Sung scholar, Chen Te-hsiu (Hsi-shan, 1178–1235), who emphasized the theory of self-cultivation with a strong moral dimension. In his major work, *Hsin ching* (Classic of the Mind-and-Heart),[41] Chen collected brief quotations on the Confucian way of mind cultivation especially from the Four Books and Sung Neo-Confucian writings. It was recognized as one of the most important texts that contributed to the establishment of the orthodox Ch'eng-Chu school not only in China, but also in Korea.

In Korea, T'oegye often spoke of the term *simhak*.[42] In his Four-Seven debate with Kobong, he emphasized it in the context of self-cultivation. His extensive use of it is evident also in his other writings such as the *Sŏnghak sipto*. In the opening lines of the *Simhak to* (Diagrammatic Treatise on the Learning of the Mind-and-Heart),[43] the eighth of the *Sŏnghak sipto*, T'oegye states: "This diagram is a collection of the famous sayings of the sages and worthies on *simhak*."[44] He also spoke of *simbŏp/hsin-fa* (system of the mind-and-heart), *tohak/tao-hsüeh* (school of the Way), and *chewang chi hak/ti-wang chih hsüeh* (learning of the emperors and kings). In his *Yukcho so* (Six-Article Memorial),[45] he argues: "To establish the foundation of government is to carry out the learning of the sages sincerely. The essence of the system of the mind-and-heart in the learning of emperors and kings comes from the great Shun's mandate to his successor Yü."[46] Furthermore, "the learning of the emperors and kings is the essence of making the system of the mind-and-heart excellent and transmitting the school of the Way."[47] T'oegye's *Songge Wŏn Myŏng ihak t'ongnok* (General Records of the School of Principle in the Sung, Yüan, and Ming Periods)[48] refers to *simhak* as *ihak/li-hsüeh* and *sŏngni-hak/ hsing-li hsüeh* as well.

Given his compelling commitment to transmitting Ch'eng-Chu orthodoxy in Korea, it was obvious for T'oegye to use Chen's *Hsin ching* as a standard text for lectures at the court, holding it in great veneration. When his students asked him to compare it with other Confucian classics, he ranked it along with the Four Books and *Hsing-li ta-ch'üan* (Great Compendium of Human Nature and Principle), as well as with Chu Hsi's *Hsiao hsüeh* (Elementary Learning), *Chu Tzu ta-ch'üan* (Great Compendium of Master Chu Hsi), and *Chin-ssu lu* (Reflections on Things at Hand).[49] In his *Simgyŏng huron* (Epilogue to the *Classic of the Mind-and-Heart*), T'oegye, in fact, affirms his own faith in Chen's *Hsin ching* as his "divine spirit" and "parents."[50] According to the *Ŏnhaeng nok* (T'oegye's Words and Acts), ever since his encounter with the *Hsin ching* in his early days, it had been a continuous source of inspiration for his learning of the mind-and-heart throughout his life. He explicitly told his students in the following words: "Only after I had obtained a copy of the *Hsing ching*, did I finally understand the foundation of *simhak* and the refinement and subtlety of the method of the mind-and-heart.

Therefore, I trust this book as my divine spirit and revered it as my stern father."[51]

The question is, Why did T'oegye maintain it as his favorite text? The *Classic of the Mind-and-Heart*, or *Heart Classic* for short, has almost no mention about the rational dimension of the Ch'eng-Chu teachings, namely the "investigation of things" and "extension of knowledge."[52] Rather, its main emphasis is focused on the moral and spiritual dimension of self-cultivation. For his reason, it became the most important text for T'oegye, who quoted it frequently in discussing the Ch'eng-Chu *simhak*. What he liked about it is especially its preoccupation with an inner-directed type of moral self-cultivation, rather than a rational study of principles and things. Invoking Sung thinkers including Chen Te-hsiu as not merely as metaphysicians but more often as moralists, T'oegye's lifelong dedication to study Chen's *Heart Classic* clearly demonstrates his ultimate concern for *simhak*. Surely, it had a significant impact on T'oegye's philosophy and practice of self-cultivation that tended to move beyond traditional Ch'eng-Chu norms.

Ch'eng-Chu teachings on mind cultivation focuses on its dual concept of the mind in terms of the "human mind" (*insim/jen-hsin*) and the "moral mind" (*tosim/tao-hsin*). In the third article of his *Yokcho so*, for example, T'oegye cites the so-called Sixteen-Character Transmission of the Mind-and-Heart, an obscure passage from the *Book of History*: "The human mind is precarious; the moral mind is subtle. Remain refined and singleminded: Hold fast the Mean."[53] This instruction of the sage-king Shun to his successor Yü contrasts the "precariousness" of the human mind with the "subtlety" of the moral mind, emphasizing the practice of mind cultivation. Chu Hsi, Chen Tu-hsiu, and others utilized this passage as a short "creedal" formula of the Neo-Confucian philosophy of mind cultivation. For example, it appears in Chu Hsi's preface to the *Doctrine of the Mean*:

> The mind-and-heart as the pure intelligence and consciousness is one and undivided. But there is a difference between the moral mind and the human mind, depending on whether it arises from the selfishness identified with physical form or originates in the correctness of Heaven and destiny, in accordance with which consciousness differs. The human mind is precarious, and the moral mind is subtle. All human beings have the physical form; so, even the most intelligent people possess the human mind, while the most stupid have the moral mind. If the moral mind and the human mind are not distinguished, then we do not know why we have to control them. Accordingly, the

> precarious will become even more precarious, the subtle will become even more subtle, and the impartiality of Heaven's principle (*ch'ŏlli/t'ien-li*) will have no way of overcoming the selfishness of human desires (*inyok/jen-yü*).[54]

This passage was cited also in the opening passages of Chen Tu-hsiu's *Heart Classic.* Of course, Chu Hsi contrasted the "precariousness" and "instability" of the human mind with the inherent goodness of the moral mind; the former is always "prone to error" and "partial" involving both good and evil, whereas the latter is always "subtle" and "impartial." For him, then, the way of mind cultivation means to overcome selfish desires aroused from the human mind. However, it is not that the "moral mind" is one and the "human mind" is another.[55] Chu Hsi meant that "the moral mind is the master of the human mind, and the latter takes the former as its moral norm."[56] More specifically, the human mind refers to the mouth's desire for taste, the eyes' desire for color, and so on, whereas the moral mind refers to the "moral principles" such as humanity, righteousness, propriety, and wisdom.[57] Nevertheless, all of these belong to human nature because even the sages like Yao, Shun, and Confucius had their desires for food and color, and even the most ignorant people have a human sense of moral consciousness.[58] How does T'oegye understand this kind of distinction between the human mind and the moral mind?

In his Four-Seven debate with Kobong, T'oegye did not talk directly about the moral mind and the human mind; as we have observed, rather, Yulgok discussed them extensively. In addressing the fundamental difference between the Four Beginnings and the Seven Emotions, T'oegye did address the relationship between the mind, human nature, and feelings, although he did not directly quote Chu Hsi's statements about the distinction between the human mind and the moral mind. For example, he politely urged Kobong to clearly distinguish the Four from the Seven, so that Kobong will not have an "unfortunate consequence" of misunderstanding *i* as *ki*.[59] He means that the Seven, unlike the Four, are basic physical desires and emotions without a moral status. In other words, the emotion of anger, for example, is not a moral virtue or feeling; therefore, it must come from *ki*, which can transform it into the "precarious" and "selfish" dimension of the mind. From a concrete standpoint of self-cultivation, T'oegye argues: "The feeling of anger [one of the Seven] is especially excessive and difficult to control. When one is angry, one should immediately forget one's anger and examine the right and wrong of the matter at hand, according to principle (*i/li*)."[60]

For him, this is the main reason for distinguishing the Four from the Seven in a conceptual and moral context.

In his other philosophical letters and treatises, T'oegye follows Chu Hsi's interpretation to clarify the way of mind cultivation. He maintains that the human mind represents the selfish desires and feelings identified with physical form, whereas the moral mind pertains to moral principles and feelings. The following passage illustrates his point: "The human mind is the source of human desires; therefore, our selfish desires come from it. The mind-and-heart (*sim/hsin*) aroused from physical form is called the human mind, for even the sages have it. The activity of human desires (*inyok/jen-yü*) really starts from this; therefore, the human mind is called the source of selfish human desires. The mind-and-heart of the ordinary people who act against Heaven becomes indulged by material desires. The material desires are wicked."[61] Unlike Chu Hsi, T'oegye sees more explicitly that the precariousness and instability of the human mind cause evil. For him, the human desires can be selfish, materialistic, and wicked. The question is, How does one cultivate the so-called human mind? For T'oegye, it can be rectified and become good. From a standpoint of self-cultivation, he argues that: "The so-called human mind and moral mind are already in opposition to each other. The former belongs to its own substance of selfishness; however, because it can follow the latter's command, it can become one with the moral mind. Although the human mind is completely blended with the moral mind, we cannot say simply that the two are one."[62] All evil is due to "selfish material desires" caused by the human mind, and *ki* stimulates the human mind. Implicit in this argument is that one must, therefore, exercize a sincere and serious effort to preserve and nourish the moral mind; to do so, one must hold fast to the command of one's moral will over one's unstable and precarious human mind. This is precisely why T'oegye emphasized the necessity of transforming the "selfish desires" issued from the human mind into the ultimate goodness of the moral mind or "Heaven's principle" (*ch'ŏlli/t'ien-li*).

As T'oegye argued in his Four-Seven letters to Kobong, Heaven's principle refers to what Mencius called the *original goodness of human nature*, what the *Doctrine of the Mean* called *human nature endowed by Heaven*, or what Chang Tsai and Chu Hsi meant by *original human nature*.[63] In his *Sŏnghak sipto*, T'oegye also asserts that it implies what Ch'eng I and Chu Hsi meant by *human nature is i* and what Chang Tsai and Chu Hsi referred to as *the nature of Heaven and Earth*.[64] All of these phrases mean the Four Beginnings, not the Seven Emotions, referring to "*i* in itself" or the "original essence of human nature." Of course, Heaven's principle pertains to the genuine source of moral self-cultivation. As T'oegye told Kobong, one's unwillingness not to distinguish *i* from *ki* means to misidentify the moral qualities (like the Four) aroused by Heaven's principle with the selfish human desires (like the Seven) aroused by external stimuli.[65]

By citing Chen's *Hear Classic*, T'oegye articulates his position on the Ch'eng-Chu learning of the mind-and-heart in the following words: "*Simhak* is . . . none other than two ideas such as suppressing human desires and preserving Heaven's principle. To suppress human desires belongs to the work of the human mind, and to preserve Heaven's principle belongs to the work of the moral mind. If not so, why would Chen Tu-hsiu conclude at the end of his *Heart Classic* that 'overcoming and controlling' and 'preserving and nourishing' both help one's effort at *simhak*?"[66] For T'oegye, then, the Ch'eng-Chu *simhak* should be based on the suppressing and overcoming of the human mind and the preserving and nourishing of the moral mind. However, a relevant question arises here, How does such a way of *simhak* relate to his Four-Seven thesis in terms of human nature (*sŏng/hsing*) and feelings (*chŏng/ch'ing*)?

In his Four-Seven thesis, T'oegye cites Chang Tsai's and Chu Hsi's doctrine that "the mind commands human nature and feelings."[67] The mind combines, comprehends, and directs both human nature and feelings. T'oegye means Chu Hsi's sayings that "the mind unites *i* and *ki*"[68] and that "Human nature consists of principles embraced in the mind, while the mind is where these principles are united. Human nature is principle. The mind is its reservoir that issues it forth into operation."[69] In the *Sim mu ch'eyong pyŏn* (Critique on the Saying "the Mind Does Not Have Substance and Function"),[70] he discusses the mind in terms of "substance" and "function": "We refer to what is tranquil as substance (*ch'e/t'i*) and what moves as function (*yong/yung*), and this is based on the *Book of Changes*.[71] We refer to the unmanifest state as substance and the manifest state as function, and this is based on the *Doctrine of the Mean*.[72] We refer to human nature as substance and feelings as function, and this is based on Mencius.[73] These texts are all about the substance and function of the mind."[74] The unmanifested state of the mind refers to human nature, whereas the manifested state of the mind feelings. T'oegye is, of course, clarifying the Ch'eng-Chu theory that the mind has both substance and function, meaning that the former is human nature and the latter is feelings. Human nature is the mind before it is aroused, whereas the feelings are the mind after it is aroused. To put it in another way, the former is the ontological reality of the mind, the mind-in-itself, whereas the latter is the concrete, experiential manifestation of the mind. For this reason, the mind is said to unite, command, and apprehend human nature and feelings. Chu Hsi wrote in this regard: "The mind is the master of human nature and feelings,"[75] as it is "the master of the self."[76] T'oegye adds: "What is stimulated by external things is the mind, and that by which the mind moves is feelings."[77] What is bestowed by the mind and becomes manifest to function is feelings.[78] Because feelings are inevitable expressions of the mind, it follows that self-cultivation must require one to attain the so-called centrality of the mind in its absolutely pure state before the issuance of feelings.

Why do "selfish desires" arise? This question is, of course, relevant to T'oegye's Four-Seven thesis. Selfish desires occur when the mind, the master of the self, does not control aroused feelings properly, leading them to become selfish desires. The Seven Emotions can become evil, if they do not attain their due degree and measure. This is due to the activity of *ki* that can always cause "selfish desires." We can use T'oegye's rider-horse analogy to explain it in the following manner: when *i* (like the rider) is undisturbed by the *ki* (the horse) that follows it, we have good feelings like the Four Beginnings; however, if *i* is controlled by the distorted *ki*, we have evil feelings like the disharmonized Seven Emotions. In other words, we have good when the moral mind commands the human mind, whereas evil arises when the latter does not comply with the former's moral guideline. In T'oegye's dualistic way of *moral reasoning*, this can be expressed in terms of the Four and the Seven as well; that is to say, good can prevail when the Four dominate over the Seven; evil can prevail when the Seven dominates over the Four. The problem with the Seven is their excessiveness; therefore, they must be controlled so that they do not cause selfish desires. "The Seven may become evil, if they do not attain their due degree and measure."[79] There are proper ways to be joyful, angry, sorrowful, fearful, loving, hating, and desiring; otherwise, they become selfish and evil. For this reason, T'oegye emphasized that these emotive feelings and desires, which are not necessarily morally grounded or oriented, necessarily require a discipline of emotional control and moral cultivation. To practice such a discipline, however, one first need to understand the conceptual and ethical distinction between *i* and *ki* and, hence, between the Four and the Seven. This is, indeed, part of the essence of his Four-Seven thesis that Kobong finally accepted.

The key to *simhak* is to control one's selfish desires issued by *ki*; it is to hold fast to *i*, which issues the Four as moral forces. Hence, one should have a clear distinction of "Heaven's principle" and "selfish desires": the former is what enables aroused feelings to become morally and emotionally harmonized, whereas the latter may lead them to evil. In his *Sŏnghak sipto* written few years after the debate with Kobong, T'oegye argues that it is extremely crucial to be "very clear on the distinction of principles and desires," so that one can "illuminate Heaven's principle" and put it into practice.[80] One's grasp of the distinction "depends on whether or not one's mind governs one's feelings."[81] It is precisely in this concrete context of self-cultivation that T'oegye, unlike Chu Hsi, not only affirmed the self-manifesting capability of *i* in concrete phenomena including moral virtues (such as the Four), but also formulated a more rigorous view of selfish desires as "wicked" and "evil." T'oegye must have formulated this argument from an experiential standpoint of his own practice of self-cultivation.

T'oegye's *simhak* certainly justifies his Four-Seven thesis in the sense that moral cultivation means to preserve the Four Beginnings and to control the Seven Emotions. To assert that the Four, the essential moral qualities of human nature, are not aroused by *i*, or that they are aroused by *ki* in the same fashion as the Seven are aroused, is, in T'oegye's view, totally wrong in both theoretical and practical contexts. Such an assertion would be absurd not only metaphysically and ethically, but also in the Neo-Confucian context of self-cultivation. In other words, benevolence is a moral virtue; therefore, the moral feeling of "commiseration" (the beginning of benevolence) must be different from the emotion of "anger" (one of the Seven) aroused by *ki*. As T'oegye argued in his Four-Seven thesis, the way of *simhak* means to suppress the dehumanizing tendencies of the Seven that are manifestations of *ki* and, therefore, easily become evil. This points to what he calls "the way of suppressing *ki* by means of *i*."[82]

Surely, the Mencian doctrine of human nature demands one's effort to "seek our lost mind" or to return to the original goodness of human nature. This is part of the reason that T'oegye referred to *simhak* as "the learning of principle" (*ihak/li-hsüeh*), "the learning of human nature and principle" (*sŏngnihak/hsing-li hsüeh*), and "the learning for sagehood" (*sŏnghak/sheng-hsüeh*) as complementary designations. On the whole, his *simhak* emphasizes "suppressing human desires and preserving Heaven's principle."[83] It suggests a way of experiencing Heaven's principle as moral principles embodied in the Four Beginnings; this is the core of his *simhak,* which he maintained in his Four-Seven thesis as well as other major writings. In fact, his entire philosophy of self-cultivation is based on such a theme. It developed especially as a fruitful result of his debate with Kobong.

T'oegye's admiration for the Sung Neo-Confucian Li T'ung (Yen-p'ing, 1088–1163), one of Chu Hsi's teachers, reveals how seriously he committed himself to the practice of mind cultivation. As revealed in his major works and biographical records, the topic of quiet sitting and *simhak* became an important topic of instruction to his disciples. This conveys the degree of Li T'ung's influence on T'oegye. For Li T'ung, quiet sitting served as a contemplative exercise to help one penetrate into the essence of one's inner nature.[84] As he told his disciples, what T'oegye found useful in Li's method is a way to experience the mind-in-itself.[85] As he asserts, Li referred to it as a method of "examining the unmanifest mind (*mibal/wei-fa*) in the state of quietude before the arousal of feelings."[86] The core of T'oegye's *simhak* is the self-realization of it. Unlike Li T'ung, however, T'oegye argues that such an experience should not preclude an establishment of relation with the mind in its "manifest" state (*ibal/i-fa*). In other words, the role of the manifest mind is significant in the whole process of moral self-cultivation: "Only after the practice of quiet sitting, can one collect the body and the mind so that moral principles can be united together."[87] For the practice of *simhak*, then, the first thing to do is to "collect" the dispersed self according to moral principles; this helps one's search for the "original substance" (*pen-t'i/ponch'e*) of human nature. In other words, it is a *contemplative, spiritual discipline* that ought to integrate one's intellectual insight and moral effort simultaneously. T'oegye refers to it as the essence of becoming a sage. For this reason, he consistently maintained the Ch'eng-Chu idea that principles are inherent in human nature, urging Kobong to accept his view that the Four Beginnings of virtue must be manifest from *i*.

For T'oegye, human nature in itself is identical to Heaven's principle, the absolutely good and pure reality. From an experiential standpoint of self-cultivation, his theory and practice of *simhak* emphasize the virtuous and transcendent dimension of *i* as something to be contemplatively realized and internally cultivated in the mind-and-heart. T'oegye's approach to *simhak* addresses *kyŏng/ching* or "reverential seriousness"[88] as the most important the virtue to be cultivated in quiet sitting and mind cultivation. This is the focus of our next inquiry.

Sagehood and the Learning of Reverential Seriousness (*Kyŏnghak*)

To get rid of evil and follow good is, according to T'oegye, to "abide in reverential seriousness" (*kŏgyŏng/chü-ching*).[89] This approach leads one to realizing Heaven's principle, the ultimate reality of sagehood. T'oegye speaks of *kyŏnghak/ching-hsüeh* (learning of reverential seriousness) and *sŏnghak/sheng-hsüeh* (learning for sagehood) as complementary terms, and this is clearly stated in his major writings such as *Sŏnghak sipto*, *Ch'ŏnmyŏng tosŏl*, and *Yukcho so*.

The locus classicus for the Confucian idea of *kyŏng/ching* includes the *Book of Changes*, *Book of Rites*, and *Analects*. According to the first classic,

"The superior person applies reverential seriousness in order to straighten the inner life and righteousness in order to square the outer life."[90] In the *Book of Rites* as well, we read: "The superior person never lacks reverential seriousness."[91] And Confucius emphasized: "Be serious and reverent in handling all affairs."[92] Sung Neo-Confucians cited these passages to emphasize reverential seriousness in the Confucian way of self-cultivation. Ch'eng Hao, for example, said: "Reverential seriousness simply means a way of managing oneself."[93] It also means "unselfishness." When one lacks it, "thousands of selfish desires arise to injure one's humanity."[94] As Ch'eng I said, "self-cultivation requires reverential seriousness."[95] Chu Hsi emphasized that one should apply it to the practice moral cultivation and maintain righteousness in handling daily affairs. For example, he said that "one must cultivate one's mind with reverential seriousness"[96] and "be serious and reverent at all times."[97] On the whole, then, these Chinese Neo-Confucians interpreted reverential seriousness as an attitude of reverent piety toward Heaven and Earth, as well as an intellectual and moral seriousness in handling things and human relationships.

How did T'oegye interpret this key Confucian concept in the context of his Four-Seven thesis and *simhak*? Reverential seriousness is his central goal and method of moral and spiritual cultivation. Chu Hsi merely emphasized it in the Neo-Confucian learning of mind cultivation, without giving an elaborate interpretation of it. On the contrary, T'oegye preached in Korea that *kyŏng* is the most important virtue to be cultivated. It is said to be the foundation of his great synthesis of the Ch'eng-Chu Neo-Confucianism of self-cultivation.[98] In his view, *simhak* is none other than *kyŏnghak*, the key to the learning for sagehood. In the *Ch'ŏnmyŏng tosŏl*, T'oegye refers to the "learning of the superior persons" (*kunja chi hak/chün-tzu chih hsüeh*) as the "learning of reverential seriousness" (*kyŏnghak/ching-hsüeh*),[99] maintaining the Mencian doctrine that the task of "preserving [the mind-and-heart] and nourishing [human nature]" is the essence of *kyŏnghak*. He articulates it in terms of the mind before and after the arousal of feelings: "If one does not take reverential seriousness to be the first principle of learning, how can one establish the original mind? Hence, before the mind is manifest, the learning of the superior person is to take reverential seriousness as the first principle and to give full effort to preserving and nourishing. After the mind is manifest, it is to give full effort to self-examination and self-reflection. This is, then, the reason why the learning of reverential seriousness completes the beginning and end [of the learning for sagehood]."[100] In the context of his Four-Seven thesis, this passage implies that one has to be conscientious about not only the observable patterns of one's behavior, but also the incipient tendencies of one's inner feelings and desires. The term *kyŏng* also means "mindfulness,"[101] conveying the Neo-Confucian technique of maintaining serious determination and constant concentration in mind cultivation. In fact, *reverence* may refer to the inner motivation that inspires the practice of self-regulation. The cultivation of reverential seriousness pertains to the Mencian doctrine of preserving the mind in itself and nourishing the original goodness of human nature. It also takes the manifest mind as the basis for self-introspection and self-realization. To T'oegye, then, this represents the essence of learning for sagehood.

Summarizing his major work, *Sŏnghak sipto,* in terms of reverential seriousness, *kyŏng,*[102] T'oegye argues: "Reverential seriousness is the beginning and end of the learning for sagehood (*sŏnghak/sheng-hsüeh*)."[103] He does not ignore the traditional Confucian teaching that the external dimension of self-cultivation is to maintain a good character according to the proper observation of the rules of propriety. For example, "be cautious and watchful in the hidden, secluded places" and "be properly ordered and controlled, grave, and quiet."[104] As he instructs his disciples, "When I am inactive, I am watchful of myself and cultivate reverential seriousness."[105] The following passage from the *Sŏnghak sipto* articulates his point further: "The method [of *simhak*] is to be gravely cautious and watchful over what is not seen and heard, as well as to be more reverential and serious. It is to practice self-watchfulness and self-reflection in a more refined way where things are invisible or subtle and when one is alone."[106]

From the same standpoint of self-cultivation, T'oegye emphasizes, in his Four-Seven thesis, that a self-possessed state of mind should be maintained by "concentrating on one thing without departing from it," as well as by preserving its internal "refined" state.[107] The whole process of cultivating reverential seriousness involves the external method of "concentrating on one thing" and the internal method of "being cautious and self-watchful." As T'oegye argues further, "Neither of these can be neglected. Regulating the exterior to nourish the interior is an even more urgent matter."[108] Furthermore, his disciples report: "The master's learning is that which takes the effort of [holding fast to] reverential seriousness; it penetrates the beginning and end and pertains to both substance and function."[109] To attain what the *Doctrine of the Mean* calls the *centrality* of the mind before the issuance of feelings, one must cultivate *kyŏng* and develop a way of continuous mind cultivation. In this way, the substance and function of the mind can become united: "The centrality [of the mind] can be grasped, while the mind concentrates on its state of refinement and single-mindedness."[110]

According to T'oegye, the Ch'eng-Chu doctrine of "holding fast reverential seriousness" (*chigyŏng/ch'i-ching*) means that reverential seriousness is "the master of making efforts to preserve the mind-and-heart."[111] Another quotation deserves our attention here: "To abide in reverential seriousness, one has to remain at the center of the myriad things and make sure that reverential seriousness and the myriad things do not deviate from one another. . . . Even for a single moment, one cannot neglect reverential seriousness."[112] Self-cultivation requires quiet-sitting meditation as a key practice to "collect the body and the mind according to moral principles"; "If the self is dispersed and not collected, one's body and mind will be in darkness and disorder, while moral principles cannot be united together."[113] Such a method is a way of experiencing the tranquil interiority of one's mind by keeping it in a quiet and peaceful atmosphere. For the practice of "self-reflection" and "self-correction," *simhak* serves as the basis for controlling and overcoming distracting thoughts, feelings, and desires; therefore, T'oegye's *simhak* is more of a contemplative approach that involves, the exercise of "suppressing selfish human desires" and "preserving Heaven's principle."[114] In the *Sŏnghak sipto*, T'oegye proclaims that self-cultivation is impossible without the virtue of *kyŏng*, the motivating and nourishing power of *simhak*. As he writes further, "When one is sincerely able to hold fast to *kyŏng* and very clear on the distinction between principles and desires, one's effort of preserving [the mind] and nourishing [human nature] will be deep. If the effort of mental self-examination and self-correction is sincerely and profoundly continued for a long period of time, then the state of refined single-mindedness will be attained."[115]

One should not deviate from nourishing the mind-and-heart with reverential seriousness even for a single moment. Accordingly, self-cultivation means to grasp what T'oegye calls "true knowledge" (*chinchi/chen-chih*). This expounds his compelling belief that the "learning for entering sagehood" (*sŏngmun chi hak/sheng-men chih hsüeh*) is complete only when *kyŏng* is internally cultivated in the mind-and-heart and then externally put into actual practice. T'oegye argues: "One should personally experience and get a taste of the meaning of reverential seriousness. One should caution oneself while using reverential seriousness for self-introspection in the course of daily life and whatever comes to the mind-and-heart. If one assimilates it in this way, one will never doubt that it is the beginning and end of the learning for sagehood."[116]

The self-realization of Heaven's principle means to grasp one's own nature through cultivating *kyŏng*. Because *kyŏng* is "the master of the self," it follows for T'oegye that if the mind is in the state of "refined oneness," one can hold fast to *kyŏng*, and one's mind remains as the master of all feelings, thoughts, desires, and so on. T'oegye theory and practice of *kyŏnghak* correspond to the underlying theme of his *Four-Seven thesis* in terms of holding fast to the Four Beginnings (issued by *i*) and controlling the Seven Emotions (issued by *ki*). They also hold to his *simhak* in the sense that one has to transform the selfish desires into the ultimate goodness of Heaven's principle. Accordingly, T'oegye urged Kobong to make a clear distinction of Heaven's principle (represented by *i*) and selfish desires (represented by *ki*). This, then, brings us to examine the ethico-spiritual dimension of such a topic, the focus of the following section.

Self-Cultivation as an Ethico-Spiritual Ideal

As we have already observed, T'oegye's approach to *simhak* emphasizes Heaven's principle and reverential seriousness. In searching for a convincing way of self-cultivation within the Ch'eng-Chu context, he accepted its general doctrine that "human nature is principle"; this is explicitly evident especially in his Four-Seven thesis. Hence, the general feature of his *simhak* and *kyŏnghak* received the philosophical and moral justification of the Ch'eng-Chu tradition. But its emphasis on the self-manifesting role of principle extends from metaphysics to quiet-sitting meditation and spiritual cultivation.

T'oegye's *simhak* and *kyŏnghak* reveal certain religious dimension; this was a result of his creative synthesis of Ch'eng-Chu teachings. We need to look at it from a cross-cultural standpoint of comparative religion. The religious dimension of the Chinese Confucian tradition has been addressed in terms of its spiritual teachings of self-cultivation; in fact, this has been one of the most popular areas of research, one that need not be rehearsed here.[117] Even though Neo-Confucianism is often considered merely as a form of "ethical humanism" or "metaphysical humanism," such a conventional categorization is misleading because it does not articulate the spiritual vitality of Neo-Confucianism.[118] In a strict sense, it is incorrect, especially if we reflect on T'oegye's Neo-Confucianism in particular.[119] We need to examine the ways in which T'oegye intensifies Neo-Confucian religiosity in terms of spiritual cultivation. Of course, his ultimate quest for sagehood is very relevant here. Another issue is to understand how it relates to his *Four-Seven thesis*. If we want to understand the vitality of T'oegye's Neo-Confucianism, we should address its religiosity.

According to his disciples, T'oegye's "mind-and-heart was bright and transparent like the moon and ice."[120] A man of peace, purity, and benevolence, he was regarded as a moral and spiritual practitioner who "united the inner and outer life" and "made no distinction and separation between himself and things."[121] T'oegye consistently engaged himself in quiet-sitting meditation and mind cultivation especially when he was alone at night. Criticizing Wang Yang-ming's method of self-cultivation, he clarifies the Ch'eng-Chu form of quiet sitting and mind cultivation: "The learning of quiet sitting comes from the two Ch'eng masters, and I doubt if it is really Zen. For Li T'ung and Chu Hsi, it was the foundation of *simhak*, but it is not Zen."[122] T'oegye, therefore, recommended the Ch'eng-Chu *simhak* of "self-examination" and "self-reflection," emphasizing the realization of Heaven's principle and the cultivation of reverential seriousness with a single-minded determination and concentration. As he says in his lecture to the king, "This is the true learning. It is not enough to read the teachings of the sages and worthies in the morning or afternoon. When the mind-and-heart is tranquil at night, one must experience Heaven's principle in oneself. Every morning and afternoon one should examine what one has done and put self-examination and self-reflection into practice. Once you get used to such a practice, you will realize the truth of the learning for sagehood."[123] For self-cultivation, T'oegye practiced quiet sitting as a contemplative activity that may be described as what Julia Ching calls a *form of inner concentration*.[124] As he says, "When my spirit is clear and my material force is undisturbed, I am austere and solemn, and my mind-and-heart naturally holds itself firm without me having to grasp it."[125] In the context of his Four-Seven thesis, one who can calm the activity of the mind, can realize in oneself Heaven's principle or the "unmanifest" state of the mind prior to the arising of the feelings and thoughts.

In Chu Hsi's philosophy, the focus of the investigation of things is generally on the search for knowledge through one's intellectual comprehension of the essence of things.[126] This process of investigation was part of self-cultivation and became an extensive, if not exhaustive, path that involves both intellectual aims and ethical implications. According to T'oegye's own experience, however, the task of self-cultivation is simply *simhak*. As his Four-Seven thesis illustrated, it is to be integrated by preserving the mind-and-heart and nourishing human nature in one's daily life. He says: "One's effort at learning should be maintained with solemnity as [one's self is] controlled and united. . . . One's mind-and-heart must be calmed down in accordance with the reality of moral principles only. If this is done over a long period of time, one's mind-and-heart will be realized naturally and be in the state of quietude, so that one can overcome the maladies of forgetting and hurrying."[127] Self-cultivation means a path to realization of human nature in itself as the authentic manifestation of Heaven's principle; that is to say, one's transformed self should form a unity with Heaven's principle, moral principles, and all phenomena. This is *why* T'oegye repeatedly affirmed *i/li* as a self-manifesting and self-sustaining principle capable manifesting, for example, the Four Beginnings. The essential feature of his *simhak* is that the mind-and-heart is the intellectual, moral, and psychological master of the self that commands and apprehends human nature and feelings. In the context of his Four-Seven thesis, it also entails integrating all feelings by maintaining the command of the moral virtues such as Four over the physical-mental emotions and material desires such as the Seven.

According to T'oegye's *kyŏnghak*, Heaven's principle is not just a philosophical and moral concept; it has religious meanings and implications. The fundamental Ch'eng-Chu teaching is that "human nature is principle." This implies that "Heaven's principle is the principle of human nature." To realize the ultimate truth of human nature is, in the Mencian sense, to look inward to seek its inherent goodness. In the spirit of *Doctrine of the Mean*, T'oegye's notion of human nature refers to what one may call "potentially a genuine manifestation of Heaven."[128] In the process of self-cultivation, the self can penetrate deeply into its own ground of existence, so that the mind-and-heart establishes a harmonious rhythm with Heaven, Earth, and all phenomena. This quest for self-realization is identified with sagehood. From a standpoint of comparative religion, it does have a significant religious dimension for T'oegye's spirituality. By *spirituality* we mean a disciplined life of spiritual-mindedness, self-realization, and spiritual exercise. For T'oegye, it involves a combination of intellectual insight, contemplative practice, and spiritual development. It is expressed in terms of *simhak*, *kyŏnghak*, and sagehood; however, it is equipped with a religious goal and method of self-transcendence, a higher state of intellectual insight, virtuous life, and spiritual consciousness. This portrays the degree to which T'oegye appreciated quiet sitting as the way to unite the inner and the outer. Meditation was a major part of his spiritual exercise of self-transformation within the Ch'eng-Chu Neo-Confucian context. The ethico-religious dimension of T'oegye's Neo-Confucianism reveals spiritual experience of unity between the self and the universe. Implicit in his practice of cultivating Heaven's principle as sagehood points to what Tu Wei-ming calls a *covenant* with Heaven, for it is to "fulfil the highest human aspirations of forming a trinity with Heaven and earth."[129] This perspective corresponds to T'oegye's faith that if human nature is endowed by Heaven's principle, the realization and nourishment of it is possible as an experienced reality both theoretically and practically.

In the Neo-Confucian tradition, such a conviction demands a spiritual discipline; nevertheless, it means to realize the ultimate truth of human nature as sagehood in daily existence. This religious path to self-transcendence involves what one can call "the relationship between Heaven as a religious absolute and the sage as a transformed person."[130] For T'oegye, however, it is quite different from one's theistic quest as an isolated person in an ascetic, monastic setting. As far as he is concerned, quiet-sitting meditation plays an important role in one's search for Heaven's principle right in one's inner nature. T'oegye's own experience suggestes a balancing synthesis of intellectual insight, emotional integration, contemplative reflection, moral effort, and spiritual cultivation, which can be complete only when it forms a continuum and harmony between the interior and the exterior.

The religious dimension of T'oegye's theory and practice of *simhak* also corresponds to his Neo-Confucian view of selfish human desires as evil. Obviously, it grew out of his *Four-Seven thesis* that sharply set the virtuous and spiritual order of principle before the emotional and material order of material force. In T'oegye's view, human nature in itself is to be found in sagehood because it shares the same reality with Heaven's principle. Hence, the key to his *kyŏnghak* is that one must experience the ultimate reality of Heaven's principle as one own inner nature. In a sense, this is *religious*, insofar as T'oegye maintains that such a process should be done contemplatively and spiritually in the mind-and-heart, not through one's theoretical speculation or textual study. In his view, the mind is not only a rational and emotional entity in the immanent sense, but, more important, something that has its own ultimate reality in the form of human nature in itself. He identified it as sagehood or Heaven's principle. Obviously, Neo-Confucian religiosity addresses the immanent-yet-transcendent dimension of human nature: in the case of T'oegye, it suggests a religious process of self-cultivation, the ultimate goal of which is to cultivate sagehood. This topic is discussed further in the concluding chapter.

V

Practical Implications for Yulgok

Current scholarship on the Korean Neo-Confucianism of Yulgok has made a significant contribution to our growing understanding of the subject. But most works, including those in English, are concerned primarily with the metaphysical patterns of Yulgok's Neo-Confucianism; his modern interpreters are impressed mainly by his philosophical writings, considering them a great systematization of the Ch'eng-Chu tradition in Korea.[1] But we are yet to understand the practical dimensions of his thought that closely relates to his Four-Seven thesis.

This chapter addresses this neglected, but important, topic: the context of Yulgok's Four-Seven thesis and its practical implication for self-cultivation. Our inquiry focuses on his interpretation of material force (*ki/ch'i*), as well as on its vital relationship with what he called the *nourishment of ki* (*yanggi/yang-ch'i*), *learning of sincerity* (*sŏnghak/ch'eng-hsüeh*) and *practical learning* (*sirhak/shih-hsüeh*). Because he presented his own experiences and insights, we shall look at a few previously untranslated materials as well, especially those from his mature philosophical works and his biographical accounts that were written after his Four-Seven debate with Ugye. In short, we will see that the practicality and vitality of Yulgok's Four-Seven thesis closely relate to his theory and method of self-cultivation with emphasis on its realistic and pragmatic dimension. To address such a topic is significant not only for a broader comprehension of Ch'eng-Chu Neo-Confucianism in general, but, more important, for a better understanding of Yulgok's Four-Seven thesis and its implications for the Confucian way of life.

Good and Evil: The Nourishment of *Ki*

Yulgok makes a clear observation on the problem of good and evil. For him, good and evil can never be two separate ideas nor ontological entities directly opposed to each other. His philosophy of *i* and *ki* closely relates to his Four-Seven thesis. In his own words, "what is manifest is *ki* and the reason for its manifestation is *i*."[2] "This is the earlier Confucian scholars' opinion," and "even if a sage arises again, he cannot dare change this statement."[3] This theory is central to his entire Neo-Confucian metaphysics and ethics. Because *i* is a "metaphysical" and "passive" principle, whereas *ki* is a "physical" and "active" force, it follows that "what is irregular and different" in cosmic transformation is due to the activity of *ki*. In his *Sŏnghak chipyo* (Outline of the Learning of the Sages),[4] a work compiled few years after his Four-Seven debate with Ugye, Yulgok articulates his view further: "What rides on the subtle moving and activating power of *ki* is *i*. . . . *I* is what is formless (*muhyŏng/wu-hsing*) and passive (*muwi/wu-wei*); hence, it is the master of what has form (*yuhyŏng/yu-hsing*) and is active (*yuwi/yu-wei*). *Ki* is what has form and is active; it is the concrete thing of the formless and passive *i*. This is the great beginning of the investigation of *i* and *ki*."[5] In all concrete phenomena, such as feelings and self-cultivation, *ki* is what acts and becomes manifest, although there must be *i* as the principle of, or ground for, the process of *ki*'s manifestation. Hence, any dualistic view of *i* and *ki* destroys the fundamental Ch'eng-Chu doctrine of the inseparability of *i* and *ki*.

One important philosophical concept in the history of Neo-Confucianism is *ki*. In Ch'ing Chinese intellectual history, it was often associated with such eminent thinkers as Wang Fu-chih (1613–1692), Yen Yüan (1635–1704), and Tai Chen (1724–1777), all of whom are known for their emphasis on the meaning and implication of *ki* in learning and self-cultivation. As Irene Bloom has amply indicated, however, the first Chinese thinker to develop such a philosophy was the Ming thinker Lo Ch'in-shun, who launched a significant change within the Ch'eng-Chu school.[6] In his *K'un-chih chi*, Lo criticized Chu Hsi's dualistic philosophy of *i* and *ki*, as well as its connection with the moral philosophy of mind, human nature, and feelings. In Tokugawa Japan, the philosophy of *ki* was advocated by the prominent Japanese scholars of the Chu Hsi school (Shushigaku), especially Hayashi Razan (1583–1657) and Kaibara Ekken (1630–1714).[7] Lo's *K'un-chih chi* was, in fact, an influential text for Hayashi Razan and Kaibara Ekken.[8] Regardless of philosophical differences among these them, these Neo-Confucians all opposed the self-autonomous and transcendent reality of *i* as something that can exist independent of the physical and immanent reality of *ki*. In Chosŏn Korea, Yulgok advocated a similar philosophy in the mid-sixteenth century. But we see strong traces of the influence of Lo Ch'in-shun especially his rethinking of Chu Hsi's metaphysics *i* and *ki*. Yulgok gave prominence not only to Kobong's Four-Seven thesis, but also Lo's interpretation of human nature and of *i* and *ki*. Lo's *K'un-chih chi* was an important text that Yulgok apparently admired.[9]

As we have seen in his Four-Seven thesis, Yulgok emphasized the physical and empirical reality of *ki*, while utilizing Lo's philosophy. The role of *ki* plays a vital current in Yulgok's theory and practice of self-cultivation. His understanding of good and evil is closely associated with his interpretation. The question is, Why does human nature lead to either good or evil when it is manifest in feelings, desires, or thoughts? This is, Yulgok argues, because, although *i* is purely and originally good, *ki* is not always pure and good in human beings. The original essence of *ki* is *i* itself; however, when turbid or impure *ki* controls the issuing process of feelings, it may lead one to evil. The following passage from his commentary will suffice to portray his conception of good and evil further: "What is *good* in the feelings rides on the clear and bright *ki* and is manifested straight from Heaven's principle, without deviating from the Mean. It may be viewed as the beginning of humanity, righteousness, propriety, and wisdom; hence, it refers to the Four Beginnings. Although what is *evil* in the feelings is also founded on *i*, it is already disturbed by impure and turbid *ki* which may cause excess in some cases or deficiency in other cases."[10] For this reason, as Yulgok points out, Ch'eng I said that good and evil are all due to Heaven's principle,[11] and Chu Hsi said that human desires are due to Heaven's principle.[12] Nevertheless, other scholars, such as T'oegye, who do not understand such theories consider the manifestation of *i* to be good feelings as the Four and the manifestation of *ki* to be evil feelings as the Seven. Yulgok argued, in his Four-Seven thesis, that T'oegye used a metaphysical and ethical *i-ki* dualism as the basis of his interpretation. Hence, he criticized T'oegye for presenting a dualistic analysis of the Four and the Seven in terms of the opposition of good and evil as well.

According to Yulgok, only after self-cultivation is established, can human nature be manifest as good, without being disturbed by physical form. The following passage describes his early determination to self-cultivation through what he calls the *nourishment of ki* (*yanggi/yang-ch'i*): "*Ki* can be transformed by nourishing it. Everyone is born with it. When it is well nourished, it comes under the control of our mind; when it is not nourished properly, our mind becomes its servant. When one's mind controls *ki*, one's body can serve as the master; therefore, one can become a sage or wise person. But when one's mind obeys *ki* . . . one cannot avoid becoming a foolish or crazy person. It was Mencius who, among ancient people, nourished *ki* well."[13] Given the Ch'eng-Chu doctrine that physical dispositions are divergent in terms of "clarity" and "purity," Yulgok argued that the learning of sagehood (*sŏnghak/sheng-hsüeh*) cannot be completed equally or satisfactorily by every one.[14] To accomplish the learning of sagehood, the method of self-cultivation, then, requires one to nourish *ki*. And everyone is capable of accomplishing it because each person is originally born with "upright" and "penetrating" *ki*. In his Four-Seven debate with Ugye, Yulgok makes an interesting statement about the task of self-cultivation:

> Heaven and Earth received what is perfectly upright and penetrating in *ki*; therefore, they have the fixed nature and, as a result, there is no change in them. The myriad things received what is partial and blocked; therefore, they also have fixed nature and, as a result, no change in them. Human beings received what is upright and penetrating in *ki*. But they have myriad variations of clarity, turbidity, or impurity and, thus, do not have the same purity of Heaven and Earth. And yet, the mind is open, clever and penetrating with the myriad principles complete in it. For this reason, what is turbid can be transformed to become clear, and what is impure can be transformed to become pure. Because only human beings have the effort at the practice of self-cultivation, they have to bring about the ultimacy of such a practice, just like the case that Heaven and Earth remain in fixed places. We can nourish and accomplish the myriad things. Only after this is done, our works will be complete.[15]

Here Yulgok means to do full justice to the Neo-Confucian conviction that human beings receive the best of *ki*, with a wide range covering various grades of purity. The sages are endowed with "the purest *ki*" and, therefore, able to "serve as the norm of others," in the same way as Heaven and Earth do as "the norm for the sages."[16] In other words, the achievement of sagehood is theoretically and practically possible in human beings only.

Self-cultivation is achieved by transforming the physical endowment of human nature. In his *Kyo kijil* (Straightening of Physical Endowment), a treatise on self-cultivation, Yulgok emphasizes: "One must straighten and control what is partial and turbid in one's physical endowment of *ki*."[17] Hence, Chang Tsai's saying that "the great benefit of learning lies in the transformation of physical nature"[18] corresponds to his own approach.[19] One should rectify and nourish *ki*[20] and should integrate one's practice of self-examination and self-correction.[21] This is, then, what Yulgok means by the nourishment of *ki* from a practical standpoint of self-cultivation. Such a discipline, of course, involves the moral and emotional harmonization of feelings, the focus of our next inquiry.

Self-Cultivation and Emotional Integration

In his Four-Seven thesis, Yulgok maintained that if one knows and nourishes the functioning of one's *ki*, then one's mind will follow moral principles.[22] Otherwise, self-cultivation is very difficult because one's feelings and desires attain their selfishness, as the mind becomes precarious. In the context of Yulgok's theory of the nourishment of *ki*, the underlying theme of his Four-Seven thesis suggests a positive view of feelings and desires. That is to say, the human feelings and desires are basically a good and natural part of human nature. When properly harmonized, all feelings and desires, including the Seven, are good. By affirming the human feelings and desires not as the source of evil, Yulgok opposed T'oegye directly and Chu Hsi indirectly, revealing his intellectual ability and scholarly confidence to challenge and reinterpret established authority. He criticized T'oegye for presenting a highly dualistic analysis of the Four and the Seven in terms of the opposition of good and evil. For Yulgok, one cannot say that Heaven's principle (*i*), as the source of our virtuous and moral behavior, represents the Four Beginnings, whereas the emotional and physical desires (*ki*), as the source of evil, represent the Seven.[23] His argument means that one cannot make any exclusive distinction or contrast between the virtuous behavior and the emotional and physical desires, between the moral mind and the human mind, and between the original human nature and the physical human nature. In other words, the Four and the Seven have what he calls a *mutual relationship* of continuum and interaction.

According to Yulgok's Four-Seven thesis, the "original human nature" refers to its unmanifested state without evil; when it is manifest in feelings, it can have either good or evil. All human beings respect moral principles such as benevolence, righteousness, and so on; these kinds of feelings refer to the innate feelings of virtuous behavior. And the state of acting on these moral principles refers to the moral mind.[24] Also, the "individual physical needs" of human beings (e.g., the desire of food and comfort), although they commonly originate from the same human nature, are not necessarily moral virtues and, thus, refer to the human mind.[25] The same argument is also evident in Yulgok's *Insim tosim tosŏl* (Diagrammatic Treatise on the Human Mind and the Moral Mind),[26] a work compiled few years after his Four-Seven debate with Ugye. Yulgok gives specific examples: "Aroused feelings include wanting to be filial to parents, wanting to be loyal to rulers, commiserating with a child falling into a well, having shame and dislike, discerning right and wrong, and showing courtesy and modesty when passing by an ancestral temple. These kinds of feelings are all aroused for moral rightness; therefore, they refer to the 'moral mind.' There are also those feelings like wanting to eat when hungry, wanting to put on clothes when cold, wanting to relax when tired, and wanting sex when one's semen is abundant. These kinds of feelings are aroused for specific physical needs; therefore, they refer to the 'human mind.'"[27] The moral mind and the human mind are the aroused states of deliberating for "moral principles" and "physical desires," respectively. Though the mind is one, the former represents the moral and ethical realm of the mind, whereas the latter represents the psychological and physiological realm of the mind. The fundamental difference between them is that the moral mind is purely good because it accords with Heaven's principle (that is, moral principles) and the human mind is either good or evil because it includes both Heaven's principle and human desires.[28] In Yulgok's view, due to "the principle of human nature" all human beings eat when hungry and put on clothes when cold, and this is also true for the sages and worthies who cannot avoid doing these natural things.[29] The sages are not different from ordinary people; however, they preserve the moral mind by overcoming selfish desires.

Embedded in Yulgok's argument is that all human feelings and desires are basically cognitive because they are aroused as the consciousness of our mind responds to external stimuli. His notion of emotion is somewhat similar to modern cognitive theories of emotion, according to which emotions are either wholly or partially cognition or dependent on consciousness. From Western perspectives, we can refer to it in terms of what is sometimes called the *behavioral theory* of emotion.[30] Those emotions that pertain to our physical, individual "needs" are aroused from what Western philosophers and psychologists call *physical sensations-perceptions*[31] accompanied by physiological disturbances.[32] Those emotions that belong to our moral virtuous behavior are aroused from value judgments.[33] Yulgok also says elsewhere: "Evil comes from one's physical endowment of nature confined to material desires, but it is not the original substance of human nature."[34] Even the wisest people, such as sages and worthies, have natural and physical feelings and desires because it is the principle of nature. In the "Sugi" (Self-Cultivation),[35] the first and most important part of his famous *Sŏnghak chipyo*, Yulgok states: "To be joyful when one should be joyful and to be angry when one should be angry refers to good feelings, while to be joyful when one should not be joyful and to be angry when one should not be angry refers to bad feelings."[36]

As revealed in his Four-Seven thesis, the fundamental implication of his argument is a significant moral issue. Addressing a concrete way of emotional integration, Yulgok emphasizes the "harmony-disharmony" link between the Four and the Seven. Although feelings are considered to be basically good, they can become evil if they are not properly harmonized and expressed. This is, he argues, due to one's excessive craving for physical, emotional, and material desires (food, pleasure, comfort, sex, and so on). The feelings and desires of sages and worthies follow moral principles. By contrast, those of inferior persons arise excessively, leading to evil; this is because their physical endowment is highly "turbid" and "impure."

According to Yulgok, the concrete prerequisite is to "make the resolve" (*ipchi/li-chih*) before the practice of nourishing *ki* and of harmonizing feelings. A key passage from his "Sugi" (Self-Cultivation) elucidates it as follows: "Nothing is prior than to make the resolve. If one's resolve is not established first, one cannot achieve one's learning completed. Thus, in this chapter on self-cultivation, I put the section on the making the resolve at the beginning."[37] As he argues, even the king must make sure that his resolve for learning and self-cultivation is clear and firmly established before he can establish a good, virtuous government.

One's goal of self-cultivation should be clear and determined. "One must have one's resolve first and model oneself after the norm of the sages."[38] In his *Manŏn pongsa* (Ten Thousand-Character Memorial),[39] a political treatise presented to the king, Yulgok argues that the prerequisite needed in the proper way of governing people is "to model himself after the sages."[40] Furthermore, the *Kyŏngmong yogyŏl* (Essential Instructions of Kyŏngmong), a systematic guide of learning, and the *Hakkyo mobŏm* (Model for an Academy), a treatise on the education of youth, illustrate a practical message that beginners of learning should, first, make their resolve and work toward the "goal of sagehood."[41] Yulgok urges the significance of making a resolve in terms of *ki*: "Resolve is the commander of *ki*. If it is one and undivided, there is nothing that *ki* moves. When one is unsuccessful . . . it is only due to the fact that one's resolve is not quite established."[42] In other words, one needs to be determined, and one's will toward learning should be firm before one attempts to nourish *ki*.

The unique feature of Yulgok's philosophy is precisely a pragmatic teaching: making the resolve is the basis of self-cultivation, and the nourishment of *ki* is the practical method of self-cultivation. It means to seek one's self-transformation right in one's established resolve. An important question arises here, How does one establish one's resolve for self-cultivation? Yulgok explicitly states: "When one is sincere, one's resolve is naturally established."[43] "Sincere will" is what really accomplishes self-cultivation. We can now examine this topic in relation to Yulgok's Four-Seven thesis and its implications for self-cultivation.

Sagehood and Learning Sincerity (*Sŏnghak*)

According to Yulgok, one can neither nourish one's *ki* nor harmonize one's feelings and emotions, unless one cultivates sincerity (*sŏng/ch'eng*).[44] In the *Sŏnghak chipyo* he argues that sincerity is the basis for the Neo-Confucian learning of sagehood (*sŏnghak/sheng-hsüeh*).[45] Sincerity is viewed by him as the fundamental virtue for nourishing *ki*, and the learning of "self-cultivation and governing people" must be founded on it. In fact, he identifies the learning for sagehood with "learning for sincerity" (*sŏnghak/ch'eng-hsüeh*), which constitutes the whole theme of his *Sŏnghak chipyo*.

The locus classicus for the Confucian idea of sincerity includes the *Great Learning*, *Doctrine of the Mean*, and Neo-Confucian writings especially those by Chou Tun-i (1017–1073). According to a famous credo in the first source, for instance, one should cultivate sincerity to investigate things, to rectify the mind-and-heart, to regulate one's family, and to bring peace and order to the world.[46] In other words, the virtue of sincerity means the source of intellectual, ethical, and socio-political development. Affirming sincerity as sagehood itself, the *Doctrine of the Mean* states: "Only those who are absolutely sincere can transform others."[47] An absolutely sincere person is a sage: "Sincerity is the Way of Heaven. To think how to be sincere is the way of human beings. A sincere person is one who hits upon what is right without effort and apprehends without thinking. Such a person is a sage. One who tries to be sincere is a person who chooses the good and holds fast to it."[48]

Embedded in this passage is the idea that the Confucian way of self-cultivation results from the cultivation of sincerity. Speaking more in the light of the *Doctrine of the Mean*, Chou Tun-i said: "Sincerity is the foundation of the sage."[49] He talked about both metaphysical and ethical aspects of the idea of sincerity. Sincerity is not only the source of all cosmic phenomena, but also the foundation of our moral nature: "Sagehood is nothing but sincerity. It is the foundation of the Five Constant Virtues (humanity, righteousness, propriety, wisdom, and faithfulness) and the source of all activities. When tranquil, it is in the state of non-being, and when active, it is in the state of being. It is perfectly correct and clearly penetrating. Without sincerity, the Five Constant Virtues and all activities will be wrong."[50] Chou meant that sincerity can be spoken of as having substance and function. In its state of tranquil reality, sincerity is has no activity; in its state of active manifestation, it is called the subtle, moving virtue. The idea of sincerity is so important that he considered it as the basis of his metaphysics and ethics.[51] As Chou argues, "The sage is the one who is in the state of sincerity."[52] A sage is, then, the most sincere person who is truthful to human nature, as well as to Heaven, Earth, and the myriad things.

What is Yulgok's interpretation of sincerity? His interpretation of sincerity appears in most of his philosophical works, especially the *Sŏnghak chipyo*, the *Sŏngch'aek* (Treatise on Sincerity),[53] the *Saja ŏnsŏng ch'aek* (Treatise on Questions About the Statements on Sincerity in the Four Books),[54] and his political memorials.[55] In his Four-Seven thesis, Yulgok argues that self-cultivation is "to make one's will sincere first" and to harmonize feelings.[56] Following the *Doctrine of the Mean* and Chou Tun-i's philosophy, he believed that the sincere will is the foundation of the moral nature, and one can arrive at sagehood through self-cultivation with it. According to his *Sŏnghak chipyo*, "to make the will sincere" is the most important basis for the "learning for sagehood."[57] In the light of the *Great Learning*, he argues that "to make oneself sincere" is the beginning and end of one's effort at the learning for sagehood, and it includes "the investigation of things" and then putting it into practice.[58] Sincerity is what enables one to nourish one's *ki*, and the extension of knowledge is invalidated unless it is always accompanied by sincere self-determination. It is thought to be the absolute "truth without any falsehood," which is identical to "Heaven's principle."[59] This implies that sincerity is the real authentic mind of the human being.

For Yulgok, one can become a sage if one follows Heaven's principle in complete sincerity, attaining what he calls the *totality of sincerity* that can reach Heaven, Earth, and the mind-and-heart. A statement from the *Sŏngch'aek* elucidates Yulgok's point further: "Heaven has the merit of transformation and nourishment [of all things] with its real principle (*silli/shih-li*).[60] The human being has a real mind (*silsim/shih-hsin*)[61] and can bring about reciprocity and response of what is felt and penetrating. The real principle and the real mind are nothing but sincerity itself. One who possesses the purity of Heaven's principle and acquires complete sincerity entirely is a sage. One who truly possesses a part of Heaven's principle and acquires partial sincerity is a wise person."[62] The reality of Heaven's principle and the reality of the human mind-and-heart are understood in the sense of forming a harmony in sincerity. Sincerity refers to the constant substance of Heaven's principle. In the *Sŏnghak chipyo*, Yulgok says: "Human beings have a real mind; therefore, their effort of learning can become broad and bright without any flaw. If one does not preserve it, one deviates from Heaven's principle."[63] For him, then, the starting point and final end of the learning for sagehood must be founded on sincerity, from which all rational and moral endeavors take their proper places.

Speaking in the light of the *Doctrine of the Mean*, Yulgok writes: "It is said that even the investigation of principle is impossible without sincerity."[64] This is, he argues, because sincerity is the source of self-cultivation required for the gradual path to sagehood. Even the extension of knowledge is invalidated unless it accompanies sincere will. Yulgok thus underscores that, when one investigates the principles of things to the utmost in sincerity, one will attain what he calls *true knowledge* (*silchi/shih-chih*) and become a sage.[65] Sincerity consists of both "substance" and "function." In this regard, Yulgok followed Chou Tun-i but moved beyond his understanding of sincerity. He states: "As foundation, sincerity is extremely subtle and mysterious. As function, sincerity is absolutely manifest and supremely broad. Its substance is everything and becomes the beginning and end of things. Therefore, origination, flourishing, advantage, and firmness[66] are the sincerity of Heaven; benevolence, righteousness, propriety, and wisdom are the sincerity of human nature."[67] Commenting on the practice of self-examination, Yulgok also argues: "Sincerity is the real principle of Heaven and the original substance of the mind-and-heart."[68] The substance (reality) of sincerity is said to be very "subtle"; however, when it is manifest in human beings, it functions as moral principles. To put it in another way, sincerity is something that the human being already possesses as an inherent moral virtue within the mind (*sim/hsin*).

The Neo-Confucian concept of the mind is understood as the master of one's body and the commander of human nature and feelings. Yulgok states: "Without sincerity, the original essence of Heaven's principle cannot exist."[69] Because sincerity itself combines Heaven's principle as its substance and the mind of the human being as its function, it can be realized and nourished in human beings. Yulgok writes: "Sincerity is the truth that has no falsehood; it is that which has the real principle. What is called knowledge can be discussed from the standpoint of sincerity."[70] The mind can be conceived of as the essence of the effort of uniting oneself with Heaven. As Yulgok asserts, the *way of Heaven* (*ch'ŏndo/t'ien-tao*) refers to the "real principle," whereas the *human way* (*indo/jen-tao*) is called the "real mind."[71] Furthermore, the principle characterized by sincerity refers to the clear and pure physical nature of the sage; therefore, sagehood can be attained by cultivating complete sincerity.[72]

What does Yulgok mean? In the light of *Doctrine of the Mean*, he means that *sincerity-in-itself* refers to the Heavenly way as the real principle, and the human way can become sincere to realize and preserve it. The Confucian conviction is that Heaven by nature is completely sincere; hence, the profound responsibility of human beings is to transform themselves into sincere persons in accordance with moral principles endowed by Heaven's principle, or real principle, itself. As Tu Wei-ming comments, the reason that one has to cultivate the sincere will is because "our nature is originally so endowed"[73] from Heaven's principle. Sincerity is the essential force that makes one a true human being so that one can relate oneself to Heaven, Earth, and other human beings. From Yulgok's epistemological and moral standpoint, it includes both the real principle for actualization of things and the real mind as the originator of knowledge. On the metaphysical level, it is equivalent to *i*-in-itself; in concrete phenomena, however, it can be cultivated and realized in one's mind-and-heart. In sincerity, then, human beings can be united with moral principles and the myriad things. If one acquires complete sincerity, one can become a sage: "Nothing can exist without sincerity. The nature of the sages is sincerity. A superior person is the person of sincerity."[74] The sages are, therefore, completely authentic and sincere. This is why Yulgok believes that even the superior persons and ordinary people cannot lack sincerity; one must strive for it constantly, so that one can cultivate "complete sincerity." When one possesses sincerity, one will become a morally upright person.

In his letter to Ugye, a letter written prior to their Four-Seven debate, Yulgok describes variations of success in learning and self-cultivation in terms of difference between the "sage" (*sŏngin/sheng-jen*), the "superior person" (*kunja/chün-tzu*), and the "learning person" (*hakja/hsüeh-che*): "one who investigated things to the utmost, extended knowledge to the utmost, made the will sincere to the utmost, and rectified the mind to the utmost is a sage"; one who tried all of these but "could not achieve them to the utmost" is a superior person; and one who "wishes to do them" is a learning person.[75] In this regard, sincerity itself is thought to be "true knowledge."[76] Accordingly, the sincerity shown by the sage is the norm that others should follow. One's attainment of true knowledge is impossible without cultivating sincerity.

Another important question is, How does Yulgok's idea of sincerity relate to his Four-Seven thesis, as well as to his understanding of the nourishment of *ki*? In the *Sŏnghak chipyo*, he asserts that the original substance (*ponch'e/pen-t'i*) of the mind is "tranquil, void, and bright like a clean mirror and a still beam of a balance."[77] He explains further: "But when it is stimulated by external things, the Seven Emotions are aroused and respond to them. This is the functioning of the mind. When *ki* is confined to selfish desires, the original substance of the mind cannot be established; therefore, the functioning of the mind deviates from its correctness."[78] The principles of myriad things are, Yulgok argues, complete in the mind; for example, the benevolence of two sages, Yao and Shun, the righteousness of King Wu, and the Way of Confucius and Mencius are all innate characteristics of human nature.[79] But when they are disturbed by selfish material desires, a good person will be confused. Sincerity extends the mind-in-itself ("real mind") that is "the real principle of Heaven" and "the original substance of the mind" as well; therefore, in pursuing self-cultivation, one must first make one's will sincere.[80] Because the mind is the full manifestation of Heaven's principle, it follows for Yulgok that it can fully realize sincerity. Obviously, this argument corresponds to his theory of "the nourishment of *ki*." In the context of his *Four-Seven thesis,* it also means emotional harmony in the practice of self-cultivation. Because the mind commands and directs human nature and feelings, to control the Seven Emotions is embodied within one's cultivation of sincerity.

How does one learn to be sincere and abide in sincerity? More specifically, what is the actual method of attaining complete sincerity? According to the *Doctrine of the Mean,* human nature is said to be a genuine manifestation of Heaven because it is imparted from Heaven.[81] From the Confucian ontological and moral standpoint, the human way and the way of Heaven share the same reality. Sincerity itself is, therefore, the means of uniting the Heavenly way and the human way; in complete sincerity lies the harmony and union between Heaven, Earth, and human beings. Yulgok says: "When one has already made one's learning sincere, one must, then, rectify the distortion of physical endowment to recover one's original human nature."[82] This is precisely the reason why he emphasized the nourishment of the physical endowment of one's nature through the moral integration of one's feelings and desires. Of course, his Four-Seven thesis, which is focused on a philosophy of *ki,* is highly relevant to his philosophical and moral arguments about the idea of sincerity.

The Confucian understanding of sincerity does not imply an extraordinary or unusual state of our mind. The virtue of sincerity is, rather, to be nourished in daily life. To borrow Wing-tsit Chan's terminology, it means to be understood as something relevant to the "ordinary deeds" of "ordinary" persons.[83] It involves a constant process of moral cultivation and action. For Yulgok, it is the essence of human nature, and the completion of a person is not possible without cultivating it and without extending it to other beings and things. The beginning and end of the learning for sagehood are, Yulgok argues, sincerity from which the practice of other Confucian virtues take their proper place in the external and physical reality of *ki.* As Young-chan Ro correctly points out in his recent study of Yulgok's philosophy, "Making reality sincere is inseparable from the individual's own personal cultivation of sincerity, as the individual's sincere mind must necessarily find expression—through into action—in the world around him."[84] For Yulgok, then, the task of self-cultivation is to illuminate goodness that innately culminates in sincerity. The cultivation of sincerity and the actual practice of it in one's daily life are equally significant.

As the foundation of self-cultivation, sincerity enables one to nourish one's own *ki*, such that one can transform bad thoughts, feelings, and desires. Perhaps, Yulgok argued from a standpoint of his own experiences and insights. He means that sincerity is not merely a specific concept of moral action, but, more important, pertains to the metaphysical and ethical foundation of all phenomena. This somewhat accords with the tradition of the *Doctrine of the Mean* and Chou Tun-i's interpretation, which explained sincerity in a similar manner. However, Yulgok's interpretation seems to go beyond the Chinese tradition by addressing specific questions and issues in both metaphysical and ethical contexts, as well as by relating them to the other theoretical themes and practical implications of his Neo-Confucianism, notably emotional integration and the nourishment of *ki* according to his Four-Seven thesis. As the foundation of all reality, sincerity ties principle and the mind together, thereby providing the theoretical and practical basis that sagehood through the self-cultivation of sincerity is possible.

Presenting Yulgok's philosophy of sincerity in terms of the unity between theory and practice, Young-chan Ro correctly points out that it has a "pragmatic" theme that closely relates to his philosophy of the mind. But Ro goes on to argue that "the practice of *ch'eng* (sincerity) is not limited to the moral and intellectual dimensions, but extends to a *religious dimension* as well"[85] and "through the concept of *ch'eng* this process of moral cultivation takes on a decidedly *religious meaning*, embodying a vision of the total transformation of social and cosmic orders as well."[86] Ro's argument seems to suggest that, from a standpoint of the ultimate reality of sincerity, Yulgok tended to affirm the continuum of the transcendent and the immanent and the inseparability of metaphysics and ethics. Nevertheless, Ro's interpretation does not seem to clarify the extent to which the "religious dimension," or "religious meaning," of Yulgok's thought, if any, is relevant to what he calls the *pragmatic* themes of it.

As revealed in Yulgok's Four-Seven thesis, as well as in its implications for self-cultivation, he was not concerned with the inner-directed, religious practices of Neo-Confucianism. Unlike T'oegye, he did not talk about spiritual exercises such as quiet-sitting meditation and personal cultivation. On the basis of what we have observed so far in this chapter, we can see why

Yulgok rejected T'oegye's Four-Seven thesis, as well as its implications for the contemplative and inner-directed way of self-cultivation that closely relates to T'oegye's philosophy of *i*. A pragmatic thinker and active politician, he was more interested in formulating an empirical philosophy of *ki* as the basis of his Four-Seven thesis and other writings. In other words, he addressed the realistic dimensions of the Neo-Confucian way of learning and self-cultivation, especially in the context of such a philosophy. This is why he emphasized the following points: first, *ki*, not *i*, is manifest in all cosmic phenomena including feelings; second, *ki* should be nourished in the process of learning and self-cultivation; third, one must establish one's revolve for such a task; and finally, one must cultivate sincerity to nourish *ki* and harmonize feelings and desires. Unlike T'oegye's version of Ch'eng-Chu Neo-Confucianism, then, Yulgok's version is more practically oriented toward the objective reality of *ki* in relation to the matters of daily life including politics and society. Hence, we have no evidence to suggest that Yulgok's systematization of Neo-Confucianism involves any religious dimension.

To Yulgok, then, the "learning for sincerity" must extend goodness to one's active daily life. The completion of a "sincere person" is impossible unless it forms a concrete network with all levels of Confucian culture. This process is significant, especially for establishing and maintaining a healthy and prosperous Confucian society. By *sage* Yulgok means an ideal political ruler as well. In articulating a philosophy of sincerity in ethico-political terms, he developed it further into a political ideal. The core of his theory and practice of self-cultivation thus points to such a pragmatic theme. It developed into what he calls *practical learning* (*sirhak/shih-hsüeh*), the focus of our next investigation.

Practical Learning (*Sirhak*) as an Ethico-Political Ideal

According to Yulgok, practical learning for "self-cultivation and governing people" must be founded on sincerity.[87] This is, indeed, a vital theme in most of his writings. To understand it, we have to examine his political thought more closely, so that we can determine what kind of practicality it contains and how it relates to his philosophy of *ki* and self-cultivation, the central theme of his Four-Seven thesis. We should also analyze his political reform ideas in the Neo-Confucian context; this is significant not only because Yulgok took government administration as a serious matter of the Confucian way of life, but also because the Neo-Confucian idea of sagehood is an attainable goal that required a Confucian model of learning, self-cultivation, and socio-political responsibility. It is particularly under this aspect that sagehood became a profoundly ethicopolitical ideal in his Neo-Confucianism.

First of all, we need to address the extent to which Confucianism is a practical learning, as such a topic has been debated in current scholarship. Confucianism (*yugyo/ju-chiao*; literally meaning "the learning of the literati") was a common intellectual, ethical, and spiritual tradition in East Asia. Even as a form of "ethical humanism," "socio-political ideology," or "secular religion," we may call it a practically oriented tradition. It maintained its humanistic teachings and their practical implications for transforming human beings through a universal path of learning and self-cultivation, as well as for promoting moral order and socio-political harmony. For this reason, the paramount spirit of classical Confucianism and Neo-Confucianism endeavored to be "practical" as opposed to "theoretical." But the Confucian tradition, like some other major philosophical or religious traditions of the world, involved a good deal of classical learning, intellectual inquiry, and moral cultivation. Whether the philosophical doctrines and ethical norms of the Ch'eng-Chu school were "pragmatic" enough from a strict Western standpoint of developing "functional" or "utilitarian" ideas, values, and results is a challenging question that is still open to debate.[88] This question involves the extent to which they fostered economic growth or scientific revolution. It is, indeed, a sophisticated subject to talk about the Neo-Confucian notion of "practical learning."

On the whole, the entire Confucian tradition offered a rationalistic learning in the context of emphasizing the unity of knowledge and action. It was not purely a positivistic or utilitarian learning, however. In his comparative work on religion and social change, the German sociologist and comparative religionist Max Weber interpreted the negative roles of Confucianism as a fundamental factor in hindering economic development and socio-political modernization in traditional China.[89] In recent years, East Asian critics analyzed Neo-Confucianism in similar ways, arguing that it did not produce any serious interest in economy, science, and technology.[90] Chu Hsi's Neo-Confucianism addresses the investigation of things and the extension of knowledge, with a strong demand for applying them to self-cultivation and social and political orders. In this regard, we may still argue that it was practical and did have its own empirical and scientific dimensions.[91]

The Chinese and Japanese Neo-Confucian notions of practical learning have been articulated elsewhere with more expertise than is necessary here.[92] What we need to clarify, however, is its subtle meanings and implications. Etymologically speaking, *sil/shih* means "seed" and "fruition," signifying the idea of a concrete phenomenon with respect to actual existence, concrete knowledge, and fruitful consequence. In both ordinary and philosophical languages, it means "truth," "reality," "substantiality," or "practicality" (as a noun), and "true," "real," "substantial," or "practical" (as an adjective). "Practicality" and "practical" are accepted as two standard renderings for it. Because the term *hak/hsüeh* means "learning," the Neo-Confucian notion of *sirhak/shih-hsüeh* refers to "practical learning," "learning for practicality," "substantial learning," "real learning," and so on. This points to the importance of inquiring concrete things and empirical principles; such a learning is intended for a goal of bringing about real and fruitful outcomes for the sake of both personal and communal progress. Regarding the ethical and psychological philosophy of the Ch'eng-Chu tradition, it also requires the practice of self-cultivation. In short, its flexible meanings and implications closely interrelate to each other, not only linguistically but also philosophically and ethically.

It was originally Sung Chinese Neo-Confucians who spoke of *sirhak/shih-hsüeh*. As de Bary points out, Ch'eng I and Chu Hsi used the term *sil/shih* to preach the "real," "solid," and "substantial" features of their systems of thought in reaction to the Han and T'ang Confucian tradition of textual commentary, as well as in opposition to what they saw as the negativism and quietism of the Buddhists and Taoists.[93] From the Confucian standpoint of moral values and socio-political responsibilities, they criticized especially Buddhism as an "impractical" or "empty" learning. Chu Hsi spoke of practical learning in the context of unifying the inner and outer dimensions of the world. He defended Neo-Confucianism as the most constructive way of learning, arguing that it assimilates philosophical ideas, moral values, and socio-political concerns. His Neo-Confucianism can be considered a practical learning in the sense of synthesizing "broad learning, scholarly mastery of the classics and literature, a humane concern for fellowman, and dedication to public service."[94]

By *practical learning* Chu Hsi meant that when one studies principles (*i/li*), one should do it with respect to concrete phenomena and their implications for daily matters.[95] He rejected the mere practice of self-cultivation that ignores the objective investigation of principles, as well as any rational learning that does not apply concrete principles to self-cultivation and socio-political responsibilities. In other words, "the practicality of moral values" entails "both the experiential and empirical aspects of principles as seen in things and affairs."[96] Chu Hsi's method of learning addresses intellectual, moral and spiritual growth at the same time. As Cheng Chung-ying points out, although it had "moral practicality" in terms of emphasizing "morality," "social interaction," and "political activity," it lacked "utilitarian practicality."[97] From a strict standpoint of contemporary thought, it offers no explicit set of pragmatic ideas, functional methods, and utilitarian concerns for promoting economy, science, or technology. This is partly why the advocates of the later Practical Learning school criticized it as a scholastic tradition of book learning with emphasis on textual study and theoretical knowledge. Nonetheless, we need to appreciate the flexible scope of Chu Hsi's Neo-Confucianism; that is to say, it recognized practical learning not only in relation to the empirical study of concrete things and principles, but also in the original Confucian context of maintaining moral, social, and political orders.

How did Yulgok view Chu Hsi's notion of practical learning? For Yulgok, it was too broad and diffuse. In other words, it lacked a clear-cut path needed for urgent economic, social, and political needs of Korean society. Yulgok realized that it did not single out direct political guidelines in terms of political systems and institutions. One may see his criterion for practical learning in terms of personal determination, pragmatic methods, and effective actions. On the basis of this criterion, he urged an effective way of learning and government administration. Commenting on Yulgok's metaphysics, Young-chan Ro points out that Yulgok emphasized harmony between theory and practice. Ro argues that its "pragmatic" theme gave rise to the *sirhak* school in Korea: "[Yulgok's] view of sincere reality as a natural and necessary outcome of the individual cultivation of sincerity led Yulgok to establish *a type of pragmatism, the forerunner of what would later be called 'practical learning'*."[98] This is a worthwhile reading of Yulgok's philosophy of sincerity in the Neo-Confucian sense of self-cultivation. But we need to articulate more clearly the interrelationship between Yulgok's "pragmatism" and the Practical Learning school in Korea.

A strikingly common feature of Yulgok's major writings is the central theme of "practical learning" as a political ideal. The *Sŏnghak chipyo,* which was written shortly after his Four-Seven debate with Ugye, is a good example that illustrates his political view that sincerity and *sirhak* are the ultimate means to sagehood through establishing and enlarging a proper political "ideology of governing people."[99] The idea of "practicality" (*sil/shih*) in relation to sincerity and practical learning occupies a central position in Yulgok's political thought. This appears almost everywhere, including his philosophical treatises and recorded sayings. In addition to the *Sŏnghak chipyo,* his political memorials, such as the *Manŏn pongsa,*[100] *Simu yukcho kye* (Six-Article Memorial for Current Affairs),[101] and *Tongho mundap* (Tongho Questions and Answers),[102] are all addressed to the king and demonstrate his ethico-political theory that sincerity and practicality are two fundamental things needed to rectify the mind-and-heart, to rule the country and, thus, to follow the way of the sage-kings. All of these works are quite systematic in style and pragmatic in content. The vocabulary presented clearly reveal Yulgok's conviction that Neo-Confucian learning must be empirical and realistic for daily ethical, economic, and socio-political matters. Yulgok himself was concerned with practical ideas and interests, rather than theoretical and subjective dimensions of Neo-Confucianism. Although the spirit of his *Sŏnghak chipyo* is Neo-Confucian, he formulated a political ideology of practical learning in a series of systematic themes and consistent discussions.

To Yulgok's mind, Confucian learning is not only for "extending knowledge," but, more important, for putting it into *practice* in daily life. In his eighth Four-Seven letter to Ugye, Yulgok addressed "three grades of knowledge," from an epistemological standpoint of Neo-Confucianism: first, those who read "books of sages and worthies," "simply follow what is said," and "acquire a literal meaning" belong to the worst group of scholars who attained the "lowest level of knowledge"; second, those who read books, get the literal meaning, and "acquire real insights" belong to the next group of scholars who attained "the middle level of knowledge"; and finally, those who not only "understand the former sages and worthies' sayings" and "acquire insights from personal experience," but also "put them into actual daily practice" belong to the best group because they actually attain "the highest level of knowledge by realizing the truth to the utmost."[103] To explain his argument further, he uses a concrete example of mountain climbing:

> It is like mountain climbing. When one ascends the mountain, one can see a view which is not the same as hearing about it from others. Furthermore, when one reaches the peak, one commands the entire view, becoming completely liberated from a partial view from one side or the partial reports of others. In other words, those who never saw the mountain and know generally about it simply by hearing from others' words belong to the lowest class; those who never climb up to the peak and know the mountain incompletely by seeing it partially from one side belong to the middle class; those who actually reach the peak and command the entire view from there, becoming completely liberated from a partial view from one side or from the partial reports of others, belong to the highest class.[104]

Similarly, those who follow the words of sages and worthies blindly without understanding the subtle meanings of their sayings are the scholars of the lowest group. In this case, Yulgok argues, they can easily misunderstand the actual meanings of the former sages and worthies' teachings or they can be misled by ambiguous statements.[105] Of course, the implication of the Four-Seven thesis is very relevant here.

Yulgok says in the *Hakkyo mobŏm*, a treatise on the education of youth, that "the empty words of bad scholars has no practicality."[106] For learning, then, one must work hard on actions; otherwise, "our learning is nothing but a vulgar affair."[107] For Yulgok, Confucian learning is not a "nominal" process; students must concentrate on the "practicality of learning."[108] Good scholars must seek the practical implications of learning.[109] In other words, they are simultaneously good thinkers and politicians. In the *Kyŏngyŏn ilgi* (A Diary of Lectures Before the Throne),[110] Yulgok argues that the king cannot govern the nation properly if his learning and self-cultivation are not practically oriented.[111]

The *Sŏnghak chipyo* underscores the practical unity of "knowledge" and "action": "In the effort of self-cultivation are both the way of knowledge and the way of action. The way of knowledge is to illuminate good, and the way of action is to make the self sincere."[112] In another passage, we read: "Only after the investigation of principle is properly done, can one put oneself into practice. Hence, there must be the practical mind (*silsim/shih-hsin*) before one can have any practical achievement."[113] The underlying theme of Yulgok's argument means that the mind-and-heart" (*sim/hsin*) is the master of knowledge and action; it is what makes one's learning possible and useful. It is thus crucial to maintain the practically oriented mind: "Without the practical mind, one cannot understand the myriad things and cannot put them into practice. If one's mind is practical, all phenomena are true, and they can be all understood. This is why Chou Tun-i said: 'Sincerity is the foundation of the sages.'[114] I think that sincerity is the foundation of self-cultivation and government administration."[115] In the context of Yulgok's Four-Seven thesis, one's efforts at straightening physical nature, nourishing *ki,* and investigating the principles of things can be fruitful.[116] Without practical learning, then, one can neither achieve self-cultivation nor put what one learned into practice.

In most cases, Yulgok refers to *sirhak* not as a theory of practical learning, but as a tangible process of functional and fruitful ethico-political actions. It is a method to obtain what he calls *practical result* and *practical achievement.* But all of these cannot be achieved unless they are accompanied by "established resolve" and "sincere effort." Yulgok's *sirhak* is focused on the following themes: first, one should have one's "practical mind" and extend it to seek "practical principles"; second, one puts it into "actual practice"; third, one should deal with "practical affairs and works"; and finally, one experiences "practical result." All of these correspond to the Neo-Confucian notion of the term *sil/shih* and its implications for the Confucian way of life. Yulgok means practical learning in terms of the usefulness and practicality of its ethico-political relevance. The process of attaining a sagely government and society must begin at the top with the ruler's commitment to learning and self-cultivation. Given such a commitment to the political relevance of Neo-Confucianism, Yulgok criticized the existing social structures and political institutions of the Chosŏn dynasty and, thus, formulated a set of concrete reform measures.

Yulgok's political career reveals his vigorous commitment to addressing urgent national needs. As his official positions in various areas demonstrate, the scope of his *sirhak* is remarkable, covering many areas from ethics to historical research, law, popular education, social structures, military strategies, and politics. In 1569 Yulgok, an influential junior statesman, submitted to the king the *Tongho mundap*, a political treatise, which consists of eleven articles on political reform, including the policy for "securing people's welfare" and the popular "education of people."[117] In 1574 he submitted to the king the *Manŏn pongsa* in which he presents the ethico-political essence of his *sirhak* that for self-cultivation one must have "practical achievement" (*silgong/shih-kung*) and "to comfort the people" one must have a "practical mind-and-heart" (*silsim/shih-hsin*).[118] In addition, he points out seven national problems that are caused by lack of "practical achievement" in maintaining an effective system of government administration.[119] As minister of defense, he also wrote in 1583 the *Simu yukcho kye*, a critical political treatise, proposing six urgent programs for government reform, including the education of people.[120] He advocated other reform measures as well, such as "government for people" and government by "public opinion," which tend to correspond to the spirit of modern democracy.[121] All of these reformist tendencies reveal his serious dedication to practical learning and its concrete implications for government administration and socio-political reform. Although never accepted by the conservative Chosŏn bureaucracy,[122] they did address economic progress and socio-political reform with a practical and functional way of establishing and enlarging an egalitarian and prosperous society in the Neo-Confucian context.

During the eighteenth and nineteenth centuries, most reformers in Ch'ing China, Chosŏn Korea, and Tokugawa Japan criticized especially the orthodox Chu Hsi tradition as an abstract or impractical learning that maintained its traditional and nonreformist affinities. The Korean Practical Learning (Sirhak) scholars, such as Yi Ik (Sŏngho, 1681–1763), Pak Chega

(Ch'och'ŏng, 1750–1805), and Chŏng Yagyong (Tasan, 1762–1836), argued that it failed to comprehend new ideas and values. Although these men were initially trained in the Chu Hsi tradition, they condemned it as an "empty" or "lip-service" learning that could not confront new historical conditions, especially the urgent economic and socio-political problems.[123] Defining the term *sirhak* in the context of promoting a direct beneficial affluence on the daily lives of people, they made a clear-cut distinction between traditional Neo-Confucianism and their *sirhak*.[124] In this regard, *sirhak* was a new learning not only for reforming the bureaucratic institutions of the nation, but also for developing economy, science, and technology. And yet, the empirical and pragmatic features of Yulgok's philosophy of *sirhak* and their implications for economic and political reform exerted a significant impact on the rise of Practical Learning school among Korean Neo-Confucian reformers. This will be discussed further in the next chapter.

If we define *utilitarian practicality* in terms of ordering the state, transforming the society, and benefiting the people through concrete economic and political measures, then Yulgok's *sirhak* has an utilitarian practicality. Even if we define it in terms of a pragmatic way to reform and modernize the state or a functional way to deal with new economic and social needs, Yulgok's *sirhak* qualifies well as a Neo-Confucian form of utilitarian learning. On the contrary, if it is defined in the strict contemporary (but narrow) sense of advancing science and technology, then the practical, pragmatic, and reformist dimension of his *sirhak* fail to satisfy such a definition. Empirical rationality and functional practicality are two important features of Yulgok's Neo-Confucianism. It was philosophically and ethically appropriate for Yulgok to reinterpret the theoretical and practical patterns of Ch'eng-Chu Neo-Confucianism. Realizing the lack of a concrete political guide in the Ch'eng-Chu tradition, he offered an integrated ethico-political system of realistic strategies and applications, one that could deal with an utilitarian reform appropriate for the contemporary Korean context. Although the essence of his *sirhak* is based on Ch'eng-Chu Neo-Confucianism, it is carefully furnished with a systematic framework in which he strived to strengthen Neo-Confucian political ideas and ideals. Its vital implications for sagehood and political reform are based on his philosophy of *ki* that grew especially out of his *Four-Seven thesis*. This, then, concludes our analysis of the practical implications of Yulgok's Four-Seven philosophy, bringing us to a comparative study of T'oegye and Yulgok in the following chapter.

VI

Conclusions: A Comparison of T'oegye and Yulgok

The underlying theme in the foregoing chapters has been the Korean Neo-Confucian Four-Seven thesis and its implications for self-cultivation and other related themes. In this final chapter, it is my intention to interpret the unfolding results of the preceding chapters in terms of certain polarities between T'oegye and Yulgok that I find present within the whole framework of the subject matter. Undoubtedly, both harmony and tension are exhibited between metaphysics and ethics, between theory and practice, and between goal and method, as the two Korean thinkers themselves realized. We need to examine, at closer range, the fundamental similarities and differences between the philosophy of T'oegye, on the one hand, and the philosophy of Yulgok, on the other hand. It is also necessary to make references to Chu Hsi and other Neo-Confucians, whenever this is helpful in our understanding of the two Korean thinkers.

I believe that the preceding textual, comprehensive, and systematic discussion of T'oegye and Yulgok has settled certain issues that arose from the topic. Before moving further, the key patterns of commonality must be stated here: first, for both T'oegye and Yulgok at least, the significance of the Four-Seven controversy has a close link to the problem of the relationship between mind, human nature, and feelings-emotions; second, they committed themselves seriously to the task of understanding the role of feelings-emotions in the practice of self-cultivation; third, each thinker's own interpetation of it shaped his Four-Seven thesis; fourth, its central and vital motif was neither speculative nor abstract, but rather resulted from personal experiences and insights; fifth, the ways in which both thinkers interpreted the norms of Ch'eng-Chu Neo-Confucianism reveal not only philosophical concepts, but also ethico-spiritual concerns for the ultimate goal of cultivating sagehood; and last, each man maintained a remarkable consistency in his Four-Seven thesis and its implications for his proposed methods of self-cultivation.

Generally speaking, T'oegye and Yulgok tend to agree with certain Neo-Confucian norms. More specifically, they were able to make some compromise between their Four-Seven theses and Chu Hsi's Neo-Confucianism. As the two leading thinkers of the orthodox Sŏngnihak tradition in sixteenth century Korea, they shared a common scholarly commitment to the Ch'eng-Chu school. Given such a commitment, it was natural for them to clarify and reinterpret the existing Ch'eng-Chu literature. Each thinker's vocabulary indicates fundamental patterns of philosophical continuity, including such ideas as *i* and *ki*, the Four Beginnings and the Seven Emotions, human nature, mind-and-heart, reverential seriousness, sincerity, sagehood, self-cultivation, and practical learning. In fact, all of these ideas come from the basic Confucian texts, especially the Four Books and Ch'eng-Chu Neo-Confucian writings. Both thinkers discussed enough of the original materials not only to support their own theoretical and practical arguments, but also to enable their challengers to contemplate on their own philosophizing.

As we have noticed, however, both T'oegye and Yulgok realized a few fundamental problems and issues of the subject matter in classical texts and Ch'eng-Chu teachings. It was, of course, a sign of fretful ambiguity at the heart of this Neo-Confucian orthodoxy that the Four-Seven debate continued to remain a wellspring of controversial but creative thought for them and their challengers, who all confessed that the debate should move beyond orthodox teachings. There is no doubt that, with respect to the metaphysics of *i* and *ki* and the method of self-cultivation, each thinker engendered a definite shift within the Korean Sŏngnihak tradition, and the shift occurred according to his own philosophical and moral reasoning. On the basis of personal experiences and insights, both thinkers formulated their own ideas and values to give fresh meanings to the old vocabulary, thereby producing two rejuvenated but divergent interpretations. As the two Korean paradigms of the Ch'eng-Chu school, they sought to ground rationality, morality, and spirituality on such a tradition. And yet, this still reveals certain patterns of *change* and *synthesis* especially in terms of their own sets of experiential and hermeneutical categories.

As far as T'oegye's and Yulgok's interpretations of learning and self-cultivation are concerned, it is not possible to speculate on any concrete phenomenon of the universe without relating it to mind, human nature, and feelings. In other words, the Neo-Confucian doctrine of human nature and its philosophical and moral psychology of mind and feelings must be understood in the light of its metaphysics of *i* and *ki*. Any separate treatment of specific metaphysical, ethical, or psychological issues alone does not do full justice to the whole Neo-Confucian tradition in general and T'oegye and Yulgok in particular; such an exclusivist approach would be improper for understanding Neo-Confucian rationality, morality, and spirituality as a whole. These aspects of the two Korean thinkers' Four-Seven theses are inseparable from one another and, therefore, most effectively understood in the context of addressing them together. In fact, they demonstrated Neo-Confucian belief in the harmonious link between metaphysics and ethics, between philosophical assumptions and concrete practices, and between theoretical goals and practical methods. We need to realize that, in addressing the status and role of feelings and emotions and their implications for self-cultivation, sagehood, and other related matters (including government administration especially for Yulgok), both T'oegye and Yulgok point to such a subtle yet diffused relationship between the self and the universe according to their respective experiences and insights.

At the first glance, one may argue that T'oegye is a somewhat "conservative" thinker who depended substantially on the textual authority of the Ch'eng-Chu school. On the one hand, his usual habit was to defend Chu Hsi against all opposing views or ideas; on the other hand, however, he articulated, under Kobong's challenge, his own views by moving beyond Chu Hsi's original thinking. Yulgok appears to be more an original and critical thinker who was not afraid of criticizing not only his senior T'oegye but also Chu Hsi, whenever he found their views unclear or unreasonable. Although quoting a great deal of classical and Ch'eng-Chu teachings, he still managed to maintain himself as an independent thinker who depended less on their literal authority and more on his own ideas and interpretations.

In regard to Neo-Confucian metaphysics, T'oegye's Four-Seven thesis deliberately maintains the ontological "separability" and conceptual "distinction" of *i* and *ki*. From an epistemological standpoint, T'oegye definitely maintains a clear-cut theory of the distinction between the transcendent and virtuous realm of *i,* on the one hand, and the physical, emotional, and material realm of *ki,* on the other. In this regard, we may consider him a dualistic thinker. On the whole, however, he emphasizes the priority of *i* especially in the context of moral and spiritual self-cultivation. In other words, he is an *idealist* who points to the importance of holding fast to the transcendent and virtuous world of *i*. By contrast, Yulgok's version of the Four-Seven thesis focuses on the mutual relationship of what he calls "inseparability" and "interdependence" between *i* and *ki* from a phenomenalistic standpoint of concrete phenomena. For this reason, we can call Yulgok a nondualistic thinker, especially in comparison to T'oegye. In fact, he criticized T'oegye for making what he considers an unreasonable distinction between *i* and *ki*.

For Yulgok, only *ki* plays the dynamic role in all phenomena including feelings and self-cultivation. He tends to be a *realist* who emphasized the natural, physical, and emotional realm of *ki*, affirming the actual reality of the phenomenal world. He is an objective thinker, insofar as his Four-Seven thesis features such a philosophy of *ki* in the context of addressing not only practical learning and self-cultivation, but also government administration and sociopolitical reform.

With respect to the moral and psychological philosophy of mind, human nature, and feelings, T'oegye remains a *dualistic* thinker to formulate a dichotomous system of thought attributing *i* to the Four Beginnings, original human nature, moral mind, and moral principles as purely good, on the one hand, and *ki* to the Seven Emotions, physical human nature, human mind, and physical feelings and desires as potentially evil, on the other. As a moral and spiritual idealist, he certainly prefers to set the former over the latter. In his Four-Seven thesis and his other major writings, T'oegye maintains a recurring emphasis on his ontological and conceptual distinction between *i* and *ki*, the Four and the Seven, and moral principles and physical feelings-desires. Embedded in his Four-Seven thesis is an idealistic form of the Ch'eng-Chu tradition in both philosophical and ethical contexts. By contrast, Yulgok's interpretation reveals his fundamental belief that the Four-Seven relationship cannot be understood through such a dualistic way of philosophical and moral reasoning. Given his view of the inseparability of *i* and *ki*, Yulgok, as a *nondualistic* thinker, maintains the relationship of continuum and complementarity between the Four and the Seven and between other original human nature and physical human nature, between moral mind and human mind, and between good and evil.

In the Ch'eng-Chu context, both thinkers generally agree that both the Four and the Seven belong to aroused human feelings that involve *i* and *ki* together in the process of their issuance after the mind is stimulated by external things. In T'oegye's view, however, it is reasonable to analyze the Four and the Seven separately, just as *i* and *ki* can be spoken of separately in an ontological and conceptual sense. In other words, although they involve both *i* and *ki*, one should not fail to recognize the critical distinction between them in the practice of moral self-cultivation; it is crucial to understand their differences in terms of origin, meaning, and quality. In Yulgok's view, on the other hand, the Four and the Seven are interrelated and, thus, cannot be spoken of separately in terms of any dichotomy of *i* and *ki* because they are all aroused states of the mind referring to the one and total realm of feelings. The Four and the Seven are not two opposing kinds of feelings and do not have two separate ontological sources.

T'oegye does full justice to his belief that the Four Beginnings of benevolence, righteousness, propriety, and wisdom should be understood in terms of *i* and the Seven Emotions such as pleasure, anger, sorrow, and joy, in terms of *ki*. To him, what Mencius singled out as the Four does not refer to the feelings manifest from *ki*. There must be a necessary and clear distinction between the manifestation of *i* and the manifestation of *ki*. Unlike the Seven, the Four are the innate seeds of moral self-cultivation. For T'oegye, then, the Four should be conceived of as our moral intuitions and feelings, which are always pure and good expressions of the mind-and-heart, whereas the Seven are our ordinary physical and emotional responses to external stimuli. The peculiarity and ingenuity of his argument abide in his ability to formulate a creative theory, from the outset, that what Mencius called the *Four* are moral qualities initiated by *i*, which is full of goodness and truth. The *Seven* are to be understood as the manifestation of *ki* because they are easily agitated by physical and material conditions. To say, for example, that commiseration (the beginning of benevolence), unlike the emotion of anger, is manifest from *i* is, therefore, to emphasize the innate moral status of the Four in the Mencian spirit. T'oegye's task was, in fact, to provide a meaningful theory of the Four and the Seven in such a context.

The question is, Why did T'oegye accept the fundamental Neo-Confucian doctrine that *i* and *ki* are inseparable in things and phenomena, on the one hand, but insist on analyzing the Four and the Seven by separating them into two, and distinguishing them from each other, in terms of the dichotomous system of *i* and *ki*, on the other hand? As we have observed before, this is a moral issue with profound implications for the practice of self-cultivation. T'oegye's dilemma was to formulate a morally oriented interpretation of the Four-Seven contrast. Throughout the whole debate with Kobong, he urged Kobong to make a clear "distinction" of *i* and *ki*, so that the purely moral nature of the Four (aroused by *i*) is not confused with the emotional and physical nature of the Seven (aroused by *ki*) in both conceptual and ethical contexts. In other words, the practice of *moral self-cultivation* requires such an understanding of the Four-Seven contrast.

From Yulgok's standpoint, however, T'oegye is wrong. The question is, Why did Yulgok reject T'oegye's Four-Seven thesis? Because *i* and *ki* are always inseparable in concrete things and phenomena, including the emanation of all feelings, it is not possible to have one group of feelings (the Four) as manifestations of *i* and the other group of feelings (the Seven) as manifestations of *ki*. For this reason, Yulgok, like Kobong, opposes T'oegye's dualistic Four-Seven thesis. T'oegye emphasizes the Four-Seven distinction in terms of an ontological and conceptual *i-ki* dichotomy and an ethical good-evil contrast. By contrast, Yulgok emphasizes their "mutual relationship" of continuum in the context of addressing a phenomenalistic *i-ki* inseparability and an ethical good-evil link. Any of the Four can be related to the Seven in one way or another because the Seven represent the "totality" of all feelings, while the Four are rooted within the Seven as the "subset" of good feelings. In this regard, Yulgok was profoundly influenced by Kobong's Four-Seven thesis.

T'oegye's interpretation points to the importance of preserving the Four and of suppressing the Seven. By contrast, Yulgok takes the Seven as an important part of experience in human life. To emphasize a concrete way of emotional integration, his nondualistic Four-Seven thesis definitely means the "harmony-disharmony" link between the Four and the Seven in the sense that their fundamental difference pertains to the question of whether feelings are expressed and harmonized properly. In other words, the goodness of the Four is no different from the goodness of the harmonized Seven. The implication of Yulgok's argument is a *moral issue* from a Confucian standpoint of self-cultivation: the Four do not have their own ontological and ethical ground outside of the Seven. Embedded in this argument is that the moral expressions of the mind-and-heart do not exist outside of the Seven Emotions. For example, to be pleased in seeing others one loves is the emotion of love, and to be sorrowful on account of bereavement is the emotion of sorrow. As two of the Seven Emotions, love and sorrow refer to what Mencius calls "the mind-and-heart of commiseration" or "the beginning of benevolence." Furthermore, to know properly when one should, or should not, be pleased (angry, sorrowful, etc.) is, Yulgok argues, no different from what Mencius calls "the mind-and-heart of right and wrong" or "the beginning of wisdom." In other words, the Four serve only as the moral norms of the Seven. For example, the mind-and-heart of commiseration is the moral norm of the emotion of love.

Yulgok refuses to make any conceptual separation or ethical distinction between the Four and the Seven. Any dualistic interpretation implies that there are two ontological and moral bases: one for the Four as good and the other for the Seven as evil. In his view, then, T'oegye's interpretation is a misunderstanding of Confucian teachings on feelings and self-cultivation. For this reason, Yulgok criticizes T'oegye for attributing two different sources for goodness. The Four and the Seven must not be understood in terms of any good-evil opposition or contrast in such a strictly exclusive way. Rather, the former should refer to good only, while the later, the totality of feeling, embraces both good and evil. Because the Seven refer to the total realm of feelings, it is especially true of Yulgok that evil cannot have its own ontological ground.

With respect to human nature, both T'oegye and Yulgok generally affirm the Ch'eng-Chu theory that "original human nature" refers to *i* only and "physical human nature" includes *i* and *ki* combined. In other words, the former refers to human nature in itself without including its physical endowment, whereas the latter refers to the concrete reality of human nature in terms of its physical endowment. Yulgok also agrees with T'oegye that the Four pertain to the former as good alone, whereas the Seven pertain to the latter as good and evil together. T'oegye's argument implies, however, that, just as human nature can be spoken of as two distinct natures, feelings can also be divided into the Four and the Seven. But Yulgok rejects his senior's claim by maintaining that feelings are one, just as human nature is one; in other words, the physical human nature includes the original human nature, just as the Seven include the Four. Instead, Yulgok's interpretation offers a theory in terms of "one nature" and "two names," maintaining that what we call "human nature" in the concrete sense is actually the physical human nature because *i* already exists in *ki*; as a result, what is called the *original human nature* is only an abstract ideal.

Another key ramification of the Four-Seven controversy is the problem of the mind. Both Korean thinkers agree on Chu Hsi's theory that the mind has both "substance" and "function": the unmanifested state is the substance of the mind, whereas the manifested state is the function of the mind. Hence, the Ch'eng-Chu doctrine that "the mind commands human nature and feelings" denotes that *human nature* refers to the substance of the mind, whereas *feelings* are called the function of the mind. In other words, it means that, in comprehending and managing human nature and feelings, the mind serves as the master of the self on all levels including moral and emotional ones.

As a dualistic thinker, T'oegye separates the mind into two parts: the moral mind and the human mind, assigning the former to the Four or Heaven's principle, and the latter to the Seven or selfish desires. T'oegye maintains a strict distinction of them for the ultimate purpose of self-cultivation. The learning of the mind-and-heart (*simhak*) is "to suppress human desires and to preserve Heaven's principle (moral principles)"; the former pertains to the human mind and the latter to the moral mind.[1] For T'oegye, then, the path to self-cultivation should be based on the controlling and overcoming of the human mind and the preserving and nourishing of the moral mind.

By contrast, Yulgok argues that the mind is fundamentally one and cannot be separated into two minds. This is because the Seven, the "totality of feelings," include both the moral mind and the human mind as a whole. From this perspective, he does not believe that, in the true Neo-Confucian spirit, the moral mind and the human mind are two ontological bases for the Four and the Seven. His interpretation focuses on their mutual relationship of continuum in both ontological and ethical contexts. If one relates the mind to the feelings in such a way that the moral mind issues the Four and the human mind issues the Seven, then it follows that there is a certain moral dichotomy between the Four and the Seven, and that there are two separate sources of feelings in opposition to each other. For Yulgok, then, this would be a complete *misunderstanding* of not only the mind but also the Four-Seven relationship. In other words, one cannot talk about the moral mind and the human mind as two different minds, or the Four and the Seven as two separate kinds of feelings. Undeniably, this controversy goes back to Chu Hsi's original thinking that maintains a fundamental distinction between the moral mind and the human mind. Yulgok emphasizes that the moral mind and the human mind are simply "two names referring" to two dimensions of one mind, virtuous-moral and emotional-physical. To him, their relationship is never a fixed or rigid one; it is, rather, a dynamic relationship of interdependence because the mind, as the master of the self, participates in both the realm of moral principles and virtues and the realm of emotional feelings and physical responses. It also pertains to the intellectual dimension of human nature that comprehends and directs these dimensions. Accordingly, the whole issue here deals with all of these interrelated tendencies of the mind-and-heart (*sim/hsin*). Yulgok did not argue exactly along this line of reasoning, but his understanding of the mind does suggest that the mind includes the intellectual, moral, and psychological dimensions of our nature. In the Neo-Confucian context, we may put it this way: there is only one mind that participates in *manifold realms* relating to moral virtues, rational principles and insights, emotional responses, physical feelings and desires, and so on.

Although T'oegye fully committed himself to self-cultivation in the tradition of Mencius and Tzu-ssu and to Chu Hsi's interpretation, he was not always consistent in explaining the relationship of *i* and *ki* in the context of Chu Hsi's original thinking. One major problem of his Four-Seven thesis is, of course, his shifting views. For example, his *hobal* (alternate manifestation) theory indicates that, although it is revised, due to Kobong's convincing challenge, to accommodate the fundamental doctrine of the inseparability of *i* and *ki* in concrete phenomena including feelings, it still reveals T'oegye's basic position to maintain a strict distinction of the Four and the Seven in terms of *i* and *ki*, as well as of good and evil. Furthermore, it means that *i* is manifest in the case of the Four, whereas *ki* is manifest in the case of the Seven. His rider-horse analogy also indicates such a dualistic position; it tends to draw a not only ontological, but also phenomenalistic, theory of *i* and *ki* that one is prior and the other is posterior in the issuance process of feelings. T'oegye considers the Four as the manifestations of *i* because *i* dominates in the process of their issuance, and the Seven as the manifestations of *ki* because *ki* has dominates in the process of their issuance. For Yulgok, however, T'oegye went too far to formulate such an antithetical interpretation of the Four-Seven thesis. Undeniably, the major problem of T'oegye's thought, as Yulgok himself realized to some extent, is that T'oegye definitely affirms the *self-manifesting* capability of *i*. In Chu Hsi's philosophy, however, the actual dynamism is assigned to *ki* only. According to it, *i* is the formless and passive principle that is not capable of moving by itself or manifesting itself. For T'oegye, however, *i* is the active principle that actually has its own self-manifesting capability. As revealed in his Four-Seven thesis and his other major writings, *i* is actually able to move on its own. In this regard, Yu Ch'i-myŏng (Chŏngjae, 1777–1861), one of T'oegye's followers, defended T'oegye's thesis by arguing that it is based on the fact that "*i* is the active entity." If *i* has no manifesting activity, then it is what Yu calls "a dead thing like ash."

Yulgok's view, however, T'oegye's *hobal* (alternate manifesting) theory of *i* and *ki* is improper for understanding the Four-Seven relationship because it implies that *i* and *ki* are "two separate entities, one being prior and the other being posterior," "each manifesting independently."[2] For Yulgok, the problem of T'oegye's Four-Seven thesis is such a dualistic view of *i* and *ki*.[3] From a standpoint of self-cultivation, Yulgok argues that it does not accord with to the Confucian sages' and worthies' teachings on feelings and self-cultivation.[4] In other words, T'oegye's interpretation destroys the fundamental Neo-Confucian doctrines that *i* and *ki* are inseparable in all concrete phenomena (including feelings) and that *ki* is manifest and the reason for its manifestation is *i*. It incorrectly affirms the self-manifesting capability of *i* in concrete phenomena like the Four. Only *ki* has such a self-manifesting power. As Yulgok said, "T'oegye could not quite understand the 'mysterious inseparability' of *i* and *ki*."[5] Following Yulgok, Song Si-yŏl, a leading thinker of Yulgok's school in the mid-seventeenth century, rejected T'oegye's theory of *i* dynamism, criticizing T'oegye for not understanding that *i* cannot be an acting agent in the process of cosmic transformation.[6]

What did T'oegye really mean by arguing that *i* can manifest itself in the case of the Four? This is really the critical issue that I have discussed before in the context of his understanding and practice of self-cultivation. Of course, this is what Yulgok did not quite understand. Although his criticism of T'oegye is an important issue, it is valid only in a textual and theoretical context. Like Yulgok, one can argue that T'oegye formulated a controversial theory of principle. Although T'oegye's interpretation is, strictly speaking, does not accord with Chu Hsi's original thinking, our main concern is the question of why he emphasized it as the essence of his Four-Seven thesis. He was, of course, aware that Chu Hsi attributed the dynamism of cosmic transformation only to the active role of *ki*, not *i*. And yet he meant that principle, which is a formless and static concept in Chu Hsi's thinking, can manifest itself to issue moral feelings like the Four in one's practice of self-cultivation. His fundamental belief is that *i* must be distinguished from *ki* in both conceptual and ethical contexts.

For T'oegye, *i* represents moral principles and virtues (such as the Four), whereas *ki* represents physical-psychological emotions and desires (such as the Seven). The latter can easily become "selfish" or "evil." His task was, in fact, to provide a morally grounded interpretation in terms of the distinction between *i* and *ki*. His holistic mission was to emphasize the transcendent, virtuous, and spiritual reality of *i* over the physical, emotional, and material reality of *ki*. This is why he maintains a dualistic approach in terms of an ontological and conceptual *i-ki* dichotomy and an ethical good-evil contrast. On the one hand, such an approach justifies the Mencian doctrine that the Four are our dynamic, moral qualities inherent in our nature, the moral basis for self-cultivation; on the other, it accords with the Ch'eng-Chu doctrine that *i* is human nature full of goodness, truth, and moral principles. Accordingly, *i* is an "active" principle capable of issuing its moral and spiritual power. Such a philosophy of *i* dynamism is intended for the ultimate purpose of self-cultivation; in this regard, *i* must have priority over *ki* in terms of moral and spiritual values. Although T'oegye did not argue exactly along this line of reasoning, he claimed that his interpretation was no more than an explanation of what Chu Hsi had intended to mean all along. Undoubtedly, he definitely gave a new compelling interpretation, which is highly unique and significant, insofar as it has implications for *moral* and *spiritual* self-cultivation. We must understand his Neo-Confucianism in such a context. Precisely for this reason, Yulgok's criticism of T'oegye does not justify the vitality of T'oegye's Four-Seven thesis.

On the whole, we may consider T'oegye as the Korean synthesizer of the Ch'eng-Chu learning of the mind-and-heart (*simhak*). His synthesis of the Ch'eng-Chu *simhak* focuses especially on what he calls "the learning of reverential seriousness" (*kyŏnghak*). It suggests an inner-directed method of self-cultivation, one that emphasizes "suppressing human desires" and "preserving Heaven's principle." Of course, T'oegye attributes the former to the Seven (aroused by *ki*) and the latter to the Four (aroused by *i*). Hence, it is crucial to distinguish *i* from *ki*, so that one does not misidentify physical, emotional and material desires with Heaven's principle (moral principles and virtues). This serves as the whole basis of his Four-Seven thesis and it implications for self-cultivation. Formulating such a philosophy of *simhak*, he made it compatible with his philosophy of *i* dynamism. He, unlike Chu Hsi, presents a more explicit view of "human desires" as "selfish," "precarious," and potentially "evil." This certainly conveys what de Bary calls a moral *rigorism* found in Chen Te-hsiu's *Heart Classic.*[7] For this and other related reasons already mentioned, we can borrow de Bary's use of the term *puritanical* in the Neo-Confucian context of interpreting T'oegye's thought. In fact, T'oegye's view of human desires represents the moral basis of his Four-Seven thesis. Regardless of other possible labels we can use to explain it, we need to note that this morally strict attitude partly comes from Chen Te-hsiu's *Heart Classic.*

The question is, Why did T'oegye accept it as part of orthodox Chu Hsi teaching and develop it much further especially in his Four-Seven thesis and in his other major writings of his mature philosophy? And how did it affect Yulgok's Neo-Confucianism and the subsequent development of Sŏngnihak in Korea? In the Chinese Confucian classics and Ch'eng-Chu commentaries except Chen's *Heart Classic,* we have no clear-cut discussion of the problem of human desires as evil. By carefully choosing and systematically interpreting fundamental quotations from the *Book of Mencius, Doctrine of the Mean,* Ch'eng-Chu writings, and especially Chen's *Heart Classic,* T'oegye drew serious attention to a rigoristic dichotomy of Heaven's principle as purely good and human desires as potentially evil. Also, he articulated Chen's distinction of Heaven's principle and human desires further to reconcile it with the whole metaphysical and ethical basis of his Four-Seven thesis. This corresponds to my initial comment that the ethico-spiritual dimension of his *simhak* was indirectly influenced by the *Heart Classic.* Nonetheless, T'oegye moved well beyond Chu Hsi's original thinking as well as Chen's philosophy; that is to say, we must to recognize the strong religious overtone of T'oegye's *simhak* that emphasizes the moral contrast between good and evil.

Current scholarship on T'oegye suggests that his synthesis of Chu Hsi's Neo-Confucianism points to an integrated balance between the external study and the internal cultivation, as it is generally revealed in his works especially the *Sŏnghak sipto* and *Chŏnsumnok nonbyŏn* (Critique of Wang Yangming's *Instruction for Practical Living*).[8] Commenting on his *Sŏnghak sipto,*

Michael Kalton, for example, argues: "T'oegye *emphasizes the external approaches*, but by no means excludes a moral, internalistic, and even meditative, approach to mental recollection."[9] This is a possible reading of T'oegye in general; however, it does not do enough justice to the fundamental vitality of his *simhak,* which closely corresponds to his Four-Seven thesis and its implications for self-cultivation. With respect to the practice of self-cultivation, T'oegye definitely moved in the direction of giving far more attention to an *inner-directed* path than to an external investigation of things and principles. Unlike Chu Hsi, he has a stronger tendency toward quiet sitting and *simhak* as a *contemplative* way of self-cultivation. As we have noted, T'oegye sees the external process of investigation as part of self-introspection and self-realization in which meditation and the cultivation of *kyŏng* play the most important roles in his moral and spiritual quest for sagehood. Undoubtedly, this is a major shift from Chu Hsi's emphasis on the intellectual knowledge of principles into T'oegye's emphasis on the self-realization of principles inherent in human nature. T'oegye's harsh criticism of Lu Hsiang-shan's and Wang Yang-ming's philosophy of mind accords with such a method of self-cultivation formulated in the Ch'eng-Chu context.[10] The conventional historical image of T'oegye as the "Chu Hsi of Korea" suggests his valuable contribution to transmitting the Chu Hsi tradition in Korea. In doing so, unlike the followers of the Chu Hsi tradition in Yüan-Ming China, T'oegye not only transmitted it to his followers in Korea,[11] but also succeeded in preventing the development of the Lu-Wang school of the mind during his time.[12]

The key to self-cultivation, as understood by T'oegye, is to transcend selfish feelings and desires, so that one can experience Heaven's principle as the essence of one's inner nature. The truth of human nature shares the same reality with Heaven's principle. As T'oegye claimed, "the moon as such" is "the real moon in the sky," not "the reflected moon on water." For the learning for sagehood, his *simhak* decisively emphasizes Heaven's principle as the ultimate reality to be experienced in oneself. The essence of his *simhak* addresses such a theme, and the impact of his Four-Seven thesis on it is quite significant. Such an approach means the cultivation of *kyŏng* as well in both moral and spiritual contexts. Unlike Sung Neo-Confucian thinkers including Chu Hsi, T'oegye therefore calls the *simhak* simply as the *kyŏnghak* (learning for reverential seriousness). *Kyŏng* is not only mental seriousness and determination in handling things and affairs, but also a kind of religious reverence toward Heaven's principle. T'oegye used it elucidate his conviction in the harmonious unity between the self and the universe. The cultivation of Heaven's principle should be done contemplatively and spiritually in the mind-and-heart, not through one's theoretical speculation or textual study. These points definitely represent an inner-directed and contemplative form of the Chu Hsi tradition. T'oegye was not only concerned with the moral implications of Chu Hsi's philosophy, but also emphasized *i* as the inherent source of self-transformation. His practice of *simhak* corresponds to his view of selfish human desires as evil. It definitely bears a religious way of self-cultivation that irresistibly represents an innovative departure from the orthodox system of Chu Hsi.[13] His synthesis of *i*, *simhak*, and *kyŏnghak* is a religious strain of the Ch'eng-Chu tradition. Although it is an elaborated form of the inward dimension of Chu Hsi's Neo-Confucianism, it goes much beyond Chu Hsi's original thinking and Chen's interpretation. We are talking about T'oegye's Neo-Confucian spirituality[14] that reveals his *religious* quest for sagehood. Obviously, it grew out of his Four-Seven thesis that sharply set the transcendent, virtuous, and spiritual order of *i* before the physical, emotional, and material order of *ki*.

According to Judaism, Christianity, and Islam, "God" is believed to be the ground of all reality and the ultimate basis for the cosmic, moral, and spiritual order. The question is, Are belief in and worship of God relevant to Neo-Confucian religiosity? Both historically and theologically speaking, in these Western religious traditions the spiritual experiences of self-transcendence are usually expressed in terms of the "union" between the human soul (or humanity) and God (or divinity). This, of course, signifies the "I-Thou" binding (*religio*) relationship in which the two parties, however, must always remain distinct from each other. T'oegye's Neo-Confucianism does not address any absolute Divine Being as a personal deity who completely transcends the phenomenal world. The binding relationship, or *religio* (if we were to call it that from a cross-cultural standpoint of comparative religion), between human nature and Heaven's principle is not that of the transcendent "God" and the immanent "human beings."

However, T'oegye's Neo-Confucianism does not lack reference to transcendence. More specifically, it underscores the transcendent ground of human nature in terms of Heaven's principle, the transcendent yet immanent reality of sagehood. The core of his *simhak* and *kyŏnghak* is an intrinsic-yet-subtle way of self-transcendence, one that is predicated on a mutual unity between the self and Heaven's principle. The practice of "preserving Heaven's principle" and "eliminating desires" and its art of quiet sitting and self-reflection accord with T'oegye's method of self-cultivation that is aimed at sagehood. In this regard, his vision of sagehood, or the truth of human nature, constitutes the religious core of his Neo-Confucianism.[15] It points to a sense of religiosity, insofar as there must be "faith"[16] in a network of continuum between human nature, Heaven's principle, and sagehood. The way of realizing such a network emphasizes a teleological, spiritual journey to self-cultivation. This is, strictly speaking, a religious faith in the goodness of human nature and in its search for Heaven's principle, its transcendent ground of existence. Even as a Neo-Confucian scholar, T'oegye seems to have maintained himself as a religious thinker and practitioner. It seems reasonable to argue that, after having reached the peak of his thought, he must have captured certain insights into the depth of Ch'eng-Chu Neo-Confucianism, especially its spiritual teaching and practice, moving beyond the tradition of its textual authority and its philosophical inquiry.

In comparison to T'oegye, Yulgok offers a nondualistic approach to *simhak* and demands a measure of control over *ki,* which involves a way to harmonize one's feelings, emotions, and desires properly in daily life. It emphasizes the "nourishment of *ki*" that requires one's established resolve, sincere determination, and practical effort. The physical, empirical, and cultural order of *ki* was more important for Yulgok. This definitely supports his Four-Seven thesis that focuses on his emphasis on the role of *ki* in cosmology and self-cultivation. We can readily consider it as a "philosophy of *ki.*" By contrast, T'oegye's Neo-Confucianism can be considered as a philosophy of *i.*

We can examine this further in terms of the development of "new" approaches within the Korean Sŏngnihak tradition. This can help us to clarify the issue of "orthodoxy" regarding T'oegye's and Yulgok's philosophies. In other words, the Four-Seven controversy can be understood from a standpoint of doctrinal orthodoxy and "power struggle." Formulating a creative philosophy of *i,* T'oegye moved in the direction of emphasizing *i* over *ki*; criticizing T'oegye and presenting his own interpretation, Yulgok, too, moved in the direction of emphasizing *ki* over *i.* Here, our major concern is *not* which Korean thinker, T'oegye or Yulgok, defended or interpreted the orthodox Chu Hsi school more correctly or more clearly. Nevertheless, this became precisely the textual and political issue among most followers of T'oegye and of Yulgok, who engaged in the Four-Seven controversy to address such a hair-splitting issue in relation to the question of the Korean tradition of Neo-Confucian orthodoxy, which lasted from the late sixteenth century to the beginning of the twentieth century. Yulgok's followers opposed T'oegye's philosophy of *i* dynamism and defended their master as the "right" interpreter of the orthodox Chu Hsi school in Korea. At the same time, they criticized T'oegye as an "*i*-ist" (*churi*) thinker, or a philosopher who emphasizes the primacy of principle, charging him with misunderstanding Chu Hsi's Neo-Confucianism. Meanwhile, T'oegye's followers criticized Yulgok for being a "*ki*-ist" (*chugi*) thinker who emphasized the primacy of *ki* and, thus, misinterpreted Chu Hsi's Neo-Confucianism. They also claimed that T'oegye's philosophy represents the "true" transmission of the Ch'eng-Chu school in Korea, praising their master as the "Chu Hsi of Korea." Subsequently, in the late sixteenth century, this spilt the whole Sŏngnihak tradition in Korea into the Yŏngnam "school of the primacy of *i*" (Churip'a) identified with T'oegye and the Kiho "school of the primacy of *ki*" (Chugip'a) identified with Yulgok. These two major schools of thought developed Korean Neo-Confucianism until the opening of the twentieth century. The Epilogue of this book will discuss this topic further in the context of the Four-Seven and *i-ki* controversy.

For Yulgok, learning is not only extending knowledge but, more important, putting it into practice in an active way. Interestingly, Yulgok's emphasis on extending good feelings into one's daily life and on the unity of practical knowledge and practical action moves him a step closer to the fundamental spirit of Wang Yang-ming in the sense that the way of self-cultivation is to pursue the good with sincere will. This does not mean in any sense that he was a Korean follower of Wang Yang-ming. Rather, I am suggesting that even as a follower of the Ch'eng-Chu school, he had a diverse intellectual interest and was probably influenced by some of Wang's thought. Although my own reading of Yulgok has no written evidence to justify that he used Wang's writings, he probably knew Wang's philosophy enough to accommodate it into his Neo-Confucianism.[17]

In contrast to T'oegye who emphasizes the cultivation of reverential seriousness, Yulgok focuses on the cultivation of sincerity as the basis for the learning for sagehood. For Yulgok, sincerity is not a mere speculative concept but a concrete way of Confucian life. It refers to one's sincere attitude toward emotional integration and the nourishment of one's *ki* as the practical method of self-cultivation. As a pragmatic thinker, Yulgok addresses the empirical and practical dimension of Neo-Confucian learning and self-cultivation. Sincerity is that which can transform and complete human nature, bringing the individual, society and government together in harmony.[18] "Sincere learning" (*sŏnghak*) is a tangible goal and method of attaining sagehood. The completion of "sincere learning" must form a concrete network with all levels of Confucian culture. Articulating a philosophy of sincerity in this way, Yulgok developed it into the "practical learning" (*sirhak*) of sagehood as an ethico-political ideal. Moving beyond the Chinese tradition of the Four Book and Sung thinkers, he argues more explicitly that sincerity is the ethico-political basis for government administration.

On the whole, Yulgok's *sirhak* focuses on the *outer-directed* and *active* form of learning and self-cultivation with ethical and socio-political implications. Yulgok transcended the Ch'eng-Chu tradition of textual authority and theoretical inquiry. This suggests the shift from a philosophy of *i* to a philosophy of *ki*. Such a shift was not only his philosophical understanding of the Ch'eng-Chu tradition, but also his direct critique of T'oegye's Four-Seven thesis; furthermore, it appears to have resulted from his personal challenge to the subjective and inner-directed tendency of T'oegye's Neo-Confucianism. As I have indicated before, we cannot ignore the influence of Lo Ch'in-shun on Yulgok. The latter respected the former's nondualistic view of the inseparability of *i* and *ki* in concrete phenomena. Especially appealing to Yulgok was the empirical and objective reality of *ki*; in this regard, Lo's *K'un-chih chi* had a significant impact on his Four-Seven thesis that relates to his philosophy of *ki*. But it was still his acceptance of basic Ch'eng-Chu doctrines that the spirit of his *sirhak* receives its justification. We can consider Chu Hsi's philosophy and Lo's reformulation of it as the basis for Yulgok's practical thinking. And yet, Yulgok opened a new direction within Korean Neo-Confucianism in the context of his argument that the philosophical tradition of the past can continue only if it provides new intellectual and ethical insights and relevant socio-political implications. He did not literally follow the canonized teachings of Sung Neo-Confucianism. Maintaining its general rational and ethical foundation, he utilized Lo's philosophy to criticize T'oegye's (and Chu Hsi's) dualistic theory of *i* and *ki*. But many passages in Yulgok's writings, indeed, convey the fact that he did have considerable respect for Chu Hsi's and T'oegye's intellectual integrity and their serious commitment to Confucian scholarship. According to his conception of "orthodoxy," however, to maintain orthodoxy does not mean one's blind adherence to its old doctrines only. As he argued in his Four-Seven thesis, the continuity of orthodoxy should involve a necessary process of clarifying and reinterpreting existing materials with personal experiences and insights, even if it requires a modification of certain doctrines. The whole process should be practical for daily matters including learning and self-cultivation.

If we ponder on this issue further in the context of the entire Neo-Confucian tradition in East Asia, the development of practical learning within the Ch'eng-Chu school applies also to Ch'ing China and Tokugawa Japan in the later periods. Despite the considerable historical and cultural differences between Chosŏn Korea and these two countries, a few Chinese and Japanese thinkers of the Ch'eng-Chu school, like Yulgok, were influenced by Lo Ch'in-shun's philosophy of *ki* in the seventeenth and eighteenth centuries. This was an inevitable development within the orthodox tradition. There are certain patterns of intellectual and ethical commonality between Yulgok, Chinese Neo-Confucians such as Wang Fu-chih (1613–1692), Yen

Yüan (1635–1704), and Tai Chen (1724–1777), and Japanese Neo-Confucians such as Kaibara Ekken (1630–1714).[19] In their critical reactions to the dominant trend of theoretical learning and subjectivist and contemplative self-cultivation, they not only formulated similar philosophies of *ki* in terms of addressing the physical, empirical, and cultural order of *ki*, but also emphasized fundamental needs for philosophical reinterpretation, practical learning, and socio-political progress. Nevertheless, we have to note that, both historically and philosophically speaking, such a Neo-Confucian philosophy of practical learning was formulated and advocated to a considerable extent by Yulgok in Korea in the mid-sixteenth century, that is, at least a half century before either Chinese or Japanese Neo-Confucians developed it in the seventeenth and eighteenth centuries.

Like the Japanese Neo-Confucian Kaibara Ekken, Yulgok paid primary attention to the empirical and practical learning of Ch'eng-Chu Neo-Confucianism, extending its scope to historical research, government administration, economy, law, and education.[20] In fact, his political treatises and his active political career clearly reflect his serious interests in these fields. Like Yen Yüan in Ch'ing China and Kaibara Ekken in Tokugawa Japan, Yulgok saw himself within the revised line of Chu Hsi orthodoxy and believed that his contribution was a necessary clarification of what Chu Hsi had intended.[21] Obviously, these general comparative observations point to another important area of our future research, one that deserves a more-detailed philosophical and historical inquiry into the fundamental patterns of continuity, change, and synthesis among the parallel wings of the Chu Hsi tradition in Korea, China, and Japan. In addition, we have to reexamine more clearly and thoroughly the intellectual and historical continuum between Yulgok's Neo-Confucianism, his "school of the primacy of *ki*" (Chugip'a), and Practical Learning (Sirhak) school in Korea during the eighteenth and nineteenth centuries.

There are several general observations that should be stated here. First, the practical implications of his Four-Seven thesis shaped Yulgok's philosophy of *ki* and *sirhak*. Second, the extent to which he critically advocated a reform of Chosŏn dynasty's socio-political institutions represents the dynamic and practical spirit of his political thought. Third, Yulgok's philosophy of "practical learning" is not only a matter of moral practice, but also a political ideology that can promote tangible benefits for many forms of Confucian culture at large. Finally, there is a systematic consistency of his argumentation in his proposed goal and method of political reform.

The question is, Why did Yulgok emphasize the practical learning of Neo-Confucianism and use it as the basis for his political thought? And what implications did this have for Korea during his time? As a Neo-Confucian scholar-official, Yulgok realized that the Ch'eng-Chu tradition in Korea had neglected, relatively speaking, the empirical study of economy and socio-political institutions. He found *sirhak* significant for dealing with the new compelling problems and needs that could not be settled by philosophical or moralistic solutions only. Hence, he maintained himself an active participant in applying it to concrete socio-political needs of the state. As a pragmatic thinker, he believed in the actual practice, not mere theory, of Neo-Confucian *sirhak* as his lifetime mission in his personal and public life. In this regard, he significantly differed from his contemporaries in Korea because he advocated the Neo-Confucian idea of sagehood especially in *ethico-political* terms. Neo-Confucianism can never be an individually oriented way of learning and self-cultivation. For this reason, his philosophy of *sirhak* emphasizes the unity of the "real mind," "practical knowledge," and "practical action" that extends from learning and self-cultivation to politics. Realizing the lack of a concrete political guide in the Ch'eng-Chu tradition, Yulgok offered an integrated system of egalitarian ideas and functional strategies, one that addressed an utilitarian socio-political reform appropriate for the contemporary Korean context.

The Practical Learning (Sirhak) school developed in eighteenth and nineteenth century Korea, but it was not a simple phenomenon because it had a philosophical and historical background in Korean Neo-Confucianism. Although it opposed the orthodox Sŏngnihak tradition, it was significantly influenced by Yulgok in particular. Current scholarship on Korean thought and history generally regards it merely as an independent school of thought, claiming that it developed in criticism of the Ch'eng-Chu school, as well as in response to Western thought, religion, and culture.[22] In such a context, most studies have emphasized its empirical interests in historical research, socio-political reform, economy, science, and so on. More to the point, they tend to agree that Sirhak scholars generated a modern movement to liberate the Korean Neo-Confucian mind from an old ethico-metaphysical and scholastic tradition to a modern scientific outlook. However, such a view is, strictly speaking, a narrow oversimplification or a shallow generalization; in fact, it is quite incorrect in the context of Neo-Confucian *sirhak* in general and Yulgok's *sirhak* in particular. We must note the historical fact that, in the unfolding process of Neo-Confucianism in sixteenth century Korea, Yulgok openly advocated a practical form of Neo-Confucianism, while formulating Confucian-based reform measures that are closely associated with economic development and socio-political progress. The empirical nature of his philosophy of *ki* and the pragmatic and egalitarian spirit of his *sirhak* exerted a good deal of influence on some of the early advocates of Sirhak school in the eighteenth century, especially Yi Ik (Sŏngho, 1681–1763), who was originally a member of Yulgok's school of the primacy of *ki*. In fact, Yi Sŏngho admired Yulgok as a great Korean scholar-official of practical learning and political reform. Indeed, we can consider Yulgok as a forerunner of the early form of Sirhak school in Korea. The basic spirit of Sirhak school can be traced back to Yulgok's *sirhak* and its implications for government and society.

The rationality and morality of Yulgok's Neo-Confucianism originate in Ch'eng-Chu Neo-Confucianism. Unlike T'oegye, he was not interested in its subjectively inner-directed and contemplative dimensions. Yulgok must have captured certain insights to the *pragmatic* and *reformist* significance of the Ch'eng-Chu tradition, undercutting especially its theoretically abstract and practically contemplative tendencies. This does not mean in any sense that he was a Neo-Confucian genius of revolutionary or utopian thinking. For example, he was not a radical thinker and revolutionary reformer like Chŏng Yag-yong (Tasan, 1762–1836), the greatest name among Korean Sirhak thinkers, who attempted to transform the established system and order of Chosŏn dynasty in the nineteenth century. Tasan, originally a student of Sŏngnihak, advanced empirical and pragmatic ideas under the influence of Western thought and science; however, the egalitarian spirit of his sociopolitical reform measures relates to Yulgok's political thought. We may argue that Yulgok's *sirhak* was, indeed, an inspiring intellectual force that facilitated developing more-advanced tendencies of practical learning in the Korean Sirhak school.

Yulgok was a Neo-Confucian reformer. The issue is not how he criticized past philosophy and tradition, but it closely relates to the ways in which he formulated new ideas and pragmatic methods needed for reforming a Confucian government. His *sirhak* points to the importance of maintaining the unity between scholarship, self-cultivation, government administration, and cultural progress. For him, it must integrate empirical objectivity, ethical rationality, social reality, political reform, and utilitarian practicality, which were essential for establishing and enlarging a modernized Confucian society with economic and socio-political progress. This was how he tried to synthesize tradition and modernity; such an approach indicates his belief in the meaningful link between these two intellectual-cultural realities.

From a standpoint of historical background as well, we can compare the reasons that T'oegye and Yulgok differed from each other, as well as from orthodox Ch'eng-Chu thought. Given the available historical information, it is possible to give a meaningful interpretation consistent with their Four-Seven theses and their practical implications for self-cultivation and other related matters discussed previously. The historical background of T'oegye corresponds to the basic features of his philosophy, notably his ontological and conceptual distinction of *i* and *ki*, his ethical contrast of good and evil, and his skeptical understanding of emotions and desires. T'oegye was influenced by the contemporary social and political settings of his life. From the early to the middle stages of his life, he had experienced political corruption, as well as three serious purges of Neo-Confucian scholars. Realizing the need for retirement from official life into a quiet and scholarly life, he probably took a somewhat negative view of contemporary government and society and made numerous attempts to withdraw from his public career.[23] As a serious scholar who was never interested in becoming a statesman, he maintained an inner-directed and contemplative attitude toward the Confucian life of learning and self-cultivation. His Four-Seven debate with Kobong took place from 1559 to 1566. In this period T'oegye, an old man in his sixties, developed his mature philosophy. In accordance with his old age and his life of retirement, he developed a philosophy of *i* that focuses on the spiritual tendencies of Ch'eng-Chu Neo-Confucianism. As we have seen, this is clearly indicated in his Four-Seven thesis and its implications for self-cultivation that relates to his theory and practice of *simhak*.

Yulgok's philosophy fits well with the contemporary political settings of his life. Yulgok became a government official after the three harsh purges of Neo-Confucian literati were over. As the conservative political party of government bureaucracy gradually declined, he saw a new future with the possibility of change and reform. Such a historical circumstance corresponds to his emphasis on the physical, material, and cultural world of *ki*. Yulgok formulated his Four-Seven thesis in 1572 when he was thirty-seven years old. As a relatively young philosopher, he established his reputation as one of the leading scholar-officials, who had written a few important works while serving several high-ranking government positions. His young age and active political life tend to accord with his Four-Seven thesis and its implications for self-cultivation that focus on an empirical and practical philosophy of *ki*. This pertains to his two positive views that emotions and desires are an inherent and important part of human experience and that emotional integration and the nourishment of one's *ki* form the core of self-cultivation. As a pragmatic thinker and active politician, Yulgok must have wished to formulate a philosophy that could integrate learning, self-cultivation, and concrete sociopolitical matters. In other words, he naturally developed such an outer-directed philosophy that could actively contribute to the Confucian sociopolitical ideal and progress.

We arrive, then, at an important question: How relevant are both Korean thinkers' Four-Seven theses to us and to our contemporary ways of life? What, if anything, do they have to offer us? More specifically, do their practical implications still provide us with something meaningful and practicable? Of course, these questions vary according to the different ways of life that are conditioned by our diverse intellectual, ethical, and psychological faculties. The *whole thrust* of the Korean Four-Seven thesis points to the way of moral self-cultivation and emotional integration; that is to say, it still addresses the important issue of how to be "human" in a genuine sense of its meaning. To borrow traditional Neo-Confucian terminology, it calls for no more than the "human way" of daily life that is "near at hand." The way of pursuing it is to affirm and experience the authentic goodness of human nature inherent in every person's mind-and-heart. Clearly, the individual's potential for, and ability of, achieving self-transformation in various situations is a vital component of his or her natural endowment. The Korean Four-Seven thesis is still an important topic for us to understand especially in the context of moral reasoning and moral life. Its vitality emphasizes the self-cultivation of our minds-and-hearts through the realization of moral principles, values, and feelings, as well as through the dynamics of emotional nourishment and interpersonal-social contact. In other words, it is about the question of how people can integrate themselves intellectually, morally, psychologically, and spiritually. It addresses the issue of understanding the fundamental controversy on the dynamic status and role of the mind-and-heart in the practice of self-cultivation. Affirming the perfectibility of the self as a possible human avenue, it points to the significance of the ethical integration of our mental emotions, physical feelings, and material desires through the process of proper *controlling* and *channeling*. We are talking about the fundamental Confucian creed that the inherent goodness of our "Heaven-endowed" nature provides every person with the theoretical basis for self-transformation. Each of us has the innate knowledge to fully actualize the goodness of his or her inner nature; in this regard, wise or intelligent persons and people of simple intelligence or little education are the same in kind. On the practical level, however, embedded in this profound commonality of human nature is an austere demand for self-reflection and self-realization with consistent effort; one needs to have a great deal of serious courage and sincere commitment.

T'oegye's Four-Seven thesis has something to offer us in the sense of appreciating the ethico-spiritual dimension of human existence and experience. His philosophy of the self-manifestation of principle advocates the self-sustaining and self-regulatory ability of our nature. Because his Neo-Confucian conviction is that "principle is human nature," it implies that we have the innate ability to transform ourselves into ideal persons. For T'oegye, the intellectually sensitive and ethically responsible person embodies moral principles and values consistently in daily life, so that he or she can fully realize the natural goodness of human nature and integrate it effectively in his or her practice of moral and spiritual self-cultivation. Moral principles, virtues, and intuitions are the essential qualities of human nature; for T'oegye, therefore, one must properly distinguish them from the selfish emotions, feelings, and desires that are physically, mentally, and materialistically oriented. In a sense, T'oegye's thought points to a kind of moral idealism that is still relevant to our ways of moral reasoning and moral life.

Yulgok prefers balance between rationality, morality, emotionality, and practicality. Affirming emotions and feelings basically as a natural and good part of human nature, his Four-Seven thesis considers moral self-cultivation as a way of emotional integration in terms of harmonizing and channeling them properly. For Yulgok, the moral principle or virtue of benevolence is no different from the harmonized emotions of joy and love, and the moral discernment of right and wrong pertains to the harmonized emotions of anger and hatred. In other words, morality and moral life do not exist outside the boundaries of human emotions and feelings. The mind-and-heart is one, just as human nature is one; therefore, there is the relationship of continuum, and no strict gap, between its intellectual, ethical, emotional, and other related dimensions. In this context, then, the ideal human being is a sincere person who is truthful to himself or herself and to other human beings and who is sensitive to concrete phenomena, including the ways of ordering and enriching society and government. In addition, Yulgok's Four-Seven thesis suggests that the way of emotional integration has the potential to promote those other aspects of human culture, such as literature, art, music, and so on. This is something that we still cannot ignore even in our present-day world. Generally speaking, a wholesome culture can be based on a healthy and comprehensive philosophy with implications for various realms of human life and society. T'oegye's and Yulgok's philosophies are still relevant to us in this regard.

The Four-Seven debate as a whole has its own cultural significance within the Korean context as well. It was both significant historically and philosophically in terms of initiating not only a *creative source* of clarifying and interpreting Neo-Confucian learning and self-cultivation, but also a *powerful model* of sophisticated scholarly communication among leading Korean intellectuals. The depth and vitality of T'oegye's Neo-Confucianism contributed to generating a unique Korean Neo-Confucian form of creative thinking, moral reasoning, and spiritual practice, one that has significant ethico-religious implications for the inner-directed and contemplative way of Confucian life. The breadth and practicality of Yulgok's Neo-Confucianism made a significant contribution to provoking another unique Korean Neo-Confucian form of critical reasoning, systematic argumentation, and pragmatic action, one that has its own practical implications for the outer-directed and active way of Confucian life including socio-political responsibilities.

Furthermore, the genuine value of T'oegye's and Yulgok's Four-Seven theses lies in their intellectual competence and scholarly willingness for interpreting and reconciling selected elements of ambiguous and conflicting doctrines, ideas, and values, as well as for constructing, out of this mighty way, new meaningful theories and practical implications that are relevant to their respective visions of the Confucian way of life. Each thinker's own set of *explanatory* and *experiential* categories reveals that, instead of defending or validating old teachings, it is carefully articulated with personal practice, insight, and interpretation in an innovative direction. Another interesting pattern of commonality is that, rather than seeking to formulate a sequential series of textual statements and theoretical arguments, each thinker's Four-Seven thesis often strives to convince his challenger and modern readers (like us) to engage themselves in their own reflections and hermeneutics.

As we look back four centuries to the beliefs, experiences, and insights of T'oegye and Yulgok, we may be led, as were the two leading Korean Neo-Confucians themselves, to the fundamental conclusion that the human way of *self-transcendence* is to retain and nourish the essential goodness of human nature inherent in the mind-and-heart and to control and harmonize our emotions, thoughts, and desires accordingly. Indeed, this is the central vitality of both thinkers's understanding of the Four-Seven controversy and its implications for moral self-cultivation in the spirit of Mencius and the *Doctrine of the Mean,* respectively. As Mencius said, just as all human beings have a common taste for good flavor in their mouths, a common sense for natural beauty in their eyes, and so on, what is also in common to our mind-and-hearts is our innate moral virtues and feelings that please our mind-and-hearts in the similar way as material things please our senses. At the end of this comparative study of the Korean Four-Seven philosophy of T'oegye and Yulgok, I believe it may serve well to quote Mencius: "The organs of hearing and sight are unable to think and can be obscured and misled by external things. The material things act on the senses and lead them astray. That is all. The mind-and-heart (*sim/hsin*) can think. If we think, we will find the answer; otherwise, we will not find it. This is what Heaven gave to us. If one first makes one's stand on what is greater importance, then what is of smaller importance cannot conquer it. It is simply this that makes us great human beings."[24]

EPILOGUE

The *I-Ki* and Four-Seven Controversy after T'oegye and Yulgok

After the T'oegye-Kobong and Yulgok-Ugye debates, the Korean tradition of Sŏngnihak divided into two major schools of thought: the Yŏngnam "school of the primacy of *i*" (Churip'a) identified with T'oegye and the Kiho "school of the primacy of *ki*" (Chugip'a) identified with Yulgok. This split occurred in the late sixteenth century and underwent further development over the next three centuries. It is the major intellectual and historical event in the entire history of Korean Neo-Confucianism; three centuries of doctrinal disputes between the followers of T'oegye and those of Yulgok resulted in a great deal of philosophical development. However, let me emphasize that, unlike T'oegye's and Yulgok's Four-Seven theses, this philosophical development focused more on textual and theoretical issues of the *i-ki* controversy, without articulating their implications for self-cultivation and other related matters.

In general, those Neo-Confucians belonging to the Churip'a faction criticized Yulgok's Four-Seven thesis, especially his emphasis on the primary role of *ki* in all phenomena including feelings, while defending T'oegye's philosophy, especially his emphasis on the dynamic role of *i* regarding the same subject. At the same time, they reiterated and justified T'oegye's dualistic theory that *i* and *ki* are conceptually "two" and "distinct," his emphasis on the ontological and ethical priority of *i*, and his view that "*i* is the master and *ki* is the servant" in the process of all concrete phenomena. T'oegye's theory of *i* dynamism that *i* is the active principle capable of manifesting itself in concrete phenomena also remained a central doctrine among most Churip'a members. The Churip'a faction also defended T'oegye's Four-Seven thesis that the Four and the Seven are distinct from each other in terms of "origin," "meaning," and "quality"; that is to say, it sustained T'oegye's views that the Four refer to manifestations of *i* and the seven manifestations of *ki* and that the former means innate moral virtues and feelings and the latter emotional feelings and physical desires. T'oegye's Four-Seven philosophy became the central teaching of the Churip'a legacy.

Meanwhile, the members of the Chugip'a faction opposed it and defended Yulgok's nondualistic interpretation of *i* and *ki*, especially by making specific references to his emphasis on the inseparability of *i* and *ki* and his view that, with respect to all concrete phenomena including feelings, *ki* is manifest and *i* is the reason for *ki*'s manifestation. In their critical reaction to T'oegye's philosophy of *i* dynamism, they also maintained Yulgok's emphasis on the primary role of *ki* in cosmic transformation and self-cultivation. With respect to the Four and the Seven, they discussed Yulgok's theory of the "mutual relationship" of continuum and complementarity between the Four and the Seven, as well as his view that the Four and the Seven are interrelated and, therefore, cannot be spoken of separately in terms of any dichotomy of *i* and *ki*. Also, his argument that the Four and the Seven are not two separate kinds of feelings and do not have two separate ontological and ethical sources remained intact among most members in the Chugip'a legacy. Yulgok's Four-Seven philosophy constituted the underlying doctrine of this school.

In addition to the Churip'a and Chugip'a traditions, another major school of thought that arose at the same time is the so-called eclectic school (Chŏlch'ungp'a). The Chŏlch'ungp'a tradition was established by those independent scholars who joined neither Churip'a nor Chugip'a. These scholars stood between the two other schools. They did not fully support either T'oegye or Yulgok and formulated their own eclectic interpretations of *i* and *ki* and of the Four and the Seven. Some of them, of course, attempted a compromise between T'oegye's and Yulgok's philosophies.

The School of the Primacy of *I*

In the late sixteenth and early seventeenth centuries, the Churip'a school was led by Yi Chŏng (1512–1571), Cho Ho-jik (Chisan, 1545–1601), Yu Chin (Suam, 1582–1635), Yi Ku (Hwalchae, 1613–1654), and Yi Hyŏn-il (Karam, 1617–1704). Yi Chŏng was known for compiling his commentaries on the *Great Learning* and Chen Tu-hsiu's *Hsin ching*. As one of T'oegye's disciples, he defended his master's philosophy of the primacy of *i*. He did so maintaining Chu Hsi's theories that "with respect to origin, *i* is prior and *ki* is posterior" and that "with respect to concrete things, *i* and *ki* exist simultaneously in concrete things and, thus, cannot be separated from each other."[1] Cho Ho-jik was another leading disciple of T'oegye and defended especially his master's *hobal* (alternate manifestation) theory of *i* and *ki*. Following his master, he argued that *i* has its own self-manifesting power. As he asserted,

"*I* is passive and *ki* is active; however, when *ki* moves, *i*, which exists in *ki*, also moves and becomes manifest."[2] For him, *i* and *ki* become manifest simultaneously and together. He also defended T'oegye's thesis that when one speaks of *i*, one refers to the Four Beginnings; when one speaks of *ki*, one refers to the Seven Emotions. Like Yi Chŏng and Cho Ho-jik, Yu Chin addressed T'oegye's philosophy by quoting Chu Hsi's theory that "if spoken from the standpoint of beginning, *i* is prior and *ki* is posterior."[3] In other words, *i* is prior to *ki* in the ontological sense.

Yi Ku was another direct disciple of T'oegye. He is considered the first scholar of the Churip'a school, who attacked Yulgok's emphasis on the primary role of *ki*. In his critique of Yulgok's theory of *i* and *ki* (*Pyŏnnon iki sŏ*), he followed his master to formulate a dualistic interpretation of *i* and *ki*, one that emphasizes the primacy of *i*. He contended, in the familiar ontological sense, that *i* is prior to *ki*, although the former already exists right in the latter. He rejected Yulgok's assertions that "*i* is the passive and nonacting principle," and that "what becomes manifest is only *ki*." To put it in another way, he maintained his master's theory of *i* that *i* is the active and self-manifesting principle in both cosmic transformation and moral self-cultivation.

Yi Hyŏn-il was an influential scholar-official who held several high-ranking government positions. He provided the Churip'a faction with the first major critique of Yulgok's Four-Seven thesis, entitled *Yulgok Issi ron sadan ch'ilchŏng sŏ pyŏn* (Critique of Yi Yulgok's Letters on the Four Beginnings and the Seven Emotions).[4] According to him, Yulgok was completely wrong in rejecting T'oegye's theory of *i* manifestation, and Yulgok's view of *i* as a "passive" principle is unacceptable in the context of Chu Hsi's metaphysics and ethics. Defending T'oegye's concept of *i* as the active and transforming agent of all phenomena, he criticized Yulgok further: "Although *i* is formless and passive, it is the source of all phenomena. According to Yulgok, it cannot be the source of all things simply because it is vacuous and empty. He also maintained that only through the transformation of *ki*, the process of all phenomena is possible. This theory is wrong."[5] In this statement, Yi Hyŏn-il is reaffirming T'oegye's conception that *i* has the self-manifesting power that is, in his view, the dynamic function of *i*. For him, then, *i* must have priority over *ki* not only in the ontological context of origin, but also in the phenomenalistic context of concrete phenomena.

Chŏng Si-han (Udam, 1675–1707), a friend of Yi Hyŏn-il, is well known for his *Sach'il pyŏnchŭng* (Treatise on the Four and the Seven), a detailed comparison of T'oegye and Yulgok that consists of forty-one short sections.[6] Criticizing Yulgok's Four-Seven thesis, he defends T'oegye's version by arguing that the latter's philosophy of principle is based on the Neo-

Confucian view that *i* is always the "master" and *ki* is its "servant." Although "*i* exists in *ki*, it is neither limited nor commanded by *ki*"; rather, "*i* commands *ki* as the latter acts as the former's servant."[7] In other words, *i* is prior to *ki* in both ontological and phenomenalistic contexts.

Yi Sang-chŏng (Taesan, 1722–1781) was the most influential thinker of the Churip'a school in the mid-eighteenth century. His fellow members respected him as the "Young T'oegye," who compiled many important philosophical works including the following: *Iki tongjŏng sŏl* (Movement and Tranquility of *I* and *Ki* Explained),[8] *Iki sŏnhu sŏl* (Priority and Posterity of *I* and *Ki* Explained),[9] *Sadan ch'ilchŏng sŏl* (The Four Beginnings and the Seven Emotions Explained),[10] *T'oegye sŏnsaengsŏ chŏryo* (Essentials of Master T'oegye's Letters), and *Chujasŏ chŏryo* (Essentials of Master Chu Hsi's Sayings). Unlike other Churip'a members, Yi Sang-chŏng explained the *i-ki* relationship systematically. Of course, he emphasized the primacy of *i* in both ontological and phenomenalistic contexts. In his *Iki tongjŏng sŏl*, a short essay on the dynamic nature of *i*, he articulates T'oegye's interpretation of *i* and *ki* in terms of his theory that "*i* is the master, whereas *ki* is the material" (*iju kija/li-chu ch'i-tsu*).[11] For him, *i* is that which commands *ki*, whereas *ki* is the material device of *i*. In cosmic transformation and moral self-cultivation, *i* limits and controls the activity of *ki*. This is, then, why he criticized Yulgok for saying that *i* is "passive and nonacting," and for implying that *ki* is the only active agent in the process of cosmic transformation and moral self-cultivation. His conclusion is that Yulgok made a serious mistake in seeing *i* as a "dead" entity.

In the mid-nineteenth century, the Churip'a school was revived under the leadership of Yu Ch'i-myŏng (Chŏngjae, 1777–1861) and others. Yu Ch'i-myŏng took over Yi Sang-chŏng's theory that "*i* is the master and *ki* is the material." He elaborated on it further by arguing that "*i* has both movement and tranquility," and that "*ki* is the material instrument of *i*."[12] For him, "*i* is an active entity."[13] If one says that *i* has no activity at all, one incorrectly means that *i* is a dead thing like "ash."[14] For this reason, he criticized that Yulgok is incorrect in seeing *i* as a "passive and nonacting" entity.

Yi Hang-no (Hwasŏ, 1792–1868) was also an influential scholar who wrote many important works including the following: *Sadan ch'ilchŏng tosŏl* (Diagrammatic Treatise on the Four Beginnings and the Seven Emotions),[15] *Inmulsŏng tongi sŏl* (Treatise on the Similarity and Difference Between Human Nature and the Nature of Things),[16] *Insim tosim sŏl* (Treatise on the Human Mind and the Moral Mind),[17] *Sŏngchŏng chunghwa tosŏl* (Diagrammatic Treatise on the Centrality and Harmony of Human Nature and Feelings),[18] and *T'aegŭk sŏl* (Treatise on the Great Ultimate).[19] His philosophy is based mainly on the conventional Churip'a view that "*i* is the master and *ki* is its servant"; this theory developed into his own theory that "*i* is noble and *ki* is low" (*ijon kibi/li-tsun ch'i-pei*).

Yi Chin-sang (Hanju, 1818–1885) was another leading Churip'a thinker in the mid-nineteenth century. He was well known for many important works including the following: *Sach'il pyŏn* (Discourse on the Four and the Seven), *Simjŭkli sŏl* (Treatise on "the Mind Is Principle"), *Inmulsŏng tongil sŏl* (Treatise on the Sameness and Oneness of Human Nature and the Nature of Things), *Chuja ŏllon tongi kopyŏn* (Inquiry into Agreements and Disagreements with Chu Hsi's Sayings), *Konjigi pyŏn* (Discourse on Lo Ch'in-shun's *Knowledge Painfully Acquired*), *Taehak ch'aŭi* (Acquired Meaning of the *Great Learning*), *Chungyong ch'aŭi* (Acquired Meaning of the *Doctrine of the Mean*), *T'aegŭk tosŏl ch'aŭi* (Acquired Meaning of the Diagram of the Great Ultimate), and *Ihak chŏnyo* (General Essentials of the School of Principle).[20] The uniqueness of Yi Chin-sang's philosophy focuses on the new doctrine that "the mind is principle." This became a controversial theory within the Churip'a school because it sounds exactly identical to Wang Yang-ming's central doctrine that opposed the orthodox Ch'eng-Chu school's doctrine that "human nature is principle." However, what did Yi Chin-sang really mean? He was never a follower of the Wang Yang-ming school that did not even develop into an independent school of Neo-Confucian thought due to the impact of the entire Sŏngnihak tradition in Korea. In criticizing Yulgok's philosophy, he wanted to formulate a theory to justify his belief that the moral mind is identical to what Mencius and T'oegye emphasized as the original goodness of human nature. As a follower of the Ch'eng-Chu school, he considered *i* as the center of the mind, or what he called the *true mind* (*chinsim/chen-hsin*) identified with the original human nature. According to Chu Hsi's philosophy, the so-called mind-in-itself, in fact, refers to human nature in such a context.

Finally, Ki Chŏng-jin (Nosa, 1798–1876) founded the so-called *yurihak* (exclusivist philosophy of *i*). He transformed the Churip'a philosophy of the primacy of *i* into an extreme *i*-ist philosophy. Rejecting Yulgok's emphasis on the role of *ki* in all concrete phenomena, he argued that *i* and *ki* form one substance. However, *ki* is not an independent entity that can exist by itself or act on its own because its manifestation and activity are all due to *i*. As he argued, *i* is the master that commands *ki*, whereas the latter is the former's servant. In other words, *i* is prior to *ki* in ontological, phenomenalistic, and moral contexts. This was, of course, a new philosophical movement within the Churip'a tradition and became the dominant trend of this school in the late nineteenth century.

The School of the Primacy of *Ki*

Kim Chang-saeng (Sagye, 1548–1631), a disciple of Yulgok, was one of the first Chugip'a thinkers. Rejecting T'oegye's theory of "alternating manifestation of *i* and *ki*," he claimed that Yulgok was correct in arguing that, in all things and phenomena, what is manifest is only *ki* and the reason for its manifestation is *i*.[21] In his view, then, T'oegye's theory of the "self-arrival of *i*" in one's practice of moral cultivation is wrong because *i* cannot move by itself or manifest itself on its own.[22]

In the middle and late seventeenth century, the great scholar-politician Song Si-yŏl (Uam, 1607–1689), a disciple of Kim Chang-saeng, was the leading thinker of the Chugip'a tradition who held many high-ranking official positions. To defend Yulgok's thought, he reaffirmed Yulgok's emphasis on the dynamic role of *ki* in all phenomena, as well as his theory of the inseparability of *i* and *ki*. Criticizing T'oegye theory of "self-arrival of *i*" and his belief in the self-manifesting capability of *i*, he followed Yulgok to argue that *i* is the "passive" principle without any form, whereas *ki* is the "active" agent of cosmic transformation. For this reason, he rejected T'oegye's philosophy of *i* dynamism, supporting Yulgok's emphasis on the role of *ki* in the process of self-cultivation.

In the early eighteenth century, Kŏwn Sang-ha (Sangam, 1641–1721), the eldest disciple of Song Si-yŏl, was the most influential scholar of the Chugip'a scholar. He emphasized Yulgok's theory of the inseparability of *i* and *ki*, maintaining that there is neither priority nor posteriority between them. "According to Yulgok, what is manifest is *ki*, and the reason for its manifestation is *i*. This is why T'oegye's theory of alternate manifestation is wrong."[23] Defending Yulgok's theory of the oneness of the mind, he also argued that what Yulgok meant is: "*Ki* is the function of the mind (*simjiyong/hsin-chih-yung*), and *i* is the substance of the mind (*simjich'e/hsin-chih-t'i*)."[24]

Han Nam-dang (Wŏnjin, 1682–1751), Kwŏn Sang-ha's disciple, was known for many important works including the following: *Insim tosim sŏl* (Treatise on the Human Mind and the Moral Mind),[25] *Ponyŏnjisŏng kigiljisŏng sŏl* (Treatise on the Original Human Nature and the Physical Human Nature),[26] *Iil punsu sŏl* (Treatise on "the Oneness of Principle and the Diversity of its Particularization"),[27] *I ch'eyong sŏl* (Treatise on the Substance and Function of Principle),[28] and *Wang Yang-myŏng chipoyŏn* (Critique of Wang Yang-ming's Collected Works), a long and systematic critique of Wang's philosophy.[29] Following Yulgok's interpretation, Han Nam-dang criticized T'oegye's dualistic view of *i* and *ki*. For him, Chu Hsi confused everyone by saying that *i* and *ki* can be spoken of as being prior and posterior, respectively, and at the same time that the two are inseparable. Such a confusion is due to Chu Hsi's theory that if viewed from the standpoint of their origin, *i* and *ki* can be spoken of as prior or posterior. According to him, the mind unites *i* and *ki*; however, when it is spoken of in contrast to human nature, the mind is *ki* and human nature is *i*.

In the late eighteenth century, Im Sŏng-ju (Nokmun, 1711–1788) transformed the Chugip'a philosophy into what he called *yugihak* (exclusivist philosophy of *ki*), a philosophy of *ki* monism. His basic thesis is that human nature and the mind are one and the same. The unique feature of his philosophy focuses on his thesis that "human nature is *ki*." Of course, this deviates significantly from the Ch'eng-Chu metaphysical and ethical doctrine that "human nature is *i*," one that Yulgok himself consistently maintained in his Four-Seven thesis. Rejecting Chu Hsi's and T'oegye's conceptual distinction of *i* and *ki*, he went far beyond Yulgok by arguing that *ki* is the only active agent of all phenomena and that all concrete phenomena are particularizations of *ki*, not *i*. In reaction to the development of the Churip'a school, this was, of course, an innovative philosophical movement within the Chugip'a tradition. It addressed Ch'eng-Chu Neo-Confucianism in terms of *ki* only with respect to its metaphysics, ethics, self-cultivation, and so on.

Nokmun's philosophy later had a significant influence on Ch'oe Hanki (Hyegang, 1803–1879) and Ch'oe Che-u (Suŭn, 1824–1879), who formulated new empirical and positivist ideas. Ch'oe Han-ki based his *yugi* philosophy on his knowledge of European thought and science that were pouring into Korea at the end of the Chosŏn dynasty. He also put together a coherent, comparative, and scientific critique of Sŏngnihak Neo-Confucianism. Formulating his epistemology on the basis of European empiricism, he argued that all knowledge is a product of human experience. One cannot talk about phenomena before one experiences them. In addition, to rule a nation it is necessary to understand physical things and natural laws. In his major philosophical work *Ch'uch'ŭk nok* (Speculations), he presented a philosophy of *ki* according to which the world is a material product of *ki* that penetrates everywhere, integrating and disintegrating everything. Like Im Nokmun, he asserted that *ki* is one in the ontological context of origin and that it is many in the phenomenalistic context of the myriad things.

Ch'oe Che-u was originally another member of the Chugip'a tradition during the mid-nineteenth century. He founded Eastern Learning (*Tonghak*)[30] thought in 1860. Even though a Neo-Confucian thinker and reformer, he incorporated his *yugi* philosophy into his pseudo-religious system of Tonghak, a synthesis of the basic tenets of Confucianism, Christianity, Buddhism, and even indigenous shamanism.[31] This school became a religious and socio-political reform movement, concerned mainly with the peasantry and the betterment of the conditions in which they lived. Tonghak was formed in reaction to Western Learning (*Sŏhak*)[32] identified with Catholicism (*Ch'ŏnjuhak*), which was flourishing in the region of the capital in the nineteenth century. Ch'oe called for reform of the corrupt government and urged that the nation be strengthened and the livelihood of the people be improved.

The Eclectic School

The first leading scholar of the Eclectic school was Chang Hyŏn-kwang (Yŏhŏn, 1554–1637), who originally came from the Yŏngnam Chu-rip'a tradition associated with T'oegye's Neo-Confucianism. He wrote a few significant works such as *Insim tosim sŏl* (Treatise on the Human Mind and the Moral Mind),[33] *Sim sŏl* (Treatise on the Mind),[34] and *T'aegŭk sŏl* (Treatise on the Great Ultimate).[35] Following Yulgok, he argued that *i* and *ki* are inseparable in concrete things. But he stood between T'oegye's emphasis on distinction of *i* and *ki* and Yulgok's emphasis on the inseparability of *i* and *ki*. As he argued, although *i* and *ki* are conceptually distinguishable from each other, they are one in the ontological and phenomenalistic context. He said: "*I* is the warp of the Way and *ki* is the woof of the Way. How can there be two sources? We refer to what is always one as *i* and what becomes transformed as *ki*. The former is truly the warp of the latter, while the latter is the woof of the former."[36] The reason that they are spoken of in such a manner is, according to him, to clarify the oneness and distinction of *i* and *ki* in the sense that the former is "substance" and the latter is "function."

Cho Sŏng-ki (Cholsujae, 1638–1687), an independent scholar who studied Ch'eng-Chu Neo-Confucianism by himself and attempted to reconcile T'oegye and Yulgok. In his famous *T'oeYul yang sŏnsaeng sadan ch'ilchŏng indo iki sŏl hupyŏn* (Second Treatise on T'oegye's and Yulgok's Theories of the Four and the Seven, the Moral Mind and the Human Mind, and *I* and *Ki*),[37] he criticized T'oegye's philosophy for being incomplete because it focused too much on the ontological separability and conceptual distinction of *i* and *ki*. In addition, Yulgok's philosophy is only partially correct because it emphasized only the inseparability of *i* and *ki* in phenomena, neglecting what T'oegye saw as important about a certain conceptual distinction of *i* and *ki*. Thus, it is, Cho asserted, equally true that *i* and *ki* are conceptually two and distinct from each other and that they are inseparable in the ontological and phenomenalistic context. Like T'oegye and Yulgok, he stressed the typical Ch'eng-Chu thesis that the mind unites *i* and *ki*, but rejected Yulgok's assertion that "*i* is passive and *ki* is active." For him, *ki* is the material source that actualizes *i* in things, whereas *i* is the master of *ki*. "*I* and *ki* wait for each other to act and are merged one into the other in the mind."[38] Cho also agreed with Yulgok's Four-Seven view that the Seven Emotions include the Four Beginnings and *ki* is manifest in both the Four and the Seven. However, this view is correct only from the standpoint of the unity of *i* and *ki* in the mind. Like T'oegye, he argued that, when viewed from the standpoint of the Four in contrast to the Seven, the feelings can be distinguished as being principally backed by *i* or *ki*, respectively.

Im Yŏng (Ch'anggye, 1649–1696) was an eclectic scholar who originally belonged to the Kiho Chugip'a school. He accepted Yulgok's emphasis on the inseparability of *i* and *ki*, but rejected his theory that, in all phenomena, *ki* is manifest and *i* simply rides on *ki*. He also agreed with T'oegye that the Four are good, moral feelings because *i* is manifest in their issuance, whereas the Seven can be either good or evil because *ki* is manifest in their issuance.[39] Accordingly, T'oegye's interpretation is correct because from the standpoint of conceptual distinction, either *i* or *ki* is manifest depending on whether one speaks of the Four or the Seven.

Kim Ch'ang-hyŭp (Nongam, 1651–1708) attempted to incorporate T'oegye's Four-Seven thesis into Yulgok's theory of *i* and *ki*. In his *Sadan ch'ilchŏng sŏl* (Discourse on the Four Beginnings and the Seven Emotions),[40] he accepted Yulgok's views that "*i* is formless and passive," whereas "*ki* has form and is active," and that in all phenomena *ki*, not *i*, is manifest. Supporting T'oegye, he, like Im Yŏng, also argued that, in the conceptual context, one can distinguish the Four from the Seven by comparing them in terms of *i* or *ki*.[41] Kim Ch'ang-hŭp (Samŭn, 1653–1722), Kim Ch'ang-hyŭp's younger brother, supported T'oegye's emphasis that *i* and *ki* are logically unmixable, while, at the same time, maintaining Yulgok's assertion that they are inseparable in things and phenomena.[42] In other words, he accepted both T'oegye's ontological and conceptual distinction of *i* and *ki* and Yulgok's theory of their phenomenological inseparability.

Kim Wŏn-haeng (Miho, 1702–1772) took Kim Ch'ang-hŭp's position further and argued that *i* and *ki* are unmixable in the ontological and conceptual context, but inseparable from each other in the phenomenalistic context of concrete things. In his view, *i* cannot be independent of *ki* and must be attached to *ki*: "When there is this *i*, there is this *ki*, and vice versa. Although *i* and *ki* are two entities, they are not separated from each other. They do not mix with each other, although they are inseparable."[43]

In the early nineteenth century, O Hŭi-sang (Noju, 1763–1832) made a meaningful compromise between T'oegye and Yulgok on the theory of *i* and *ki*. Like the former eclectic thinkers, he maintained both the inseparability and unmixability of *i* and *ki* in the light of Chu Hsi's original thinking. He wrote: "*I* is the foundation of *ki*, whereas *ki* is the material of *i*. Without the material, the foundation cannot be understood, and without the foundation, the normative law of the material cannot be understood."[44] According to him, then, *ki* transforms and develops all phenomena, whereas *i* is the master of *ki* that makes *ki* act in that way. Like Yulgok, he pointed out that *i* and *ki* are inseparable because the former is a "passive" principle and the latter is an "active" material force. It is, therefore, right to say that there is neither priority nor posteriority between *i* and *ki*. As he wrote, "one origin refers principally to *i* and the diversity of particularizations refers principally to *ki*."[45] "Although *i* and *ki* are inseparable, they are not mixed; although *i* and *ki* are unmixable, they are not separated."[46] For him, *i* and *ki* are "one foundation." At the same time, however, he supported T'oegye's theory that there must be the conceptual distinction between what is "formless" (*i*) and what "has form" (*ki*). It is, then, clear that most eclectic thinkers attempted to synthesize T'oegye's and Yulgok's different views of *i* and *ki* and of the Four Beginnings and the Seven Emotions in the light of Chu Hsi's metaphysics.

APPENDIX 1

T'oegye's Diagram of the Mind, Human Nature, and Feelings[1]

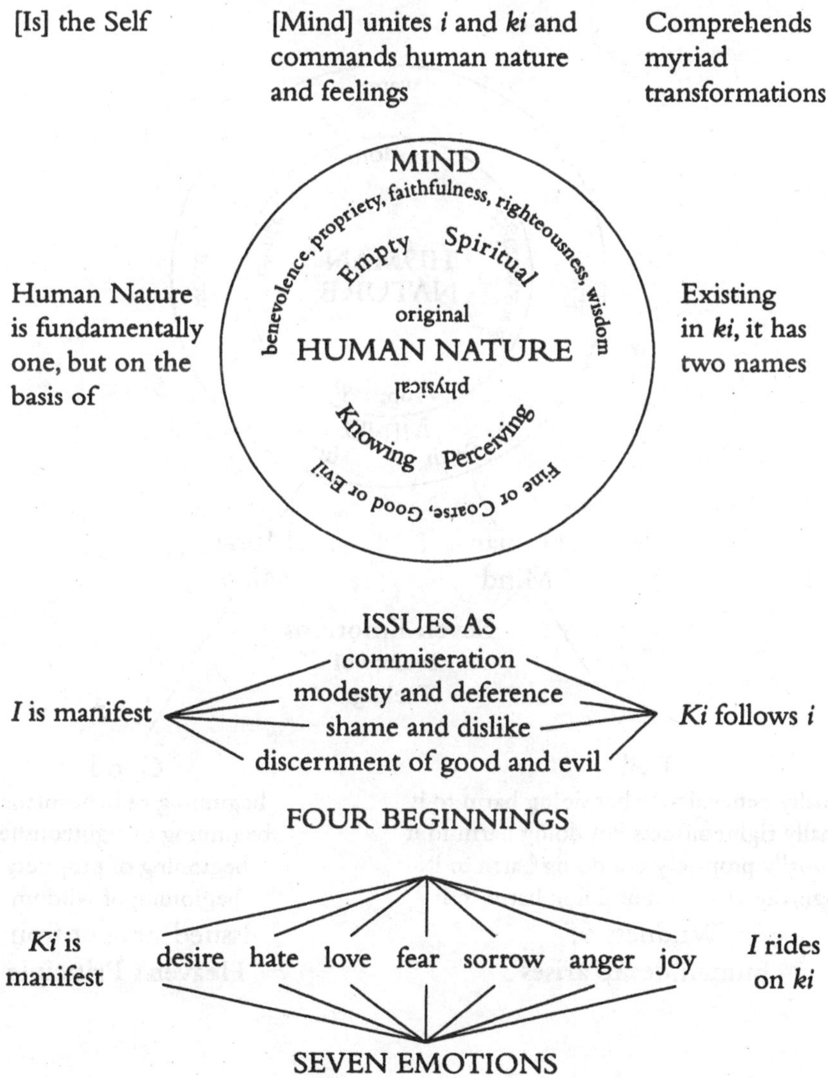

APPENDIX 2

Yulgok's Diagram of the Human Mind and the Moral Mind[2]

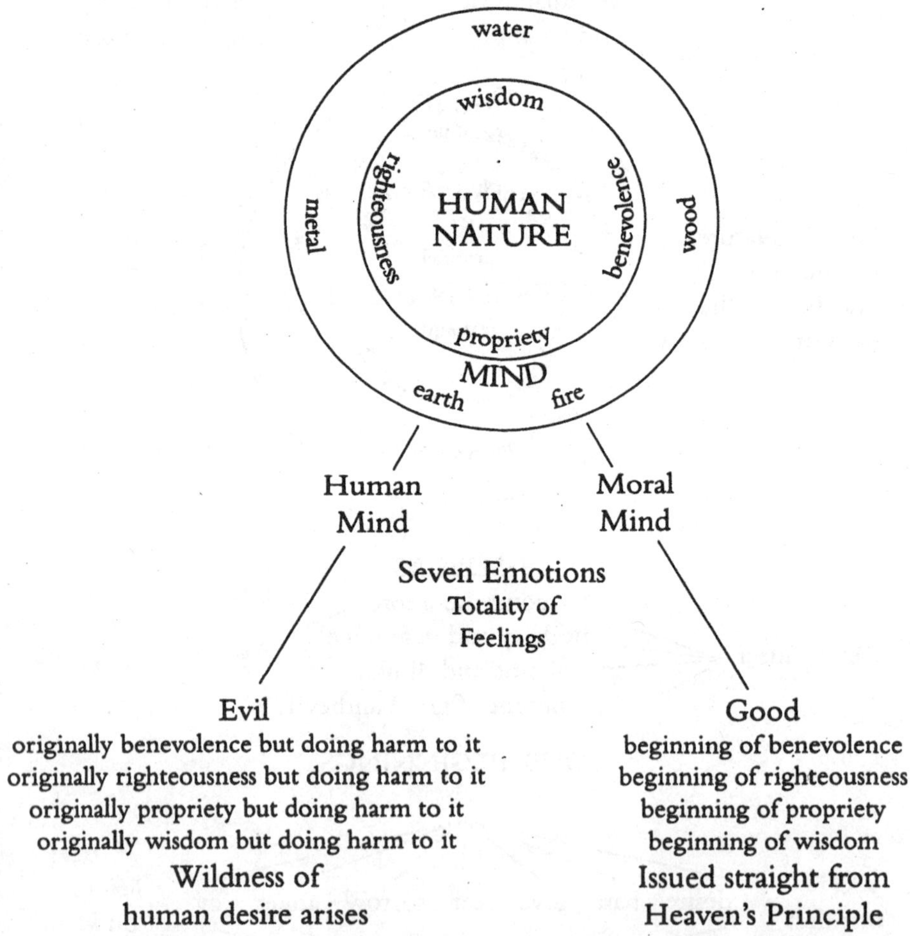

APPENDIX 3

A Chronological and Annotated List of Yi T'oegye's Major Writings Cited

Year	Title and Brief Description
1553	*Ch'ŏnmyŏng tosŏl* (Diagrammatic Explanation of the Mandate of Heaven). This philosophical treatise contains a key statement correlating the Four Beginnings and the Seven Emotions, the statement that initiated the historic Four-Seven debate between T'oegye and Kobong. It is T'oegye's first major work, a ten-section treatise on the diagram. See *T'oegye sŏnsaeng sokjip* (Supplementary Collection of Master T'oegye's Writings), 8:11a–20b, in *TC,* vol. 3, pp.140–144. The original *Ch'ŏnmyŏng to* (Diagram of the Mandate of Heaven) was composed by Chŏng Ch'u-man (Chiŭn, 1509–1561). Chŏng's diagram and T'oegye's revised version of it are collected in *TC* 41:11a (vol. 2, pp. 321–326).
1557	*Kyemong chŏnŭi* (Problems Regarding the Study of Changes), *TC,* vol. 3, pp. 209–248, was written as a result of T'oegye's early interest in the *Book of Changes* and his respect for Chu Hsi's *I-hsüeh ch'i-meng* (Instruction for the Beginners in the Study of the *Book of Changes*). In this text, T'oegye examines Chu Hsi's comments to clarify ambiguous philosophical points in the *Book of Changes.*
1558	*Chujasŏ chŏryo* (Essentials of Master Chu's Correspondence), *TC,* vol. 2, pp. 348–372, is a collection of about one-third of Chu Hsi's letters selected by T'oegye. These letters, according to T'oegye, emphasize particularly Chu Hsi's moral character and learning, as well as his philosophy of self-cultivation. The *Chujasŏ chŏryo* became one of the standard texts for many Korean Neo-Confucians, as well as for Japanese Neo-Confucians such as Fujiwara Seika and Hayashi Razan, who

admired not only T'oegye himself as the great Korean scholar, but also his edition of Chu Hsi's letters.

1558 *Chasŏng nok* (Record for Self-Reflection), *TC*, vol. 3, pp. 153–190. This is a collection of about 100 letters that T'oegye wrote, in his fifties, to his friends and disciples. Most of them address T'oegye's understanding of Neo-Confucian learning and self-cultivation.[3] In fact, this text had a great impact on the rise and development of the Japanese Chu Hsi school, becoming one of the most important texts among the Japanese Neo-Confucians including Hayashi Razan and Yamazaki Ansai.

1559 *Songge Wŏn Myŏng ihak t'ongnok* (Comprehensive Records of the School of Principle in the Sung, Yüan, and Ming Periods), *TC*, vol. 3, pp. 249–552. One of T'oegye's most important works, this is an encyclopedic compendium consisting of many historical and philosophical records about Chu Hsi, his disciples, Chen Te-hsiu, and many other Chinese Neo-Confucians who, in T'oegye's view, transmitted the orthodox Ch'eng-Chu school in China. In eleven fascicles of *Ponjip* (Original Collection) and one more fascicle of *Oejip* (Outer Collection), T'oegye reviews Chu Hsi and over 500 other Chinese scholars, recording all the available data on their biographies and the essential features of their philosophies.[4]

1559–1566 Three "Four-Seven Letters," *TC* 16:8a–17:6b (vol. 1, pp. 405–430).

1566 *Paeksa Sigyo Chŏnsŭmnok ch'ojŏn insŏ kihu* (Postscript to a Conveyed Copy of Ch'en Hsien-chang's *Instructions Through Poetry* and Wang Yang-ming's *Instruction for Practical Living*), *TC* 41:29b–35b (vol. 2, pp. 335–338). In this critical and influential essay, T'oegye defends Ch'eng-Chu orthodoxy and condemns Wang Yang-ming's philosophy of mind and self-cultivation presented in his *Ch'uan-hsi lu* (Instructions for Practical Living) and Ch'en Hsien-chang's individualistic thought presented in his *Shih chiao* (Instructions Through Poetry). Ch'en Hsien-chang (Pai-sha, 1428–1500)[5] was a mid-Ming period Neo-Confucian who was originally a disciple of Wu Yü-pei (1391–1469), a leading member of the orthodox Ch'eng-Chu school. In this critical essay, T'oegye argues that Ch'en Hsien-chang departed radically, either in theory or practice, from Chu Hsi's philosophy. As he asserts,

Ch'en's "individualistic" thinking and esoteric practice and Wang's philosophy of mind and self-cultivation all "come from the thought of Lu Hsiang-shan that focuses on the mind alone" and "generally speaking, they are both Zen Buddhist in nature" (*TC* 41:30b, vol. 2, p. 335). In particular, Wang is charged with rejecting Ch'eng-Chu doctrines on the "extension of knowledge" (ibid.). In T'oegye's own view, then, Lu, Ch'en, and Wang provided no systematic guidance for the Neo-Confucian way of Neo-Confucian learning and self-cultivation.

1566 *Chŏnsŭmnok nonbyŏn* (Critique of Wang Yang-ming's *Instruction for Practical Living*), *TC* 41:23b–29b (vol. 2, pp. 332–336), is the first major and most influential criticism of Wang yang-ming's *Ch'uan-hsi lu* in Korea. T'oegye's full commitment to the heritage of the Chu Hsi school is vividly illustrated in this essay. Calling it orthodoxy (*chŏnghak/cheng-hsüeh*; literally, "right learning"), he expresses his extreme discomfort with Wang's philosophy of mind cultivation. As its leading critic in Korea, T'oegye condemned any deviation like Wang's thought as "heterodox learning" or "Zen Buddhist." For example, he declares that Wang's theory of "the mind is principle" is a "false" view because it abolishes the whole process of the Neo-Confucian learning of human nature and principle. In his view, Wang felt uncomfortable with the Ch'eng-Chu doctrine of "investigating the principles of things"; therefore, he spoke of the mind only, "betraying the teachings of the sages and worthies" (*TC* 41:26b, vol. 2, p. 333). T'oegye criticizes Wang further: "Is this [Wang's teaching] not the same as the Buddha's teaching? Wang sometimes attacked the Buddha in order to prove that his ideas did not come from Buddhism itself. This means that he cheated not only himself but also others" (ibid.). We need to note the historical fact that T'oegye, as the leading guardian of the Ch'eng-Chu tradition in Korea, played a major role in suppressing any substantial historical development of the Wang Yang-ming school in Korea.[6] T'oegye's absolute faith in the orthodox Chu Hsi school is expressed also in his biographical work of Neo-Confucianism, *Songgye Wŏn Myŏng ihak t'ongnok*.

1566 *Heoam sŏnsaeng haengjang* (Biographical Account of Master Chu Hsi), T'oegye's own biography of Chu Hsi. This piece of work illustrates his deep concern with transmitting Chu Hsi orthodoxy in Korea.

1568 *Yukcho so* (Six-Article Memorial), *TC* 6:36b–59b (vol. 1, pp. 181–193). This is T'oegye's greatest political treatise, advising the young ruler on six fundamental matters of the Confucian way of learning, self-cultivation, and government administration. Of course, the serious practice of ethico-spiritual self-cultivation is emphasized for establishing a good government.

1568 *Sŏnghak sipto* (Ten Diagrams on the Learning of Sagehood), *TC* 7:4b–35a (vol. 1, pp. 195–211).[7] T'oegye compiled it in his late sixties (1568), several years after his Four-Seven debate with Kobong. The impact of his Four-Seven thesis on the *Sŏnghak sipto* is quite significant. In particular, the *Sim t'ong sŏngchŏng tosŏl* (Diagrammatic Treatise on the Saying "the Mind Commands Human Nature and Feelings),[8] the sixth part of the *Sŏnghak sipto*, T'oegye gives two concise diagrammatic summaries of his Four-Seven thesis in terms of some of the key ideas examined in this book. As I have pointed out, the *Sŏnghak sipto* is one of his most important works that gives a great summation and synthesis of the entire framework and linkage of the Neo-Confucian metaphysics, ethics, and psychological theory. It went through many printings during the Chosŏn dynasty, and now it exists in at least three modern Korean translations. It was also introduced to Tokugawa Japan, where it became one of the most popular texts among Japanese Neo-Confucians.

1569 *Sasŏ haeŭi* (A Commentary on the Four Books), *TC*, vol. 3, pp. 191–208. This is the first Korean commentary written in contemporary Korean readable for nonscholars, including young people.

No date *Samgyŏng haeŭi* (Commentary on the Three Classics), *TC*, vol. 5, pp. 27–168. T'oegye wrote this in the same contemporary form of Korean language, probably during his later life; that is, roughly around the same time when the *Sasŏ haeŭi* was compiled. It is a collection of his commentaries on the *Book of Poetry*, *Book of History*, and *Book of Changes*.

No date *Sim mu ch'eyong pyŏn* (Critique on the Saying "the Mind Does Not Have Substance and Function"), *TC* 41:16b–19a (vol. 2, pp. 328–330). This treatise explains the Ch'eng-Chu thesis that the mind-and-heart unites *i* and *ki*: human nature is the principle (*i*) of the mind, whereas feelings are the function of the mind.

No date *Pi iki wi ilmul pyŏnchŭng* (Treatise on the Saying That "*I* and *Ki* Are Not One"), *TC* 40:21b (vol. 2, p. 330). T'oegye makes a strict ontological and conceptual distinction of *i* and *ki* more explicit than did Chu Hsi.

APPENDIX 4

A Chronological and Annotated List of Yi Yulgok's Major Writings Cited

Year	Title and Brief Description
1555	*Chagyŏng mun* (Letter of Resolution), *YC* 14:40a–41b (vol. 1, pp. 300–301). This early self-disciplinary letter was written when Yulgok was only nineteen years old. It consists of eleven articles in which he claims that, after a year-long period of Buddhist study and meditation, he finally decided to follow Ch'eng-Chu Neo-Confucianism. In this famous letter, he compares Neo-Confucianism and Buddhism and argues that Neo-Confucianism (especially its practical way of learning, self-cultivation, political order, and social prosperity) is superior to the monastic Buddhist way of meditation and mind cultivation.
1558	*Ch'ŏndo ch'aek* (Treatise on the Way of Heaven), *YC* 14:54a–60b (vol. 2, pp. 307–310). This is Yulgok's first major philosophical work. Yulgok, then twenty-two years old, wrote it during the highest civil service examination in Seoul. As a philosophical treatise on Ch'eng-Chu Neo-Confucianism, it is an outstanding work consisting of 2,500 words interwoven with his broad knowledge of Neo-Confucian metaphysics, ethics, and political thought. It also reflects his extensive reading of the Taoist texts of Lao Tzu and Chuang Tzu that he mastered in his late teens. It not only won a high reputation in Chosŏn Korea, but also was introduced to Ming China where it received respect among Ming Chinese Neo-Confucians.
1569	*Tongho mundap* (Tongho Questions and Answers), *YC* 15:2a–33b (vol. 1, pp. 314–329). This is one of Yulgok's major political treatises, a systematic and critical essay on the way of righteous government with practical measures of government administration. Yulgok wrote it and submitted it to the king after he was

appointed minister of justice. Its eleven articles address political reform, revealing his strong Confucian conviction that a sagely and kingly government must be achieved by establishing practical and necessary changes in government administration. Among these articles are the following proposals: the "recruitment of talented persons from both commoners and Neo-Confucian literati," the policy for "securing people's welfare," and the popular "education of people."

1571 *Sŏwŏn hyangyak* (Community Code of Sŏwŏn) was written when Yulgok became the magistrate of Ch'ŏngju county. It is a systematic political guideline for the local government, consisting of the four main objectives: mutual encouragement of morality, mutual supervision of misconduct, mutual decorum in social order, and mutual cooperation in time of difficulty and hardship.[9]

1572 Yulgok's nine Four-Seven letters, *YC* 9:32b–10:40a (vol. 1, pp. 192–216). The Yulgok-Ugye debate took 1572, that is, six years after the end of the T'oegye-Kobong debate and a year after the death of T'oegye.

1574 *Manŏn pongsa* (Ten-Thousand Character Memorial), *YC* 5:10b–39a (vol. 1, pp. 95–109). This long political treatise demonstrates Yulgok's serious interests in, and concern for, not only practical learning (*sirhak*) but also statecraft. It presents his pragmatic, functional, and egalitarian programs for socio-political reform. In addition to learning and self-cultivation, the central part of this text addresses what Yulgok calls "the seven points of trouble" caused by "the lack of practical achievement" in maintaining an effective system of government administration: first, "there is no real trust between the country and the people"; second, "government officials are not practical in carrying out their duties and responsibilities"; third, "there is no practical role in maintaining the virtue of the king"; fourth, "although wise and talented people are recruited, they are not practically utilized"; fifth, "when there is a national disaster, the government's response to [the will of] Heaven is not practically oriented"; sixth, "most government policies are not practical in ruling (literally saving) the people"; and finally, "in the process of transforming the people's mind-and-heart, there is no practical achievement" (*YC* 5:16b, vol. 1, p. 98). As Yulgok argues, if these are not rectified, "to secure the country and to comfort the people will have no public result, even if the ruler has the sagely mind-and-heart" (*YC* 5:24b, vol. 2, p. 102). Regarding the question of "comforting the people," Yulgok recommends that the king should do five things: first, seek and unite the feelings (*chŏng/ch'ing*) of many ministers by extending the sincere mind-and-heart (*sŏngsim/ch'eng-hsin*) to them; second, reform public servants' rules and regulations to abolish the political corruption of their seizing people's goods through illegal acts; third, rectify the social malady of people's excessive spending, and establish a system of self-regulatory saving; fourth, change the legal system of recruiting slaves (public and private) to relieve the suffering of those people belonging to slavery classes; and finally, change military policies to strengthen the country's defense systems in case of emergency (*YC* 5:25a, vol. 2, p. 102).

1575 *Sŏnghak chipyo* (Essentials of the Learning of the Sages), *YC* 20:1a–20:38b (vol. 1, pp. 428–527, and vol. 2, pp. 1–81). This is Yulgok's most extensive work, which consists of eight volumes divided into twenty-six *kwŏn* (fascicles) on many related topics. It contains the major fundamentals of learning, self-cultivation, and statecraft that are addressed directly to the ruler. Generally speaking, it is patterned after the style of the late Sung scholar Chen Te-hsiu's *Ta-hsüeh yen-i* (Extended Meaning of the *Great Learning*).[10] Like T'oegye's *Sŏnghak sipto*, Yulgok's *Sŏnghak chipyo* is also a great systematization of Ch'eng-Chu Neo-Confucian metaphysics, ethics, and philosophical psychology. Quotations from the entire Ch'eng-Chu literature are carefully selected and systematically structured, and Yulgok presents his own views, insights, and interpretations as well. In contrast to T'oegye's *Sŏnghak sipto*, the *Sŏnghak chipyo* has no diagrams, but is longer and more comprehensive and systematic in style. In addition, it is written as an ethico-political manual; its last two major parts are devoted specifically to the subject of government administration that presents his specific ethico-political ideas and ideals. On the whole, the *Sŏnghak chipyo* clearly illustrates Yulgok's serious concern for practical learning and government administration.

1577 *Kyŏngmong yokyŏl* (Essential Instructions of Kyŏngmong), *YC* 27:3a–21b (vol. 2, pp. 82–91). This systematic text consists of ten short, specific sections devoted to various themes of the Confucian way of life. Unlike Yulgok's other major philosophical works, it covers not only such topics as "establishing the resolve [for learning]," "reading," "self-regulation," and public servants' duties, but also practical guidelines for family regulation, the maintenance of Confucian human relationships, and the proper observance of Confucian rituals including ancestor veneration. This text clearly demonstrates Yulgok's broad interest in many aspects of Confucianism.

1581 *Kyŏngyŏn ilgi* (A Diary of Lectures Before the Throne), *YC* 28:1a–30:94b (vol. 2, pp. 99–228). This is a massive and critical record of crucial historical and political events that took place in Korea from 1556 to 1581. Yulgok wrote it as a result of his practical learning (*sirhak*) of historical research and political administration.

1582 *Hakkyo mobŏm* (Model for an Academy), *YC* 15:34a (vol. 1, p. 330). As a systematic treatise on the education of youth, it gives specific guidelines to beginners of learning. For example, it emphasizes Yulgok's belief that the beginners of learning should, first, establish their resolve.

1582 *Insim tosim tosŏl* (Diagrammatic Treatise on the Human Mind and the Moral Mind), *YC* 14:4a–17a (vol. 1, pp. 282–284). This philosophical treatise is a brief, diagrammatic summary of Yulgok's Four-Seven thesis, which was presented to the king. Yulgok gives a clear discussion of the relationship between mind, human nature, and feelings, especially in terms of the moral mind and the human mind and the Four Beginnings and the Seven Emotions. The Four are described as the good part of the Seven issued from Heaven's principle or the goodness of human nature, and the Seven refer to the totality of all feelings that includes both the moral mind and the human mind.

1583 *Simu yukcho kye* (Six Article Memorial of Current Affairs), *YC* 8:18a–23b (vol. 1, pp. 169–172). This political memorial was presented to the king when Yulgok became the minister of defence in 1583. It is shorter than the *Manŏn pongsa.* As a systematic political essay on the practicality (*sil/shih*) of learning, self-cultivation, and government administration, it contains his six specific reform proposals for education, economy, society, and politics: first, recruit talented and virtuous people; second, preserve and nourish people and army; third, make sufficient revenue for the nation; fourth, keep defense ready in case of emergency; fifth, prepare combat horses; and finally, educate and transform people.

No date *Sŏngch'aek* (Treatise on Sincerity), *Sŭbu* (Supplements), 6:14a–18b, in *YC,* vol. 2, pp. 569–571. In this short philosophical essay, Yulgok presents a systematic interpretation of the Neo-Confucian idea of sincerity, discussing his own understanding of sincerity and sagehood in terms of the practicality of Neo-Confucian learning and self-cultivation. In this regard, then, the essential feature of the *Sŏngch'aek* is similar to that of the *Sŏnghak chipyo,* which suggests that Yulgok probably wrote it in his forties.

No date *Saja ŏnsŏng ch'aek* (Treatise on Questions About the Statements on Sincerity in the Four Books), *Sŭbu,* 6:38a–40a, in *YC,* vol. 2, pp. 581–582. This is another brief essay on Yulgok's understanding of the idea of sincerity according to the Four Books. Like the *Sŏngch'aek* mentioned previously, it emphasizes the cultivation of sincerity as an important part of practical learning and self-cultivation. Like the *Sŏngch'aek,* this essay was probably written in his later years.

No date *Yŏksu ch'aek* (Treatise on the *Book of Changes*), *YC* 14:47a–54a (vol. 1, pp. 304–307). This brief commentary on the *Book of Changes* is presented especially in terms of Chu Hsi's metaphysics of *i* and *ki* and shows Yulgok's basic philosophical views that *i* is the "metaphysical and passive" principle and *ki* is the "physical and active" material force, and that *i* and *ki* are phenomenalistically inseparable in concrete things. Its basic content is similar to that of the *Chŏndo ch'aek,* Yulgok's first philosophical treatise, suggesting that Yulgok probably wrote it in his mid-twenties.

No date *Sasaeng kwisin ch'aek* (Treatise on Life and Death, Ghosts and Spirits), *Sŭbu* (Miscellaneous Writings), 4:20b–26b, in *YC,* vol. 2, pp. 540–543. This interesting essay presents Yulgok's interpretation of ghosts and spirits. It is discussed especially in terms of his philosophy of *ki.* In addition, Yulgok emphasizes the Confucian virtue of filial piety and, therefore, its practice of ancestor veneration.

No date *Sinsŏn ch'aek* (Treatise on Spirits and Immortals), *Sŭbu,* 5:2a–7a, in *YC,* vol. 2, pp. 548–550. Like the former, this is another philosophical essay on the question of spirits and immortals discussed especially in terms of his philosophy of *ki.* However, Yulgok, as a pragmatic and practical thinker, emphasizes the empirical and phenomenal world of human beings and concrete things.

No date *Kunchŏng ch'aek* (Treatise on Military Defense), *Sŭbu*, 5:2a–7a, in *YC*, vol. 2, pp. 548–550. This political treatise was presented to the king and addresses Yulgok's specific reform measures for the contemporary system of government administration and military defense: first, maintain government administration by moral examples; second, feed and nourish people to make them healthy and happy; third, make available sufficient public revenue for all people; and finally, keep all defense systems ready and sharp. The basic content of this short essay suggests that Yulgok probably wrote it when he was serving as minster of defence in 1583, a year before he died.

Notes

Preface

1. The word *Ch'eng-Chu* refers to the two family names of Sung Chinese Neo-Confucians, such as two bothers, Ch'eng Hao and Ch'eng I, and Chu Hsi.

2. It is called the *Chujahak* because Chuja/Chu Tzu ("master Chu") refers to the philosopher's honorific title "master" (*cha/tzu*) and his family name Chu, as this tradition of Neo-Confucianism was established by him.

3. It is called *sŏngnihak* because it refers to the "learning" or "school" (*hak/hsüeh*) of two metaphysical and ethical concepts, *i/li* (principle) and *sŏng/hsing* (human nature). In the Ch'eng-Chu transmission of Neo-Confucianism, these concepts are the two most important single terms of its entire tradition of metaphysics and ethics in China, Korea, and Japan.

4. Every educated Korean would know something about T'oegye and Yulgok. The life, personal character, and moral teaching of these two Neo-Confucians usually appear in the textbooks on ethics or society for primary, middle, and high school students. In addition, there are the so-called Institute of T'oegye's studies and Institute of Yulgok's studies in Seoul; these two research centers have been publishing books and articles, while promoting national and international conferences on their thought.

5. For primary, middle, and high school students, textbooks on ethics and society include these basic aspects of the Korean Confucian tradition.

6. Wm. T. de Bary, and JaHyun Kim Haboush, eds., *The Rise of Neo-Confucianism in Korea* (New York: Columbia University Press, 1985), p. vii.

7. I am referring to Michael Kalton's *To Become a Sage: The Ten Diagrams on Sage Learning by Yi T'oegye* (New York: Columbia University Press, 1988).

8. See Young-chan Ro's *The Korean Neo-Confucianism of Yi Yulgok* (Albany: SUNY Press, 1989), which mainly deals with Yulgok's metaphysics and his philosophy of the mind.

9. See Julia Ching's article on Yulgok's Four-Seven thesis, Tu Weiming's article on T'oegye's Four-Seven thesis, and Wing-tsit Chan's article

on T'oegye's writings. These and two other brief studies on T'oegye and Yulgok are collected in de Bary and Haboush, eds., *The Rise of Neo-Confucianism in Korea.*

10. For a detailed discussion of these terms, see the first section of Chapter I.

11. See the works by Yi Pyŏng-do, Yi Sang-ŭn, Yun Sa-sun, Pae Chong-ho, and others in Bibliography, part II, sec. A.

12. See Bibliography, part I, sec. A.

13. This is done from literary Chinese. In premodern Korea, academic books and scholarly works, including Confucian and Neo-Confucian texts, were written in literary Chinese because they were intended for the literati classes of educated people.

14. See Bibliography, part I, sec. B.

15. See Bibliography, part I, sec. B.

16. See Bibliography, part I, sec. C.

17. These include the works by Ch'ien Mu, Mou Tsung-san, Abe Yoshio, Takahashi Susume, Yi Pyŏng-do, Yi Sang-ŭn, Yun Sa-sun, Pae Chong-ho, and others. See Bibliography, part II, sec. A.

18. See de Bary and Haboush, eds., *The Rise of Neo-Confucianism in Korea*; Kalton, *To Become a Sage,* and Ro, *The Korean Neo-Confucianism of Yi Yulgok.*

Historical Background: Korean Neo-Confucianism

1. From 57 B.C.E. to 668 C.E., the Korean peninsula was divided into three kingdoms: Koguryŏ (37 B.C.E.–668 C.E.), Paekche (13 B.C.E.–668 C.E.), and Silla (57 B.C.E.–668 C.E.). Koguryŏ occupied the top half, Paekche the southwestern quarter, and Silla the southeastern quarter. Silla conquered the other two kingdoms in 668 C.E. and ruled the whole peninsula until 935 C.E.

2. For example, the eminent monk Wŏnkwang emphasized Confucian moral precepts, such as filial piety and truthfulness, for the secular life of self-cultivation and public service. See Kim Pu-sik, *Samguk sagi* (Historical Records of the Three Kingdoms) (Seoul: Eulyoo Munhwasa, 1983). Fur-

thermore, it is also said that he "mastered the major Buddhist scriptures as well as Confucian classics." See Ilyon, *Samguk yusa: Legends and History of the Three Kingdoms of Ancient Korea*, trans. Ha Tae-Hung and Grafton Mintz (Seoul: Yonsei University Press, 1972), bk. 4, ch. 5, sec. 97.

3. Three-year Confucian mourning was known to the people of Koguryŏ as well. But the Buddhist custom was more popular because most people found it much less demanding. See *Samguk sagi*, 4:4.

4. This academy adopted the key teachings of Taoism and Buddhism as well, together with martial arts. The Silla youth learned about the "Five Confucian Virtues" (benevolence, righteousness, propriety, wisdom, and truthfulness) and the "Six Ways to Serve the Government" (sagely minister, good minister, loyal minister, wise minister, virtuous minister, and honest minister). See Kim Pusik, *Sạmguk sagi*, 4:4 (King Chinhŭng).

5. See *Koryŏsa* (History of Koryŏ) (Seoul: Asea munhwasa, 1973), 73:2a-b.

6. The purpose of *chesul kwa* was to select candidates on the basis of their ability to compose Chinese literary forms such as poetry (*shih*), rhyme prose (*fu*), sacrificial ode (*sung*), and the problem essay (*ts'e*), while the *myŏnggyŏng kwa* examined one's knowledge of the Five Classics. Both examinations were conducted for the purpose of selecting officials, but the former was regarded as especially important because the aristocratic classes of this era esteemed literary accomplishment more than the theoretical knowledge of Confucian classics. Literary composition was more important in both China and Korea not only because it was more practical in daily life, but also because the Five Classics were generally thought to be too hard and theoretical. The *chap kwa* was used to select specialists to serve in areas, such as law, medicine, divination, and accounting, that required technical knowledge and skill. The status of this examination was, therefore, lower than that of the literary composition and classics examination.

7. *Koryŏsa*, 93:19a (Biography of Ch'oe Sŏng-no).

8. Ibid., 3:22b. The Chinese state shrine system began in the Han dynasty but was fully established by the T'ang dynasty. In the Three Kingdoms period (57 B.C.E.–668 C.E.), there was a Korean royal shrine system, called the Seven-Generation Ancestors Shrine that prospered for venerating former kings. From the end of the Koryŏ period, Confucian ceremonies for Confucian sages and worthies (including eminent Korean Confucians) were

strictly observed throughout the country. The state policy of the Chosŏn dynasty later solidified them much further.

9. Ibid., 3:24b.

10. Ibid., 3:24a.

11. Ibid. The Hyanggyos served as important local Confucian academies in the Chosŏn dynasty. In South Korea, there are 231 Hyanggyos, which still serve as local ritual sites, meeting halls, and classrooms for Confucian ethical education. The former Chinese and Korean Confucian sages and worthies are periodically venerated at many of these places, and other traditional rituals are observed. Also, these Hyanggyos provide people in local areas with knowledge about Confucian rituals and genealogical information.

12. See his biography in *Koryŏsa*, 95:1a–9a. The nine courses are as follows: Pleasure of Sagehood; Great Mean; Illumination of Sincerity; Reverential Effort; Discussion of the Way; Following Nature; Progress of Virtue; Great Harmony; and Serving and Calling. Ch'oe seems have based these ideas mainly on the Four Books. In particular, the second, third, sixth, and eighth are the ideas found in the *Doctrine of the Mean*, one of the Four Books.

13. *Koryŏsa*, 95:5a-b.

14. Ibid., 95:5b–6a.

15. Ibid., 73:2b–3a.

16. Ibid., 31a–32a. Each program is devoted the study of one of the following: *Book of Changes*, *Book of Rites*, *Book of Poetry*, *Book of History*, *Spring and Autumn Annals*, *Rites of Chou*, and military studies.

17. In this regard, see Yi Pyŏng-do, *Han'guk yuhak saryak* (An Outline History of Korean Confucianism) (Seoul: Asea munhwasa, 1986), p. 56.

18. These six colleges include National College (Kukhak), High College (T'aehak), Four-Portal College (Samunhak), Law College (Yurhak), Calligraphy College (Sŏhak), and Accounting College (Sanhak). The most important entrance requirement for students was the differences of official ranks of their families: National College admitted the sons of the top three rank officials; High College, the sons of the fourth and fifth rank officials; Four-Portal College, the sons of the sixth and seventh rank officials; and the sons of the eighth and ninth rank officials attended either the last three colleges of technical specialties or local schools (*hanggyo*).

19. For example, a daughter of Khubilai of the Yüan married the crown prince of Koryŏ who later became King Ch'ungyŏl in 1270. And at the Yüan's request, a government bureau was established to arrange marriage between Korean girls and Yüan officials.

20. *Koryŏsa*, 105:28a–31a.

21. Consult Yi Pyŏng-do, *Han'guk yuhak saryak*, p. 68; Ki-baik Lee, *A New History of Korea*, trans. Edward Wagner (Seoul: Ilchogak, 1983), p. 166; Park Chong-hong, "Historical Review of Korean Confucianism," *Korea Journal* (Sept. 1963): 6; K. P. Yang and G. Henderson, "An Outline History of Korean Confucianism, Part I: The Early Period and Yi Factionalism," *Journal of Asian Studies* 18 (1958): 85.

22. *Koryŏsa*, 106:1a–2b.

23. See Hyŏn Sang-yun, *Chosŏn yuhaksa* (A History of Korean Confucianism) (Seoul: Hyŏnŭmsa, 1948; reprint 1982), p. 18; Yun Yong-gyun, *Shushigaku no denrai to sono eikyō ni tsuite* (On the Transmission of the Chu Hsi School and Its Influence) (Seoul, 1933), p. 21.

24. *Koryŏsa*, 105:31a.

25. Ibid., 105:31a. It is stated that he even took his pen name, Hoehŏn, and the Sino-Korean character Hoe comes from Chu Hsi's own pen name, Hoeam (Hui-an in Chinese).

26. Ibid., 106:2a-b.

27. Ibid.

28. Ibid., 105:30a.

29. At present, it is affiliated with a public secular university called Sŏnggyun'gwan Taehakkyo in Seoul. But the Sŏnggyun'gwan itself still serves as the headquarters of Confucianism in Korea, whereas Sŏnggyun'gwan University maintains its College of Confucianism and Department of Korean Philosophy that offer a variety of courses on the subject of Confucianism including the Korean tradition. The Sŏnggyun'gwan is organized into the eight areas of the Confucian tradition: rituals, classics, culture, education, newspapers, and so on. Only in South Korea, is Confucianism still practiced formally through public organizations, rituals, meetings, and seminars on both national and local levels. It is, therefore, strong enough to be institutionalized, if necessary, even as an organized religion. The Confucian Yurim (literally, "forest of literati") organization consists of active Confucian

elites and ordinary citizens who expand their network at both national and local levels. Many leaders of the Sŏnggyun'gwan and the Yurim are academic professors of Confucianism and Korean philosophy at Sŏnggyun'gwan University and other universities. The national organization of the Yurim is the Yudohoe Ch'ongbonbu (General Organization for the Confucian Way) established in 1970. In the countryside, there are 231 Hyanggyos (local government academies in the Koryŏ and Chosŏn periods), which now serve as local ritual sites, meeting halls, and classrooms for Confucian ethical education. Official rituals are performed at the Sŏnggyun'gwan; for example, the celebration of Confucius' birthday is still observed there, and Chinese and Korean Confucian sages and worthies, including eminent Korean scholars like T'oegye and Yulgok, are periodically venerated at the Sŏnggyun'gwan and Hyanggyos. Ancestor worship and other rituals (especially funeral ceremonies) are formalized and observed. For more information on this and related topics, see my articles: "Confucianism and Women in Modern Korea: Continuity, Change, and Conflict," in Arvind Sharma and Katherine Young, eds, *The Annual Review of Women in World Religions*, vol. 3. (Albany, N.Y.: SUNY Press, 1994), pp. 142–188; "Confucianism in Contemporary Korean Society: Some Reflections on Continuity and Change," *Korean Studies in Canada* 1 (1993): 17–33; and "Confucianism: A Living Religious Tradition in Contemporary South Korea," *Korean Studies in Canada* 2 (December 1994): 11–23.

30. *Koryŏsa*, 107:15a.

31. Ibid., 109:21a. U T'ak seems to be the first Korean Neo-Confucian scholar who studied the *Book of Changes* and Chu Hsi's commentary seriously.

32. King Ch'ungsŏn went to the Yüan capital with Paek I-jong in 1298 and developed a close relationship with Yüan scholars. He returned to Koryŏ ten years later to succeed to the throne. When he was removed from the throne in 1313, he went to Yüan China again, accompanied by Yi Chehyŏn and other Koryŏ scholars. There, he associated with Yüan Neo-Confucians as before and built the Hall of Ten Thousand Volumes in the Yüan capital.

33. *Koryŏsa*, 74:31b–32a.

34. For a biographical account of Chŏng, see *Koryŏsa*, 117:1a–20a and *Poŭn munjip* (Literary Works of Chŏng Poŭn), *kwŏn* 3 and 4. Since his early years, Chŏng liked to study the *Great Learning* and *Doctrine of the Mean* (*Koryŏsa*, 117:1b). For Korean secondary sources on Chŏng, see Hyŏn Sang-

yun, *Chosŏn yuhaksa*, p. 13; Yi Pyŏng-do, *Han'guk yuhak saryak*, pp. 47–77; and Pak Chong-hong, "Tongbang ihakŭi cho rosŏŭi Chŏng Poŭn" (Chŏng Poŭn, the Founder of the Korean Neo-Confucian School of Principle), in his *Han'guk sasangsa nongo yuhak p'yŏn* (Essays on the History of Korean Thought, edition on Confucianism) (Seoul: Sŏngmundang, 1977), pp. 24–26.

35. Although this general distinction is generally convenient for us to distinguish the two schools of thought, it is, in the strict sense, misleading. I will discuss this problem further in Chapter IV, in the second section on feelings and the learning of the mind-and-heart.

36. *Koryŏsa*, 117:2a.

37. In the Three Kingdom period, the Confucian custom of a three-year mourning had been known to the people of Koguryŏ and Silla, but the Buddhist custom of 100-day mourning was more popular (*Samguk sagi*, 4:4).

38. *Koryŏsa*, 115:9b.

39. This text was introduced to Korea sometime during the early fourteenth century. For an English translation of it, see Patricia B. Ebrey, trans., *Chu Hsi's Family Rituals* (Princeton, NJ: Princeton University Press, 1991).

40. China's family shrine system was established in the Sung dynasty following Chu Hsi's *Chia li*. According to this text, a man of virtue should construct a Confucian shrine to the east of the main house. All noble families of the Chosŏn dynasty were asked by the government to build a family shrine. Those who did not have it were punished and even degraded to the status of commoner. Confucian ceremonies were performed at family shrines by noble families; commoners gradually developed their own. Poor nobles and commoners had a small household altar in a corner of the front hall of their houses, which was more popular than expensive independent shrines.

41. *Koryŏsa*, 115:7b–8a (Biography of Chŏng Mong-ju).

42. Ibid., 113:34b (Biography of Yi Saek).

43. Ibid., 117:10b (Biography of Yi In-jok).

44. Ibid., 120:32a-b (Biography of Kim Cha-su).

45. Ibid. (Biography of Pak Cho).

46. For a brief English discussion of the rise and development of this school, see Yi U-sŏng, "Confucian Politics in Chosŏn Period and the Existence of Sallim," in *Main Currents of Korean Thought* (Seoul: Korean Commission for UNESCO, 1983), pp. 147–161.

47. For more information on this subject, consult the following Korean sources: *Koryŏ hugi pulgyo chŏngaesa yŏn'gu* (Studies on the History of Buddhism in the Late Koryŏ Dynasty) (Seoul: Minjoksa, 1986); Yi Chong-ik, "Chosŏnŭi pibul chŏngch'aekkwa bulkyohoe t'ong sasang" (Anti-Buddhist Policy and the Entire Tradition of Buddhist Thought in the Chosŏn Dynasty), in *Han'guk sasangŭi simch'ung yŏn'gu* (Studies on Korean Thought) (Seoul: Usŏk, 1986), pp. 142–159; and Han Woo-keun (U-gŭn), "Yŏmal Sŏnch'oŭi pulgyo chŏngch'aek" (The Policy Toward Buddhism During the Koryŏ-Chosŏn Transitional Period), in *Seoul Taehakkyo nonmunjip* (Collected Articles of Seoul University), vol. 6 (Dec. 1957), pp. 3–80.

48. His biography is found in *Koryŏsa*, 109:1a–30a, as well as in *Sambong chip* (Collected Works of Chŏng To-jŏn) (Seoul: Kuksa p'ŏynch'an wiwŏnhoe, 1961), *kwŏn* 14. For a general discussion on his life and thought, see Chai-sik Chung, "Chŏng To-jŏn: Architect of Yi Dynasty Government and Ideology," in de Bary and Haboush, *The Rise of Neo-Confucianism in Korea*, pp. 59–88. A good Korean source is Han Yong-u, *Chŏng To-jŏn sasangŭi yŏn'gu* (A Study of Chŏng To-jŏn's Thought) (Seoul: Seoul National University Press, 1985).

49. For this text, see *Sambong chip*, pp. 204–207. It was compiled in 1394 and outlines a new constitutional order for the Chosŏn dynasty. Chŏng based it on several Chinese texts, especially the *Rites of Chou* (*Chou-li*) that he referred to as an ideal model for political reform.

50. Ibid., pp. 128–203. This text was compiled in 1395 and describes how the duties and functions of government officials were codified over the course of China's history. Also, it presents Sambong's own suggestions for the Chosŏn government.

51. Ibid., pp. 295–358. Unlike the preceding, it outlines the moral and political duties of the ruler.

52. For this text, see ibid., pp. 280–288. The first part deals with Sambong's critique of Buddhism in terms of mind (*sim/hsin*) and the second part presents his critique of Taoism in terms of material force (*ki/ch'i*). In the third part, entitled "Principle Admonishes Mind and Material Force," Sambong defends Confucianism in the context of his critique of both Buddhism

and Taoism. This last part of the *Simgii p'ŏyn* is translated by John B. Duncan in Peter H. Lee et al. eds. *Sourcebook of Korean Civilization* (New York: Columbia University Press, 1993), vol. 1, pp. 454–458.

53. *Sambong chip*, ibid., pp. 280–288.

54. See ibid., pp. 256–269. It consists of twenty short chapters. For an English translation of two chapters dealing with Sambong's critique of the Buddhist doctrine of *karma* and *samsara* and his critical comparison of Neo-Confucianism and Buddhism respectively, see Lee, *Sourcebook of Korean Civilization*, vol. 1, pp. 377–383.

55. For Ch'eng I's criticism of Buddhism, see *I-shu* (Surviving Works) 18:10a–11b, in *Erh-Ch'eng ch'üan-shu* (Complete Works of the Two Ch'engs) (SPPY ed.). For Chu Hsi's, consult his *Chu Tzu wen-chi* (hereafter abbreviated *CTWC*) (Literary Works of Master Chu) 6:36a–38 and 67:19–20, in *Chu Tzu ta-ch'üan* (Great Compendium of Literary Works by Master Chu) (SPPY ed.), and *Chu Tzu yü-lei* (hereafter abbreviated *CTYL*) (Classified Conversations of Master Chu) (comp. Li Ching-te, 1880 ed.), 126:1–7. For selected translations of these works, see Wing-tsit Chan, *A Source Book in Chinese Philosophy* (hereafter abbreviated *Source Book*) (Princeton, N.J.: Princeton University Press, 1963), pp. 564–565, 646–653.

56. *Sambong chip*, pp. 254–256, 264–265.

57. Ibid., pp. 261–262.

58. Ibid.

59. See *Yangch'on chip* (Collected Works of Kwŏn Yangch'on) (Seoul: Minjok munhwa ch'ujinhoe, 1979).

60. Ibid., 16:15a.

61. Ibid., 22:16b.

62. Ibid., 15:14b.

63. For the *Iphak tosŏl* in original Chinese, see Pae Chong-ho, ed., *Han'guk yuhak charyo chipsŏng* (Collected Source Materials on Korean Neo-Confucianism), 3 vols. (Seoul: Yŏnsae University Press, 1980), vol. 1, pp. 3–17.

64. For this diagram in original Chinese, see Pae Chong-ho, ibid., vol. 1, pp. 77–78. For John Duncan's English translation of it, see Lee et al. *Sourcebook of Korean Civilization*, vol. 1, p. 458–460. For a good discussion of

this diagram, see Michael Kalton, "The Writings of Kwŏn Kŭn: The Context and Shape of Early Yi Dynasty Neo-Confucianism," in de Bary and Haboush, *The Rise of Neo-Confucianism in Korea*, pp. 107–113. For East Asian sources, consult Yi Pyŏng-do, *Han'guk yuhak saryak*, pp. 84–86 and Takahashi Susumu, "Kwŏn Kŭn sasangŭi yŏksajŏk ŭimiwa T'oegye" (Historical Meaning of Kwŏn Kŭn's Thought and T'oegye) in *Yi T'oegyewa kyŏngŭi sasang* (Yi T'oegye and His Philosophy of Reverence), trans. An Pyŏng-ju (Seoul: Sin'gu munhwasa, 1986), pp. 31–47.

65. *Iphak tosŏl*, 1:2a.

66. Herbert Fingarette, *Confucius—The Secular as Sacred* (New York: Harper and Row, 1972).

67. These include three classes in the following order: (1) the middle class (*chungin*), who held the technical posts as medical officers, translator-interpreters, accountants, artists, etc; (2) free-born commoners (*sangmin*) like farmers and merchants; and (3) low-born slaves (*ch'ŏnmin*). Furthermore, the *yangban* class itself also had some distinctions: the military order received much less respect than the civil order. Likewise, *soja* (Sons of *yangban* by secondary wives, their descendants, and sons and grandsons of *yangban* widows who remarried) could not sit for examinations to qualify for civil office appointments.

68. JaHyun Kim Haboush, "Confucianization of Korean Society," in Gilbert Rozman, ed., *The East Asian Region: Confucian Heritage and Its Modern Adaptation* (Princeton, N.J.: Princeton University Press, 1991), pp. 91–103.

69. This subject of Korean Neo-Confucianism in the Chosŏn dynasty has been studied to a ceratin extent, which added a great deal to articulating the socio-political structures and historical differences of Chosŏn Korea. See Haboush, ibid. This article is a historical survey that discusses the Korean process of Confucianizing the society in terms of "education," "government, "meritocracy," "ancestor worship," and "patriarchy." It covers from the ancient period to the late Chosŏn dynasty, focusing more on the Koryo-Chosŏn transitional period. See also Martina Deuchler's recent book, *The Confucian Transformation of Korea: A Study of Society and Ideology*, Harvard-Yenching Institute Monograph Series 36 (Cambridge, Mass.: Harvard University Press, 1992), which presents the fundamental ways in which the Chosŏn dynasty used Neo-Confucian ideology as a "political vehicle" to alter many aspects of Koryo's life, including the social structure, position of women, ancestor veneration, and inheritance. For other relevant studies, see the following: Edward Y. J. Chung, "The Wang Yang-ming School of Neo-

Confucianism in Korean Intellectual History," *Korean Culture* 13, no. 3 (Fall 1992): 14–23; JaHyun Haboush Kim, *A Heritage of Kings: One Man's Monarchy in the Confucian World* (New York: Columbia University Press, 1988); James Palais, "Confucianism and the Aristocratic/Bureaucratic Balance in Korea," *Harvard Journal of Asiatic Studies* 44, pt. 2 (1984): 427–466; J. Palais, *Politics and Policies in Traditional Korea*, Harvard East Asian Series 82 (Cambridge, Mass.: Harvard University Press, 1975); and Chun Shin-yong, ed., *Upper-Class Culture in Yi-Dynasty Korea* (Seoul: The Si-sa-yong-o-sa Publishers, 1982).

70. For the examination system of the Chosŏn dynasty, consult Yong-ho Ch'oe, *The Civil Examinations and the Social Structure in the Early Yi Dynasty Korea: 1392–1600* (Seoul: The Korea Research Center, 1987) and Yi Sŏngmu, "The Influence of Neo-Confucianism on Education and the Civil Service Examination in Fourteen and Fifteenth-Century Korea," in de Bary and Haboush, eds., *The Rise of Neo-Confucianism in Korea*, pp. 59–88. For a Korean source, see Yi Pyŏng-do, *Han'guk yuhak saryak*, pp. 99–101.

71. For a good monograph on these literati purges and institutional power struggles, see Edward W. Wagner, *The Literati Purges: Political Conflict in Early Yi Korea* (Cambridge, Mass.: East Asian Research Center, Harvard University Press, 1974).

72. For this subject, consult Sakai Tadao, "Yi Yulgok and the Community Compact," in de Bary and Haboush, eds., *The Rise of Neo-Confucianism in Korea*, pp. 323–348.

73. The village code was embodied basically in four objectives: mutual encouragement of Confucian morality, mutual supervision of wrong doing, mutual observance of social relationships, and mutual help in times of trouble and disaster. It was later developed further by such scholars as T'oegye and Yulgok.

74. Hyŏn Sang-yun, *Chosŏn yuhaksa*, pp. 47–49, classified it as an independent school of thought in the early sixteenth century.

75. In 1608 these private schools numbered more than 100; and those *sŏwŏn* supported by the state also increased in number at the same time.

76. These are collected in the *Hwadam chip* (Collected Works of Hwadam), 2:11b–15a. See Pae Chong-ho, *Han'guk yuhak charyo chipsŏng*, vol. 1, pp. 77–78. For Michael Kalton's translation of Hwadam's *T'aehŏ sŏl*, see Lee et al., *Sourcebook of Korean Civilization*, vol. 1, p. 608.

77. Pae Chong-ho, ibid., 2:14b. Translation adapted from Lee, et al., ibid., vol. 1, p. 608.

78. Pae Chong-ho, ibid., 2:12a-b.

79. Ibid., 2:14a.

80. For T'oegye's criticism of Hwadam, see *TC* 14:8b (vol. 1, p. 364).

81. For Yulgok's comments on Hwadam, see *YC* 10:37b (vol. 2, p. 214).

82. Hoejae's philosophy of *i* and *ki* is found in *Hoejae chip* (Collected works of Yi Hoejae), 5:5a–12a. See Pae Chong-ho, *Han'guk yuhak charyo chipsŏng*, vol. 1, pp. 63–71.

83. *Ilchae chip* (Collected Works of Yi Ilchae), 7b–8a. Pae Chong-ho, ibid., vol. 1, pp. 85–86.

84. For the life and teaching of Lo Ch'in-shun, see I. Bloom, trans., *Knowledge Painfully Acquired: The K'un-chih chi of Lo Ch'in-shun* (New York: Columbia University Press, 1987).

85. This is found in *TC* 41:10b. T'oegye revised it and gave his own ideas. T'oegye's *Ch'ŏnmyŏng sindo* (New Diagram of Heaven and Destiny) is in *TC* 41:11a.

86. For my brief discussion of Kwŏn's philosophy, see the second section (Neo-Confucianism in the Chosŏn Dynasty) of this chapter.

87. *TC* 41:10b.

88. For the *locus classicus* for the two ideas of "moral mind" and "human mind," as well as Chu Hsi's commentary, see Chapter I ("Philosophical Introduction"), section on The Ch'eng-Chu Interpretation in China and Chapter III ("Yulgok's Four-Seven Thesis"), section on Moral Mind and Human Mind.

89. See *Sojae sŏnsaeng naejip* (Collected Inner Works of Master Sojae), 2:1a–7a. See Pae Chong-ho, *Han'guk yuhak charyo chipsŏng*, vol. 1, pp. 269–272. Chu Hsi's theory of the human mind and the moral mind was discussed more extensively by T'oegye and Yulgok in their Four-Seven debates.

90. *Sojae chip* (Collected Works of No Sojae), 7:16a-b.

91. Bloom, *Knowledge Painfully Acquired,* p. 51. Yulgok was influenced by Lo's philosophy; he also argues that the mind is one because the moral mind is always included in the human mind.

92. *Sojae sŏnsaeng naejip,* 2:5a, in Pae Chong-ho, *Han'guk yuhak charyo chipsŏng,* vol. 1, p. 271.

93. Tu Wei-ming, "Yi Hwang's Perception of the Mind," *T'oegye hakpo* 19 (1978), p. 467.

94. Abe Yoshio, ed., *Chōsen no Shushigaku Nihon no Shushigaku* (Korean Chu Hsi School and Japanese Chu Hsi School) in *Shushigaku taikei* (Great Compendium on the Chu Hsi School) (Tokyo: Meitoku Shuppansha, 1977), vol. 12, p. 9.

95. *T'oegye sŏnsaeng ŏnhaengnok* (Words and Conduct of Master T'oegye), 6:21a, in *TC,* vol. 4, p. 254. For Yulgok's account of T'oegye, see also *T'oegye sŏnsaeng ŏnhaengnok,* 6:15b–17a, *TC,* vol. 4, pp. 251–252.

96. Ibid.

97. In this regard, see Abe Yoshio, "Development of Neo-Confucianism in Japan, Korea, and China: A Comparative Study," *Acta Asiatica* 19 (1970): 22.

98. See Abe Yoshio, *Nihon Shushigaku to Chōsen* (The Chu Hsi School in Japan and Its Relation to Korea) (Tokyo: Tokyo University Press, 1965).

99. See *TC,* vol. 3, pp. 153–190. For a brief description of this text, see Appendix 3.

100. This is found in *TC,* vol. 2, pp. 348–372. See Appendix 3.

101. Except as otherwise noted, most of the biographical information that follows is drawn from his *Yŏnbo* (Chronological Biography) in *TC,* vol. 3, pp. 576–620.

102. Many of his poems are found in *TC* 1:1a–5:43a (vol. 1, pp. 47–162). For an introductory work on his poetry, consult Wang Su, *T'oegye sihak* (T'oegye's Poetry) (Seoul: T'oegyehak yŏn'guwŏn, 1981).

103. This compendium contains extensive quotations from Chu Hsi and many other authors on such subjects as Neo-Confucian metaphysics and ethics. As one of the most widely read reference books, it played a major role in establishing the orthodox Ch'eng-Chu school in both China and Korea.

104. See *T'oegye sŏnsaeng ŏnhaengnok*, 1:1b, in *TC*, vol. 4, p. 169.

105. For an English discussion of Chen Te-hsiu and his *Hsin ching*, see Wm. T. de Bary, *Neo-Confucian Orthodoxy and the Learning of the Mind-and-Heart* (hereafter abbreviated as *Neo-Confucian Orthodoxy*) (New York: Columbia University Press, 1981), pp. 67–205. For a Korean study of T'oegye and this text, see Kim Pyŏng-t'ae, "T'oegyewa *Simgyŏng puju*" (T'oegye and the *Classic for Mind-and-Heart* Supplemented and Annotated) in *Han'gukŭi ch'ŏrak*, no. 8 (Dec. 1979): 67–81, and his "*Simgyŏng puju* yuhuron ponŭi kanbon" (Publication of Editions of the *Classic for the Mind-and-Heart* with T'oegye's Epilogue), *T'oegyehak yŏn'gu*, no. 6 (Dec. 1979): 83–113.

106. *TC*, vol. 4, p. 169.

107. *TC*, vol. 4, pp. 169–171, and vol. 2, p. 326.

108. *TC*, vol. 2, p. 328.

109. T'oegye accepted such appointments as the minister of rites, the minister of public works, the minister of personnel, the head of high offices, and so on. In 1552 he was forced to serve, for a short period of time, as the head of the Sŏnggyun'gwan, the most respected position for a Neo-Confucian scholar. When he heard in 1567 the news that his friends and disciples were urging King Sŏnjo (r. 1567–1607) to appoint the leading scholar T'oegye prime minister, he accepted only a position in the royal lectures.

110. Yi Sang-ŭn, *T'oegyeŭi saengaewa hangmun* (T'oegye's Life and Learning) (Seoul: Sŏmundang, 1973), pp. 44–48.

111. For a chronological and annotated description of these and other works, see Appendix 3.

112. T'oegye's Four-Seven letters are found in *TC* 16:8b–30a (vol. 1, pp. 405–442).

113. *YC* 3:21a (vol. 1, p. 56).

114. Cited in Yi Pyŏng-do, *Yulgokŭi saengaewa sasang*, p. 28.

115. Song Si-yŏl was a leading thinker-politician in the mid-seventeenth century. He was a leading disciple of Yulgok's disciple Kim Changsaeng; that is, he came from the Kiho tradition of Chugip'a (school of the primacy of material force). He held many high-ranking official positions, including prime minister and the tutor to the king in the middle and late seventeenth century. For a brief description of his comments on the Four-Seven controversy, see the Epilogue (section on The School of the Primacy of *Ki*).

116. See *Songja taejŏn* (Great Compendium of Master Song), *kwŏn* (fascicle) 19, p. 444.

117. *YC* 35:3b–4a (vol. 2, pp. 342–343).

118. See Song Sŏk-ku, *Han'gukŭi yubul sasang* (Confucian and Buddhist Thought in Korea) (Seoul: Sangsawŏn, 1985), p. 393.

119. As we will see later in the chapter on self-cultivation, Yulgok's interpretation of self-cultivation puts great emphasize on the transformation of *ki* by nourishing it. This seems to have been influenced by his early study of Buddhism.

120. This is found in *YC* 14:40a–41b (vol. 1, pp. 300–301).

121. *YC* 35:4a (vol. 2, p. 343).

122. *TC*, *kwŏn* 23, Letter to Cho Sa-kyŏng.

123. *TC* 14:17b–18a (vol. 1, p. 367).

124. For a chronological and annotated list of these and other writings, see Appendix 4.

125. For this subject, see Edward Y. J. Chung, "Yi Yulgok, a Neo-Confucian Political Reformer in Sixteenth-Century Korea," in Bernard H. Luk, ed., *Contacts Between Cultures (Eastern Asia: History and Social Sciences)* (Lewiston, Queenston, and Lampeter: Edwin Mellen Press, 1992), vol. 4, pp. 171–175.

126. See *Simu yukcho kye*, *YC* 8:18a–23b.

127. When the Japanese invaded Korea soon after Yulgok died, Yu showed his admiration of Yulgok by praising him as a true sage with a clear, far-reaching vision of history. Modern Korean historians suggest that, had Yulgok's proposal been adopted, Korea would not have suffered from Hideyoshi's massive invasion.

128. For my chronological and annotated list of these and other writings, see Appendix 4.

129. These are found in *YC* 9:34b–10:40a (vol. 1, pp. 192–217).

130. This school of thought was influential especially in Seoul and in Kyŏnggi and Ch'ungch'ŏng provinces, areas of central Korea near the capital.

131. See Julia Ching, "The Goose-Lake Monastery Debate (1175)," *Journal of Chinese Philosophy* 1 (1974): 161–178.

132. Edward Y. J. Chung, "The Wang Yang-ming School of Neo-Confucianism in Korean Intellectual History," *Korean Culture* 13, no. 3 (Fall 1992): 20.

133. The Sino-Korean term *chŏng* means "correct," "right" or even "orthodox," referring to Ch'eng-Chu orthodoxy.

134. This is found in *TC,* vol. 3, pp. 249–551. For a brief description of this text, see Appendix 3.

135. *TC* 41:23b–29b (vol. 2, pp. 332–335). See Appendix 3.

136. For Japanese Neo-Confucian schools of thought, see Masao Maruyama, *Studies in the Intellectual History of Tokugawa Japan* (Princeton, N.J.: Princeton University Press, 1975) and Abe Yoshio, "The Characteristic of Japanese Confucianism," *Acta Asiatica* 25 (1970): 1–20. For studies in the Japanese Shushigaku, consult Wm. T. de Bary and I. Bloom, eds. *Principle and Practicality: Essays in Neo-Confucian and Practical Learning* (New York: Columbia University Press, 1979) and his *Neo-Confucian Orthodoxy and the Learning of the Mind-and-Heart.* For Japanese sources, see Abe Yoshio, *Nihon Shushigaku to Chōsen*; Abe Yoshio et al., eds. *Chōsen no Shushigaku Nihon no Shushigaku. Shushigaku taikei,* vol. 12.

137. As the second major debate after the Four-Seven controversy, it focused on the philosophical and moral issue of whether or not human nature and the nature of things are identical, which appears to be another ambiguous topic in Chu Hsi's philosophy. It is also closely related to Yulgok's Four-Seven thesis. In the eighteenth century, two new schools of thought, Hohak (Ho learning) and Nakhak (Nak learning), emerged out of the Kiho tradition of Yulgok's Chugip'a. The former school was founded by Kwŏn Sangam and Han Namdang, who argued that human nature and the nature of things are different due to the purity and physical endowment of their *ki* and that human nature is morally superior to the nature of things. By contrast, Yi Kan, another follower of Yulgok, argued that human nature and the nature of things are identical: according to Ch'eng-Chu teachings, because nature is principle and ontologically one, the "original nature" is one and the same for myriad things. Yi established the so-called Nakhak school. The Horak tradition is also known as Horon (Ho theory), and the name itself refers to Ch'ungch'ŏng Province, in which the founders and their followers

lived. Similarly, the name of Nakhak refers to Seoul or surrounding Kyŏnggi Province, in which the founder and his followers lived.

Chapter I. Philosophical Introduction: The Fruitful Four-Seven Legacy

1. *Mencius*, 2A:6. See D. C. Lau, tran., *Mencius* (New York: Penguin Books, 1970), pp. 82–83.

2. This Chinese term means both the mind and the heart without separation. It can also be translated as "feeling" because Mencius often refers to it as the human feelings of commiseration, shame and dislike, and so on. For example, Wing-tsit Chan rendered it as "feeling" and D. C. Lau as "heart" (Chan, *Source Book*, p. 65; Lau, *Mencius*, pp. 82–83). However, these two translations do not fully render the Mencian concept of *sim/hsin*. As I have mentioned before (in my Note on Style and Translation), this Confucian term means both the mind and the heart, often signifying the intellectual, moral and psychological continuum and integration of the mind and the heart together.

3. *Mencius*, 2A:6. Lau, *Mencius*, p. 82.

4. *Mencius*, 2A:6; Lau, *Mencius*, pp. 82–83.

5. *Mencius*, 2A:6; Lau, *Mencius*, p. 83.

6. See Charles Wei-hsun Fu, "The Mencian Theory of Mind and Nature: A Modern, Philosophical Approach," *Journal of Chinese Philosophy* 10 (1983): 389.

7. *Mencius*, 6A:6; Lau, *Mencius*, p. 163.

8. *Mencius*, 6A:8; Lau, *Mencius*, p. 165.

9. *Mencius*, 7A:1; Lau, *Mencius*, p. 182.

10. Chan, *Source Book*, pp. 50–51.

11. In this book, I am using the two English words *feeling* and *emotion* interchangeably, although I am aware of a difference in nuance in their meaning. The distinction between feeling and emotion in the English usage is necessary here. As we know, the English term *emotion* refers to "a moving, stirring, agitation and perturbation"; by contrast, the term *feeling* usually means "the sense of touch in the looser acceptance of the term, in which it includes all physical sensibility not referable to the special senses of sight,

hearing, taste, and smell" (*The Compact Edition of the Oxford English Dictionary*). The Confucian notion of the idea of *chŏng/ch'ing* usually means both feeling and emotion, relating to not only the body, but also the mind-and-heart. Emotion, as in the case of the "Seven Emotions," refers to an aroused mental, physical, or psychological state, often the result of a stimulation or disturbance of the mind; feeling is a physical, physiological sensation or perception through the sense of touch or general sensibility of the body. Despite the overlapping of the two terms, Confucianism refers to more or less different kinds of human experience.

12. See James Legge, trans., *The Chinese Classics* (Hong Kong: Hong Kong University Press, 1970, reprint), vol. 1, p. 379.

13. *Doctrine of the Mean*, Chapter 1. See Chan, *Source Book*, p. 98.

14. For a good English discussion of the *Doctrine of the Mean*, see Tu Wei-ming, *Centrality and Commonality: An Essay on Chung-yung* (Honolulu: University of Hawaii Press, 1976), esp. pp. 1–28. This book was reprinted as Tu Wei-ming, *Centrality and Commonality: An Essay on Confucian Religiousness* (A revised and enlarged edition of *Centrality and Commonality: An Essay on Chung-yung*) (Albany: SUNY Press, 1989).

15. For example, see A. Graham, "The Background of the Mencian Theory of Human Nature," *Tsing Hua Journal of Chinese Studies* (Dec. 1967): 215–274.

16. Note that Mencius used the "mind-and-heart of respect and reverence" interchangeably with the "mind-and-heart of courtesy and modesty" to refer to it as the beginning of propriety.

17. *Mencius*, 6A:6; Lau, *Mencius*, p. 163.

18. See my Note on Style and Translation in this book.

19. *Mencius*, 7A:21; Lau, *Mencius*, p. 186.

20. *Mencius*, 7B:24; Lau, *Mencius*, p. 198.

21. *Mencius*, 7A:15; Lau, *Mencius*, p. 184.

22. Chan, *Source Book*, p. 50.

23. Ch'eng Hao and Ch'eng I, *I-shu*, 18:1a.

24. Ibid.; Chan, *Source Book*, p. 559.

25. *I-shu*, 18:17b; Chan, *Source Book*, p. 567.

26. *I-shu*, 18:17b, the emphasis is added.

27. *Mencius*, 7A:1.

28. *Doctrine of the Mean*, Chapter 1.

29. *I-shu*, 18:14b–15a.

30. *CTWC* 67:21a. This is a direct quote from Ch'eng I's saying in *I-shu*, 18:1a.

31. Ibid.

32. Chu Hsi's commentary on *Mencius*, 2A:6, *Meng Tzu chi-chu ta-ch'üan* (Great Compendium of Collected Commentaries on Mencius), in *Kyŏngsŏ* (Four Books) (Seoul: Sŏnggyun'gwan University Press, 1972), p. 516. See also *CTYL* 53:9a.

33. *CTYL* 53:20a.

34. *CTYL* 53:10b.

35. *CTYL* 53:20a.

36. The relevant literature includes the following: Wing-tsit Chan, "Chu Hsi's Completion of Neo-Confucianism," in *Etudes Song: In Memoriam Etienne Balazas*, ed. Francoise Aubin, (Ser. II, no. 1, 1973), pp. 59–90; Chan, "The Evolution of the Neo-Confucian Concept of *Li* as Principle," *Ch'ing-hua hsüeh-pao* (Tsing Hua Journal of Chinese Studies) new series 4, no. 2 (Feb. 1964): 123–148; Chan, trans., *Reflections on Things at Hand: The Neo-Confucian Anthology by Chu Hsi and Lü Tsu-ch'ien* (New York: Columbia University Press, 1967); Chan, ed., *Chu Hsi and Neo-Confucianism* (Honolulu: University of Hawaii Press, 1986); Ch'ien Mu, *Chu Tzu hsin hsüeh-an* (A New Philosophical Study of Chu Hsi), 5 vols. (Taipei: San-min shu-chü, 1971), esp. vol. 1, pp. 238–262; Mou Tsung-san, *Hsin-t'i yü hsing-t'i* (Substance of Mind and Substance of Human Nature), 3 vols. (Taipei: Cheng-chung shu-chü, 1975), esp. vol. 3, pp. 407–424; Tang Chün-i, *Chung-kuo che-hsüeh yüan-lun: yüan hsing p'ien* (Sources of Chinese Philosophy: A Volume on Human Nature) (Taipei: Hsüeh-sheng shu-chü, 1973), esp. pp. 358–411; and Tomoeda Ryūtarō, *Shushi no shisō keisei* (The Formation of Chu Hsi's Thought) (Tokyo: Shunjūsha, 1969).

37. See Tang Chün-i, *Chung-kuo che-hsüeh yüan-lun: yüan hsing p'ien* (Sources of Chinese Philosophy: A Volume on Human Nature) (Taipei: Hsüeh-sheng shu-chü, 1973), pp. 188–189.

38. *Chang Tzu ch'üan-shu* (Complete Works of Master Chang) (SPPY edition), 14:2a. See also *CTYL* 5:9a. Note that the term *t'ung* has been rendered as "command" by contemporary scholars. But it also conveys other meanings, such as "master, "comprehend," "combine," and "control." So, the whole four-character theory, *hsin t'ung hsing ch'ing*, can be understood as follows: the mind-and-heart embodies, masters, and comprehends human nature and feelings, combining and commending these two features of human reality into a dynamic totality.

39. See the two Ch'eng brothers' *I-shu*, 18:17b and 22A:11a; Chan, *Source Book*, pp. 567 and 569. See also Chu Hsi's numerous citations of it in, for example, *CTYL* 5:7a.

40. *I-shu*, 18:17b; Chan, *Source Book*, p. 567.

41. *CTYL* 5:3b.

42. *CTWC* 32:24b–25a.

43. *Chang Tzu ch'üan-shu*, 14:2a.

44. *CTYL*, 53:9a.

45. *CTYL* 53:20b.

46. *CTYL* 53:10a.

47. *CTWC* 67:21a.

48. See *CTYL* 87:16a-b.

49. Ibid.

50. *CTWC* 67:28b.

51. Chu Hsi's commentary on *Mencius*, 2A:6, *Meng Tzu chi-chu ta-ch'üan* (Great Compendium of Collected Commentaries on Mencius), in *Kyŏngsŏ*, p. 516.

52. For this subject, see Mou Tsung-san, *Hsin-t'i yü hsing-t'i*, vol. 3, pp. 416–425.

53. For the *locus classicus* for the ideas of the "moral mind" and "human mind," see Chapter III ("Yulgok's Four-Seven Thesis"), section on Human Mind and Moral Mind, p. 86.

54. See Chu Hsi's preface to *Chung-yung chang-chü* (Commentary on the Words and Phrases of the *Doctrine of the Mean*), in *CTWC* 76:21b.

55. *CTYL* 61:5a-b.

56. *CTYL* 5:4a.

57. *Chu Tzu ch'üan-shu*, 42:6b; Chan, *Source Book*, p. 616.

58. *Tung-shu* (On Understanding the *Book of Changes*), Chapter 1.

59. *I-shu*, 18:19b.

60. Quoting Chang Tsai in *Chang Tzu ch'üan-shu*, SPPY ed., 2:18b.

61. Ibid.

62. *CTYL* 4:11a-b.

63. *CTYL* 4:12b.

64. *CTYL* 4:13b.

65. M. Kalton, *To Become Sage: The Ten Diagrams on Sage Learning by Yi T'oegye*, p. 136.

66. Tu Wei-ming, "Tu Wei-ming, "Yi T'oegye's Perception of Human Nature: A Preliminary Inquiry into the Four-Seven Debate in Korean Neo-Confucianism," in de Bary and Haboush, eds., *The Rise of Neo-Confucianism in Korea*, p. 264.

67. See Julia Ching, "Yi Yulgok on the Four Beginnings and the Seven Emotions," in de Bary and Haboush, ibid., p. 305.

68. Tu Wei-ming, "Yi T'oegye's Perception of Human Nature," p. 276 and p. 272, respectively.

69. *CTYL* 53:17b.

Chapter II.
T'oegye's Four-Seven Thesis

1. T'oegye and Kobong each wrote three letters to the other. These letters are found in *TC* 16:8a–17:6b and 17:28a–30a (vol. 1, pp. 405–430 and 441–442).

2. Yi Sang-ŭn, *T'oegyeŭi saengaewa hangmun*, p. 86.

3. Tu also said: "The seriousness and open-mindedness with which T'oegye entertained Kobong's pointed questions set a high standard of inspiration for those who assumed responsibility for elucidating the classics through demonstration and argumentation." See his "Yi T'oegye's Perception of Human Nature," p. 262.

4. T'oegye entitled it *Ch'ŏnmyŏng kudo* (Old Diagram of Heaven's Imperative) and included it in his *Ch'ŏnmyŏng tosŏl husŏ pudo* (Treatise on the Diagram of Heaven's Imperative: A Post-Description with Diagrams), *TC* 41:10b (vol. 2, p. 325). He revised it and called it *Ch'ŏnmyŏng sindo* (New Diagram of Heaven's Imperative). This is in *TC* 41:11a.

5. For my brief discussion of Kwŏn's philosophy and the notes, see the second section (Neo-Confucianism in the Chosŏn dynasty) of the introductory chapter ("Historical Background"). In Korea, Kwŏn was, of course, the first Neo-Confucian who spoke of the Four and the Seven; however, he did not directly mention the terms *Four Beginnings* and *Seven Emotions* in his *Ch'ŏnin simsŏng habil chi to*, although he assigned benevolence, righteousness, propriety, and wisdom to human nature, and the Seven Emotions to the mind-and-heart.

6. See T'oegye's *Ch'ŏnmyŏng kudo*, *TC* 41:10b.

7. *CTYL* 53:20a.

8. See T'oegye's *Ch'ŏnmyŏng sindo*, *TC* 41:11a.

9. *TC* 16:1b (vol. 1, p. 402).

10. This is Kobong's first letter to T'oegye, entitled *Pu Ki Myŏng-hŏn pi sadan ch'ilchŏng pun iki pyŏn* (Ki Myŏng-hŏn's Treatise Against the Distinction Between the Four Beginnings and the Seven Emotions in Terms of *I* and *Ki*), in *TC* 16:12b–14b.

11. *TC* 16:12b–13b (vol. 1, pp. 407–408).

12. See *CTYL* 87:16a-b.

13. *TC* 16:14a (vol. 1, p. 408).

14. *TC* 16:13b (vol. 1, p. 408). Kobong cited the *Doctrine of the Mean*, Chapter 1, which states: "Before pleasure, joy, anger, and sorrow are aroused, it is called equilibrium. After these feelings are aroused and all attain due degree and measure, it is called harmony."

15. *TC* 16:13b (vol. 1, p. 408).

16. Yi Sang-ŭn, "Yi Hwangŭi ch'ŏrak: sach'il nonpyŏn" (Yi T'oegye's Philosophy: The Four-Seven Debate), in *Han'guk ch'ŏrak yŏn'gu* (Studies in Korean Philosophy), vol. 2, (Seoul: Tongyŏngsa, 1979), p. 233.

17. *Doctrine of the Mean*, Chapter 1.

18. *TC* 16:14a (vol. 1, p. 408).

19. *TC* 16:13b (vol. 1, p. 408).

20. As Tu Wei-ming correctly points out in this regard, "Kobong suggests that the Four are the roots of those feelings in the Seven that are eventually harmonizable." Tu Wei-ming, "Yi T'oegye's Perception of Human Nature," p. 269.

21. *TC* 16:14a (vol. 1, p. 408).

22. *TC* 16:13b (vol. 1, p. 408).

23. Ibid.

24. Ibid.

25. *TC* 16:14a (vol. 1, p. 408).

26. This is called T'oegye's "First Letter to Kobong on the Four Beginnings and the Seven Emotions." See in *TC* 16:8a–12b (vol. 1, pp. 405–407).

27. *TC* 16:8b (vol. 1, p. 405).

28. Tu Wei-ming, "Yi T'oegye's Perception of Human Nature," p. 268.

29. *TC* 16:8b (vol. 1, p. 405).

30. *TC* 16:9a-b (vol. 1, p 406).

31. For this reason, Yi Sang-ŭn correctly pointed out that there is a "dichotomous tendency" in T'oegye's philosophy of human nature. See Yi Sang-ŭn, "Yi Hwangŭi ch'ŏrak: sach'il nonpyŏn," p. 238.

32. *TC* 16:9b (vol. 1, p 406).

33. Mencius referred to the Four as our *inborn roots* of moral self-cultivation. Here, we can recall that he mentioned specifically the "mind-and-heart" of commiseration, shame and dislike, courtesy and modesty, and right and wrong as the Four Beginnings of such virtues as benevolence, righteousness, propriety, and wisdom. His assertion that we all have the Four is based on the belief that all human beings have "the mind-and-heart that cannot bear to see the suffering of others." What he means to say regarding the fourfold beginning is that, for instance, whenever one sees an infant falling into a well, one's mind-and-heart functions spontaneously and naturally.

34. *Mencius*, 7B:35.

35. The *Sim t'ong sŏngchŏng tosŏl* describes the basic elements of Neo-Confucian moral and psychological theories of the mind, human nature, and feelings. It consists of three subdiagrams. For the third diagram in English, see Appendix 1; for the original diagram in Chinese, see *TC* 7:22b–25a (vol. 1, pp. 204–206). For a complete English translation with notes and comments, see M. Kalton, *To Become a Sage: The Ten Diagrams on Sage Learning by Yi T'oegye*. T'oegye compiled the *Sŏnghak sipto* in his late sixties (1568), several years after his Four-Seven debates with Kobong. He borrowed the first diagram from a Chinese source that contains the major ideas of Ch'eng-Chu theory that "the mind commands human nature and feelings" and that pays special attention to the unity and duality of the mind in terms of "substance" and "function." According to T'oegye, it was originally compiled by Ch'eng Fu-hsin (Lin-yin, 1279–1358), a Yüan Chinese Neo-Confucian, who was best known for his *Ssu-shu chang-t'u* (Diagrams of the Chapters of the Four Books), a book that T'oegye obtained in 1560. He held Ch'eng in high esteem; there is an account of Ch'eng in his *Ihak t'ongnok*, 10:31b–32a (*TC*, vol. 3, p. 519). The second and third diagrams were compiled by T'oegye himself; they present not only a detailed philosophy of basic ideas presented in the first diagram, but also a carefully formulated summary of T'oegye's final position on the Four-Seven controversy. According to T'oegye, the second diagram focuses on the original human nature from the standpoint of *i* only, whereas the third diagram is a general summary of his Four-Seven thesis on the physical human nature from the standpoint of *i* and *ki* combined.

36. *TC* 7:4b–35a (vol. 1, pp. 195–211). For a brief description of T'oegye's *Sŏnghak sipto*, see Appendix 3. For a complete English translation of it with notes and comments, see Kalton, *To Become a Sage*.

37. *TC* 7:24a (vol. 1, p. 209).

38. According to T'oegye, all of their sayings represent the meaning of the second diagram in his *Sim t'ong sŏngchŏng tosŏl*. However, he added a new point that the Seven Emotions, if they are harmonized and good, also come from the original human nature. For the second diagram of the *Sim t'ong sŏngchŏng tosŏl*, see Kalton, *To Become a Sage*, p. 122.

39. *TC* 7:24a–24b (vol. 1, pp. 204–205). According to T'oegye, this is the basis of the third diagram that explains the Four and the Seven in terms of the physical human nature. For the third diagram in English, see Appendix

1; for the original diagram in Chinese, see *TC* 7:22b–25a (vol. 1, pp. 204–206).

40. *TC* 16:10a (vol. 1, p. 406).

41. *TC* 16:8b–9a (vol. 1, pp. 405–406).

42. *TC* 16:10a (vol. 1, p. 406).

43. *CTYL* 87:16a-b.

44. In my reading of their writings, these statements were never quoted by T'oegye, Kobong, or Yulgok.

45. *CTYL* 53:17b.

46. Quoting *Mencius*, 2A:6.

47. *Doctrine of the Mean*, Chapter 1.

48. *TC* 16:10b (vol. 1, p. 406).

49. *Doctrine of the Mean*, Chapter 1.

50. See *I-shu*, 18:1a and 17a.

51. Quoting Chu Hsi's statement in *CTWC* 46:24a.

52. *TC* 16:11a (vol. 1, p. 407).

53. This alludes to Chu Hsi's saying. See especially *CTYL* 1:1a–3a; *CTWC* 46:24a-b and 59:45b.

54. *CTYL* 53:20a.

55. *TC* 16:12a (vol. 1, p. 407).

56. Lo was the most prominent scholar of the Ch'eng-Chu school in Ming China. For his biography and philosophy, see Lo Ch'in-shun, *K'un-chih chi* (Knowledge Painfully Acquired), *Chung-kuo che-hsüeh Ming-chu chi-ch'eng*, vol. 41 (Taipei, 1978). For a recent English translation, see Irene Bloom, trans., *Knowledge Painfully Acquired: The K'un-chih chi by Lo Ch'in-shun* (New York: Columbia University Press, 1987).

57. *TC* 16:11a (vol. 1, p. 407).

58. *CTWC* 46:24a.

59. Bloom, *Knowledge Painfully Acquired*, p. 69. Lo also said: "*Li* is only the *li* of *ch'i*. It must be observed in the phenomenon of revolving and turn-

ing of *ch'i*. . . . What acts and reacts is *ch'i*, while the fact that a particular action involves a particular reaction without there being the slightest possibility of error is principle. . . . I have, therefore, said that *li* must be identified as an aspect of *ch'i*" (p. 174).

60. For the Ch'eng-Chu doctrine of "principle is one, but its particularizations are diverse," see *CTYL* 1:2a. This is originally formulated by Ch'eng I in his *Ts'ui-yen* (Pure Words), 1:24a and his *I chuan* (Commentary on the *Book of Changes*), 3:3b.

61. *Mencius*, 3A:1 and 6A:6.

62. This is a statement advanced by Mencius' disciple Kung-tu. See *Mencius*, 6A:6.

63. Bloom, *Knowledge Painfully Acquired*, p. 66.

64. Ibid., p. 64.

65. *TC* 16:11a (vol. 1, p. 407).

66. *TC* 16:12a (vol. 1, p. 407).

67. See "Kobong tap T'oegye ron sadan ch'ilchŏng sŏ" (Kobong's Letter to T'oegye's Doctrine on the Four Beginnings and the Seven Emotions), *Sach'il iki wangbok sŏ* (Correspondences on the Four and the Seven, *I* and *Ki*), 1:6b–28b in *Kobong chŏnjip* (Complete Works of Ki Kobong) (Seoul: Sŏnggyun'gwan University Press, 1976).

68. Ibid., 1:9b.

69. Ibid., 1:17a-b.

70. Ibid., 1:19a.

71. Ibid., 1:10b.

72. Ibid., 1:12a–17b.

73. Ibid., 1:17b, 25b.

74. Ibid., 1:8b.

75. Ibid., 1:8b. This is Chu Hsi's saying in *CTYL* 4:12a.

76. Ibid., 1:13b. This is Chu Hsi's saying taken from *CTYL* 4:12a.

77. See Yi Sang-ŭn, "Yi Hwangŭi ch'ŏrak sach'il nonpyŏn," in *Han'guk ch'ŏrak yŏn'gu*, p. 250.

78. This is based on his *Yŏnbo* (Chronological Biography), found in *Kobong chŏnjip*. According to it, Kobong had a debate with No Sojae (1515–1590), another leading scholar in Korea, on the problem of the moral mind and the human mind, which took place in the winter of the twentieth year (1564) of King Myŏngjong's reign, four years after the beginning of the Four-Seven debate with T'oegye. In the year following this debate, Kobong wrote a discourse on the *K'un-chih chi* in response to Sojae's argument based on it. But his second Four-Seven letter to T'oegye was written in the summer of 1560. If his biography is correct, then this indicates that Kobong did not read the *K'un-chih chi* prior to or during his Four-Seven debate with T'oegye not until 1564 when he read it probably for the first time.

79. This is called T'oegye's *second Four-Seven letter.* See *TC* 16:19a–39a (vol. 1, pp. 411–421).

80. *TC* 16:23a-b (vol. 1, p. 413).

81. *TC* 7:22b (vol. 1, p. 204). T'oegye also makes this point clearly in his *Sim t'ong sŏngchŏng tosŏl* (Treatise on the Diagram of the Saying "the Mind Commands Nature and Feelings"), the sixth part of his *Sŏnghak sipto.* The impact of Kobong's argument on T'oegye' Four-Seven thesis is quite evident in the second diagram of his *Sim t'ong sŏngchŏng tosŏl,* where the good feelings of the Seven are listed alongside the Four as manifestations of human nature. For the diagram in Chinese, see *TC* 7:22b (vol. 1, p. 204); see also Michael Kalton's English translation of it in his *To Become Sage,* p. 122.

82. *TC* 16:21a (vol. 1, p. 412).

83. *TC* 16:25a–28a (vol. 1, pp. 414–415).

84. This statement alludes to Chu Hsi's saying in *CTYL* 4:12a.

85. *TC* 16:29a–30a (vol. 1, p. 416).

86. *TC* 16:30a (vol. 1, p. 416).

87. *TC* 16:30b (vol. 1, p. 416).

88. *CTYL* 53:20a.

89. *TC* 16:30a (vol. 1, p. 416).

90. *TC* 16:30b (vol. 1, p. 416).

91. Ibid.

92. *TC* 16:31a (vol. 1, p. 416).

93. Ibid.

94. Ibid.

95. Ibid.

96. *TC* 16:32a (vol. 1, p. 417).

97. Ibid. T'oegye stated this theory of the alternate manifestation of *i* and *ki* also in the third diagram of his *Sim t'ong sŏngchŏng tosŏl*, the sixth diagram of his *Sŏnghak sipto*. For the original diagram in Chinese, see *TC* 7:22b (vol. 1, p. 204), and see Appendix 1 for my translation of it.

98. *TC* 16:32b–33a (v. 1, p. 418).

99. It may be said that in the case of the Four, *i* (like the rider on horseback) is in command; therefore, as *i* wills, controls, and directs, *ki* (like the horse) follows. There is some possibility that the horse may disobey what the rider orders. In T'oegye's view, however, to say that the rider does not know where he or she wants to go is not possible in the Mencian spirit of morality. In other words, in the case of the Four, *i* actually manifests itself, guiding *ki* according to what it "wishes."

100. *TC* 16:33a (vol. 1, p. 418).

101. *TC* 16:32a-b (vol. 1, p. 418).

102. *TC* 16:33b (vol. 1, p. 418).

103. Ibid.

104. *TC* 16:34a (vol. 1, p. 418).

105. *TC* 16:34b (vol. 1, p. 418).

106. This argument his clearly indicated in the third diagram of T'oegye's *Sim t'ong sŏngchŏng tosŏl*, the sixth of his *Sŏnghak sipto*, *TC* 7:22b (vol. 1, p. 204). See Appendix 1 for this diagram. In this diagram, the Four are put on top of the Seven.

107. *TC* 16:35b (vol. 1, p. 419).

108. *TC* 16:35a (vol. 1, p. 419).

109. *TC* 16:36b (vol. 1, p. 419).

110. See *Ming-tao wen-chi*, 3:1a-b in *Erh-Ch'eng ch'üan-shu*, SPPY ed.

111. *TC* 16:37b (vol. 1, p. 419).

112. Ibid.

113. Ibid.

114. See Kobong's *Sach'il iki wangbok sŏ*, 2:1a.

115. *TC* 16:33b (vol. 1, p. 418).

116. *TC* 16:30a (vol. 1, p. 416) and *TC* 16:34a (vol. 1, p. 418).

117. *Sach'il iki wangbok sŏ*, 2:6a.

118. Ibid., 2:10a.

119. Quoting *CTYL* 53:20a.

120. *Sach'il iki wangbok sŏ*, 2:8a.

121. Ibid., 2:10a.

122. This is found in his *Chosuljae sŏnsaeng munjip* (Collected Literary Works of Master Cholsujae), 11:1a–9a. For more information, see Epilogue (section on the Eclectic School).

123. *Sach'il iki wangbok sŏ*, 2:10a.

124. For example, in the second diagram of the *Sim t'ong sŏngchŏng tosŏl*, he added a new point that if the Seven Emotions are harmonized and good, they also come from original human nature. In addition, the good feelings of the Seven are listed alongside the Four as manifestations of human nature. T'oegye utilized Kobong's suggestion in the third diagram of the *Sim t'ong sŏngchŏng tosŏl*: the Four and the Seven are not put in opposition to each other, rather the former is placed on top of the latter. For the second and third diagrams in English, see Kalton, *To Become a Sage*, pp. 122–123. For my own translation of the third diagram, see Appendix 1. For both diagrams in the original Chinese, see *TC* 7:22b (vol. 1, p. 204).

125. Ibid.

126. Here, I should point out that this is precisely the line of reasoning that Yulgok, in turn, used in his Four-Seven debate with Sŏng Ugye. Following Kobong, Yulgok, as will see later, argued more systematically that *ki* is what is manifest in both the Four and the Seven, whereas *i* is what makes its manifestation possible.

127. Kobong probably borrowed it from *CTYL* 94:41b–42a, which reads: "Fundamentally speaking, there is only one Great Ultimate; however, everything is endowed with it, and everything in itself possesses the Great

Ultimate in its entirety. This is similar to the fact that there is only one moon in the sky, but when its light is scattered upon rivers and lakes, it is seen everywhere. We cannot say that the moon has been split." Note that Chu Hsi's idea is similar to the "one in all" and "all in one" doctrines in the Hua-yen school of Buddhism, and that his moon-moonlight analogy originates from the Hua-yen metaphor of the moon and its many reflections.

128. See Kobong's *Sach'il iki wangbok sŏ*, 2:7b.

129. Ibid., 2:8a.

130. For the Ch'eng-Chu doctrine of "principle is one, but its particularizations are diverse," see *CTYL* 1:2a. This was originally formulated by Ch'eng I in his *Ts'ui-yen* (Pure Words), 1:24a, and his *I chuan* (Commentary on the *Book of Changes*), 3:3b.

131. *Sach'il iki wangbok sŏ*, 2:10a.

132. Ibid.

133. Ibid.

134. *TC* 17:4b (vol. 1, p. 429).

135. *I-shu*, 18:17b.

136. *I-shu*, 18:17b.

137. *I-shu*, 18:17b.

138. *TC* 17:6b (vol. 1, p. 430).

139. See Kobong's *Pu Ki Myŏnghŏn sadan ch'ilchŏng ch'ongron* (Ki Kobong's Summary on the Four Beginnings and the Seven Emotions), in *TC* 17:28a–30a (vol. 1, pp. 441–442). This is also included in Kobong's *Sach'il iki wangbok sŏ*, 2:25a–27a.

140. In my view, however, had Kobong decided to challenge T'oegye's Four-Seven thesis further, it might have stimulated T'oegye to revise some of his basic philosophical and moral views. Of course, this could have engendered the subsequent patterns of the Four-Seven debate between Yulgok and Ugye, and, in turn, those between T'oegye's followers and Yulgok's followers in the later periods. We can only raise the following question, In what sense and to what extent could this have altered the philosophical and historical development of Sŏngnihak after T'oegye and Yulgok?

Chapter III.
Yulgok's Four-Seven Thesis

1. These letters are collected in *YC* 9:32b–10:40a (vol. 1, pp. 192–216).

2. T'oegye's *Sim t'ong sŏngchŏng tosŏl* describes the basic elements of Ch'eng-Chu Neo-Confucianism especially its moral and psychological theories of the mind, human nature, and feelings. It consists of three subdiagrams with T'oegye's comments. Ugye is referring to the third diagram in particular. In this diagram, T'oegye gives a basic summary of his Four-Seven thesis including his *hobal* theory. For my translation of it, see Appendix 1; for the original diagram in Chinese, see *TC* 7:22b–25a (vol. 1, pp. 204–206); for a brief description of T'oegye's *Sŏnghak sipto*, see Appendix 3; and for a complete English translation with notes and comments, see M. Kalton, *To Become a Sage: The Ten Diagrams on Sage Learning by Yi T'oegye.* T'oegye compiled the *Sŏnghak sipto* in his late sixties (1568), several years after his Four-Seven debate with Kobong; obviously, Ugye had a copy of it and studied it thoroughly.

3. See *YC* 19:37a (vol. 1, p. 193). For T'oegye's *hobal* theory, see *TC* 7:24b (vol. 1, p. 205).

4. Ibid.

5. *YC* 9:37b (vol. 1, p. 193).

6. Ibid.

7. Ibid.

8. *YC* 9:38a (vol. 1, p. 194).

9. *Book of History*, "Counsels of Great Yü." See J. Legge, trans., *The Chinese Classics*, vol. 3. p. 61.

10. For a good English discussion of Chen Te-hsiu and his *Hsin ching*, see Wm. T. de Bary, *Neo-Confucian Orthodoxy and the Learning of the Mind-and-Heart* (hereafter *Neo-Confucian Orthodoxy*) (New York: Columbia University Press, 1981), pp. 67–205.

11. Chu Hsi's preface to *Chung-yung chang-chü* in *CTWC* 76:21b.

12. *CTYL* 61:5a-b.

13. *CTYL* 5:4a.

14. Here, Ugye is citing Chu Hsi's comment on the *Doctrine of the Mean*, in *Ssu-shu chi-chu* (Collected Commentaries on the Four Books), SPPY ed., Preface to *Chung-yung*, p. 1. See also Chu Hsi's Preface to *Chung-yung chang-chü* (Collected Commentaries on the *Doctrine of the Mean*) in *CTWC* 76:21b. This also appears in the opening chapter of Chen Te-hsiu's *Hsin ching*, 1a.

15. Ibid.

16. *YC* 19:37a-b (vol. 1, p. 193), emphasis is added.

17. *YC* 19:37a (vol. 1, p. 193). See also Chu Hsi's saying in *CTWC* 67:19b.

18. *YC* 9:35b (vol. 1, p. 192).

19. *YC* 9:36a (vol. 1, p. 192).

20. *YC* 9:34b (vol. 1, p. 192) quoting Chu Hsi. These statements appear in Chu Hsi's *Treatise on the Examination of the Mind*, in *CTWC* 67:19a. See also his Preface to the *Doctrine of the Mean*, in *Ssu-shu chi-chu*, SPPY ed., p. 1, and his Preface to *Chung-yung chang-chü*, in *CTWC* 76:21b.

21. *YC* 9:34b (vol. 1, p. 192). This alludes to what Chu Hsi said in his *Treatise on the Examination of the Mind*, in *CTWC* 67:19a.

22. Ibid. Quoting Chu Hsi's "Treatise on the Examination of the Mind," in *CTWC* 67:19a.

23. Ibid.

24. Chu Hsi's saying in his Preface to the *Doctrine of the Mean*, in *Ssu-shu chi-chu*, p. 1. See also his Preface to *Chung-yung chang-chu*, in *CTWC* 76:21b.

25. *YC* 9:35a (vol. 1, p. 192).

26. See his *Yulgokŭi saengaewa sasang* (Yulgok's Life and Thought) (Seoul: Smundang, 1973), p. 79. As far as Chu Hsi, Yulgok, and even T'oegye are concerned, the human mind has to overcome its "selfish desires" by holding fast to the command of the moral mind. In other words, the moral mind does not "overcome" the human mind; rather it guides and controls the human mind by serving as the virtuous "master" of the latter.

27. *YC* 9:36a (vol. 1, p. 192).

28. Ibid.

29. Ibid.

30. *YC* 10:10b (vol. 1, p. 201).

31. Ibid.

32. *YC* 10:4a (vol. 1, p. 199).

33. Ibid.

34. Ibid. This idea alludes to *CTYL* 61:5a-b.

35. *YC* 10:4b (vol. 1, p. 198).

36. *YC* 10:4a-b (vol. 1, p. 198).

37. This is found in *YC* 14:4a–17a (vol. 1, pp. 282–284). For my translation of this diagram, see Appendix 2.

38. *YC* 14:4b (vol. 1, p. 198).

39. For a brief description of this text, see Appendix 4. For my discussion of this text in relation to the implications of Yulgok's Four-Seven thesis, see Chapter V.

40. Quoting Chu Hsi in his "Treatise on the Examination of the Mind," *CTWC* 67:19a.

41. *YC* 20:58a (vol. 1, p. 456).

42. *YC* 10:4b (vol. 1, p. 198).

43. Ibid.

44. This is Chu Hsi's saying in his Preface to the *Doctrine of the Mean*, in *Ssu-shu chi-chu*, SPPY ed., p. 1, and in his Preface to *Chung-yung chang-chü* in *CTWC* 76:21b.

45. *YC* 10:4b (vol.1, p. 198), emphasis is added.

46. *YC* 10:12a (vol. 1, p. 202).

47. *YC* 10:12b (vol. 1, p. 202).

48. *YC* 10:13a (vol. 1, p. 202).

49. Ibid.

50. *YC* 10:14b–15a (vol. 1, p. 203).

51. *YC* 10:15a (vol. 1, p. 203).

52. *YC* 10:15b (vol. 1, p. 203).

53. *YC* 10:16a (vol. 1, p. 204).

54. *YC* 10:15b (vol. 1, p. 203).

55. Ibid.

56. Ibid.

57. *YC* 10:7b (vol. 1, p. 199).

58. Ibid.

59. Ibid.

60. *YC* 14:5a (vol. 1, p. 284).

61. *YC* 10:29a (vol. 1, p. 210).

62. *TC* 40:9b (vol. 2, p. 307). For a detailed discussion of this topic, see Chapter IV.

63. *TC* 25:20a (vol. 2, p. 10), Letter to Chŏng Cha-chung.

64. Yulgok's theory of the oneness of the moral mind and the human mind might have been influenced by the Mahayana Buddhist notion of the oneness of the mind, according to which the mind can be understood in terms of "the mind of integration and disintegration" (the phenomenal mind) and "the mind of Tathata" (the true mind). Historically speaking, this is a strong possibility because, as I have discussed in Yulgok's biography, he was attracted to Buddhism in his early years, studying Buddhist scriptures especially those of Zen and Hua-yen. Song Sŏk-ku, for example, argues that Buddhism had a good deal of impact on Yulgok's philosophy of the oneness of the mind. See his "Pulgyowa Yi Yulgokŭi ch'ŏrak" (Buddhism and Yi Yulgok's Philosophy) in his *Han'gukŭi yubul sasang* (Confucian and Buddhist Thought in Korea), pp. 402–404. However, we should not underestimate the fact that Yulgok was a Neo-Confucian scholar of the Ch'eng-Chu tradition. His philosophy of the moral mind and the human mind is fundamentally Neo-Confucian, insofar as it is, as I have mentioned, based on Chu Hsi's philosophy.

65. See Young-chan Ro, *The Korean Neo-Confucianism of Yi Yulgok* (Albany: SUNY Press, 1989), pp. 46–50.

66. *YC* 10:7b (vol. 1, p. 199).

67. As Yulgok states elsewhere: "Because the human mind and the moral mind are not two different minds, the Four and the Seven are not two different kinds of feelings." *YC* 12:23a (vol. 1, p. 250).

68. *YC* 9:34b (vol. 1, p. 192).

69. Ibid.

70. *YC* 9:35a (vol. 1, p. 192).

71. Ibid.

72. *Mencius*, 2A:6 and 6A:6.

73. *YC* 9:35b (vol. 1, p. 192).

74. *YC* 9:35b–36a (vol. 1, p. 192).

75. See *CTYL* 87:16a-b. Like Kobong, Yulgok never quoted these statements by Chu Hsi.

76. See *YC* 9:38b (vol. 1, p. 195).

77. Ibid.

78. Ibid.

79. Ibid.

80. Ibid.

81. Ibid.

82. Ibid.

83. Quoting the *Doctrine of the Mean*, Chapter 1.

84. *YC* 9:38a (vol. 1, p. 195).

85. *YC* 9:39a (vol. 1, p. 195).

86. Ibid.

87. *YC* 9:39b (vol. 1, p. 195).

88. See also Kobong's argument in *TC* 16:13b (vol. 1, p. 408).

89. *YC* 10:7a (vol. 1, p. 199).

90. *CTYL* 53:20a.

91. *YC* 9:35b (vol. 1, p. 192).

92. *YC* 10:5a (vol. 1, p. 198).

93. Ibid.

94. Quoting the *Doctrine of the Mean*, Chapter 1.

95. *YC* 14:5b (vol. 1, p. 283).

96. *YC* 20:56b (vol. 1, p. 455). Yulgok's *Sŏnghak chipyo* was compiled in 1575, almost three years after the Yulgok-Ugye debate, which took in 1573. Another quotation from this text illustrates his understanding of good and evil in terms of the role of *ki*: "What is called good in the feelings rides on clear and bright *ki*, coming straight from Heaven's principle. Because this refers to the beginning of benevolence, the beginning of righteousness, the beginning of propriety, and the beginning of wisdom, we call it the Four Beginnings. Although what is not good in the feelings also originates from *i*, it is already disturbed by impure and turbid *ki* and, therefore, does injury to this *i*. Because this does not refer to the beginning of benevolence, the beginning of righteousness, the beginning of propriety, and the beginning of wisdom, we cannot call it the Four Beginnings" (*YC* 20:57a).

97. *YC* 14:32b (vol. 1, p. 296).

98. *YC* 10:7a-b (vol. 1, p. 199).

99. *TC* 16:9b (vol. 1, p. 406).

100. Ch'eng I and Chu Hsi generally mentioned the following three points: the mind-and-heart of commiseration is an innate seed of the virtue of benevolence; "benevolence is human nature"; and love is a common mental "feeling" that may not be a virtuous root of morality. For more information, see Chapter I.

101. *YC* 9:35b (vol. 1, p. 192).

102. Ibid.

103. *YC* 10:9a (vol. 1, p. 200).

104. The Ch'eng-Chu school speaks of human nature as constituting "original human nature" and "physical human nature." According to Ch'eng I, it would be "incomplete" to talk about human nature without mentioning *ki* at the same time, and it is "unintelligent" to talk about *ki* without including human nature (*I-shu*, 6:2a). Chu Hsi also said that original human nature is perfectly good (*CTYL* 4:11a). It would be the same as the nature described by Mencius as "naturally good," by Chou Tun-i as "pure," by Ch'eng I as

"the fundamental character of our nature," and by Chang Tsai as "the nature of Heaven and Earth." When one speaks of this nature, one is said to be referring to principle alone; however, when one speaks of the physical human nature endowed, one must refer to principle and material force combined (*CTYL* 4:12a).

105. *YC* 10:7b (vol. 1, p. 199).

106. *YC* 10:10b (vol. 1, p. 201).

107. *YC* 10:22a (vol. 1, p. 207).

108. *YC* 10:22a (vol. 1, p. 207).

109. Ibid.

110. *YC* 10:22b (vol. 1, p. 207).

111. Ibid.

112. *YC* 10:29b (vol. 1, p. 210).

113. *YC* 10:29b–30a (vol. 1, pp. 210–211).

114. *YC* 14:32a (vol. 1, p. 296).

115. Ibid.

116. Ibid.

117. *YC* 20:57b (vol. 1, p. 455).

118. See *YC* 19:37a (vol. 1, p. 193). For T'oegye's *hobal* theory, see *TC* 7:24b (vol. 1, p. 205).

119. *YC* 9:37b (vol. 1, p. 193).

120. Ibid.

121. *YC* 9:36a (vol. 1, p. 192).

122. *YC* 10:4b (vol. 1, p. 198).

123. Ibid.

124. *YC* 10:5a (vol. 1, p. 198). In this regard, we can refer to Han Nam-dang (Wŏnjin, 1682–1750), a scholar of Yulgok's school, who defended Yulgok's argument that, in all cosmic phenomena, what can move and become tranquil is *ki*, and what makes it to do so is *i*. According to him, Chu Hsi confused everyone by saying that, on the one hand, *i* and *ki* are

ontologically two entities that can be spoken of being prior and posterior and that, on the other hand, the two are inseparable in concrete phenomena.

125. *CTYL* 53:20a.

126. *YC* 9:35b (vol. 1, p. 192).

127. *YC* 10:5a (vol. 1, p. 198).

128. *YC* 10:5b (vol. 1, p. 198).

129. *YC* 10:5a (vol. 1, p. 198). Kim Chang-saeng (Sagye, 1548–1631), a disciple of Yulgok, argued that Yulgok's saying means that "*i* is only the passive principle; therefore, it cannot move or be manifest by itself." And "what really acts and becomes manifest in all phenomena is only *ki*." See *Sagae chŏnsŏ* (Complete Works of Kim Sagae), *kwŏn* 17, "Reply to Han Saang's Letter."

130. Ibid.

131. *YC* 10:5a (vol. 1, p. 198).

132. *YC* 10:6a (vol. 1, p. 198).

133. Ibid.

134. *YC* 10:6b (vol. 1, p. 198).

135. Ibid.

136. Ibid.

137. Yulgok seems to say here that although Lo's interpretation of *i* and *ki* is correctly formulated, it tends to put too much emphasis on the oneness of *i* and *ki* while deviating from Chu Hsi's philosophy of *i* and *ki*. In his view, Lo saw correctly that *i* and *ki* are inseparable, but went too far in seeing *i* and *ki* as fundamentally one and, therefore, *i* almost is *ki*, without discussing clearly their conceptual distinction, which happens to be the basis of Chu Hsi's philosophy.

138. *YC* 10:8b (vol. 1, p. 200).

139. *YC* 10:12a (vol. 1, p. 202).

140. Ibid.

141. Ibid.

142. *YC* 10:23b (vol. 1, p. 207).

143. *YC* 10:31b (vol. 1, p. 211).

144. *YC* 10:33a (v. 1, p. 212).

145. *YC* 10:29a (vol. 1, p. 210).

146. *YC* 14:4b (vol. 1, p. 282).

147. *YC* 20:55b (vol. 1, p. 454). Yulgok's *Simsŏngchŏng sŏl* is a short philosophical treatise included in his famous *Sŏnghak chipyo.*

148. Pae Chong-ho points out that in Korea Yulgok succeeded Chu Hsi's view of *i* and *ki.* See his "Yi Iŭi ch'ŏrak sasang" (Yi Yulgok's Philosophical Thought), in *Han'guk ch'ŏrak yŏn'gu* (Studies in Korean Philosophy) (Seoul: Tongmyŏngsa, 1978), vol. 2, p. 299.

149. *Sŏnghak chipyo,* vol. 2, "Sugi" (Self-Cultivation), sec. 4, "Investigation of Principle," in *YC* 20:57b (vol. 1, p. 455)

150. *YC* 9:39a (vol. 1, p. 194).

151. Ibid. For this doctrine, see *CTYL* 1:2a. It was originally formulated by Ch'eng I in his *Ts'ui-yen* (Pure Words), 1:24a, and *I chuan* (Commentary on the *Book of Changes*), 3:3b.

152. The similar statement is presented in his letter to An Ŭng-hyu: "Why does *i* take on myriad differentiations? *Ki* is not uniform, and *i* rides on *ki.* When the latter flows and circulates, it takes on its myriad variations. How can *i* flow and circulate? This is because when *ki* circulates, *i* rides on its subtle, activating moving force of *ki.*" See *YC* 12:20a (vol. 1, p. 248).

153. Ibid.

154. To put it in another way, *i* is to be conceived with respect to substance and function simultaneously: "With respect to its oneness, it refers to the substance of *i*; with respect to its myriad differentiations (in things), it refers to the function of *i.*" See *YC* 12:20a (vol. 1, p. 248, Letter to An Ŭng-hyu).

155. *YC* 9:39a (vol. 1, p. 194).

156. For this Ch'eng-Chu doctrine, see *CTYL* 1:2a; *Ts'ui-yen,* 1:24a; and *I chuan,* 3:3b.

157. *YC* 9:39a-b (vol. 1, p. 194).

158. *YC* 10:2a (vol. 1, p. 197).

159. Ibid.

160. *YC* 10:2a-b (vol. 1, p. 197).

161. In the "General Discourse on Mind, Human Nature, and Feelings" in his *Sŏnghak chipyo,* Yulgok presents the same kind of argument: "Someone [probably Ugye] asked me, 'Are *i* and *ki* one or two?' I replied that 'according to the former scholars, they are one yet two and two yet one.' *I* and *ki* are in perfect harmony, having no space between them. They cannot be called *two things* because they were never originally inseparable. Consequently, Ch'eng I said, 'The concrete things are also the Way and the Way is also the concrete things.'" See the *Sŏnghak chipyo,* vol. 2, "Sugi" (Self-Cultivation), sec. 4, "Investigation of Principle," in *YC* 20:59b (vol. 1, p. 455).

162. Without giving a clear explanation, Yi Pyŏng-do generally points out, in this regard, that Yulgok's thought is based on what he calls a *monistic dualism of i and ki,* which seems to be an ambiguous description. See his *Yulgokŭi saengaewa sasang,* p. 67, and *Han'guk yuhak saryak,* p. 170. Yi probably means here that Yulgok's theory is based on the ontological distinction of *i* and *ki* and their relationship of inseparability in things and phenomena.

163. *YC* 10:2a–3a (vol. 1, p. 197).

164. See Julia Ching, "Yi Yulgok on the Four Beginnings and the Seven Emotions," in de Bary and Haboush, *The Rise of Neo-Confucianism in Korea,* p. 311.

165. Ibid.

166. *YC* 10:3b (vol. 1, p. 197).

167. Ibid.

168. *YC* 10:8b (vol. 1, p. 200).

169. *CTWC* 46:24a.

170. I. Bloom, trans., *Knowledge Painfully Acquired: The K'un-chih chi by Lo Ch'in-shun,* p. 58.

171. Ibid., p. 174.

172. This is found in *YC* 14:54a–60b (vol. 1, pp. 307–310). For my brief description of this text, see Appendix 4.

173. *YC* 14:55a (vol. 1, p. 308). In the *Yŏksu ch'aek* (Treatise on Changes), another important work, he also states in the spirit of Chu Hsi: "That which exists without form is the *i* of nature, and that which exists within form is the *ki* of nature. As there is this *i*, there is this *ki*. As there is *ki*, there must be the myriad things created. . . . *Ki* is what moves and become tranquil, while *i* is what makes *ki* move and become tranquil." See *YC* 14:48b (vol. 1, p. 304). For a brief description of this text, see Appendix 4.

174. *YC* 10:13b (vol. 1, p. 202).

175. It is not surprising that Yulgok was quoting Buddhism here because, as I have pointed out before, Yulgok was well versed in Buddhist scriptures, especially those of Hua-yen and Ch'an, which he studied in his early years.

176. *YC* 10:13a (vol. 1, p. 202).

177. This is, as Yulgok himself mentioned, originally a Buddhist analogy that the essence of air (principle) is pervasive in phenomena, taking various particularizations in them, just as the air in different bottles is one and the same, taking on various forms of shape.

178. *YC* 10:22a (vol. 1, p. 207).

179. Ibid.

180. *Ŏrok* (Collected Sayings of Yulgok), part 2, in *YC* 31:16b (vol. 2, p. 267).

181. *YC* 12:21b (vol. 1, p. 249).

182. *YC* 10:25b (vol. 1, p. 208).

183. Ibid. In a letter to his friend An Ŭng-hyu, Yulgok also argued that in all phenomena *ki* is what actually moves and becomes tranquil and *i* is what makes *ki* act in this way: "That which has form and is active, being in movement and tranquility is *ki*; that which is no form and nonactive is *i*. Without *i*, *ki* has no root; therefore, it is said that *i* has neither form nor action and that *ki* has both form and action. The former is the master of the latter." See *YC* 12:20b (vol. 1, p. 248).

184. As Song Si-yŏl (Udam, 1607–1689) commented, with respect to concrete phenomena, *i* and *ki* are inseparable in things because the former is located inside of the latter. He argued that "since *i* is formless and passive, it

is only *ki* that actually acts, becoming manifest." See *Songja taejŏn* (Great Compendium of Master Song), *kwŏn* 91, Letter to Yi Yŏ-ku.

185. *YC* 10:29a (vol. 1, p. 210).

186. *YC* 10:26a (vol. 1, p. 209). This can also be translated as "*i* penetrates and *ki* limits."

187. *YC* 10:26a (vol. 1, p. 209).

188. *YC* 10:33a (vol. 1, p. 212).

189. *YC* 10:26a (vol. 1, p. 209).

190. See *Chuang Tzu*, Chapter 22. Yulgok probably formulated his theory under some influence from Chuang Tzu, although we have no written proof to justify this claim because he never directly quoted Chuang Tzu. As I pointed out before, he was well versed in the Taoist texts such as the *Tao Te Ching* and *Chuang Tzu*, which he had studied in his early years.

191. According to the Hua-yen philosophy, "principle" constitutes the noumenal world that is said to be empty, static, formless, and characterless, whereas "facts" pertain to the manifestations of the mind that make up the phenomenal world with active, concrete, and particular things and phenomena. The realm of principle and the realm of facts are said to be in harmony through their mutual interaction and penetration.

192. These ideas appear in *Shih Hsan-men* (Ten Mysterious Gates). See *Hua-yen ching* (Flowery Splendor Scripture) or Chan, *A Source Book in Chinese Philosophy*, pp. 411–413. According to Yi Pyŏng-do, Yulgok borrowed these ideas from the Hua-yen school. See Yi Pyŏng-do, *Yulgokŭi saengaewa sasang*, p. 69. Pae Chong-ho disagrees with him by arguing that Yulgok's theory relates more to the orthodox Ch'eng-Chu doctrine on *i* and *ki*. See his "Yi Iŭi ch'ŏrak sasang," in *Han'guk ch'ŏrak yŏn'gu*, vol. 2, p. 307. In my view, however, the Ch'eng-Chu theory of *i* and *ki* originally has unmistakable Hua-yen imprints; in other words, the issue is not as simple as both Yi and Pae make out.

193. Yi Pyŏng-do makes a debatable observation that Yulgok formulated his philosophy of *i* and *ki* under the direct influence by Hua-yen Buddhism. See his *Han'guk yuhak saryak*, p. 160, and *Yulgokŭi saengaewa sasang*, p. 69. Unlike the Hua-yen notion, however, Yulgok does not say that things and phenomena are simply the manifestations of the mind. In the Ch'eng-Chu Neo-Confucian context, he means that they consist of *i* and *ki* together.

In other words, the Hua-yen philosophy lacks such a view. In this regard, then, Yi Pyŏng-do's argument is incorrect.

194. *YC* 10:35a (vol. 1, p. 213).

195. Quoting *Tao Te Ching*, Chapter 40. See Chan, *A Source Book in Chinese Philosophy*, p. 160; D. C. Lau, trans., *Lao Tzu: Tao Te Ching*, p. 101. Lao Tzu meant that turning back is how the Tao works and that Being (something) and Nonbeing (nothing) generate each other, referring to the nothingness and fullness of the Way. And the myriad things in the world come from Being, but Being itself is born out of Nonbeing.

196 *YC* 10:39a (vol. 1, p. 215). It is not unusual for Yulgok to quote this Taoist text because, as I pointed out in his biography, he was well versed in both Taoist and Buddhist texts, which he studied during his early years.

197. Ibid.

198. *YC* 10:40a (vol. 1 p. 216).

199. *YC* 10:37a (vol. 1, p. 214).

200. Ibid.

201. *YC* 10:37b–38a (vol. 1, pp. 214–215).

Chapter IV. Practical Implications for T'oegye

1. For English works on T'oegye, see Michael C. Kalton's book, Tu Wei-ming's two articles, and other articles by Wing-tsit Chan, Abe Yoshio, Tomoeda Ryūtarō, and Youn Sa-soon. For East Asian works, see Abe Yoshio, *Nihon Shushigaku to Chōsen* and *Chōsen no Shushigaku Nihon no Shushigaku*; Ch'ien Mu, "Chu Tzu hsüeh liu-yen Han-kuo kao"; Takahashi Susumu, *T'oegyewa kyŏngŭi ch'ŏrak*; Pae Chong-ho, *Han'guk yuhaksa*; Yi Pyŏng-do, *Han'guk yuhak saryak*; Yi Sang-ŭn, *T'oegyeŭi saengaewa hangmun*; and Yun Sa-sun, *T'oegye ch'ŏrakŭi yŏn'gu*. For more information on these sources, see the Bibliography.

2. See Chu Hsi's *CTYL* 1:2b. The phrase *hsing-erh-hsia* can be translated also as "below physical form" or simply "physical"; it originally comes from the *Book of Changes*, "Appended Remarks," part 1, Chapter 12.

3. See Chu Hsi's *CTYL* 1:2b. The phrase *hsing-erh-shang* can be translated also as "above physical form" or simply "metaphysical"; it origi-

nally comes from the *Book of Changes*, "Appended Remarks," part 1, Chapter 12.

4. *CTYL* 94:41b–42a.

5. *CTYL* 1:2a. This is originally said by Ch'eng I in his *Ts'ui-yen* (Pure Words), 1:24a; *I chuan* (Commentary on the *Book of Changes*), 3:3b.

6. The relevant English and East Asian literature on Chu Hsi's philosophy of *li* includes those prominent works by Wing-tsit Chan, Ch'ien Mu, Mou Tsung-san, Tang Chün-i, and Tomoeda Ryūtarō. For more information, see the Bibliography.

7. *CTWC* 46:24a.

8. Ibid.

9. In this subject, see Ch'ien Mu, *Chu Tzu hsin hsüeh-an*, vol. 1, pp. 238–239.

10. *CTYL* 1:1a.

11. *CTYL* 1:2b.

12. *CTYL* 1:2b.

13. See Mou Tsung-san, *Hsin-t'i yü hsing-t'i*, vol. 3, pp. 420–421, and Ch'ien Mu, *Chu Tzu hsin hsüeh-an*, vol. 1, p. 243.

14. Chan, trans., *Reflections on Things at Hand: The Neo-Confucian Anthology by Chu Hsi and Lü Tsu-ch'ien*, p. xxi.

15. See Tu Wei-ming, "T'oegye's Creative Interpretation of Chu Hsi's Philosophy of Principle," *Korea Journal* 22, no. 2 (Feb. 1982): 4–15 and "Yi T'oegye's Perception of Human Nature: A Preliminary Inquiry into the Four-Seven Debate in Korean Neo-Confucianism," in de Bary and Haboush, *The Rise of Neo-Confucianism in Korea.*

16. *TC* 16:11a (vol. 1, p. 407). T'oegye is quoting Chu Hsi's statement in *CTWC* 46:24a.

17. *TC* 16:29b (vol. 1, p. 416).

18. *TC* 16:30b (vol. 1, p. 416).

19. *TC* 16:8b (vol. 1, p. 405).

20. *TC* 16:11a (vol. 1, p. 407).

21. This concise essay is found in *TC* 40:21b (vol. 2, p. 330). For my brief description of it, see Appendix 3.

22. Ibid.

23. *TC,* vol. 3, p. 161.

24. *TC* 35:25a (vol. 2, p. 217).

25. *TC* 12:22b (vol. 1, p. 333).

26. Ibid.

27. *TC* 35:26a (vol. 2, p. 218).

28. See his "Chu Hsi and T'oegye: Differences in Their Theories of Principle and Material Force," in de Bary and Haboush, *The Rise of Neo-Confucianism in Korea,* p. 253.

29. *TC* 16:10b (vol. 1, p. 406).

30. *TC* 16:12a (vol. 1, p. 407).

31. *TC* 16:11a (vol. 1, p. 407).

32. Ibid.

33. See *TC* 41:16b–19a (vol. 2, pp. 328–330). For a brief description of this text, see Appendix 3.

34. *TC* 39:28b (vol. 2, p. 299).

35. In his brief comment on T'oegye, de Bary correctly observed that T'oegye formulated his philosophy of *i* by following Chen Te-hsiu. This is a good point, although de Bary does not elaborate on it further. See his *Neo-Confucian Orthodoxy,* p. 197.

36. Yun Sa-soon, "T'oegye's Identification of 'To Be' and 'Ought': T'oegye's Theory of Value," in de Bary and Haboush, *The Rise of Neo-Confucianism in Korea,* p. 228.

37. Abe Yoshio, "Development of Neo-Confucianism in Japan, Korea, and China: A Comparative Study," p. 25. Without analyzing T'oegye's writings, however, Abe does not explain clearly in what sense T'oegye have a "new" interpretation of Chu Hsi.

38. Ch'ae Mu-song, *T'oegye Yulgok ch'ŏrakŭi pigyo yŏn'gu* (A Comparative Study of T'oegye's and Yulgok's Philosophies) (Seoul: Sŏnggyun'gwan University Press, 1985), p. 99.

39. *TC* 16:12a (vol. 1, p. 407).

40. De Bary points out that Shao Yung (1022–1077) was the first Sung thinker to use the term *hsin-fa* (System of the Mind-and-Heart) metaphysically for mind cultivation. See *Neo-Confucian Orthodoxy*, pp. 126–131.

41. For a more detailed discussion of the *Heart Classic*, see de Bary, ibid., pp. 73–82.

42. In an article on the transmission of the Chu Hsi school in Korea, Ch'ien Mu comments correctly that *simhak* is a predominant feature in T'oegye's thought. See his "Chu Tzu-hsüeh liu-yen Han-kuo k'ao," *Hsin-ya hsüeh-pao*, 12 (1977): 1–69.

43. This is found in *TC* 7:28b (vol. 1, p. 207). See M. Kalton, *To Become a Sage*, pp. 160–164. For my brief description of this text, see Appendix 3.

44. *TC* 7:29b (vol. 1, p. 208).

45. *TC* 6:36b–59b (vol. 1, pp. 181–193). See Appendix 3 for my brief description of this text.

46. *TC* 6:42a (vol. 1, p. 184).

47. *TC* 6:45b (vol. 1, p. 186)

48. *TC*, vol. 3, pp. 249–551, esp. pp. 254, 513. For my brief description of this text, see Appendix 3.

49. *TC*, vol. 4, pp. 169–171; vol. 2, p. 326.

50. *TC*, vol. 2, p. 328.

51. *TC*, vol. 4, p. 169.

52. For a detailed discussion of the *Heart Classic*, see de Bary, *Neo-Confucian Orthodoxy*, pp. 73–82.

53. *TC* 6:42a (vol. 1, p. 184). This is quoted from the *Book of History*, "Counsels of Great Yü." See J. Legge, trans., *The Chinese Classics*, vol. 3, p. 61.

54. Preface to *Chung-yung chang-chü*, in *CTWC* 76:21b. This is also cited in Chen Tu-hsiu's *Hsin-ching*, 1a.

55. *CTWC* 67:19b. Chu Hsi's formula is that the moral mind (the unmoved, tranquil state of the mind) is pure and always good, whereas the

human mind (the aroused mind mixed with selfish desires) includes both good and evil. See also *CTYL* 5:4a.

56. *CTYL* 61:10a.

57. *CTYL* 61:5a–b.

58. *CTYL* 118:29b.

59. *TC* 16:12a (vol. 1, p. 407).

60. *TC* 16:37b (vol. 1, p. 419).

61. *TC* 40:9b (vol. 2, p. 307).

62. *TC* 37:27a–b (vol. 2, p. 259), Letter to Yi P'yŏng-suk.

63. *TC* 16:9a-b and 16:32a-b (vol. 1, pp. 406 and 418).

64. *TC* 7:24a (vol. 1, p. 205).

65. *TC* 16:12a (vol. 1, p. 407).

66. *TC* 37:28b (vol. 2, p. 259), Letter to Yi P'yŏng-suk.

67. See also *TC* 25:19b (vol. 2, p. 10) and 7:23a (vol. 1, p. 205). This doctrine was originally Chang Tsai's saying in *Chang Tzu ch'üan-shu*, SPPY ed., 14:2a. It is used extensively by Chu Hsi; for example, see *CTYL* 53:9a.

68. *TC* 41:16b (vol. 2, p. 328).

69. *CTYL* 5:7a.

70. See *TC* 41:16b–19a (vol. 2, pp. 328–330). For my brief description of this essay, see Appendix 3.

71. T'oegye is referring specifically to the *Book of Changes*, "Appended Remarks," (SPPY ed.), 7:14b, which states: "When change is quiescent, it does not move. But when it is stimulated, it penetrates all things."

72. T'oegye is referring to the first chapter, which states: "Before pleasure, sorrow, anger, and joy are aroused, it is called equilibrium; after they are aroused and attain their due degree and measure, it is called harmony. Equilibrium is the great foundation of the world; harmony is the universal way." See Wing-tsit Chan, *A Source Book in Chinese Philosophy*, p. 98.

73. T'oegye probably means that what *Mencius* (2A:6) called the "Four Beginnings" refers to the original goodness of human nature or the substance of the mind. For him, the Four are the innate seeds of moral cul-

tivation, whereas the Seven are the basic physical sensations and mental feelings that refer to the function of the mind.

74. *TC* 41:16b (vol. 2, p. 328).

75. *CTWC* 67:1a.

76. *CTWC* 32:24b, 25a.

77. *TC* 36:2b (vol. 2, p. 226), Letter to Yi Koeng-chung.

78. *TC* 36:16a (vol. 2, p. 233), Letter to Yi Koeng-chung.

79. *TC* 7:24b (vol. 1, p. 205).

80. This is T'oegye's concluding remark in the *Sim t'ong sŏngchŏng tosŏl* (Diagrammatic Treatise of the Saying that "Mind Commands Human Nature and Feelings"), the sixth of his *Sŏnghak sipto*, *TC* 7:26b (vol. 1, p. 205).

81. *TC* 36:2b (vol. 2, p. 226), Letter to Yi Koeng-chung.

82. *TC* 16:37b (vol. 1, p. 419).

83. *TC* 37:28b (vol. 2, p. 259), Letter to Yi P'yŏng-suk.

84. Chu Hsi was cautious of quiet sitting as a convincing method of self-cultivation. In early Ming China, however, some followers of the Ch'eng-Chu school promoted it. For example, Wu Yü-pei (1391–1469), a leader of the Ch'eng-Chu tradition, and his disciple Ch'en Hsien-chang (1428–1500) are well known for it. A good English discussion of Wu and Ch'en is in Wm. T. de Bary, ed., *The Unfolding of Neo-Confucianism* (New York: Columbia University Press, 1975), especially "Introduction," pp. 19–30. For the subject of quiet sitting and Ming Chinese Neo-Confucianism, see Rodney Taylor, "The Sudden/Gradual Paradigm and Neo-Confucian Mind Cultivation" and "Meditation and Ming Orthodoxy," in his *Religious Dimensions of Neo-Confucianism* (Albany: SUNY Press, 1991), pp. 77–91 and 93–114, respectively; R. Taylor, *The Confucian Way of Contemplation: Okada Takehiko and the Tradition of Quiet-Sitting* (Columbia: University of South Carolina Press, 1988), especially pp. 123–137 and 140–144; and R. Taylor, *The Cultivation of Sagehood as a Religious Goal in Neo-Confucianism: A Study of Selected Writings of Kao Pan-lung (1525–1626)* (Missoula, Mont.: Scholar's Press/AAR, 1978).

85. *Ŏnhaeng nok* (Biographical Records of T'oegye), 1:16b and 1:23a (*TC*, vol. 4, pp. 180 and 176).

86. *TC* 41:32b (vol. 2, p. 338).

87. *Ŏnhaeng nok*, 1:16b (*TC*, vol. 4, p. 176).

88. This can be translated as "reverence" and "seriousness, as these are other standard renderings that are generally accepted.

89. *TC* 29:15a (v. 2, p. 94), Letter to Kim Yi-chŏng.

90. *Book of Changes*, "Commentary on the K'un Hexagram," (SPPY ed.), 1:16a. See J. Legge, trans., *Yi King*, p. 426, and Wing-tsit Chan, *A Source Book in Chinese Philosophy*, p. 264.

91. *Book of Rites*, "Summary of Ceremonies," (SPPY ed.), 1:1a. See J. Legge, trans., *Li Ki*, vol. 1, p. 61.

92. *Analects*, 13:19. See D. C. Lau, trans., *Confucius: Analects (Lun yü)* (New York: Penguin Books, 1970), p. 121.

93. *I-shu*, 18:19a. See Chan, *A Source Book*, p. 560.

94. *I-shu*, 15:9a.

95. *I-shu*, 18:5b.

96. *CTYL* 95:41a.

97. *CTYL* 96:2b.

98. In this regard, See Takahashi Susumu, *T'oegyewa kyŏngŭi ch'ŏrak*, especially pp. 219–254.

99. *TC*, vol. 3, p. 144.

100. *TC*, vol. 3, p. 144.

101. Kalton, *To Become a Sage*, p. 188.

102. *TC* 7:35a (vol. 1, p. 211).

103. *TC* 7:33a (vol. 1, p. 210). This is a paraphrase of *CTYL* 12:7b.

104. See T'oegye's *Ŏnhaeng nok* (Records of Words and Conduct), 1:14b–15a, in *TC* vol. 4, pp. 175–176. The former is a paraphrase of the *Doctrine of the Mean*, Chapter 1, and the latter comes from the Ch'eng brothers' *I-shu*, 15:6b.

105. *Ŏnhaeng nok*, 1:12b (*TC*, vol. 4, p. 175).

106. *TC* 7:8a (vol. 1, p. 197).

107. *TC* 16:6b (vol. 1, p. 405), Letter to Ki Myŏng-hŏn.

108. *TC* 16:6b (vol. 1, p. 405), Letter to Ki Myŏng-hŏn.

109. *Ŏnhaeng nok*, 6:5b–6a (*TC*, vol. 4, p. 246).

110. *TC* 6:44b (vol. 1, p. 185).

111. *Ŏnhaeng nok*, 1:15a (*TC*, vol. 4, p. 176).

112. *Ŏnhaeng nok*, 1:16a (*TC*, vol. 4, p. 176).

113. *Ŏnhaeng nok*, 1:16b, in *TC*, vol. 4, p. 176. This statement alludes to what Chu Hsi said about the need for scholars to "keep always collecting together [the dispersed mind] without allowing oneself to become dispersed" (*CTYL* 12:10b).

114. *TC* 37:38b (vol. 1, p. 259), Letter to Yi P'yŏng-suk.

115. *TC* 7:24b (vol. 1, p. 205).

116. *TC* 7:33a (vol. 1, p. 210).

117. The relevant English literature on this topic includes the following: Rodney Taylor, *Religious Dimensions of Neo-Confucianism*; R. Taylor, *The Way of Heaven: An Introduction to the Confucian Religious Life* (Leiden: E. J. Brill, 1986); Julia Ching, "What Is Confucian Spirituality," in I. Eber, ed., *Confucianism: The Dynamics of Tradition* (New York: Macmillan, 1986); Hans Küng and J. Ching, *Christianity and Chinese Religions* (New York: Doubleday, 1989), especially Chapter 2, "Confucianism: Ethical Humanism as Religion?" by Ching; Julia Ching, *Confucianism and Christianity: A Comparative Study* (New York and Tokyo: Kodansha International, 1976); Tu Wei-ming, *Centrality and Commonality: An Essay on Confucian Religiousness* (a revised and enlarged edition of *Centrality and Commonality: An Essay on Chung-yung*) (Albany: SUNY Press, 1989); Tu Wei-ming, "Neo-Confucian Religiosity and Human-Relatedness" in *Confucian Thought: Selfhood as Creative Self-Transformation* (Albany: SUNY Press, 1985); William T. de Bary, "Human Rites—An Essay on Confucianism and Human Rites," in I. Eber, ed., *Confucianism: The Dynamics of Tradition*; Cheng Chung-ying, "Religious Reality and Religious Understanding in Confucianism and Neo-Confucianism," *International Philosophical Quarterly* 13, no. 1 (March 1974): 33–61; Mou Tsung-san, "Confucianism as Religion," in D. Lancashire, trans., *Chinese Essays on Religion and Faith* (San Francisco: Chinese Material Center, 1981), pp. 222–243.

118. Examining the Chinese Confucian tradition, Julia Ching correctly points out: "Sagehood offers a model of self-transcendence, and the way to sagehood—by self-cultivation . . . was formulated as a way of self-transcendence, with clear religious dimensions" (Ching, *Confucianism and Christianity*, p. 10). She classified the Confucian way of self-cultivation as "a lay spirituality" (Ching, "What Is Confucian Spirituality?" p. 79). Similarly, Tu Wei-ming considered Neo-Confucianism as a "spiritual tradition" in the sense of emphasizing its inner aspects of learning and self-cultivation (Tu Wei-ming, *Confucian Thought*, p. 132).

119. Regardless of the academic discipline, a major question about Confucianism has been, Is Confucianism a religion, a philosophy, or a way of life? First of all, however, the question one has to address is, What do we mean by *religion*? Whether the philosophical doctrines and ethical practices of Confucianism were "religious" enough in the strict Western sense of believing in and worshipping "God" is a question open to debate. The English word *religion* itself, of course, has several problems of characterization. As we know, it originates from the Latin *religio,* which means "to bind (together)," and the notion of binding the individual and the monotheistic God has been the most common perspective for articulating the Jewish, Christian, and Islamic traditions. It is, nonetheless, a narrow and limited viewpoint that does not fit well into East Asian religious traditions, especially Neo-Confucianism (and philosophical Taoism and Zen Buddhism, too). As manifested in current scholarship, the Confucian tradition has widely been taken as "humanist" or "socio-political," meaning a teaching on human values, ideas, and concerns that are relevant to the goal of transforming the various aspects of society and culture. For this reason, Confucianism is generally said to be "secular" as opposed to "religious." But we must remember that the Confucian tradition approaches human nature and its ultimate reality from a different standpoint other religions like Christianity; however, this should not necessarily eliminate it from the religious context. If *religion* is defined in a general perspective, as a way of life, associated with a collective set of scriptures, beliefs, and moral codes, Confucianism qualifies well. Even if we define it as a spiritual concern to seek for the transcendental ground of human beings, Neo-Confucianism can be considered as a religion. Like other world religions, it promoted a large component of spiritual teachings and practices. T'oegye's Neo-Confucianism demonstrates this quite well.

120. *Ŏnhaeng nok*, 6:7b (*TC,* vol. 4, p. 247).

121. Ibid.

122. *TC* 41:31b (vol. 2, p. 336).

123. *Ŏnhaeng nok*, 3:22b (*TC*, vol. 4, p. 209).

124. Ching, "What Is Confucian Spirituality," p. 75.

125. *Ŏnhaeng nok*, 1:14b (*TC*, vol. 4, p. 176).

126. Here, the word *things* should be understood as including not only the objective world of the material things, but also the moral and intersubjective world of human nature and human relationships.

127. *Ŏnhaeng nok*, 5:18a (*TC*, vol. 4, p. 238).

128. To use Tu Wei-ming's terminology. See his *Centrality and Commonality: An Essay on Chung-yung* (Honolulu: University of Hawaii Press, 1976), p. 104.

129. Tu Wei-ming, *Centrality and Commonality: An Essay on Confucian Religiousness*, p. 99. Let me point out that by the idea of trinity Tu does not mean in the theistic context of Christian theology; rather, he seems to have used it from the standpoint of the *Doctrine of the Mean* that Heaven, Earth, and human nature form an unity of three. Examining the *Doctrine of the Mean*, he also argues that such a view can be "the natural outcome of an attempt to understand Confucian humanism religiously" (Ibid., p. 120).

130. Taylor, *Religious Dimensions of Neo-Confucianism*, p. 3.

Chapter V. Practical Implications for Yulgok

1. For English works, I refer to Young-chan Ro, *The Korean Neo-Confucianism of Yi Yulgok* (Albany: SUNY Press, 1989) and Julia Ching, "Yi Yulgok on the Four and the Seven Emotions," in de Bary and Haboush, eds., *The Rise of Neo-Confucianism in Korea*. For East Asian works, see Abe Yoshio, *Nihon shushigaku to Chōsen*; *Chōsen no Shushigaku Nihon no Shushigaku*; Song Sŏk-ku, *Yulgokŭi ch'ŏrak sasang yŏn'gu* (A Study of Yulgok's Philosophical Thought) (Seoul: Hyŏngsŏl ch'ulp'ansa, 1987); Yi Pyŏng-do, *Yulgokŭi saengaewa sasang*; Hwang ŭi-dong, *Yulgok ch'ŏrak yŏn'gu* (A Study of Yulgok's Thought) (Seoul: Kyŏngmundang, 1987); Yi Pyŏng-do, *Han'guk yuhak saryak*; Pae Chong-ho, "Yi Iŭi ch'ŏrak sasang"; and Pae Chong-ho, *Han'guk yuhaksa* (A History of Korean Confucianism) (Seoul: Yŏnsae University Press, 1973).

2. *YC* 9:36a (vol. 1, p. 192).

3. *YC* 10:5a (vol. 1, p. 198).

4. *YC* 20:1a–20:38b (vol. 1, pp. 428–527, and vol. 2, pp. 1–81).

5. *YC* 20:60a (vol. 1, p. 457).

6. See Bloom, trans., *Knowledge Painfully Acquired: The K'un-chih chi by Lo Ch'in-shun* and "On the 'Abstraction' of Ming Thought: Some Concrete Evidence from the Philosophy of Lo Ch'in-shun," in Wm. T. de Bary and Bloom, eds., *Principle and Practicality: Essays in Neo-Confucianism and Practical Learning* (hereafter abbreviated *Principle and Practicality*) (New York: Columbia Universirt Press, 1979).

7. The Ch'eng-Chu tradition was introduced into late sixteenth century Japan through Korean editions of Chinese Neo-Confucian works. Another Japanese Neo-Confucian school of thought was identified with the philosophy of *i* and came to be associated with Yamazaki Ansai (1618–1682) and his followers in the Kimon school; in fact, it developed under T'oegye's influence.

8. For the impact of Lo's *K'un-chih chi* on the Japanese Neo-Confucians, see Abe Yoshio, *Nihon Shushigaku to Chōsen*, pp. 514–524, and "Development of Neo-Confucianism in Japan, Korea, and China: A Comparative Study," *Acta Asiatica* 19 (1970) 16–39.

9. *YC* 10:8b (vol. 1, p. 200).

10. *YC* 14:5b–6a (vol. 1, p. 283).

11. Ibid., quoting *I-shu*, 2A:1b.

12. *Chu Tzu ch'üan-shu*, 42:18b. Cited in Chan, *A Source Book in Chinese Philosophy*, p. 618. Chu Hsi also states that "it is from the deviation in the operation of Heaven's principle that human desires arise."

13. *YC* 35:3b–4a (vol. 2, pp. 342–343).

14. *YC* 10:14b (vol. 1, p. 203).

15. *YC* 10:3a (vol. 1, p. 197).

16. Ibid.

17. *Sŏnghak chipyo*, vol. 3, "Sugi," part 2, sec. 6, in *YC* 21:6b (vol. 1, p. 465).

18. *Chang Tzu ch'üan-shu* (Complete Works of Master Chang Tsai), 12:3a. See Chan, *Source Book*, p. 516.

19. *Sŏnghak chipyo*, vol. 3, "Sugi," part 2, sec. 6, "Kyo kijil," in *YC* 21:6b (vol. 1, p. 465).

20. Ibid., sec. 7, "Yanggi" (Nourishment of *ki*), in *YC* 21:14b (vol. 1, p. 469).

21. Ibid., sec. 8, "Chŏngsim" (Rectification of the Mind), in *YC* 21:20a (vol. 1, p. 472).

22. *YC* 9:36a (vol. 1, p. 193).

23. *YC* 14:5a (vol. 1, p. 284).

24. *YC* 10:4a (vol. 1, p. 198).

25. Ibid.

26. This is found in *YC* 14:4a–17a (vol. 1, pp. 282–284). For my translation of this diagram, see Appendix 4.

27. *YC* 14:4a (vol. 1, p. 282).

28. Ibid.

29. Ibid.

30. For example, one may say that it is compatible with John Dewey's theory of emotion, which asserts three general components of emotion: (1) the object of emotion, (2) the presence of a feeling, and (3) a disposition to behave. See J. Dewey, "Feeling," in *John Dewey: The Early Works, 1882–1898*, vol. 2 (Bloomington: Southern Illinois University Press, 1967).

31. In *A Treatise of Human Nature*, David Hume formulates a theory of emotion that addresses a pure sensation theory. Indeed, in his view, emotions are simply sensations, if not specifically physical sensations.

32. In *The Principles of Psychology*, vol. 2 (New York: Dover Publications, 1950), William James, a philosopher and psychologist, argues that emotions are feelings or perceptions accompanied by physiological disturbances. It would be interesting to compare Yulgok's theory of emotion with Western theories of emotion, though it is beyond the scope of this book. We might say that Yulgok's theory of emotion somewhat corresponds to what both Hume and James have pointed out.

33. In this regard, Yulgok's theory, that good emotions such as moral innate feelings are aroused by virtuous behavior, is similar to Jean-Paul Sarte's

theory according to which emotions are value judgments—perceptions analogous to sensory perceptions.

34. *YC* 20:60a (vol. 1, p. 457).

35. This is found in *YC* 20:1a–22:29b (vol. 1, pp. 427–499). It has three major parts consisting of thirteen sections that are divided into short subsections of various themes about self-cultivation. Yulgok divides the whole chapter into the following categories: "making the resolve," "self-recollection," "investigation of principle," "sincerity of intention," "straightening of physical endowment," "nourishing *ki*," "rectification of the mind," and "self-reflection."

36. *Sŏnghak chipyo*, vol. 2, "Sugi," part 1, sec. 4, "Kungni" (Investigation of Principle), in *YC* 20:57a (vol. 1, p. 455).

37. Ibid., vol. 2, "Sugi," part 1, sec. 1, "Ipchi" (Making the Resolve), in *YC* 20:3b (vol. 1, p. 428).

38. Yulgok said this after he returned home from his study of Buddhism in the Diamond Mountain at the age of twenty. See *Chagyŏng mun* (Essay on Self-Realization), *YC* 14:40a (vol. 1, p. 300).

39. For a brief description of it, see Appendix 4.

40. *YC* 5:24b (vol. 1, p. 102).

41. *Kyŏngmong yokyŏl*, sec. 1, "Making the Resolve," in *YC* 27:3b (vol. 2, p. 82), and *Hakkyo mobŏm*, in *YC* 15:34a (vol. 1, p. 330). For my brief description of these texts, see Appendix 4.

42. *Sŏnghak chipyo*, vol. 2, "Sugi," part 1, sec. 2, "Making the Resolve," in *YC* 20:8a (vol. 1, p. 431).

43. Ibid.

44. Here, I should point out that the Western perspective of *sincerity* comes from the Latin term *sincerus* and generally means "faithfulness," "truthfulness," or "honesty" to oneself in relation to others. It does not seem to have ethico-metaphysical meanings and implications. By contrast, the Neo-Confucian notion of sincerity has both of them in the context of feelings, morality, and self-cultivation.

45. See *YC* 20:1a–22:29b (vol. 1, pp. 427–499), especially pp. 463–465, the section on sincerity in *Sŏnghak chipyo*, vol. 3, "Sugi," part 2, sec. 5.

46. See Chan, *Source Book*, p. 86.

47. *Doctrine of the Mean*, Chapter 23.

48. *Doctrine of the Mean*, Chapter 20. See Chan, *Source Book*, p. 107. In this regard, Tu Wei-ming points out that this Confucian conviction means that "the true nature of the human being and the real creativity of the cosmos are both grounded in sincerity." See Tu, *Humanity and Self-Cultivation: Essays in Neo-Confucian Thought*, p. 99.

49. *T'ung-shu* (Penetrating of the *Book of Changes*), Chapter 1, "Sincerity," part 1, in *Chou Tzu ch'üan-shu* (Complete Works of Master Chou), p. 123. Translation adapted from Chan, *Source Book*, p. 465.

50. Ibid., Chapter 1, "Sincerity," part 2, in *Chou Tzu ch'üan-shu*, pp. 124–125. Translation adapted from Chan, *Source Book*, p. 466.

51. See, for example, Huang Tsung-hsi et al., *Sung-Yüan hsüeh-an* (Records of Sung and Yüan Scholars), SPPY ed. 12:17a, 18a.

52. *T'ung-shu*, Chapter 4, "Sagehood," in *Chou Tzu ch'üan-shu*, p. 135. Translation adapted from Chan, *Source Book*, p. 467.

53. For my brief description of this text, see Appendix 4.

54. See Appendix 4.

55. See especially *Manŏn pongsa, Simu yukcho kye* (Six-Article Memorial) and *Tongho mundap* (Tongho Questions and Answers). See Appendix 4 for my description of these texts.

56. *YC* 9:36a (vol. 1, p. 192).

57. See *Sŏnghak chipyo*, vol. 3, "Sugi," part 2, in *YC* 20:1a–22:29b (vol. 1, pp. 427–499), especially the section on sincerity, pp. 463–465.

58. Ibid., vol. 2, "Sugi," part 1, sec. 1, "General Discourse on Self-cultivation," in *YC* 20:2a (vol. 1, p. 428).

59. *Sŭbu* (Miscellaneous Works), 6:38a-b, in *YC*, vol. 2, pp. 581–582.

60. This can be translated also as "true principle" or "practical principle," and it is, Yulgok argues, equivalent to Heaven's principle.

61. This can be rendered as "true mind' or "practical mind," which is, in Yulgok's view, equivalent to the "mind of Heaven" or the "mind of the sage."

62. *Sŭbu*, 6:15a, in *YC*, vol. 2, p. 570.

63. *Sŏnghak chipyo*, vol. 3, "Sugi," part 2, sec. 5, "Sincerity," in *YC* 21:5b (vol. 1, p. 464).

64. Ibid., *YC* 21:6a (vol. 1, p. 465).

65. See *Ŏrok*, part 2, in *YC* 32:13b–16a (vol. 2, pp. 265–267).

66. Paraphrasing the *Book of Changes*, commentary on hexagram no. 1, *ch'ien*. In Neo-Confucian thought, these refer to the four qualities of Heaven and Earth that are identified with the four moral virtues of the mind, such as benevolence, righteousness, propriety, and wisdom. For this subject see, for example, Chu Hsi's "Treatise on Benevolence," in *CTWC* 67:20a–21b.

67. *Sŭbu*, 6:18a, in *YC*, vol. 2, p. 571.

68. *Sŏnghak chipyo*, vol. 3, "Sugi," part 2, sec. 5, "Rectification of the Mind," in *YC* 21:35b (vol. 1, p. 479).

69. *Sŭbu*, 6:43a, in *YC*, vol. 2, p. 584.

70. Ibid., 6:38a-b, in *YC*, vol. 2, pp. 581–582.

71. Ibid., 6:39a, *YC*, vol. 2, p. 482.

72. Ibid.

73. See his *Centrality and Commonality: An Essay on Chung-yung* (Hawaii: University of Hawaii Press, 1976), p. 116.

74. *Sŭbu*, 6:18a, in *YC*, vol. 2, p. 571.

75. *YC* 9:28b (vol. 1, p. 189).

76. Ibid.

77. *Sŏnghak chipyo*, vol. 3, "Sugi," part 2, sec. 8, "Rectification of the Mind," in *YC* 21:36a (vol. 1, p. 480).

78. Ibid.

79. Ibid., vol. 2, "Sugi," part 1, sec. 4, "Investigation of Principle," in *YC*, 20:50a (vol. 1, p. 452).

80. Ibid., vol. 3, "Sugi," part 2, sec. 8, "Rectification of the Mind," in *YC*, 21:35b (vol. 1, p. 479).

81. *Doctrine of the Mean*, Chapter 1.

82. *Sŏnghak chipyo,* vol. 3, "Sugi," part 2, sec. 5, "Sincerity," in *YC,* 21:6a (vol. 1, p. 465).

83. See Chan, *Source Book,* p. 96.

84. Young-chan Ro, *The Korean Neo-Confucianism of Yi Yulgok,* p. 108.

85. Ibid., p. 112, emphasis is added.

86. Ibid., p. 115, emphasis is added.

87. See *Sŏnghak chipyo,* vol. 3, "Sugi," part 2, sec. 5, in *YC,* vol. 1, pp. 463–465.

88. The question we must first address is, What do we mean by *pragmatic, realistic, functional,* and *utilitarian*? As we know, these words are interrelated with one another in the philosophical traditions of the West. They certainly bear a good deal of ambiguity in a cross-cultural context. In ordinary languages, they usually render such meanings as "useful" and "effective" as well, pointing to concrete goals, strategic methods, and beneficial outcomes. Etymologically speaking, the term *pragmatic* comes from the Greek *pragma,* which means "thing" or "fact"; of course, it closely relates to Pragmatism, a philosophical movement of the late nineteenth and early twentieth centuries. By *pragmatic,* I mean a philosophical and ethical view that emphasizes an interpretation of ideas and values in relation to concrete things, facts, and results. The term *functional* comes from the Latin *functio* (originating from the term *fungi*) that literally means "to perform" or "to execute" a concrete thing; in general, it signifies practical theories and methods to be used for bringing about positive and functional outcomes. The term *realistic,* which derives partly from the Latin *res* (literally, "thing"), has been understood especially in a context of underscoring the reality of external things. We shall use it in the sense that the objects of knowledge should address concrete things, concepts, and thoughts. In addition, another term, *utilitarian,* comes from the Latin *utilis* (literally meaning "useful"); it generally signifies useful application and procedure to promote beneficial results. Although Western utilitarians often speak of individual motivations and acts, the value of "utility," as David Hume argued, can be an ethical one as well. By *utilitarian,* then, we can use such a perspective that the ethical principle of utility can be expressed in terms of theoretical reasoning and concrete action to promote practical results such as the "greatest good," "greatest happiness," and so on.

89. Weber argued, in a comparative context, that the Confucian tradition was too "traditionalistic," enjoying adaptation to the given world and

not the mastery of it and that it lacked an emotional and dynamic mentality like the ascetic Protestant ethic (especially Calvinist) appropriate for the development of capitalism and modernization. See Max Weber, *The Religion of China: Confucianism and Taoism*, trans. H. M. Gerth (New York: Free Press, 1968) and *Protestant Ethic and the Spirit of Capitalism*, trans. T. Parsons (London: George Allen and Unwin, 1976).

90. For example, the Japanese scholar Ishida Ishirō argued that the rigid, moralistic tendency of Neo-Confucianism inhibited any interest in empirical research and natural science. See his "Tokugawa Feudal Society and Neo-Confucian Thought," *Philosophical Studies of Japan* 5 (1964): 17–24. Similarly, Masao Maruyama also made a debatable observation that the Neo-Confucian scope of learning did not promote any scientific practicality in the context of engendering economic and industrial progress. Se his *Studies in the Intellectual History of Tokugawa Japan* (Princeton, N.J.: Princeton University Press, 1975).

91. For example, Wing-tsit Chan discussed Chu Hsi's Neo-Confucianism in terms of what he calls *Chinese scientific thought*. See Chan, "Neo-Confucianism in Chinese Scientific Thought," *Philosophy East and West* 4 (1957): 309–332. As Joseph Needham suggested, we can also consider it as qualifying for a broader requirement of scientific thought in the global context. See *Science and Civilisation in China* (Cambridge: Cambridge University Press, 1965), vol. 2, pp. 193–194.

92. See Wm. T. de Bary and Irene T. Bloom, eds., *Principle and Practicality*. This volume includes the following articles: Chung-ying Cheng, "Practical Learning in Yen Yüan, Chu Hsi and Wang Yang-ming"; Irene Bloom, "On the 'Abstraction' of Ming Thought: Some Concrete Evidence from the Philosophy of Lo Ch'in-shun"; Wm. T. de Bary, "Sagehood as a Secular and Spiritual Ideal in Tokugawa Neo-Confucianism"; Julia Ching, "The Practical Learning of Chu Shun-shui"; and Okada Takehiko, "Practical Learning in the Chu Hsi School: Yamazaki Ansai and Kaibara Ekken."

93. De Bary, *The Unfolding of Neo-Confucianism*, pp. 184–187. See also his introduction to de Bary and Bloom, eds., *Principle and Practicality*, pp. 1–36.

94. De Bary, "Sagehood as a Secular and Spiritual Ideal in Tokugawa Neo-Confucianism," in de Bary and Bloom, ibid., p. 128.

95. See Chung-ying Cheng, "Practical Learning in Yen Yüan, Chu Hsi and Wang Yang-ming," in de Bary and Bloom, ibid., pp. 37–68.

96. See de Bary's introduction to de Bary and Bloom, ibid, p. 24. He also argues that Chu Hsi's Neo-Confucianism is a practical learning "in the several senses of moral solidity, rational coherence, practical effectiveness, and experiential or empirical verification" (Ibid., p. 25).

97. Cheng Chung-ying, "Practical Learning in Yen Yüan, Chu Hsi and Wang Yang-ming," in de Bary and Bloom, ibid., pp. 37–38.

98. Young-chan Ro, *The Korean Neo-Confucianism of Yi Yulgok*, p. 108, emphasis is added.

99. *Sŏnghak chipyo*, vol. 3, "Sugi," part 2, sec. 5, "Sincerity," in *YC* 21:6a (vol. 1,.p. 465).

100. This is found in *YC* 5:10b–39a (vol. 1, pp. 95–109). For my brief description of this text, see Appendix 4.

101. *YC* 8:18a–23a (vol. 1, pp. 169–172). See Appendix 4.

102. *YC* 15:2a–33b (vol. 1, pp. 313–329). See Appendix 4.

103. *YC* 10:34b (vol. 1, p. 213).

104. Ibid.

105. Ibid.

106. *YC* 15:33b (vol. 1, p. 329). For my brief description of this text, see Appendix 4.

107. *YC* 15:48b (vol. 1, p. 337).

108. *Ŏrok*, part 1, in *YC* 31:41a (vol. 2, p. 248).

109. *YC* 7:20b (vol. 1, p. 140).

110. For a brief description of this text, see Appendix 4.

111. *YC*, vol. 2, p. 226.

112. *Sŏnghak chipyo*, vol. 2, "Sugi," part 1, sec. 1, "General Discourse on Self-Cultivation," in *YC* 20:2a (vol. 1, p. 428).

113. Ibid., vol. 3, "Sugi," part 2, sec. 5, "Sincerity," in *YC* 21:2a (vol. 1, p. 463).

114. Quoting *T'ung-shu*, Chapter 1, "Sincerity," part 1, in *Chou Tzu ch'üan-shu*, p. 123. Translation adapted from Chan, *Source Book*, p. 465.

115. Ibid., in *YC* 21:6a (vol. 1, p. 465).

116. Song Sŏk-ku, *Yulgokŭi ch'ŏrak sasang yŏn'gu*, p. 193, comments that Yulgok's learning of self-cultivation is not only about the "subjective" effort of mind cultivation, but also for the "objective," "realistic" learning of the investigation of things and the transformation of *ki*. In my view, however, it puts more emphasis on the latter aspect, which points to the active and outer-directed method of learning.

117. *YC* 15:2a–33b. For more information, see my description of this political treatise in Appendix 4.

118. *YC* 5:25b (vol. 2, p. 102).

119. *YC* 5:16b (vol. 1, p. 98). See my discussion of the *Manŏn pongsa* in Appendix 4.

120. For more information, see Appendix 4.

121. Also, Yulgok addressed a need to abolish political corruption maintained by the traditional rules and customs of government; for instance, he urged liberation of talented slaves, urging that they, as well as sons of secondary wives of the upper *yangban* class, should be appointed to government positions. For a brief discussion of this subject in relation to Yulgok's *Tongho mundap*, *Manŏn pongsa*, and *Simu yukcho*, see Edward Y. J. Chung, "Yi Yulgok, a Neo-Confucian Political Reformer in Sixteenth-Century Korea," in Bernard H. Luk, ed., *Contacts Between Cultures (Eastern Asia: History and Social Sciences)* (Lewiston, Queenston, and Lampeter: Edwin Mellen Press, 1992), vol. 4, pp. 171–175.

122. These reform programs were never brought in to actual practice because most high-ranking conservative bureaucrats strongly opposed them, criticizing Yulgok for formulating what they saw as radical programs for existing socio-political systems in sixteenth century Korea.

123. When Chosŏn Korea was shaken politically, socially, and psychologically by Japanese and Western powers especially in the second half of the nineteenth century, it experienced a state of rapid decline, overwhelmed by problems of poverty, class conflict, and political corruption. Accordingly, Korean reformers and intellectuals began to question the country's cultural heritage, particularly Neo-Confucianism. Criticizing it for causing many problems, most *sirhak* scholars including Tasan condemned its institutional bureaucracy ideology as a serious burden that prevented the country's economic and socio-political modernization.

124. We must recall, however, that the similar distinction was originally advocated by Chu Hsi and his followers in China, Korea, and Japan. In other words, many *sirhak* scholars in Korea tended to ignore the distinction drawn by earlier Neo-Confucians, while others utilized it in their attempts to condemn the Neo-Confucian orthodoxy.

Chapter VI. Conclusions: A Comparison of T'oegye and Yulgok

1. *TC* 37:28b (vol. 2, p. 259), Letter to Yi P'yŏng-suk.

2. *YC* 9:36a (vol. 1, p. 192).

3. *YC* 9:35b (vol. 1, p. 192).

4. *YC* 9:36a (vol. 1, p. 192).

5. *YC* 10:29a (vol. 1, p. 210).

6. Furthermore, Kwŏn Sang-ha (Sangam, 1641–1721), another leading follower of Yulgok also emphasizes: "There are neither priority nor posteriority between *i* and *ki*. . . . This is why T'oegye's theory of alternate manifestation is wrong." See *Hansu chip* (Collected Works of Kwŏn Sangam), *kwŏn* 21, "Sach'il hobal pyŏn" (Treatise on the Alternate Manifestation of the Four and the Seven).

7. See de Bary, *Neo-Confucian Orthodoxy and the Learning of the Mind-and-Heart*, p. 81.

8. See also T'oegye's other works such as *Yukcho so* (Six-Article Memorial), in *TC* 6:36b–59b (vol. 1, pp. 181–193) and *Songge Wŏn Myŏng ihak t'ongnok* (General Records of the School of Principle in the Sung, Yüan, and Ming Periods), in *TC*, vol. 3, pp. 249–551 (especially pp. 254 and 513). For my brief description of the *Chŏnsŭmnok nonbyŏn* and the afore-mentioned texts, see Appendix 3.

9. See Kalton, *To Become a Sage: The Ten Diagrams on Sage Learning by Yi T'oegye*, p. 185, emphasis is added.

10. It was T'oegye's interpretation of Ch'eng-Chu orthodoxy in a fashion reminiscent of not only Chen Tu-hsiu, but also the early Ming Neo-Confucian Wu Yü-pi. Also, it developed out of his reaction against the independent thinkers of the Ch'eng-Chu school, especially Ch'en Hsien-chang and Lo Ch'in-shun. From T'oegye's own standpoint, Lo's emphasis on the role of *ch'i* points to an empirical materialism, and Ch'en overemphasized the

subjectively oriented form of quiet sitting only. As he asserted, both Lo and Ch'en repudiated the Ch'eng-Chu doctrines of principle and human nature, and their views were inappropriate for the whole process of learning and self-cultivation. For T'oegye's harsh critiques of the Chinese Neo-Confucians such Lu Hsiang-shan, Ch'en Hsien-chang, and Wang Yang-ming, see his two essays: *Paeksa Sigyo Chŏnsŭmnok ch'ojŏn insŏ kihu* (Postscript to the Conveyed Copy of Ch'en Hsien-chang's *Instructions Through Poetry* and Wang Yang-ming's *Instruction for Practical Living*), *TC* 41:29b–35b (vol. 2, pp. 336–336), and *Chŏnsŭmnok nonbyŏn* (Critique of Wang Yang-ming's *Instruction for Practical Living*), *TC* 41:23b–29b (vol. 2, pp. 332–336). The latter is a more systematic critique of Wang Yang-ming, in which he defends orthodox Ch'eng-Chu teachings. For my chronological and annotated description of both essays, see Appendix 3.

11. Let me point out that it is interesting to speculate what would have happened if the Four-Seven debates had occurred in Ming China before the rise of the Wang Yang-ming school. In other words, the success of Wang Yang-ming's reformulation of the Neo-Confucian philosophy of the mind could be the reason why a T'oegye-like phenomenon never occurred in China.

12. He was well aware of the popularity of the Wang school in Ming China. T'oegye's deep concern with the Wang Yang-ming school in Ming China produced an influential essay entitled *Chŏnsŭmnok nonbyŏn.*

13. This kind of religious Neo-Confucianism had significant influence on the thinking of the Neo-Confucians of Tokugawa Japan, especially Yamazaki Ansai. Ansai, the founder of the Kimon school, synthesized Neo-Confucian rationalism with traditional religious beliefs of Shinto, and his followers followed it closely. Ōtsuka Taiya (1618–1750) and his followers in the Kumamoto school also followed T'oegye's philosophy of *i*. For this subject, see Abe Yoshio, *Nihon Shushigaku to Chōsen*, pp. 514–524.

14. As I have defined before from a cross-cultural perspective, *spirituality* can mean mind cultivation, intuitive thinking, self-introspection, self-realization, and so on. More to the point, I mean a disciplined and spiritual-minded life that involves a combination of intellectual insights and contemplative practices, integrated with a degree of self-cultivation and self-transcendence. If we think of *spirituality* as something associated with the cultivation and experience of the inner self, then T'oegye's Neo-Confucianism qualifies as spirituality.

15. Commenting on the religious dimension of Confucianism, Julia Ching points out that "Sagehood offers a model of self-transcendence" and the way to sagehood is "a way of self-transcendence, with clear religious dimensions." See Ching, *Confucianism and Christianity: A Comparative Study*, p. 10. Recognizing Confucian religiosity, Tu Wei-ming also argues: "We can define the Confucian way of being religious as *ultimate self-transformation . . . as a faithful dialogical response to the transcendent. . . .* Confucian religiosity is expressed through the infinite potential and inexhaustible strength of each human for self-transcendence." This interpretation comes from Tu's study of the *Doctrine of the Mean*. See Tu, "On Confucian Religiousness," in his *Centrality and Commonality: An Essay on Confucian Religiousness*, p. 94. Indeed, these remarks fit into my discussion of the religious dimension of T'oegye's Neo-Confucianism.

16. Here, we need to clarify what we mean by *faith*. As we know, the English word *faith* originates from the Latin *fidere,* which means a human attitude of "trust" that may or may not completely transcend our reason and emotion. However, *faith* has been identified mainly with the Jewish, Christian, and Islamic traditions. Westerners do not always call *religious* those Eastern traditions, especially Neo-Confucianism that involve an integrating dialogue of moral effort and spiritual cultivation. Nonetheless, it generally involves some relationship between human nature and its ultimate reality of being. From a cross-cultural perspective of comparative religion, then, T'oegye's faith can be considered as religious in the sense of appreciating the manifold growth of rationality, morality, and spirituality. In this regard, Neo-Confucianism in general and T'oegye in particular are still relevant to the academic discipline of religious studies, especially comparative religion.

In his work on the subject of "faith," Wilfred C. Smith argues that faith is essentially "the fundamental human category," and that "since it is an engagement, to know faith authentically is to become oneself involved, to know it in personal committed fashion in one or another of its varied forms." See Wilfred C. Smith, *Faith and Belief* (Princeton, N.J.: Princeton University Press, 1979), pp. 7 and 5–6, respectively. Smith's thesis corresponds to the Neo-Confucian understanding of faith as a human quality and effort that, as we have noted in the case of T'oegye, is expressed not only in terms of metaphysics and ethics, but more important, in terms of spiritual development. For the relevant literature on comparative religion, see especially the following works of Wilfred C. Smith: *Toward a World Theology: Faith and the Comparative History of Religion* (Philadelphia: Westminster Press, 1981); *The Faith of Other Men* (New York: Harper and Row, 1962, 1963); and *The Meaning and End of Religion: A New Approach to the Religious Traditions of Mankind*

(New York: Macmillan, 1963). For other works, see Frederick J. Streng, *Understanding Religious Life*, 3rd ed. (Belmont, Calif.: Dickenson Publishing Co., 1985); F. Streng, *Ways of Being Religious* (Englewood Cliffs, N.J.: Prentice-Hall, 1973); Paul J. Griffiths, ed., *Christianity Through Non-Christian Eyes* (Maryknoll, N.Y.: Orbis Books, 1990); Willard G. Oxtoby, *The Meaning of Other Faiths* (Philadelphia: Westminster Press, 1983); Ninian Smart, *Crosscultural Explorations of Human Beliefs* (New York: Charles Scribners Sons, 1983); and John Hick, *God Has Many Names* (London: Macmillan, 1981).

17. Yulgok neither quotes nor criticizes Wang Yang-ming in his own writings, and this is unusual because other prominent Korean scholars like T'oegye criticized Wang very severely, accusing him of being an "anti-Chu Hsi" and a "pseudo-Buddhist" thinker. It seems possible that Yulgok was influenced by Wang's practical thinking; however, he was, perhaps, afraid of being persecuted for praising it. In Chosŏn Korea, the Ch'eng-Chu school was the dominant orthodox school, and the Wang Yang-ming school was condemned as a heresy.

18. In this regard, Young-chan Ro's argument that the implication of Yulgok's concept of sincerity for moral cultivation "takes on a decidedly *religious meaning*" (Ro, *The Korean Neo-Confucianism of Yi Yulgok*, p. 115) does not correspond to what he calls the basic "pragmatic" theme of Yulgok's Neo-Confucianism. We have no evidence to suggest that Yulgok's Neo-Confucianism involves any religious dimension. As revealed in his Four-Seven thesis, as well as in its implications for self-cultivation, Yulgok's philosophy of sincerity is based on an empirical and practical philosophy of *ki*.

19. For Wang Fu-chih's philosophy, see, for example, Ian McMorran, "Wang Fu-chih and the Neo-Confucian Tradition," in de Bary, ed., *The Unfolding of Neo-Confucianism*. For Yen Yüan's philosophy of *ch'i* and practical learning, see Chung-ying Cheng, "Practical Learning in Yen Yüan, Chu Hsi and Wang Yang-ming," de Bary and Bloom, eds., *Principle and Practicality*. And a good discussion of Tai Chen's life and thought is Cheng Chung-ying, trans., *Tai Chen's Inquiry into Goodness* (Honolulu: East-West Center Press, 1971). The relevant literature on the Japanese tradition of *ch'i* and practical learning include de Bary, "Sagehood as a Secular and Spiritual Ideal in Tokugawa Neo-Confucianism," and Okada Takehiko, "Practical Learning in the Chu Hsi School: Yamazaki Ansai and Kaibara Ekken," both in de Bary and Bloom, eds., *Principle and Practicality*.

20. Here may I note that it would be an interesting study to compare Yulgok's view of practical learning with Kaibara Ekken's Japanese notion of practical learning (*jitsugaku*).

21. Undoubtedly, a unique feature Yulgok's *sirhak* developed on a political theme. Like Yen Yüan, Yulgok was a follower of the Chu Hsi school and formulated a concrete political ideology for government administration; however, as his political writings indicated, his political thought is formulated more systematically and comprehensively. Also, Yulgok is somewhat similar to Kung Tzu-chen (1792–1841), a nineteenth-century Neo-Confucian in Ch'ing China, who focused his philosophy on the concrete and utilitarian matters of economic and socio-political ideology, advancing a political reform for enriching the nation and strengthening the army. In contrast to Kung who finally rejected Neo-Confucianism completely, Yulgok formulated a similar political ideology on the basis of the Ch'eng-Chu school. Furthermore, Yulgok differs from Tai Chen, a great eighteenth-century Chinese Neo-Confucian, who formulated a philosophy of *ki* that represented one of the dominant trends of Neo-Confucian empiricism in Ch'ing China. Tai Chen eventually rejected the Ch'eng-Chu tradition to which he originally belonged. Unlike Tai, Yulgok is similar to the Japanese Neo-Confucian Kaibara Ekken in the sense of maintaining himself as a follower of the Ch'eng-Chu tradition.

22. For the Korean Sirhak traditon, see Han Yongu, "Chŏng Yagyong: The Man and His Thought," in *Main Currents of Korean Thought* (Seoul: Korean National Commission for UNESCO, 1983), pp. 185–203; Yi Ŭisŏng, "Korean Intellectual Tradition; the *Sirhak* School of Thought," in Hugh Kang, ed., *The Traditional Culture and Society of Korea: Thought and Institutions* (Honolulu: Center for Korean Studies, University of Hawaii Press, 1975), pp. 105–138; Donald L. Baker, "*Sirhak* Medicine: Measles, Smallpox, and Chŏng Tasan," *Korean Studies* 14 (1990): 136–166; and Yi Ulho, "Tasan's View of Man," *Korea Journal* 25, no. 9 (Sept. 1985). See also Han Yong-u, "Tasan's Approach to History," Cho Sung-eul, "Tasan on the Social Hierarchy," and Kŭm Chang-t'ae, "Tasan on Western Learning and Confucianism," all in *Korea Journal* 26, no. 2 (Feb. 1986). For Korean works, I recommend *Sirhak sasangŭi sin'gu* (New Studies on *Sirhak* Thought), ed. Asea munjae yŏn'guso (Seoul: Hyŏnamsa, 1985); Yi Ŭlho, *Chŏng Tasanŭi saengaewa hangmun* (Chŏng Tasan's Life and Thought) (Seoul: Paekyŏng mun'go, 1979); Chang Tonghŭi, *Chŏng Tasanŭi haengjŏng sasang* (Chŏng Tasan's Political Thought) (Seoul: Iljisa, 1986); and for Tasan's own works,

see *Yŏyudang chŏnsŏ* (Complete Works of Chŏng Tasan) (Seoul: Kyŏngin munhwasa, 1970).

23. As we have seen in his biography, T'oegye was offered many high-ranking government positions in his middle and later years, but he almost always turned them down to retire to his home.

24. *Mencius*, 6A:15.

Epilogue: The *I-Ki* and Four-Seven Controversy After T'oegye and Yulgok

1. *Kwiam chip* (Collected Works of Yi Kwiam), *kwŏn* 1, "Iki." Cited in Ryu Myŏng-jong, *Chosŏn hugi Sŏngnihak* (The School of Nature and Principle in the Late Chosŏn Period) (Seoul: Imunsa, 1985), p. 215. This statement alludes to *CTYL* 1:2b and *CTWC* 46:39b.

2. *Chisan munjip* (Collected Literary Works of Cho Chisan), *kwŏn* 6, "Iki pyŏn" (Treatise on *I* and *Ki*).

3. *Suam chip* (Collected Works of Yu Suam), "Chapnok" (Miscellaneous Writings). This alludes to *CTYL* 1:2b.

4. This is found in *Karam sŏnsaeng munjip* (Collected Literary Writings of Master Yi Karam), 18:1a–20b.

5. Ibid., 18:16a.

6. This is found in *Udam sŏnsaeng munjip* (Collected Literary Writings of Master Chŏng Udam), 7:1a–6b. See also Pae Chong-ho, ed., *Han'guk yuhak charyo chipsŏng*, vol. 1, pp. 668–670.

7. Ibid., 9:29b (Pae, *Han'guk yuhak charyo chipsŏng*, vol. 1, p. 684).

8. This is in *Taesan sŏnsaeng munjip* (Collected Literary Writings of Master Yi Taesan), 39:5b–6a. See also Pae, *Han'guk yuhak charyo chipsŏng*, vol. 2, pp. 1176–1177.

9. Ibid., 39:10b–12a. Pae, *Han'guk yuhak charyo chipsŏng*, vol. 2, pp. 1179–1180.

10. Ibid., 39:15a–22b. Pae, *Han'guk yuhak charyo chipsŏng*, vol. 2, pp. 1181–1190.

11. For his metaphysics of *i* and *ki*, see *Taesan sŏnsaeng munjip*, 39:5b–10b.

12. *Chŏngjae sŏnsaeng munjip* (Collected Literary Works of Master Yu Chŏngjae), 19:3b. See also Pae, *Han'guk yuhak charyo chipsŏng*, vol. 2, p. 1444.

13. Ibid., 19:4a or Pae, *Han'guk yuhak charyo chipsŏng*, vol. 2, p. 1444.

14. Ibid.

15. This diagrammatic treatise has one diagram on the Four and the other on the Seven and two diagrams are separated. See *Hwasŏ chip* (Collected Works of Yi Hwasŏ), 19:46a–50a or Pae, *Han'guk yuhak charyo chipsŏng*, vol. 2, pp. 1479–1482.

16. *Hwasŏ chip*, 20:44b–47b (Pae, *Han'guk yuhak charyo chipsŏng*, vol. 2, pp. 1483–1485).

17. *Hwasŏ chip*, 20:11a–14a (Pae, *Han'guk yuhak charyo chipsŏng*, vol. 2, pp. 1490–1492).

18. This explains the relationship between human nature and feelings, with an unclear diagram on it. See *Hwasŏ chip*, 21:41a–49b (Pae, *Han'guk yuhak charyo chipsŏng*, vol. 2, pp. 1500–1505).

19. *Hwasŏ chip*, 24:33a–37a (Pae, *Han'guk yuhak charyo chipsŏng*, vol. 2, pp. 1542–1544).

20. For these works, see *Hanju chip* (Collected Works of Yi Hanju) or Pae, *Han'guk yuhak charyo chipsŏng*, vol. 2, pp. 1645–1712.

21. *Sagae chŏnsŏ* (Complete Works of Kim Sagae), *kwŏn* 17, Reply to Han Sa-ang's Letter. Cited in Yi Pyŏng-do, *Han'guk yuhak saryak*, p. 177.

22. Ibid.

23. *Hansu chip* (Collected Works of Kwŏn Sangam), *kwŏn* 21, "Sach'il hobal pyŏn" (Treatise on the Alternating Manifestation of the Four and the Seven).

24. Ibid.

25. *Namdang sŏnsaeng munjip* (Collected Literary Works of Master Han Namdang), 3:1a–7a (Pae, *Han'guk yuhak charyo chipsŏng*, vol. 1, pp. 1010–1013).

26. Ibid., 7a–10b (Pae, *Han'guk yuhak charyo chipsŏng*, vol. 1, pp. 1013–1014).

27. Ibid., 30:10b–11b (Pae, *Han'guk yuhak charyo chipsŏng*, vol. 1, pp. 1014–1015).

28. Ibid., 30:11b–12a (Pae, *Han'guk yuhak charyo chipsŏng*, vol. 1, p. 1015).

29. Ibid., 27:26a–48a (Pae, *Han'guk yuhak charyo chipsŏng*, vol. 1, pp. 962–973).

30. The Sino-Korean term *tong* is a broad one that not only refers to the direction "east," but also means "East" and "Eastern" and, therefore, other aspects of East Asian culture, such as philosophy, religion, history, values, and so on. Hence, we have the name *Tonghak*. In modern Korea it is known as *Ch'ŏndogyo* (Religion of the Heavenly Way), one of the most popular "New Religions." For the history of Tonghak, see Susan Shin, "Tonghak Thought: The Roots of Cultural Revolution," in *Main Currents of Korean Thought*, pp. 204–223; Ch'oe Tong-hŭi, *Tonghak kyŏngjŏn* (Scriptures of Tonghak); and Yi Ton-hwa, *Ch'ŏndogyo ch'angŏnsa* (A History of the Founding of the Religion of the Heavenly Way).

31. Ch'oe synthesized what he thought to be the best tenets of these religions into a new nationalistic, religious ideology, borrowing certain elements, including the idea of God, from Catholicism. His syncretic ideas are expressed in his writings such as *Tonggyŏng taejŏn* (Great Compendium of Tonghak Doctrines) and *Yongdam yusa* (Hymns from the Dragon Pool). For an English study, see Young Choon Kim, *The Chŏndogyo Concept of Man: An Essence of Korean Thought* (Seoul: Pan Korea Book Co, 1978).

32. The Sino-Korean term *sŏ* is the antonym of *tong* and, therefore, refers to not only a western direction, but also means "West," "Western," or even "non-Far Eastern" or "non-Korean." It implies various aspects of Western cultures, such as religion, philosophy, history, values, and so on; hence, the name *Sŏhak*.

33. See *Yŏhŏn sŏnsaeng munjip* (Collected Literary Works of Master Chang Yŏhŏn), 5:11b–14b or Pae, *Han'guk yuhak charyo chipsŏng*, vol. 1, pp. 445–446.

34. Ibid., 14b–19a or Pae Chong-ho, *Han'guk yuhak charyo chipsŏng*, vol. 1, pp. 446–449.

35. This is a long philosophical commentary on the Neo-Confucian philosophy of the Great Ultimate. See *Yŏhŏn sŏnsaeng sŏngni sŏl* (Master

Chang Yŏhŏn's Treatise on Human Nature and Principle), 3:1a–46b or Pae Chong-ho, *Han'guk yuhak charyo chipsŏng*, vol. 1, pp. 454–476.

36. *Yŏhŏn sŏnsaeng munjip* (Literary Works of Master Chang Yŏhŏn), *kwŏn* 4, "Non kyŏngwi kaiu iki" (Treatise on *i* as Warp and *ki* as Woof).

37. This is in his *Cholsujae sŏnsaeng munjip* (Collected Literary Works of Cho Cholsujae), 11:1a–9a. See also Pae, *Han'guk yuhak charyo chipsŏng*, vol. 1, pp. 715–719.

38. Ibid., 11:1a.

39. *Ch'anggye sŏnsaengjip* (Collected Works of Master Ch'anggye), 25:23a.

40. This is in *Nongam sokjip* (Inner Collection of Kim Nongam's Works), 2:65b–75a. Pae, *Han'guk yuhak charyo chipsŏng*, vol. 1, pp. 747–752.

41. *Nongam sokjip*, 2:65b.

42. For his *Samŭn chip* (Collected Works of Kim Samŭn), see Pae, *Han'guk yuhak charyo chipsŏng*, vol. 1, pp. 755–780.

43. *Miho chip* (Collected Works of Kim Miho), *kwŏn* 5, Letter to Im Tongji.

44. *Noju chip* (Collected Works of O Noju), 24:6b or Pae, *Han'guk yuhak charyo chipsŏng*, vol. 2, p. 1400.

45. Ibid., 7:40a-b (Pae, *Han'guk yuhak charyo chipsŏng*, vol. 2, p. 1359).

46. Ibid., 7:40b (Pae, *Han'guk yuhak charyo chipsŏng*, vol. 2, p. 1359).

Appendixes

1. This is the third diagram of the *Sim t'ong sŏngchŏng tosŏl*, the sixth of T'oegye's *Sŏnghak sipto*. For this diagram in Chinese, see *TC* 7:22b (vol. 1, p. 204).

2. For this diagram in Chinese, see *YC* 14:6a (vol. 1, p. 283).

3. For a brief description of this text, see Wing-tsit Chan, "How T'oegye Understood Chu Hsi," in de Bary and Haboush, eds., *The Rise of Neo-Confucianism in Korea*, pp. 298–301.

4. For more information of this important work, see ibid., pp. 298–301.

5. Ch'en Hsien-chang was the founder of the Chang-men school, which was named after his native place. For a brief period of time, Ch'en was a student of Wu Yü-pi, a leading Neo-Confucian of the Ch'eng-Chu school in the early Ming period, who emphasized the direct relevance of Ch'eng-Chu teachings to mind cultivation. Wu affirmed the value of quiet sitting meditation and self-reflection for cultivating reverential seriousness. Although Ch'en was influenced by Wu, he claimed that his own method of self-cultivation did not come from Wu. He later rejected entirely any rational approach of the Ch'eng-Chu school (namely, the investigation of things and extension of knowledge) in favor of his own philosophy, which focuses more on quiet sitting and mind cultivation. This is illustrated in his *Shih-chiao*, a lyrical appreciation of nature, which cites very little of the Ch'eng-Chu teachings. For the life and thought of Ch'en, see Huang Tsung-hsi, *The Records of Ming Scholars*, trans. and ed. Julia Ching (Honolulu; University of Hawaii Press, 1987), pp. 70–89. For a Chinese study of Ch'en, consult Jen Yu-wen, *Pai-sha yen-chiu* (A Study of Ch'en Hsien-chang) (Hong Kong: Meng-chih shu-wu, 1970). A good English discussion of Wu Yü-pi and Ch'en Hsien-chang is in de Bary, ed., *The Unfolding of Neo-Confucianism*, "Introduction," esp. pp. 19–30.

6. For this subject, see Edward Y. J. Chung, "The Wang Yang-ming School of Neo-Confucianism in Korean Intellectual History," *Korean Culture* 13, no. 3 (Fall 1992): 14–23.

7. For a full English translation of it with commentaries and notes, consult Michael Kalton, *To Become a Sage: The Ten Diagrams of Sage Learning by Yi T'oegye.*

8. It consists of three subdiagrams and his commentaries. For my translation of the third diagram, see Appendix 1; for M. Kalton's translation of all diagrams, see Kalton, ibid.

9. In Chosŏn Korea, the village code (*hyangyak*) of the same type was first initiated by Cho Kwang-jo. From the beginning of King Sŏnjo's reign (1567–1608), it was widely put into actual practice throughout the country. For a discussion of Yulgok's village code, consult Sakai Tadao, "Yulgok and the Community Compact," de Bary and Haboush, eds., *The Rise of Neo-Confucianism in Korea*, pp. 323–348.

10. For a good English discussion of this text, see de Bary, *Neo-Confucian Orthodoxy*, pp. 106–122.

Glossary: Major Terms, Names and Titles Cited

Chagyŏng mun 自警文

Chasŏng nok 自省錄

ch'e/t'i 體

Chen Te-hsiu (Hsi-shan) 眞德秀 (西山)

Ch'en Hsien-chang (Pai-sha) 陳獻章 (白沙)

chewang chi hak/ti-wang chih hsüeh 帝王之學

chigyŏng/ch'i-ching 持敬

ch'ilchŏng/ch'i-ch'ing 七情

ch'ilchŏng kijibal/ch'i-ch'ing ch'i-chih-fa 七情氣之發

ch'ilchŏng palŏki/ch'i-ch'ing fa yü ch'i 七情發於氣

ch'ilchŏng si kijibal/ch'i-ch'ing shih ch'i-chih-fa 七情是氣之發

Chin-ssu lu 近思錄

ch'ŏlli/t'ien-li 天理

ch'ŏndo/t'ien-tao 天道

Ch'ŏndo ch'aek 天道策

chŏng/ch'ing 情

Chŏnsŭmnok nonbyŏn 傳習錄論辨

ch'ŏnmyŏng chi sŏng/t'ien-ming chih hsing 天命之性

Ch'ŏnmyŏng kudo 天命舊圖

Ch'ŏnmyŏng sindo 天命新圖

Ch'ŏnmyŏng to 天命圖

Ch'ŏnmyŏng tosŏl 天命圖說

chugi 主氣

Chugip'a 主氣派

Chujahak/Chu-tzu hsüeh 朱子學

Chujasŏ chŏryo 朱子書節要

chung/chung 中

churi 主理

Churip'a 主理派

Hakkyo mobŏm 學校模範

hobal/hu-fa 互發

Hsin ching 心經

hsin-hsüeh 心學

Hyogyŏng/Hsiao-hsüeh 孝經

hyŏng i ha/hsing-erh-hsia 形而下

hyŏng i sang/hsing-erh-shang 形而上

i/li 理

ibal/i-fa 已發

ibal/li-fa 理發

ihak/li-hsüeh 理學

Ihak t'ongnok 理學通錄

iil punsu/li-i fen-shu 理一分殊

ijon kibi/li-tsun ch'i-pei 理尊氣卑

iju kija/li-chu ch'i-tsu 理主氣資

iki hobal/li-ch'i hu-fa 理氣互發

Iki wangbok sŏ 理氣往復書

indo/jen-tao 人道

insim/jen-hsin 人心

Insim tosim tosŏl 人心道心圖說

inyok/jen-yü 人慾

ipchi/li-chih 立志

it'ong kiguk/li-t'ung ch'i-chu 理通氣局

i chi ponyŏn/li chih pen-jan 理之本然

ki/ch'i 氣

kibal/ch'i-fa 氣發

kiil punsu/ch'i-i fen-shu 氣一分殊

kijil chi sŏng/ch'i-chih hsing 氣質之性

Ki Myŏng-hŏn (Kobong) 奇明彥 (高峰)

Kobong tap T'oegye ron sadan ch'ilchŏng sŏ 高峰答退溪論四端七情書

kŏgyŏng/chi-ching 居敬

kunja chi hak/chün-tzu chih hsüeh 君子之學

kyŏng/ching 敬

kyŏnghak/ching-hsüeh 敬學

Kyŏngmong yokyŏl 擊蒙要訣

Kyŏngyŏn ilgi 經筵日記

Li T'ung (Yen-p'ing) 李侗 (延平)

Lo Ch'in-shun (Cheng-an) 羅欽順 (整菴)

Lu Hsiang-shan 陸象山

Manŏn pongsa 萬言封事

mibal/wei-fa 未發

muhyŏng/wu-hsing 無形

muwi/wu-wei 無爲

Non simsŏngchŏng 論心性情

Ŏnhaeng nok 言行錄

Paeksa Sigyo Chŏnsŭmnok ch'ojŏn insŏ kihu 白沙詩教傳習錄抄傳因書其後

pal/fa 發

palcha/fa-che 發者

Pi iki wi ilmul pyŏnchŭng 非理氣爲一物辨證

ponch'e/pen-t'i 本體

ponyŏn chi i/pen-jan chih li 本然之理

ponyŏn chi sŏng/pen-jan chih hsing 本然之性

sach'illon 四七論

sadan/ssu-tuan 四端

sadan ijibal/ssu-tuan li-chih-fa 四端理之發

sadan palŏi/ssu-tuan fa yü li 四端發於理

sadan si ijibal/ssu-tuan shih li-chih-fa 四端是理之發

Saja ŏnsŏng ch'aek 四子言誠策

sheng-hsüeh 聖學

Shushigaku 朱子學

sil/shih 實

silchi/shih-chih 實知

silgong/shih-kung 實功

silli/shih-li 實理

silsim/shih-hsin 實心

sim/hsin 心

simbŏp/hsin-fa 心法

Simgyŏng/Hsin ching 心經

simhak/hsin-hsüeh 心學

Simhak to 心學圖

simjich'e/hsin-chih-t'i 心之體

simjiyong/hsin-chih-yung 心之用

Simsŏngchŏng sŏl 心性情說

Simsŏngchŏng to 心性情圖

Simu yukcho kye 時務六條啓

Sim mu ch'eyong pyŏn 心無體用辨

Sim t'ong sŏngchŏng tosŏl 心統性情圖說

sirhak/shih-hsüeh 實學

Sŏ Kyŏng-dŏk (Hwadam) 徐敬德 (花潭)

soiyŏn/so-i-jan 所以然

soi palcha/so-i fa-che 所以發者

Songge Wŏn Myŏng ihak t'ongnok 宋季元明理學通錄

sŏng/ch'eng 誠

sŏng/hsing 性

Sŏngch'aek 誠策

sŏnghak/ch'eng-hsüeh 誠學

sŏnghak/sheng-hsüeh 聖學

Sŏnghak chipyo 聖學輯要

Sŏnghak sipto 聖學十圖

sŏngmun chi hak/sheng-men chih hsüeh 聖門之學

sŏngnihak/hsing-li hsüeh 性理學

Sŏngni taejŏn/Hsing-li ta-ch'üan 性理大全

sŏng chi ponyŏn/hsing chih pen-jan 性之本然

Sŏng Hon (Ugye) 成渾 (牛溪)

Sugi 修己

T'oegye munjip 退溪文集

tohak/tao-hsüeh 道學

tonghak 東學

Tongho mundap 東湖問答

tosim/tao-hsin 道心

Wang Yang-ming 王陽明

yanggi/yang-ch'i 養氣

yangji/liang-chih 良知

yangnŭng/liang-neng 良能

Yi Hwang (T'oegye) 李滉 (退溪)

Yi I (Yulgok) 李珥 (栗谷)

Yŏksu ch'aek 易數策

yong/yung 用

yugihak 唯氣學

Yukcho so 六條疏

yurihak 唯理學

yuwi/yu-wei 有爲

Selected Bibliography

Primary Sources and Other Older Works

Korean Neo-Confucian Works

Kwŏn Kŭn 權近. *Yangch'on chip* 陽林集 (Collected Works of Kwŏn Yang-ch'on). Seoul: Minjok munhwa ch'ujinhoe, 1979.

Chŏng To-jŏn 鄭道傳. *Sambong chip* 三峰集 (Collected Works of Chŏng Sambong). Seoul: Kuksa p'yŏnch'an wiwŏnhoe, 1961.

Ki Myŏng-hŏn 奇明彥. *Kobong chŏnjip* 高峰全集 (Complete Works of Ki Kobong). Seoul: Sŏnggyun'gwan University Press, 1976.

Yi T'oegye 李退溪. *T'oegye chŏnsŏ* 退溪全書 (Complete Works of Yi T'oegye), enlarged edition, 5 vols. Seoul: Sŏnggyun'gwan University Press, 1986.

Yi Yulgok 李栗谷. *Yulgok chŏnsŏ* 栗谷全書 (Complete Works of Yi Yulgok), 3 vols. Seoul: Sŏnggyun'gwan University Press, 1985.

Pae Chong-ho 裴宗鎬, ed. *Han'guk yuhak charyo chipsŏng* (Collected Source Materials on Korean Neo-Confucianism), 3 vols. Seoul: Yŏnse University Press, 1980.

Chinese Neo-Confucian Works

Chang Tsai 張載. *Chang Tzu ch'üan-shu* 張子全書 (Complete Works of Master Chang Tsai). SPPY ed.

Ch'eng Hao 程顥 and Ch'eng I 程頤. *Ear-Ch'eng ch'üan-shu* 二程全書 (Complete Works of the Two Ch'engs). SPPY ed.

———. I-shu 遺書 (Written Legacy), in *Ear-Ch'eng ch'üan-shu.*

Chu Hsi 朱熹. *Chu Tzu yü-lei* 朱子語類 (Classified Conversations of Master Chu Hsi), comp. Li Ching-te. 1880 ed.

———. *Chu Tzu wen-chi* 朱子文集 (Collection of Literary Works by Master Chu Hsi), in *Chu Tzu ta-ch'üan* 朱子大全(Great Compendium of Works by Master Chu Hsi). SPPY ed.

———. *Meng Tzu chi-chu ta-ch'üan* 孟子集注大全 (Great Compendium of Commentaries on Mencius), in *Kyŏngsŏ* 經書 (Collected Commentaries on the Four Books). Seoul: Sŏnggyun'gwan University Press, 1972.

———. *Chung-yung chang-chü* 中庸章句 (Commentary on the Words and Phrases of the *Doctrine of the Mean*), in *Kyŏngsŏ*.

Huang Tsung-hsi 黃宗羲 and Ch'an Tsu-wang 全祖望. *Sung Yüan hsüeh-an* 宋元學案(Records of Sung and Yüan Scholars). SPPY ed.

Translations and Anthologies

Bloom, Irene, trans. *Knowledge Painfully Acquired: The K'un-chih chi of Lo Ch'in-shun*. New York: Columbia University Press, 1987.

Li Chi: Book of Rites, trans. James Legge. *The Chinese Classics*. Reprinted by Hong Kong University Press, 1970

Chan, Wing-tsit, trans. *Neo-Confucian Terms Explained (The Pei-hsi tzu-i) by Ch'en Ch'un, 1159–1223*. New York: Columbia University Press, 1986.

———, trans. *Reflections on Things at Hand: The Neo-Confucian Anthology by Chu Hsi and Lü Tsu-ch'ien*. New York: Columbia University Press, 1967.

———, trans. *Instructions for Practical Living and Other Neo-Confucian Writings by Wang Yang-ming*. New York: Columbia University Press, 1963.

———. *A Source Book in Chinese Philosophy*. Princeton, N.J.: Princeton University Press, 1963.

Kalton, Michael C., trans. *To Become a Sage: The Ten Diagrams on Sage Learning by Yi T'oegye*. New York: Columbia University Press, 1988.

Lau, D. C., trans. *Mencius*. New York: Penguin Books, 1970.

———, trans. *Confucius: The Analects (Lun yü)*. New York: Penguin Books, 1970.

———, trans. *Lao Tzu: Tao Te Ching*. New York: Penguin Books, 1963.

Legge, James, trans. *The Chinese Classics*, 5 vols. Hong Kong: Hong Kong University Press, 1970, reprint.

Watson, Burton, trans. *The Complete Works of Chuang Tzu*. New York: Columbia University Press, 1968.

Modern Works in Korean, Japanese, and Chinese

Korean Confucianism and History

Abe Yoshio 阿部吉雄, et al., eds. *Chōsen no Shushigaku Nihon no Shushigaku* 朝鮮の朱子學日本の朱子學 (Korean Chu Hsi school and Japanese Chu Hsi school). *Shushigaku taikei* 朱子學大系 (Great Compendium on the Chu Hsi school), vol. 12. Tokyo: Meitoku shuppansha, 1977.

———. *Nihon shushigaku to Chōsen* 日本朱子學と朝鮮 (Japanese Chu Hsi School and Its Relation to Korea). Tokyo: Tokyo University Press, 1965.

———. "Ni-Sen-Min ni okeru shuriha shukiha no keifu to sono tokushitsu" (The Genealogy and Special Characteristics of the School of *Li* and the School of *Ch'i* in Japan, Yi Korea, and Ming China). *Chōsen gakuhō* 14 (1957).

Ch'ae Mu-song 蔡茂松. *T'oegye Yulgok ch'ŏrakŭi pigyo yŏn'gu* 退溪栗谷哲學 의 比較研究 (A Comparative Study of T'oegye's and Yulgok's Thought). Seoul: Sŏnggyun'gwan University Press, 1985.

——— "Kobong sŏngnihakŭi yŏn'gu" (A Study of Ki Kobong's Philosophy of Human Nature and Principle). *Asea yŏn'gu* 16, no. 1 (1973).

Ch'ien Mu 錢穆. "Chu Tzu hsüeh liu-yen Han-kuo kao" (An Examination of the Spread of Chu Hsi School to Korea). *Hsin-an hsüeh-pao* 12 (1977): 3–8.

Ch'oe Ch'ang-kyu 崔昌圭. "Yulgokŭi chŏngch'i sasang" (Yulgok's Political Thought). In Yi Chun-ho, ed., *Yulgokŭi sasang* 栗谷의 思想 (Yulgok's Thought). Seoul: Hyŏnamsa, 1975.

Ch'oe Min-hong 崔旼洪. *Han'guk ch'ŏraksa* 韓國哲學史 (A History of Korean Philosophy). Seoul: Sŏngmunsa, 1981.

Chŏn Tu-ha 全斗可. *T'oegye sasang yŏn'gu* 退溪思想研究 (A Study of T'oegye's Thought). Seoul: Tonga ch'ulp'ansa, 1974.

Hwang Ŭi-dong 黃義東. *Yulgok ch'ŏrak yŏn'gu* 栗谷哲學研究 (A Study of Yulgok's Thought). Seoul: Kyŏngmundang, 1987.

Han Yong-u 韓永愚. *Chŏng To-jŏn sasangŭi yŏn'gu* 鄭道傳思想의 研究 (A Study of Chŏng To-jŏn's Thought). Seoul: Seoul National University Press, 1985.

Hyŏn Sang-yun 玄相允. *Chosŏn yuhaksa* 朝鮮儒學史 (A History of Korean Confucianism). Seoul: Hyŏnamsa, 1948, 1982.

Kim Kil-hwan 金吉煥. "Yi Iŭi sugi simhak" (Yulgok's Learning of the Mind-and-Heart and Self-Cultivation). In Kim Kil-hwan, *Chosŏnjo yuhak sasang yŏn'gu* 朝鮮朝儒學思想研究. (A Study of Confucian Thought in the Yi Dynasty). Seoul: Iljisa, 1985.

Kim Pyŏng-t'ae. "T'oegyewa *Simgyŏng puju*" (T'oegye and the *Classic for the Mind-and-Heart* Supplemented and Annotated). *Han'guk ch'ŏrak* 8 (Dec. 1979): 67–81.

———. "*Simgyŏng puju* yuhuron ponŭi kanbon" (Publications of Editions of the *Classic for the Mind-and-Heart* with T'oegye's Epilogue). *T'oegyehak yŏn'gu* 6 (Dec. 1979): 83–113.

Kim Pu-sik 金富軾. *Samguk saki* 三國史記 (History of the Three Kingdoms). Seoul: Ulyu munhwasa, 1987.

Koryŏsa 高麗史 (History of Koryŏ). Seoul: Asea munhwasa, 1973.

Kŭm Chang-t'ae 琴章泰. *Yugyowa Han'guk sasang* 儒教와 韓國思想 (Confucianism and Korean Thought). Seoul: Sŏnggyun'gwan University Press, 1980.

Pae Chong-ho 裴宗鎬. *Han'guk yuhaksa* 韓國儒學史 (A History of Korean Confucianism). Seoul: Yŏnse University Press, 1973.

———. "Yi Iŭi ch'ŏrak sasang" (Yi Yulgok's Philosophical Thought). In *Han'guk ch'ŏrak yŏn'gu* 韓國哲學硏究 (Studies in Korean Philosophy), vol. 2. Seoul: Tongmyŏsa, 1978.

Pak Chong-hong 朴宗鴻. *Han'guk sasangsa nongo yuhak p'yŏn* 韓國思想論攷儒學篇 (Essays on the History of Korean Thought, Edition on Confucianism). Seoul: Sŏngmundang, 1977.

Pak Ch'ung-sŭk 朴忠錫. "T'oegyeŭi chŏngch'i sasangŭi sasangsajŏk ŭich'i" (Place of T'oegye's Political Thought in the History of Korean Thought). *T'oegye hakpo* 19 (1978): 332–333.

Ryu Myŏng-jong 劉明鍾. *Chosŏn hugi sŏngnihak* 朝鮮後期性理學 (Korean Neo-Confucianism in the Late Chosŏn Period). Seoul: Imunsa, 1985.

Song Sŏk-ku 宋錫球. *Yulgokŭi ch'ŏrak sasang yŏn'gu* 栗谷 의 哲學思想硏究 (A Study of Yulgok's Philosophical Thought). Seoul: Hyŏngsŏl ch'ulp'ansa, 1987.

———. "Pulgyowa Yi Yulgokŭi ch'ŏrak" (Buddhism and Yi Yulgok's Philosophy). In Song Sŏk-ku, *Han'gukŭi yubul sasang* (Confucian and Buddhist Thought in Korea). Seoul: Sangsawŏn, 1985.

Takahashi Susumu 高橋進. *T'oegyewa kyŏngŭi ch'ŏrak* 退溪와 敬의 哲學 (T'oegye and His Philosophy of Reverential Seriousness), trans. An Pyŏng-ju. Seoul: Sin'gu munhwasa, 1986.

Takahashi Tōru 高橋亨. "Chōsen no Yōmeiha" (The Wang Yang-ming School in Korea). *Chōsen gakuho* 10 (1953): 131–156.

———. "Richo jugaku-shi ni okeru shuriha shugiha no hattatsu" (The Development of the *I*-ist School and *Ki*-ist School in Korea). In Tabobashi Kiyoshi 田保橋潔 ed., *Chōsen china bunka no kenkyū* 朝鮮支那文化の硏究 (Studies in Chinese and Korean Cultures). Tokyo, 1929.

Tomoeda Ryūtarō 友枝龍太郎. "Sach'il nonbyŏne issŏsŏŭi T'oeKoŭi ipchang" (T'oegye's and Kobong's Standpoint on the Four-Seven Debate). *T'oegye hakpo* 19 (1978): 159–168.

Yi Pyŏng-do 李丙燾. *Han'guk yuhak saryak* 韓國儒學史略 (An Outline History of Korean Confucianism). Seoul: Asea munhwasa, 1986.

———. *Yulgokŭi saengaewa sasang* 栗谷의 生涯와 思想 (Yulgok's Life and Thought). Seoul: Sŏmundang, 1973.

———. *Han'guksa taekwan* 韓國史大觀 (A General Study of Korean History). Seoul: Tongbang tosŏ, 1983.

Yi Sang-ŭn 李相殷. *T'oegyeŭi saengaewa hangmun* 退溪의 生涯와 學問 (T'oegye's Life and Learning). Seoul: Sŏmundang, 1973.

———. "Yi Hwangŭi ch'ŏrak: sach'il nonpyŏn" (Yi T'oegye's Philosophy: The Four-Seven Debate). In *Han'guk ch'ŏrak yŏn'gu* 韓國哲學硏究 (Studies in Korean Philosophy), vol. 2. Seoul: Tongmyŏsa, 1979.

Yi Tong-jun 李東俊. "T'oegye sasangŭi inganhakchŏk ihae" (A Humanistic Understanding of T'oegye's Thought). *T'oegye hakpo* 19 (1978): 197–184.

Yi Wan-jae 李完栽. "*I-Ki* hobalsŏlŭi yuhak chŏnt'ong sasangjŏk chomyŏng" (A Philosophical Inquiry into Orthodox Confucian Theory of Alternate Manifestation of *I* and *Ki*). *T'oegye hakpo* 19 (1978): 191–202.

Yu Sŭng-guk 柳承國. "Han'guk yuhak sasang kaesŏl" (Introductory Review of Korean Confucian Thought). In *Han'gukŭi yuhak sasang* 韓國의 儒學思想 (Confucian thought in Korea), vol. 2. Seoul: Samsŏng ch'ulp'ansa, 1983.

Yun Sa-sun 尹絲淳. *T'oegye ch'ŏrakŭi yŏn'gu* 退溪哲學의 硏究 (A Study of T'oegye's Philosophy). Seoul: Korea University Press, 1980. (This was translated by Michael Kalton as *Critical Issues in Neo-Confucian Thought: The Philosophy of Yi T'oegye*. Honolulu: University of Hawaii Press, 1992).

———. "T'oegye ch'ŏrakŭi isang chuŭijŏk sŏnggyŏk (The Idealistic Character of T'oegye's Philosophy). *T'oegye hakpo* 19 (1978) :197–184.

Yun Yong-gyun. *Shushigaku no denrai to sono eikyō ni tsuite* (On the Transmission of the Chu Hsi School and Its Influence). Seoul, 1933.

Wang Su 王甦. *T'oegye sihak* 退溪詩學 (T'oegye's Poetry). Seoul:T'oegyehak yŏn'guwŏn, 1981.

Other References on Neo-Confucianism

Ch'ien Mu 錢穆. *Chu Tzu hsin hsüeh-an* 朱子新學案 (A New Philosophical Study of Chu Hsi), 5 vols. Taipei: San-min shu-chü, 1971.

Mou Tsung-san 牟宗三. *Hsin-t'i yü hsing-t'i* 心體與性體 (Substance of Mind and Substance of Human Nature), 3 vols. Taipei: Cheng-chung shu-chü, 1975.

Shimada Kenji 島田虔次. *Shushigaku to Yōmeigaku* 朱子學と陽明學 (The Chu Hsi School and the Wang Yang-ming School). Tokyo: Iwanami shoten, 1967.

Tomoeda Ryūtarō 友枝龍太郎. *Shushi no shisō keisei* 朱子の思想形成 (The Formation of Chu Hsi's Thought). Tokyo: Shunjūsha, 1969.

Tang Chün-i 唐君毅. *Chung-kuo che-hsüeh yüan-lun yüan hsing p'ien* 中國哲學原論原性篇 (Sources of Chinese Philosophy, Section on Human Nature). Taipei: Hsüeh-sheng shu-chü, 1973.

Western Language Works

Korean Confucianism and History

Abe Yoshio. "Development of Neo-Confucianism in Japan, Korea, and China: A Comparative Study." *Acta Asiatica* 19 (1970): 16–39.

———. "The Characteristics of Japanese Confucianism." *Acta Asiatica* 25 (1970): 1–19.

Chan, Wing-tsit. "How T'oegye Understood Chu Hsi." In Wm. T. de Bary and J. Kim Haboush, eds., *The Rise of Neo-Confucianism in Korea*. New York: Columbia University Press, 1985.

Ching, Julia. "Yi Yulgok on the Four Beginnings and the Seven Emotions." In de Bary and Haboush, eds., *The Rise of Neo-Confucianism in Korea*.

———. "Yi Yulgok on Human Nature." *Proceedings of the Asian Studies Conference II*. Seoul: Sŏnggyun'gwan University Press, 1980.

Cho Sung-eul. "Tasan on the Social Hierarchy." *Korea Journal* 26, no. 2 (Feb. 1986).

Ch'oe, Yong-ho. *The Civil Examinations and the Social Structure in the Early Yi Dynasty Korea: 1392–1600*. Seoul: The Korea Research Center, 1987.

Chun Shin-yong, ed. *Upper-Class Culture in Yi-dynasty Korea*. Seoul: The Si-sa-yong-o-sa Publishers, 1982.

Chung, Chai-sik. "Chŏng To-jŏn: Architect of Yi Dynasty Government and Ideology." In de Bary and Haboush, eds., *The Rise of Neo-Confucianism in Korea*.

Chung, Edward Y. J. "Confucianism in Contemporary Korean Society: Some Reflections on Continuity and Change." *Korean Studies in Canada* 1 (1993): 17–33.

———. "Yi T'oegye on the Learning of Reverential Seriousness (*Kyŏnghak*): A Korean Neo-Confucian Spirituality." *Korea Journal* 32, no. 1 (Spring 1992): 61–71.

———. "Yi T'oegye on the Neo-Confucian Learning of Principle and Mind: A Religious Way of Self-Cultivation." *Asian Profile* 20, no. 5 (Oct. 1992): 353–365.

———. "The Wang Yang-ming School of Neo-Confucianism in Korean Intellectual History." *Korean Culture* 13, no. 3 (Fall 1992): 14–23.

———. "Yi Yulgok, a Neo-Confucian Political Reformer in Sixteenth-Century Korea." In Bernard H. Luk, ed., *Contacts Between Cultures* vol. 4 (*Eastern Asia: History and Social Sciences*). Lewiston and Queenston: Edwin Mellen Press, 1992, pp. 171–175.

———. "Confucianism and Women in Modern Korea: Continuity, Change, and Conflict." In Arvind Sharma and Katherine Young, eds., *The Annual Review of Women in World Religions*, vol. 3, pp. 142–188. Albany: SUNY Press, 1994.

———. "Confucianism: A Living Religious Tradition in South Korea." *Korean Studies in Canada* 2 (Dec. 1994): 11–23.

de Bary, William Theodore, and JaHyun Kim Haboush, eds. *The Rise of Neo-Confucianism in Korea*. New York: Columbia University Press, 1985.

Deuchler, Martina. *The Confucian Transformation of Korea: A Study of Society and Ideology*. Harvard-Yenching Institute Monograph Series 36. Cambridge, Mass.: Harvard University Press, 1992.

———. "Reject the False and Uphold the Straight: Attitudes Toward Heterodox Thought in Early Yi Korea." In de Bary and Haboush, eds., *The Rise of Neo-Confucianism in Korea*.

———. "Neo-Confucianism: The Impulse for Social Action in Early Yi Korea." *Journal of Korean Studies* 2 (1980): 71–111.

———. "Neo-Confucianism in Early Yi Korea: Some Reflections on the Role of Ye." *Korea Journal* 15, no. 5 (May 1975): 12–17.

Haboush, Kim JaHyun. "Confucianization of Korean Society." In Gilbert Rozman, ed., *The East Asian Region: Confucian Heritage and Its Modern Adaptation*. Princeton, N.J.: Princeton University Press, 1991.

———. *A Heritage of Kings: One Man's Monarchy in the Confucian World*. New York: Columbia University Press, 1988.

Han, Woo-keun. *The History of Korea*, trans. Kyung-shik Lee, ed. Grafton K. Mintz. Honolulu: University of Hawaii Press, 1970.

Han Yongu. "Tasan's Approach to History." *Korea Journal* 26, no. 2 (Feb. 1986).

———. "Chŏng Yag-yong: The Man and His Thought." In *Main Currents of Korean Thought*. Seoul: Korean National Commission for UNESCO, 1983.

Hong I-sup. "Political Philosophy of Korean Confucianism." In *Korea Journal* 3, no. 9 (Sept. 1963): 12–16.

———. *History of Korea*. Seoul: National Commission for UNESCO, 1970.

Ilyon. *Samguk yusa: Legends and History of the Three Kingdoms of Ancient Korea*, trans. Ha Tae-Hung and Grafton Mintz. Seoul: Yonsei University Press, 1972.

Kalton, Michael. "The Writings of Kwŏn Kŭn: The Context and Shape of Early Yi Dynasty Neo-Confucianism." In de Bary and Haboush, eds., *The Rise of Neo-Confucianism in Korea.*

———. "An Introduction to Silhak." *Korea Journal* 15, no. 5 (July 1975): 12–17.

Kang, Hugh H. W., ed. *The Traditional Culture and Society of Korea: Thought and Institutions.* Honolulu: Center for Korean Studies, University of Hawaii Press, 1975.

Kim Doo-hun. "Confucian Influences on Korean Society." *Korea Journal* 3, no. 9 (Sept. 1963): 17–21.

Kim Hyong-hyo. "Confucian Thought in Korea." *Korea Journal* 17, no. 9 (Sept. 1977): 42–52.

Kŭm Chang-t'ae. "Tasan on Western Learning and Confucianism." *Korea Journal* 26, no. 2 (Feb. 1986).

Lee, Chon *urnal of Asiatic Studies* 44, pt. 2 (1984): 427–466.

———. *Politics and Policies in Traditional Korea.* Harvard East Asian Series 82. Cambridge, Mass.: Harvard University Press, 1975.

Park Chong-hong. "Historical Review of Korean Confucianism." *Korea Journal* 3, no. 9 (Sept. 1963): 5–11.

———. "T'oegye and His Thought." *Korea Journal* 11, no. 3 (March 1971): 19–23.

Ro, Young-chan. *The Korean Neo-Confucianism of Yi Yulgok.* Albany: SUNY Press, 1989.

———. "The Anthropology of Yulgok: A Nondualistic Approach to the Mind and the Problem of *Li* and *Ch'i*." Ph. D. dissertation. University of California, Santa Barbara, 1982.

Sakai Tadao. "Yi Yulgok and the Community Compact." In de Bary and Haboush, eds., *The Rise of Neo-Confucianism in Korea.*

Seoh, Munsang. "The Ultimate Concern of Yi Korean Confucians: An Analysis of the *I-Ki* Debates." *Occasional Papers on Korea,* no. 5 (Joint Committee on Korean Studies of the ACLS and the SSRC, March 1977), pp. 20–66.

Tomoeda Ryūtarō. "Yi T'oegye and Chu Hsi: Differences in Their Theories of Principle and Material Force." In de Bary and Haboush, eds., *The Rise of Neo-Confucianism in Korea.*

Tu Wei-ming. "Yi T'oegye's Perception of Human Nature: A Preliminary Inquiry into the Four-Seven Debate in Korean Neo-Confucianism." In de Bary and Haboush eds., *The Rise of Neo-Confucianism in Korea.*

———. "T'oegye's Creative Interpretation of Chu Hsi's Philosophy of Principle." *Korea Journal* 22, no. 2 (Feb. 1982): 4–15.

———. "Yi Hwang's Perception of the Mind." *T'oegye hakpo* 19 (1978): 455–467.

Wagner, Edward W. *The Literati Purges: Political Conflict in Early Yi Dynasty*. Cambridge, Mass.: Harvard University Press, 1974.

Yang, K. P. and G. Henderson. "An Outline History of Korean Confucianism, Part II: The Schools of Yi Factionalism." *Journal of Asian Studies* 18 (1959): 259–276.

———. "An Outline History of Korean Confucianism, Part I: The Early Period and Yi Factionalism." *Journal of Asian Studies* 18 (1958): 81–102.

Yi Sŏngmu. "The Influence of Neo-Confucianism on Education and the Civil Service Examination in Fourteen- and Fifteenth-Century Korea." In de Bary and Haboush, eds., *The Rise of Neo-Confucianism in Korea*.

Yi U-sŏng. "Confucian Politics in Chosŏn Period." In *Main Currents of Korean Thought*. Seoul: Korean Commission for UNESCO, 1983.

Yi Ŭisŏng. "Korean Intellectual Tradition: The *Sirhak* School of Thought." In Hugh Kang, ed., *The Traditional Culture and Society of Korea: Thought and Institutions*.

Yi Ul-ho. "Tasan's View of Man." *Korea Journal* 25, no. 9 (Sept. 1985).

Youn Sa-soon. "T'oegye's Identification of 'To Be' and 'Ought': T'oegye's Theory of Value." In de Bary and Haboush, eds., *The Rise of Neo-Confucianism in Korea*.

Other Works on Neo-Confucianism and Comparative Studies

Bloom, Irene. "On the 'Abstraction' of Ming Thought: Some Concrete Evidence from the Philosophy of Lo Ch'in-shun." In Wm. T. de Bary and Irene T. Bloom, eds., *Principle and Practicality: Essays in Neo-Confucianism and Practical Learning*. New York: Columbia University Press, 1979.

Chan, Wing-tsit, ed. *Chu Hsi and Neo-Confucianism*. Honolulu: University of Hawaii Press, 1986.

———. "Chu Hsi's Completion of Neo-Confucianism." In *Etudes Song: In Memoriam Etienne Balazas*, ed. Francoise Aubin, Ser. II, no. 1, 1973, pp. 59–90.

———. "Neo-Confucianism: New Ideas in Old Terminology." *Philosophy East and West* 18: 1–4.

———. "The Evolution of the Neo-Confucian Concept of *Li* as Principle." *Ch'ing-hua hsüeh-pao* (Tsing Hua Journal of Chinese Studies) new series 4, no. 2 (Feb. 1964): 123–148.

———. "The Neo-Confucian Solution to the Problem of Evil." Reprinted in Chan, *Neo-Confucianism Etc.: Essays by Wing-tsit Chan*, comp. by Charles K. H. Chen. New Haven: Oriental Society, 1969.

———. "Neo-Confucianism in Chinese Scientific Thought." *Philosophy East and West* 4 (1957): 309–332.

Chang, Carsun. *The Development of Neo-Confucian Thought*, 2 vols. New York: Bookman, 1957 and 1962.

Cheng, Chung-ying. "Chu Hsi's Methodology and Theory of Understanding." In Wing-tsit Chan, ed., *Chu Hsi and Neo-Confucianism*.

———. "Practical Learning in Yen Yüan, Chu Hsi and Wang Yang-ming." In de Bary and Bloom, eds., *Principle and Practicality: Essays in Neo-Confucianism and Practical Learning*.

———. "Reason, Substance and Human Desires in Seventeenth-Century Neo-Confucianism." In Wm. T. de Bary, ed., *The Unfolding of Neo-Confucianism*. New York: Columbia University Press, 1975.

———. "Religious Reality and Religious Understanding in Confucianism and Neo-Confucianism." *International Philosophical Quarterly* 13, no. 1 (March 1974): 33–61.

———. *Tai Chen's Inquiry into Goodness*. Honolulu: East-West Center Press, 1971.

Ching, Julia. "Chu Hsi on Moral Cultivation." In Wing-tsit Chan, ed., *Chu Hsi and Neo-Confucianism*. Honolulu: University Hawaii Press, 1986.

———. "What Is Confucian Spirituality?" In Irene Eber, ed., *Confucianism: The Dynamics of Tradition*. New York: Macmillan, 1986.

———. "Confucianism, a Philosophy of Man." In James D. Whitehead et. al., *China and Christianity*. Notre Dame, Ind.: University of Notre Dame Press, 1979.

———. "Chu Hsi's Theory of Human Nature." *Humanitas* 20 (1979): 77–100.

———. "Chinese Ethics and Kant." *Philosophy East and West* 28 (1978): 162–172.

———. *Confucianism and Christianity: A Comparative Study*. New York and Tokyo: Kodansha International, 1977.

———. *To Acquire Wisdom: The Way of Wang Yang-ming*. New York: Columbia University Press, 1976.

———. "The Goose Lake Monastery Debate (1175)." *Journal of Chinese Philosophy* 1 (1974): 161–178.

———. "Neo-Confucian Utopian Theories and Political Ethics." *Monumenta Serica* 30 (1972/73): 56–73.

Cua, A. S. *The Unity of Knowledge and Action: A Study of Wang Yang-ming's Moral Psychology*. Honolulu: University of Hawaii Press, 1982.

de Bary, William T. *Learning for One's Self: Essays on the Individual in Neo-Confucian Thought*. New York: Columbia University Press, 1991.

———. *The Message of the Mind in Neo-Confucianism*. New York: Columbia University Press, 1989.

———. *East Asian Civilizations: A Dialogue in Five Stages*. Cambridge, Mass.: Harvard University Press, 1988.

———. "Human Rites—An Essay on Confucianism and Human Rites." In I. Eber, ed., *Confucianism: The Dynamics of Tradition*.

———. *Neo-Confucian Orthodoxy and the Learning of the Mind-and-Heart*. New York: Columbia University Press, 1981.

———. "Sagehood as a Secular and Spiritual Ideal in Tokugawa Neo-Confucianism." In de Bary and Bloom, eds., *Principle and Practicality: Essays in Neo-Confucianism and Practical Learning*.

———, ed. *The Unfolding of Neo-Confucianism*. New York: Columbia University Press, 1975.

———. "Neo-Confucian Cultivation and the Seventeenth-Century 'Enlightenment'" In de Bary, ed., *The Unfolding of Neo-Confucianism*.

———, ed. *Self and Society in Ming Thought*. New York: Columbia University Press, 1970.

———. "Some Common Tendencies in Neo-Confucianism." In David S. Nivison and Arthur F. Wright, eds., *Confucianism in Action*. Stanford, Calif.: Stanford University Press, 1959.

———. "A Reappraisal of Neo-Confucianism." In Arthur F. Wright, ed., *Studies in Chinese Thought*. Chicago: University of Chicago Press, 1953.

——— and I. Bloom., eds. *Principle and Practicality: Essays in Neo-Confucianism and Practical Learning*. New York: Columbia University Press, 1979.

Ebrey, Patricia B., trans. *Chu Hsi's Family Rituals*. Princeton, N.J.: Princeton University Press, 1991.

Fu, Charles Wei-hsun. "The Mencian Theory of Mind and Nature: A Modern, Philosophical Approach." *Journal of Chinese Philosophy* 10 (1983): 85–410.

Fung Yu-lan. *A History of Chinese Philosophy*, trans. by D. Bodde, 2 vols. Princeton, N.J.: Princeton University Press, 1952 and 1953.

Graham, Arthur C. *Two Chinese Philosophers: Ch'eng Ming-tao and Ch'eng Yi-ch'uan*. London: Lund Humphries, 1958.

———. "The Background of the Mencian Theory of Human Nature." *Tsing-Hua Journal of Chinese Studies* (Dec. 1967): 215–274.

Griffiths, Paul J., ed. *Christianity Through Non-Christian Eyes.* Maryknoll, N.Y.: Orbis Books, 1990.

Hall, David L., and Roger Ames. *Thinking Through Confucius.* Albany: SUNY Press, 1987.

Hatton, Russell. "*Ch'i*'s Role Within the Psychology of Chu Hsi." *Journal of Chinese Philosophy* 9, no. 4 (Dec. 1982): 441–69.

Hick, John. *God Has Many Names.* London: Macmillan, 1981.

Huang Tsung-hsi. *The Records of Ming Scholars,* trans. and ed. Julia Ching. Honolulu; University of Hawaii Press, 1987.

Ishida Ishirō. "Tokugawa Feudal Society and Neo-Confucian Thought." *Philosophical Studies of Japan* 5 (1964):17–24.

Jiang, Paul Yun-ming. *The Search for Mind: Ch'en Pai-sha, Philosopher-Poet.* Singapore: Singapore University Press, 1980.

Kim, Ha Tai. "The Religious Dimension of Neo-Confucianism." *Philosophy East and West* 27, no. 3 (1977): 337–348.

Küng, Hans, and Julia Ching. *Christianity and Chinese Religions.* New York: Doubleday, 1989. Especially chapter 2, "Confucianism: Ethical Humanism as Religion?" by J. Ching.

Lau, D. C. "The Theories of Human Nature in Mencius and Shyuntzyy." *Bulletin of the School of Oriental and African Studies* 30 (1967): 353–357.

Lik, Kuen Tong. "Nature and Feeling: The Meaning of Mentality in the Philosophy of Chu Hsi." *Journal of Chinese Philosophy* 9 (1982): 1–11.

Masao Maruyama. *Studies in the Intellectual History of Tokugawa Japan.* Princeton, N.J.: Princeton University Press, 1975.

Moore, Charles A., ed. *Essays in East-West Philosophy.* Honolulu: University of Hawaii Press, 1951.

Mou Tsung-san. "Confucianism as Religion." In D. Lancashire, trans., *Chinese Essays on Religion and Faith.* San Francisco: Chinese Material Center, 1981.

Okada Takehiko. "Practical Learning in the Chu Hsi School: Yamazaki Ansai and Kaibara Ekken." In de Bary and Bloom, eds., *Principle and Practicality: Essays in Neo-Confucianism and Practical Learning.*

Oxtoby, Willard G. *The Meaning of Other Faiths.* Philadelphia: Westminster Press, 1983.

Schwartz, Benjamin. "Some Polarities in Confucian Thought." In David Nivison and Arthur F. Waley, ed., *Confucianism in Action.* Stanford, Calif.: Stanford University Press, 1959.

Smart, Ninian *Crosscultural Explorations of Human Beliefs*. New York: Charles Scribners Sons, 1983.

Smith, Wilfred C. *Faith and Belief*. Princeton, N.J.: Princeton University Press, 1979.

Streng, Frederick J. *Understanding Religious Life*. 3d ed. Belmont, Calif.: Dickenson Publishing Co., 1985.

———. *Ways of Being Religious*. Englewood Cliffs, N.J.: Prentice-Hall, 1973.

T'ang Chün-i. "Chang Tsai's Theory of Mind and Its Metaphysical Basis." *Philosophy East and West* 6 (1956): 113–136.

———. "The Development of the Concept of Moral Mind from Wang Yang-ming to Wang Chi." In de Bary, ed., *Self and Society in Ming Thought*.

Taylor, Rodney. *Religious Dimensions of Neo-Confucianism*. Albany: SUNY Press, 1991.

———. *The Confucian Way of Contemplation: Okada Takehiko and the Tradition of Quiet-Sitting*. Columbia: University of South Carolina Press, 1988.

———. *The Way of Heaven: An Introduction to the Confucian Religious Life*. Leiden: E. J. Brill, 1986.

———. *The Cultivation of Sagehood as a Religious Goal in Neo-Confucianism: A Study of Selected Writings of Kao P'an-lung*. Missoula, Mont.: Scholar Press, 1978.

———. "Neo-Confucianism, Sagehood and the Religious Dimension." *Journal of Chinese Philosophy* 2 (1975): 389–415.

Tomoeda Ryūtarō. "The Characteristics of Chu Hsi's Thought." *Acta Asiatica* 21 (Oct. 1971): 52–72.

———. "The System of Chu Hsi's Philosophy." In Wing-tsit Chan, ed., *Chu Hsi and Neo-Confucianism*. Honolulu: University of Hawaii Press, 1986.

Tu Wei-ming. *Centrality and Commonality: An Essay on Confucian Religiousness* (A revised and enlarged edition of *Centrality and Commonality: An Essay on Chung-yung*). Albany: SUNY Press, 1989.

———. "The Confucian Sage: Exemplar of Personal Knowledge." In J. S. Hawley, ed., *Saints and Virtues*. Berkeley: University of California Press, 1987.

———. *Confucian Thought: Selfhood as Creative Transformation*. Albany: SUNY Press, 1985.

———. "'Pain and Suffering' in Confucian Self-Cultivation." *Philosophy East and West* 34 (1984): 379–388.

———. "On the Mencian Perception of Moral Self-Cultivation." *Monist* 61, no. 1 (Jan. 1978): 72–81.

———. *Centrality and Commonality: An Essay on Chung-yung*. Honolulu: University of Hawaii Press, 1976.

———. "Neo-Confucian Concept of Man." *Philosophy East and West* 21, no. 1 (1971): 79–87.

———. "Neo-Confucian Ontology." *Journal of Chinese Philosophy* 7 (1980): 93–114.

Weber, Max. *The Religion of China: Confucianism and Taoism*, trans. H. M. Gerth. New York: Free Press, 1968.

———. *Protestant Ethic and the Spirit of Capitalism*, trans. T. Parsons. London: George Allen and Unwin, 1976.

Wen, Hsi-tseng. "The Status of Man in Neo-Confucianism." Ph.D. dissertation, University of Southern California, 1957.

Index

To facilitate use of this index, English equivalents or identifications are provided for all titles and philosophical terms, and dates for most historical figures and periods. The key entries are printed in boldface type. As cited in the text, East Asian names are listed according to the common East Asian fashion, with family name first and without a comma after it (e.g., Cho Kwang-jo). In addition, honorific names are given in parentheses for most Korean Neo-Confucians (see also A Note on Style and Translation). Two common phrases, the Four Beginnings and the Seven Emotions, are abbreviated as Four and Seven, respectively; Chinese Neo-Confucian and Japanese Neo-Confucian as C. Neo. and J. Neo., respectively.